Bu s Strategy

Business Strategy
An Introduction

Second edition

David Campbell, George Stonehouse and Bill Houston

ELSEVIER
BUTTERWORTH
HEINEMANN

AMSTERDAM • BOSTON • HEIDELBERG • LONDON • NEW YORK • OXFORD
PARIS • SAN DIEGO • SAN FRANCISCO • SINGAPORE • SYDNEY • TOKYO

Elsevier Butterworth-Heinemann
Linacre House, Jordan Hill, Oxford OX2 8DP
200 Wheeler Road, Burlington, MA 01803

First published 1999
Second edition 2002
Reprinted 2003, 2004

British Library Cataloguing in Publication Data
A catalogue record for this book is available from the British Library

ISBN 0 7506 5569 0

For information on all Butterworth-Heinemann publications
visit our website at www.bh.com

Typeset by Keyword Typesetting Services Ltd, Wallington, Surrey
Printed and bound in Great Britain by MPG Books Ltd, Bodmin, Cornwall

Contents

Index of key concepts

Preface to the second edition

In this second edition we have attempted to retain the first edition's core qualities of accessibility, conciseness and comprehensiveness. Feedback from our many adopters, however, has enabled us to iron out a few things and add to the text in a way that will hopefully make it more useful, especially at centres with overseas students whose need for an accessible strategy text is most pronounced.

In particular, the updating has been focused in two areas. First, the suite of cases has been significantly expanded. New cases have been added and some of the existing cases have been updated. In addition to cases written by the authors, colleagues at the University of Northumbria have kindly donated a number of excellent cases to this edition. Nigel Evans wrote MyTravel (formerly Airtours plc), the outbound tour operations industry and airline alliances. Dr Colin Combe donated the case on Amazon.com. Second, we have updated the text in terms of scholarship. There is a balance to be struck between the inclusion of the most recent research and our aim to keep the text accessible to students studying strategy for the first time. The extent to which we have met this objective is perhaps a matter of opinion, but we hope that new and existing adopters will think we have got the balance about right.

Two themes in the research literature have been particularly prominent in recent years: 'knowledge management' as a source of competitive advantage in business strategy and the debate over the ethical role of businesses in society. Up-to-date scholarship on both of these themes is reflected in the second edition whilst (we hope) not detracting from the central canon of strategic management 'doctrine'. Similarly, the development of strategic perspectives other than the 'Porteresque' competitive positioning school of thought is discussed. In particular, resource dependency theory and the 'core competence' understanding of strategic management have increased in prominence in this edition.

We have been fortunate to benefit again from the experience and scholarship of two colleagues at the University of Northumbria who are seasoned experts within their respective fields. Harry Robinson updated his chapter on products and markets (Chapter 5) and Alex Appleby added the most recent scholarship to his chapter on operations and quality (Chapter 12). We thank them both for their sterling contributions to the second edition.

David Campbell
George Stonehouse
Bill Houston

University of Northumbria
May 2002

An introduction to the strategic process

Why do we refer to business strategy as a *process*? The answer is that it is never a once for all event – it goes on and on. There is a need to continually review strategic objectives because the environment is always changing. The purpose of strategy is to make a business fit into its environment. By achieving this, the probability that it will survive and prosper are enhanced.

Furthermore, strategy is a process because it contains distinct 'stages' – three in all.

Strategic analysis

The purpose of strategic analysis is to gather information. None of us would be wise to make an important decision about anything in life without adequate and relevant information, and neither would a business.

There are two main stages in strategic analysis. Firstly, strategic analysis involves an examination of an organization's internal environment (*internal analysis*). This takes the form of a thorough analysis of the internal processes and structures of a business in much the same way as a doctor might carry out a thorough medical examination on a person. The purpose of internal analysis is to establish what the organization is good at (its strengths) and what it is not so good at (its

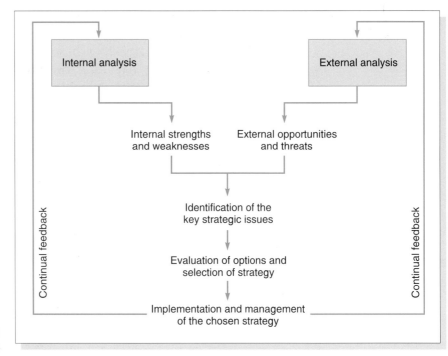

Internal analysis

External analysis

Internal strengths
and weaknesses

External opportunities
and threats

Continual feedback

Identification of the
key strategic issues

Evaluation of options and
selection of strategy

Implementation and management
of the chosen strategy

Continual feedback

A schematic of the
strategic process

weaknesses). We discuss the internal environment in Part II of this book.

The second stage in strategic analysis is an examination of the organization's external environment (an *external analysis*). This takes the form of a thorough analysis of two 'layers' of external environment – the micro or 'near' environment, and the macro or 'far' environment. We will encounter the external environment in Part III of the book.

The micro environment comprises the industry in which the business competes. The organization is usually affected by the factors in this environment often and it may be able to have an influence upon it. We sometimes refer to the micro environment as the competitive environment because it is within this sphere that an organization competes, both for resource inputs and to sell its product outputs. We discuss this in Chapter 7.

The macro environment contains a range of influences that affect not only an organization in an industry, but also the whole industry itself. It follows that a single organization is usually unable to affect the factors in the macro environment – successful strategy usually involves learning to cope and adapt to changes. This textbook explains the macro environment in terms of five main areas of influence – socio-demographic, political, economic, natural and technological influences. We discuss this in Chapter 6.

From the information gathered from the external analysis, we seek to establish which influences represent opportunities, and which are, or might develop into, threats. When these are considered alongside the internal strengths and weaknesses, we are able to construct a SWOT statement. A SWOT statement is a summary of the internal and external analyses. The SWOT factors are not strategies; they are observations resulting from the previous analyses.

The strengths and weaknesses are based on the internal analysis of an organization and the opportunities and threats are based on the analysis of the environment which is external to the organization. One key distinguishing characteristic between the strengths and weaknesses on the one hand and the opportunities and threats on the other is the degree of control that managers may have. With the internal strengths and weaknesses managers can often exert control whereas with regard to the opportunities and threats, managers are less likely to be able to control such factors. If for example the organization has a strong balance sheet (a strength) this will have resulted from managerial decisions. If, instead the organization is seen as being over-staffed (a weakness), managers can address the issue through reducing staff numbers. Conversely, by way of example, changing government policies, product changes by competitors or a war breaking out (all of, which might produce opportunities or threats to an individual organization depending on the circumstances) are beyond the control of managers.

The SWOT represents a position statement stating where the organization is at the time of the analysis in relation to its environment. It is not the strategy itself and should not involve making statements about what should be done next. Instead it provides a firm platform for planning for the future of the organization, i.e. formulating the strategy which is the next stage in the strategic process.

In presenting the SWOT a number of rules should be followed:

 ■ Too much detail should be avoided so that the key points can be clearly seen. Keep each point short and to the point so that an overview can quickly be gained. The detailed justifications for the points presented in the table should be presented separately.
 ■ Many of the points presented in the SWOT may be relative rather than absolute and consequently a matter of some judgement. Thus it is difficult to say at exactly what level a high

level of financial gearing becomes a weakness or a share of a particular market becomes a strength.

■ The SWOT should not concentrate solely on 'hard' facts (such as financial measures or market growth statistics) that can be measured or proved. Softer factors such as organizational culture or the leadership skills exhibited by managers may be more difficult to measure but they are nevertheless important for organizational performance.

■ The analysis should prioritise and combine points. The most important points should be shown first and points that are not key or strategic in nature should be excluded. In some cases it may be necessary to combine smaller points to make one large overarching point. For example, if a SWOT is partly based on a financial analysis of an organization which indicates a strong financial position, the SWOT should not have individual points on high level of profitability, low gearing, adequate liquidity, etc., for to do so would confuse the presentation. The point presented in the SWOT should be that is that the organization has a strong financial position. The justification for making such a point would be provided by the assessments relating to profitability, gearing liquidity and so on.

■ The presentation should be specific, but avoid blandness, and be realistic in its assessment.

The process sometimes involves an additional stage of condensing the strengths, weaknesses, opportunities and threats (SWOT) into a survey of the 'key issues'. These are the most pressing or most important elements of the SWOT statement – those which require the most urgent action or which the strategy should be particularly designed to address.

Once we have established the organization's internal strengths and weaknesses, and its external opportunities and threats, the challenge becomes to select a strategy that will address the weaknesses and threats whilst at the same time, will build upon its strengths and exploit its opportunities. It is important to understand that a detailed internal and external analysis is a necessary pre-requisite for the SWOT information – it emerges from the internal and external analyses.

Strategic selection

The second stage in the strategic process involves taking the important information gathered from the strategic analysis and using it to make an intelligent and informed selection of the most appropriate course of action for the future.

It is at this stage that we come to appreciate the importance of the strategic analysis. If we have gained insufficient or flawed information from the analysis, then we cannot be sure that the strategy selection we make will be the right one.

Selection therefore begins with an examination of the strategic analysis. Once we are acquainted with it, we normally generate a list of the options open to the organization, paying particular attention to how each option will address the key issues. After this, we evaluate each option using a number of criteria. Finally, the most appropriate strategic option is selected. We discuss this matter in Chapter 9.

Strategic implementation and management

The third stage in the strategic process involves taking the selected strategic option and actually putting it into practice. We discuss this stage in Part IV of the book.

This is a rather more complex process than either analysis or selection. It involves *doing* the strategy and this brings into focus a number of other managerial issues. There are a number of areas of which we need to be aware in order to effectively implement a business strategy.

Implementation typically involves taking into account the following:

- the adequacy of the organization's resource base (Chapter 10);
- the readiness of the organization's culture and structure to undertake the proposed strategy (Chapter 10);
- the management of any changes that are needed to implement the strategy (also Chapter 10);
- deciding which, if any, growth or development paths to pursue (Chapter 11);
- the readiness of the organization's operations function to pursue the proposed strategy and any quality issues that this discussion might throw up (Chapter 12);

■ the extent to which the organization positions itself in respect to its geographic coverage and international presence (Chapter 13);

■ the impact that the strategy may have upon an organization's internal or external stakeholders and a discussion (if appropriate) of the strategy's implications for the organization's relationship with society (Chapter 14).

The 'feedback' link

Finally, the progress of strategy is monitored continually through feedback from the implementation stage back to the analysis stage. As a strategy proceeds, it may affect the company's internal environment and it may have an effect on the external environment. In addition, independent influences may have brought internal or external changes about since the strategic analysis was first carried out.

In order to ensure that the selected strategy is still appropriate, therefore, a review of the strategic analysis is necessary. If nothing has changed, then the company may decide that no amendment to the strategy is necessary. If the environment (internal or external) has changed, however, some modification to the strategy may become necessary.

CHAPTER 1

Strategy and strategic management

Strategic thinking and strategic management are the most important activities undertaken by any business or public sector organization. How skilfully these activities are carried out will determine the eventual long-term success or failure of the organization. In this chapter, we introduce the most basic concepts in the study of these activities. The various definitions of the word *strategy* are discussed and then we explore the levels of decision-making in successful strategic management (at the strategic and operational levels). These are defined and the links between the levels are discussed. The different frameworks and ways of approaching strategy are introduced and then, finally, we discuss the nature of strategic objectives – who is responsible for setting them and what they are essentially about.

After studying this chapter, students should be able to:

- define the word *strategy* using Mintzberg's five Ps framework;
- distinguish between deliberate (prescriptive) and emergent strategy;
- explain what strategy contains in practice;
- describe the different frameworks by which strategy is understood;

- describe what is meant by *strategic*, *tactical* and *operational* decisions;
- explain what is meant by *hierarchical congruence* and why is it important;
- explain the stakeholder model to show how strategic decisions are arrived at.

What is strategy?

Definition

At the beginning of a book on business strategy, the question 'what is strategy?' seems to be the most obvious starting point. However, the answer to the question is rather more complicated than might at first appear.

Definitions

This is because we use the word *strategy* in many ways. You may have heard people talk about a strategy for a business, a strategy for a football match, a strategy for a military campaign or a strategy for revising for a set of exams. It was this multiplicity of uses of the term that led Henry Mintzberg at the McGill University in Montreal (Mintzberg, 1987) to propose his 'five Ps' of strategy.

Mintzberg's 5 Ps

Mintzberg suggested that nobody can claim to own the word 'strategy' and that the term can legitimately be used in several ways. A strategy can be:

- a plan;
- a ploy;
- a pattern of behaviour;
- a position in respect to others;
- a perspective.

It is important not to see any of these Ps in isolation from the others. One of the problems of dividing ideas into frameworks such as the five Ps is that they are necessarily simplified. The five Ps are not mutually exclusive – i.e. it is possible for an organization to show evidence of more than one interpretation of strategy.

Plan strategies

A plan is probably the way in which most people use the word strategy. This tends to imply something that is intentionally put in train and its progress monitored from the start to a predetermined finish. Some business strategies follow this model. 'Planners' tend to produce internal documents that detail what the company will do for a period of time in the future (say five years). It might include a schedule for new product launches, acquisitions, financing (i.e. raising money), human resource changes, etc.

Ploy strategies

A ploy is generally taken to mean a short-term strategy. It tends to have very limited objectives and it may be subject to change at very short notice. One of the best examples of a ploy strategy is that employed in a football match. If the opposing team has a particularly skilful player, the team manager may use the ploy of assigning two players to mark him for the duration of the game. However, this tactic will only last for the one game – the next game will have a completely different strategy. Furthermore, the strategy will only operate for as long as the dangerous player is on the pitch. If he is substituted or gets injured, the strategy will change mid-game.

Mintzberg describes a ploy as "a manoeuvre intended to outwit an opponent or competitor" (Mintzberg *et al.*, 1998, p. 14). He points out that some companies may use ploy strategies as threats. For example, they may threaten to decrease the price of their products simply to destabilize competitors. A boss may threaten to sack an employee if a certain performance standard is not met – not because the boss intends to carry out the threat, but because he wants to effect a change in the subordinate's attitude.

Pattern strategies

A 'pattern of behaviour' strategy is one in which progress is made by adopting a consistent form of behaviour. Unlike plans and ploys, patterns 'just happen' as a result of the consistent behaviour. On a simple level, small businesses such as scrap dealers follow pattern strategies. They are unlikely to produce elaborate plans – they simply buy as much scrap metal as they can. If there is a batch of old scaffolding, then they buy it up without thinking about it. However, they would not buy old plastics because that would be outside their pattern of business behaviour. Eventually, following this consistent behaviour makes the scrap dealer a wealthy person – a successful strategy.

Such patterns of behaviour are sometimes unconscious, meaning that they do not even realize that they actually following a consistent pattern. Nevertheless, if it proves successful, it is said that the consistent behaviour has *emerged* into a success. This is in direct contrast to planning behaviour.

Key concepts

Deliberate and emergent strategy

There is a key difference between two of Mintzberg's Ps of strategy: plan and pattern. The difference is to do with the *source* of the strategy. Mintzberg drew attention to the fact that some strategies are deliberate whereas others are emergent.

Deliberate strategy (sometimes called *planned or prescriptive* strategy) is *meant* to happen. It is preconceived, premeditated and usually monitored and controlled from start to finish. It has a specific objective.

Emergent strategy has no specific objective. It does not have a preconceived route to success BUT it may be just as effective as a deliberate strategy. By following a consistent pattern of behaviour, an organization may arrive at the same position as if it had planned everything in detail.

We discuss these concepts in more detail later in this chapter.

Position strategies

A position strategy is appropriate when the most important thing to an organization is how it relates to, or is positioned with respect to, its competitors or its markets (i.e. its customers). In other words, the organization wishes to achieve or defend a certain position. We see this a lot in sport. When a new boxing champion is crowned, his only objective is to remain the champion. He wants to retain his superior position. Accordingly, all of his efforts are invested in examining his future opponents and keeping himself in shape for the next defence of the title.

In business, companies tend to seek such things as market share, profitability, superior research, reputation, etc. It is plainly obvious that not all companies are equal when one considers such criteria. Some car manufacturers have enviable reputations for reliability and quality whereas others are not so fortunate. The competitors with a reputation to defend will use a position strategy to ensure that the reputation they enjoy is maintained and strengthened. This may even include marketing messages that point out the weaknesses in competitors' products while pointing out the features of their own.

Perspective strategies

Perspective strategies are about changing the culture (the beliefs and the 'feel', the way of looking at the world) of a certain group of people – usually the members of the organization itself. Some companies want to make their employees think in a certain way, believing this to be an important way of achieving success. They may, for example, try to get all employees to think and act courteously, professionally or helpfully.

Religious groups such as the Church of England operate something approximating to this strategy. They have a number of core religious beliefs that they encourage all members to adopt. Then, it is argued, these beliefs will outwork themselves in actions. To be a good member of the Church of England, people must adopt the world view of the church. The purpose of preaching, teaching, worship and other such practices is in large part concerned with further embedding Christian beliefs into the personalities of the believers. Success is achieved when all members think in the same way – i.e. they all believe in the core doctrines and work them out in their lives through good works.

The elements of strategy

Chandler's definition

Given the foregoing definitions by Mintzberg, we might think that writers in business strategy are unable to agree to a single definition of the word strategy. This is partly true, but some have tried to sum it up succinctly to make it easier for students to understand. One such definition, still widely quoted, was offered by Professor Chandler of Harvard Business School in 1962. Given that Chandler predated Mintzberg, it is not surprising that it is rather more simplistic than Mintzberg might have accepted.

Strategy is the *determination of the basic long-term goals* and objectives of an enterprise, and the *adoption of courses of action* and the *allocation of resources* necessary for carrying out these goals. (Chandler, 1962; emphasis added)

Three components of strategy

Chandler's is a good definition because it shows the scope of what 'good' strategy is. The italics in the above quote show the three important contents of strategy.

The *determination of the basic long-term goals* concerns the conceptualization of coherent and attainable strategic objectives. Without objectives, nothing else can happen. If you do not know where you want to go, how can you act in such a way as to get there?

The *adoption of courses of action* refers to the actions taken to arrive at the objectives that have been previously set. If your objective is to be in France, then the actions you would take would include arranging transport. You might do this by ringing travel agents, servicing your car, etc.

The *allocation of resources* refers to the fact that there is likely to be a cost associated with the actions required to achieve the objectives. If the course of action is not supported with adequate levels of resource, then the objective will not be accomplished.

Hence, strategy contains three things. In order to achieve your *objective* of being in France, you would take the *actions* of booking or arranging travel, taking leave from work and actually making the journey that will take you to France. However, the actions would not be possible if they could not be resourced. You need the *resources* of a plane, train, car or similar with a suitably qualified pilot or driver, money to pay for your travel and other such 'inputs'. If any one of these is missing, you will be unable to meet your objective.

Key concept

Resources

Resource inputs (sometimes called *factors of production*) are the inputs that are essential to the normal functioning of the organizational process. These are the inputs without which an organization simply could not continue to exist or meet its objectives. We can readily appreciate that human beings rely upon certain vital inputs such as air, water, nutrition, warmth, shelter, etc., but organizations have similar needs. An organization's resource inputs fall into four key categories:

1 *financial resources* – money for capital investment and working capital; sources include shareholders, banks, bondholders, etc.;
2 *human resources* – appropriately skilled employees to add value in operations and to support those that add value (e.g. supporting employees in marketing, accounting, personnel, etc.); sources include the labour markets for the appropriate skill levels required by the organization;
3 *physical (tangible) resources* – land, buildings (offices, warehouses, etc.), plant, equipment, stock for production, etc.; sources include estate agents, builders, trade suppliers, etc.;
4 *intellectual (intangible) resources* – inputs that cannot be seen or felt but which are essential for continuing business success, such as 'know-how', legally defensible patents and licences, brand names, registered designs, logos, 'secret' formulations and recipes, business contact networks, databases, etc.

Strategy: thinking, decisions, leadership and management

Defining the key terms

Organizations exist to serve particular purposes and to achieve related goals. Although businesses are usually concerned with providing goods and services and seeking profitability and competitive advantage over their rivals, 'not for profit organizations' such as the health service, education and charities focus on providing the best quality service with the efficient use of resources.

Earlier in this chapter, we explored some of the definitions of strategy (using Mintzberg's '5Ps' model) and we learned that there is no universally agreed definition of strategy. At the most fundamental level, an organization's strategy can be regarded as the means (plans, policies and actions) by which it seeks to achieve its long-term goal or goals. In many organizations, strategy also includes the determination of the goals and objectives themselves, as well as the means of achieving them.

Several terms are used interchangeably in the strategy literature and this can be a cause of confusion. In order to avoid confusion and to set out some of the fundamental terms used in strategy, the key terms are defined here.

Definitions

Strategic management can be viewed as a set of theories, frameworks, tools and techniques designed to explain the factors underlying the performance of organizations and to assist managers in thinking, planning and acting strategically. In simple terms, it is a vehicle through which a business can review past performance and, more importantly, determine future actions geared towards achieving and sustaining superior performance.

Strategic thinking and leadership relate to the ability of the leaders of an organization to look into its future and to think creatively about its potential development. Such thinking, vision and leadership are essential to the longer-term development of the organization. Prahalad and Hamel (1990) stressed the need for leaders to think beyond current operations so as to develop a 'strategic intent' which, they argued, shapes the organization's future strategy and development, 'stretching' it beyond its past and present achievements.

Strategic thinking is based upon strategic learning. *Strategic learning* is concerned with the processes by which leaders, managers and organizations learn about themselves, their business and environment. Strategic learning is vital to the development of the strategic knowledge upon which superior performance is based (Nonaka, 1991).

Strategic planning centres on the setting of organizational objectives, as well as developing and implementing plans designed to achieve these objectives. Rather unfortunately, strategic planning is often associated with a highly prescriptive approach to strategic management (Mintzberg, 1995). In many situations a prescriptive or deliberate approach will be inappropriate. Whilst the uncertainty of the modern business environment means that detailed and prescriptive long-term planning may be of little value, some form of broad long-term planning, related to strategic thinking and vision, is necessary if strategic intent is to be translated into action.

The debate about the 'sources' of strategy

What is the debate about?

Strategic management is a relatively young discipline and its immaturity is reflected in both the ambiguity of some of its terminology (hence the definitions above) and in the fact that there is no single agreed approach to the subject. Five distinct but often interrelated strands to strategy theory[1] can be identified:

- planned strategy (also called deliberate or prescriptive);
- competitive positioning strategy;
- core competence-based strategy (or resource-based or distinctive capability);
- emergent strategy (or learning);
- knowledge-based strategy.

Although the literature of strategic management sometimes presents these approaches as discrete and even as in conflict with each other, it is more useful to view them as interdependent and, in many ways, complementary and mutually enriching. Each approach represents a different perspective and provides analytical frameworks through which managers can gain greater understanding of the strategic capabilities of their organizations.

It is useful at this stage to consider each approach and its contribution to strategic thinking.

---

[1]McKiernan (1997) identified four strands to strategy theory, and the knowledge-based approach to strategy is sometimes subsumed into core competence- or resource-based strategy. We believe, however, that knowledge-based strategy has its own distinctive characteristics, at the same time as providing a fundamental underpinning for all the other theories of strategic management.

The planning approach

The prescriptive, deliberate or planned approach is based on long-term planning which seeks to achieve a 'fit' between organizational strategy and the environment in which it operates. This approach views strategic management as a highly systematized and deterministic process (Andrews, 1987; Ansoff, 1965; Argenti, 1974). The prescriptive paradigm of strategic management has been criticized as being unrealistic, particularly in times of rapid and turbulent change. Nevertheless, the need to set long-term objectives and to formulate broad plans and policies is necessary for the survival and progression of any organization. Detailed and inflexible long-term planning is, on the other hand, unnecessary and often counterproductive. Competitive advantage can be gained by being opportunistic and taking advantage of unforeseen opportunities.

The competitive positioning approach

The competitive positioning paradigm, drawing largely on the work of Porter (1980, 1985), dominated strategic management in the 1980s. It emphasized the idea of 'strategic fit' between the organization and its environment so as to achieve competitive advantage, referring to this as 'competitive positioning'. The approach is often described as 'outside-in' as the initial emphasis is on analysis of the environment before determining how to achieve a strategically desirable position. Porter's frameworks − the *five forces* (used for analysing the organization's competitive environment; see Chapter 7), *generic strategy* (used to identify sources of competitive advantage; see Chapter 8) and *the value chain* (used to analyse the activities and resources of the organization; Chapter 2) − still provide some of the most useful tools of strategic analysis. There are apparent limitations to Porter's tools but, as long as these limitations are recognized, they are valuable to managers seeking to make sense of complex organizations and their environments.

The emergent or learning approach

An alternative to the strategic planning movement is the emergent or learning approach (Lindblom, 1959; Mintzberg and Walters, 1985; Mintzberg *et al.*, 1995). This is based upon the view that the modern dynamic and hypercompetitive business environment will inevitably mean that there will be a gap between 'planned' and 'realized' or actual strategies. A rapidly changing environment means that organizations must incrementally change and adapt strategy on the basis of organizational learning. This does not preclude 'deliberate' strategic planning completely but implies that strategic plans must be flexible, guiding the overall direction of the organization, but adapted when changing circumstances dictate.

The core competence approach

In the 1990s, a strong movement developed which suggested that competitive advantage arises from an organization's internally developed *core competences* or *distinctive capabilities* rather than from its environment (Hamel and Prahalad, 1994; Heene and Sanchez, 1997; Kay, 1993; Prahalad and Hamel, 1990; Stalk *et al.*, 1992). Whereas Porter (1980, 1985) stressed the importance of the industry in determining competitive advantage, this approach suggests that the core competence of the organization is of far greater importance (Baden-Fuller and Stopford, 1992; Rumelt, 1991). The approach is 'inside-out', suggesting that businesses seeking competitive advantage must first examine and develop their own distinctive resources, capabilities and competences before exploiting them in their environment. Clearly, some organizations in the same industry are more successful than others, lending support to the view that competitive advantage is largely internally developed. Equally, however, there is a danger of ignoring the environment, as customers and their needs, competitors, changes in technology, etc., can play an important role in determining competitive success.

Learning and knowledge-based strategy

What is required is an holistic view of strategy that embraces all facets of the organization (resources, capabilities, core competences and activities) and its interactions with the environment (customers, suppliers, competitors, government, legislation, technology, etc.). This holistic approach is embraced by the *learning or knowledge-based approach* to strategic management which has developed in recent years (Nonaka, 1991; Nonaka *et al.*, 2000; Pemberton and Stonehouse, 2000; Stonehouse and Pemberton, 1999; Stonehouse *et al.*, 2001). In essence, this approach suggests that competitive advantage depends upon the development of new and superior knowledge through the processes of organizational learning.

In fact, Prahalad and Hamel (1990) recognized the relationship between core competences, knowledge and organizational learning, defining core competences as ". . . the collective learning of the organization . . .". Later research also suggested that businesses cannot afford to be internally or externally driven. Instead, competitive advantage depends upon the ability of the organization to develop knowledge-based core competences which are essentially market-driven strategies sensitive to customer needs, based upon organizational learning (Nonaka, 1991; Nonaka *et al.*, 2000; Prahalad and Hamel, 1990; Pemberton and Stonehouse, 2000; Stonehouse and Pemberton, 1999; Stonehouse *et al.*, 2001). Such an approach encompasses the use of any conceptual frameworks that assist in the processes of learning and the creation of new knowledge. As Mintzberg *et al.* (1995) suggested, the various approaches to strategic management can be regarded as "complementary, representing two different forms of analysis both of which must be brought to bear for improving the quality of strategic thinking and analysis".

The approach in this book: learning and knowledge-based strategy

This book adopts an holistic approach to the subject and draws upon the theories and frameworks developed within all these perspectives. Essentially, however, competitive advantage is seen as arising from new knowledge which is, in turn, created through organizational learning. In a rapidly changing world, competitive advantage can only be sustained if the process of learning is both continuous and continual. Organizations must learn by gathering information about their business, their activities, their resources, their core competences, their customers and their needs, their competitors and other aspects of the business environment. This information must then be analysed to develop new strategic knowledge which will act as the basis of new core competences and strategies which will produce superior performance.

Strategic decisions

Different 'levels'

It is useful at this stage to understand what characterizes strategic decisions. Management decisions within any organization can be clas-

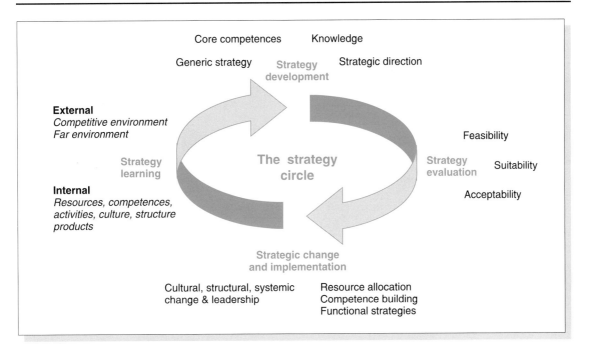

Figure 1.1
The 'strategy circle'.

sified into three broad (and sometimes overlapping) categories: strategic, tactical and operational. These can be illustrated as a hierarchy in which higher-level decisions tend to shape those at subordinate levels (see Figure 1.2).

Strategic, tactical and operational decisions within an organization differ from each other in terms of:

■ focus;
■ the level in the organization at which they are made;

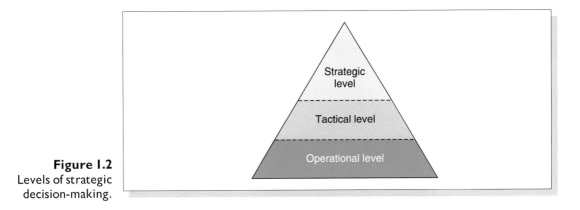

Figure 1.2
Levels of strategic
decision-making.

- scope;
- time horizon;
- degree of certainty or uncertainty;
- complexity (see Table 1.1).

The strategic level

Strategic decisions are concerned with the acquisition of sustainable competitive advantage, which involves the setting of long-term corporate objectives and the formulation, evaluation, selection and monitoring of strategies designed to achieve those objectives. Strategic decisions are made by senior managers (usually directors), they affect the whole organization, are long-term in nature, are complex and are based upon uncertain information. Managers at the strategic level require multiconceptual skills – the ability to consider the effects of multiple internal and external influences on the business and the

Table 1.1

Comparison of strategic, tactical and operational decisions

	Strategic	Tactical	Operational
Focus of decision	Achieving sustainable competitive advantage	Implementation of strategy	Day-to-day operations
Level of decision-making	Senior management, board of directors	Head of business unit or functional area	Supervisory
Scope	Whole organization	Business unit or functional area (e.g. marketing)	Department
Time horizon	Long-term (years)	Medium-term (months to years)	Short-term (days, weeks, month)
Certainty/ uncertainty	High uncertainty	Some uncertainty	High certainty
Complexity	Highly complex	Moderately complex	Comparatively simple
Examples	Decision to launch new product, enter new market, investment decision, etc.	Decision to advertise, alter price, etc.	Decision to re-order stock, scheduling of jobs

possible ways in which strategy can be adjusted to account for such influences.

The decision early on in the company's history for Easyjet to operate as a low-cost, no frills airline is an example of a strategic decision. It was taken at the most senior level, it affected the whole competitive position of the business, it was long-term in nature and it affected all members of the business.

The tactical level

Tactical decisions are concerned with how corporate objectives are to be met and how strategies are implemented. They are dependent upon overall strategy and involve its fine-tuning and adjustment. They are made at head of business unit, department or functional area level and affect only parts of the organization. They are medium-term in timescale, semi-complex and usually involve some uncertainty, but not as much as at the strategic level.

The operational level

Operational decisions are concerned with the shorter-term objectives of the business and with its day-to-day management. They are dependent upon strategy and tactics. These decisions are made at junior managerial or supervisory level, are based on a high degree of certainty and are not complex. The procedures in a sales office are typical operational activities – processing orders that have a tactical purpose in pursuit of the overall strategy.

Congruency and 'fit'

The success of strategy rests upon a very important, but rather obvious, principle. Once the strategic-level objectives have been set, the tactical and then the operational objectives must be set in such a way that they contribute to the achievement of the strategic objectives. In other words, all three levels must 'agree' or 'fit' together. This introduces the concept of *congruence*.

As shown in Figure 1.2, we can visualize the decision-making framework as a pyramid. The top, where the strategic decisions are made, is thin whereas the bottom (operational decisions) is fatter. This representation is meant to show that strategic decisions are taken infrequently whereas operational decisions are taken often. Strategic decisions are few and far between whereas operational decisions are taken weekly, daily or even hourly. For every one strategic decision, there will be more tactical decisions and possibly hundreds of individual operational decisions.

Where is a strategy actually carried out?

Although we have identified the top level in an organization's decision-making as strategic, we must not confuse this with the strategy itself, which is carried out at all levels of the organization. Strategy exists at all levels and thus it is useful to distinguish between the different levels as well as considering the relationships between them.

Network strategy

Many organizations and most businesses operate within a network of suppliers, distributors, customers and, sometimes, competitors. Although there may be no explicit strategy at this level, it is likely that the organizations will share certain objectives and information and that aspects of strategy will be devised collaboratively. Collaborative advantage through networks, strategic alliances and joint ventures can be an important source of competitive advantage. For example, collaboration between Japanese car manufacturers such as Toyota and their component suppliers, which involves the sharing of information and objectives, is at the heart of just-in-time management which, in turn, contributes significantly to Toyota's competitive edge.

Corporate strategy

Corporate strategy is at the level of the whole organization. Many organizations (especially larger ones) consist of a number of businesses which are linked together to varying degrees in terms of ownership, objectives, products, management, marketing, finance, etc. The degree of linkage can vary significantly from corporation to corporation. In terms of strategy, the degree of integration, coordination and commonality between the individual businesses can also vary enormously. It will depend upon the extent to which knowledge and core competences can be shared across the various businesses that comprise the organization. For example, Ferrari's Formula One team is heavily reliant upon the financial resources of the sports car manufacturing part of the business. At the same time, the sports car manufacturing benefits from technological developments made through Formula One racing, and the marketing effort benefits from the publicity the racing team attracts. Thus, there is a sharing of knowledge and core competences across the business and there are synergies between activities.

In some organizations, strategic decision-making takes place at the level of the business or strategic business unit (SBU). In cases where businesses within a corporation have little relationship with each other, strategic decision-making occurs largely at the level of the business or SBU. The strategic level of the organization may do little other than set broad policies and objectives, together with performance targets.

Business strategy

Much strategic decision-making takes place at the level of the business or SBU. This will be within a context set by the strategic level but which may allow considerable strategic autonomy (or not), according to whether or not there is potential for synergy and economies of scale and scope. Core competences in marketing, finance, sourcing and distribution can be shared across the whole corporation, but each business is likely to require certain distinctive competences particular to its own local geographic, competitive or industry conditions. For example, Virgin's various activities share the same brand name but different businesses demand different competences.

Functional strategy

Within the strategy of the business, each area of value-adding activity or functional area (design, procurement, production, marketing, distribution, finance, information systems, etc.) will need to design and implement a strategy that supports (i.e. is congruent with) the overall strategy of the organization. Functional strategy is of considerable importance in the successful implementation of business strategy and in its fine-tuning or tactical management.

Strategy frameworks

We have now seen that there is no single model of strategic management upon which there is general agreement. In fact, each of the strands of strategic theory makes a contribution to, and gives a complementary perspective on, how organizations achieve competitive advantage. In the same way, each strand of theory offers conceptual and analytical frameworks which assist in the process of organizational learning, strategic knowledge-building, strategic choice, strategic change and strategy implementation.

Table 1.2 summarizes some of the major analytical frameworks used in this book, their purpose and their origins.

How do businesses set strategic objectives?

Who 'owns' an organization?

Earlier in this chapter, we introduced the idea that strategic objectives, since they represent the most important level of decision-making, are set by an organization's senior management, usually the board of directors. In setting objectives, however, senior managers are sometimes influenced by a range of different groups that have an interest in the organization. Hence, a key question is: Who or what influences the senior management in their objective-setting? This question cuts to the heart of an important debate that is taking place both in universities and in business circles. This debate revolves around two different approaches towards objective-setting: the stockholder and stakeholder approaches.

The stockholder approach

The stockholder approach argues that businesses exist primarily for their owners (usually shareholders). Accordingly, any business behaviour that renders profit performance suboptimal is not only theft from shareholders but will also, eventually, lead to a level of business performance that will harm all other groups, such a employees, customers and suppliers.

In 1970, the Nobel Laureate Professor Milton Friedman contended that 'the moral obligation of business is to increase its profits'. Friedman argued that the one and only obligation of company directors (which are the legal agents of shareholders' financial interests) is to act in such a way as to maximize the financial rate of return on the owners' shares. The capitalist system upon which the Western economies are based rests in large part upon the presupposition that investments made in shares (e.g. in pension funds, unit trusts, etc.) will perform well. The profitable performance of shares lies in an increase in a share's value and in the rate of dividend per share – objectives that can only be served by financial profits. Hence, the stockholder position can usually be expressed as a 'profit maximization' dictum.

Table 1.2
A summary of analytical frameworks

Strategic process	Framework	Analytical purpose	Origin
Strategic learning: internal	Value chain	Value-adding activities	Porter – competitive positioning
	Resource	Resources	Penrose – resource-based strategy
	Core competences	Competences and core competences – competitive advantage	Prahalad and Hamel – resource/competence-based
	Products	BCG matrix	Boston Consulting Group – competitive positioning
Strategic learning: external	Five forces	Competitive environment – industry and market	Porter-competitive positioning
	Globalization drivers	Competitive environment – globalization	Yip – competitive positioning
	Strategic group	Competitive environment	Competitive positioning
	SPENT	Remote environment – social, political, economic, natural and technological (SPENT) forces	Competitive positioning
Strategy development	Knowledge – explicit and tacit	Nature of strategic knowledge	Nonaka, Stonehouse and Pemberton – knowledge-based
	Core competences	Nature and development of core competences	Prahalad and Hamel – competence-based
	Distinctive capability	Nature and development of distinctive capability	Kay – competence-based
	Generic strategy	Nature of differentiation, cost leadership and hybrid strategies	Porter – competitive positioning
	Total global strategy	Nature of global strategies	Yip – competitive positioning
Strategy evaluation	Suitability, feasibility, acceptability	Choosing appropriate strategy and direction	Competitive positioning
Strategic change and implementation	Resource allocation		Competitive positioning
	Competence-building		Competence-based
	Functional strategies		Competitive positioning
	Cultural, structural and systemic change		Organizational learning

The stakeholder approach

A stakeholder has been defined as:

> Any group or individual who can affect or [be] affected by the achievement of an organization's objectives. (Freeman, 1984, p. 46)

This definition draws in almost everybody that is, or may potentially be, involved in the life of an organization. It consequently goes without saying that not all stakeholders are equal in their influence on an organization's objectives.

The stakeholder approach (see, for example, Freeman, 1984; Donaldson and Preston, 1995) argues that organizations, like individual people, are characterized by their relationships with various groups and individuals such as employees and customers. A group or individual qualifies as a stakeholder if it has an interest in the organization's activities and has the power to affect the firm's performance and/or has a stake in it.

The implications of this proposition are far-reaching. In essence, stakeholder theory argues that shareholders are neither the sole owners of a business nor the sole beneficiaries of its activities. Although shareholders are undeniably one stakeholder group, they are far from being the only group who expect to benefit from and influence business activity and, accordingly, are just one of those groups that have a legitimate right to influence a company's strategic objectives. Some of these groups are internal to the organization whereas others are external.

Key concept

Stakeholders

A stakeholder is "any group or individual who can affect or [be] affected by the achievement of an organization's objectives". (Freeman, 1984, p. 46)

Internal stakeholders include directors, employees, employees' representatives (e.g. trades unions).

External stakeholders include shareholders, customers, suppliers, trade bodies, pressure groups, governments, competitors, local communities and 'society'.

Stakeholders and objectives

One widely used and useful model for understanding how stakeholders exert influence on an organization's objectives was proposed by Mendelow (1991). According to this model, stakeholders can be 'ranked' depending upon two variables: the stakeholder's *interest* and *power*:

- stakeholder *power* refers to the *ability* to influence the organization;
- stakeholder *interest* refers to the *willingness* to influence the organization. In other words, interest concerns the extent to which the stakeholder cares about what the organization does.

It then follows that:

$$\text{Stakeholder influence} = \text{power} \times \text{interest}$$

The actual influence that a stakeholder has will depend upon where the stakeholder is positioned with respect to ability to influence and willingness to influence. A stakeholder with both high power and high interest will be more influential than one with low power and low interest. We can map stakeholders by showing the two variables on a grid comprising two intersecting continua (Figure 1.3).

Once constructed, we can use the map to assess two things:

1 which stakeholder is likely to exert the most influence upon the organization's objectives;
2 the stakeholders that are most likely to be in potential conflict over strategic objectives (where two or more stakeholders are in close proximity in the high power–high interest part of the map).

The managing director and the board of directors are usually examples of stakeholders with both high power and high interest. This is because they not only manage the business but also depend upon it for their jobs and potential career advancement. The pub to which employees retire after or during the day's work is an example of a stakeholder with potentially high interest but low power (and therefore low total influence).

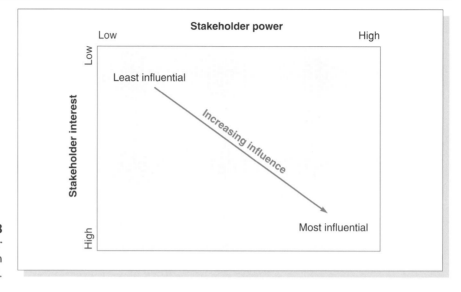

Figure 1.3
The stakeholder map (adapted from Mendelow, 1991).

Once the stakeholder map has been constructed for an organization, the competing agendas can be analysed. If, for example, two highly influential stakeholders (i.e. in the high–high quadrant) agree on corporate objectives, the momentum behind the agreed objective will be very strong. If, conversely, influential stakeholders disagree on objectives, the possibility of damaging conflict will be high. It is also important to bear in mind that the shape of the 'map' can change with time as stakeholders vary in their power and interest. A certain event, for example, might stimulate interest and push a powerful but not-as-yet-interested stakeholder into the highly influential quadrant. Similarly, high interest but low power stakeholders can sometimes increase their power by forming a joint campaign or coalition, thus moving them nearer to the high–high quadrant. The more stakeholders there are with influence, the more complex a scenario becomes when it comes to agreeing objectives.

References and further reading

Andrews, K. (1987) *The Concept of Corporate Strategy*. Homewood: Irwin.

Ansoff, H.I. (1965) *Corporate Strategy: An Analytical Approach to Business Policy for Growth and Expansion*. New York: McGraw-Hill.

Ansoff, H.I. (1991) Critique of Henry Mintzberg's the 'Design School' reconsidering the basic premises of strategic management. *Strategic Management Journal*, September, 449–461.

Argenti, J. (1974) *Systematic Corporate Planning*. Sunbury-on-Thames: Nelson.

Argyris, C. (1992) *On Organisational Learning*. Blackwell.

Baden-Fuller, C. and Stopford, J. (1992) *Rejuvenating the Mature Business*. London: Routledge.

Barney, J.B. (1991) Firm resources and sustained competitive advantage. *Journal of Management*, 17(1).

Barney, J.B. (1996) *Gaining and Sustaining Competitive Advantage*. New York: Addison Wesley.

Chandler, A.D. (1962) *Strategy and Structure*. Boston, MA: MIT Press.

Donaldson, T. and Preston, L.E. (1995) The stakeholder theory of the corporation – concepts, evidence and implications. *Academy of Management Review*, 20(1), 65–91.

Freeman, R.E. (1984) *Strategic Management: A Stakeholder Approach*. Boston: Pitman.

Grant, R. (1991) The resource based theory of competitive advantage: implications for strategy formulation. *California Management Review*, 33 (Spring), 114–135.

Grant, R.M. (1998) *Contemporary Strategic Analysis*. Blackwell.

Heene, A. and Sanchez, R. (1997) *Competence-Based Strategic Management*. John Wiley.

Kay, J. (1993) *Foundations of Corporate Success*. Oxford: Oxford University Press.

Kay, J. (1995) Learning to define the core business. *Financial Times*, 1 December.

Lindblom, C.E. (1959) The Science of Muddling Through. *Public Administration Review*, 19

McKiernan, P. (1997) Strategy past; strategy futures. *Long Range Planning*, 30(5).

Mendelow, A. (1991) Proceedings of Second International Conference on Information Systems, Cambridge, MA.

Mintzberg, H. (1987) Five Ps for strategy. *California Management Review*, Fall. Reprinted in Mintzberg, H. (1990) The Design School: reconsidering the basic premises of strategic management. *Strategic Management Journal*, March.

Mintzberg, H. and Waters, J.A. (1985) Of strategies deliberate and emergent. *Strategic Management Journal*, 6.

Mintzberg, H., Quinn, J.B. and Ghoshal, S. (1995) *The Strategy Process: Concepts, Contexts and Cases*. European Edition. Englewood Cliffs, NJ: Prentice Hall.

Mintzberg, H., Quinn, J.B. and Ghoshal, S. (1998). *The Strategy Process*. Revised European Edition. Hemel Hempstead: Prentice Hall.

Nonaka, I. (1991) The knowledge-creating company. *Harvard Business Review*, 6(8), 96–104.

Nonaka, I., Toyama, R. and Konno, N. (2000) SECI, Ba and leadership: a unified model of dynamic knowledge creation. *Long Range Planning*, 33(1), 5–34.

Pemberton, J. and Stonehouse, G. (2000) Organisational learning and knowledge assets: an essential partnership. *The Learning Organization*, 7(4), 184–193.

Penrose, E. (1959) *The Theory of the Growth of the Firm*. Oxford: Oxford University Press.

Porter, M.E. (1980) *Competitive Strategy: Techniques for Analysing Industries and Competitors*. New York: Free Press.

Porter, M.E. (1985) *Competitive Advantage*. New York: Free Press.

Prahalad, C.K. and Hamel, G. (1990) The core competence of the corporation. Harvard Business Review, May–June.

Rumelt, R.P. (1984) Towards a strategic theory of the firm. In: Lamb, R.B. (ed.), *Competitive Strategic Management*. Englewood Cliffs: Prentice Hall.

Rumelt, R. (1991) How much does industry matter? *Strategic Management Journal*, March.

Sanchez, R. and Heene, A. (1997) *Strategic Learning and Knowledge Management*. New York: John Wiley.

Senge, P. (1990) Building learning organisations. *Sloan Management Review*, Fall.

Stalk, G., Evans, P. and Shulmann, L.E. (1992) Competing on capabilities: the new rules of corporate strategy. *Harvard Business Review*, March/April, 57–69.

Stonehouse, G. and Pemberton, J. (1999) Learning and knowledge management in the intelligent organisation. *Participation and Empowerment: An International Journal*, 7(5), 131–144.

Stonehouse, G., Pemberton, J. and Barber, C. (2001) The role of knowledge facilitators and inhibitors: lessons from airline reservations systems. *Long Range Planning*, 34(2), 115–138.

Yip, G.S. (1992) *Total Global Strategy: Managing for Worldwide Competitive Advantage*. Englewood Cliffs, NJ: Prentice Hall.

Internal analysis

Purposes of internal analysis

Internal analysis is concerned with providing management with a detailed understanding of the business, how effective its current strategies are and how effectively it has deployed its resources in support of its strategies. In recent years the importance of internal analysis has been given greater emphasis because recent research has suggested that it is predominantly the actions of the business itself that determine its ability to outperform competitors. Internal analysis aims to provide the managers of a business with an understanding of its potential for competitive advantage and, equally, of those areas where it must take remedial action to ensure its survival. This section of the book introduces and evaluates the main techniques employed in internally analysing the business.

Organizations may carry out an internal analysis for some or all of the following reasons:

- to identify resources, competences and core competences to be developed and exploited;
- to evaluate how effectively value-adding activities are organized;
- to identify areas of weaknesses to be addressed in future strategy and its implementation;
- to evaluate the performance of products;
- to evaluate financial performance, particularly in comparison with competitors;
- to evaluate investment potential if finance is being sought from external sources;

■ as a first step in assessing the suitability, feasibility and acceptability of future strategies.

What are the components of an internal analysis?

An internal analysis will cover some or all of the following aspects of the business or organization:

- ■ resource analysis (Chapter 2);
- ■ competence audit and analysis, and the sources of distinctive capabilities (Chapter 2);
- ■ internal activities analysis using Porter's value chain framework (Chapter 2);
- ■ performance analysis (evaluating business performance using financial and non-financial indicators) (Chapter 4);
- ■ human resources and culture (Chapter 3);
- ■ financial resources and financial performance (Chapter 4);
- ■ products and their positions in markets (Chapter 5).

These aspects of internal analysis are covered in Chapters 2–5, which form Part II of this book. A number of 'tools' and 'frameworks' will be introduced to assist the internal analysis.

CHAPTER 2

The business organization: competences and activities

Introduction and chapter overview

In Chapter 1 we encountered the concept of competitive advantage as one of the key objectives of business strategy. There has been considerable debate in the academic literature as to the causes of competitive advantage. Essentially, the debate asks the question: How do organizations achieve superior performance? Two positions have emerged as the most prominent.

The *competitive positioning* school of thought, based primarily on the work of Michael Porter (1980, 1985), stresses the importance of how the organization is positioned with respect to its competitive environment or industry (which we discuss in Chapter 7). The *resource* or *competence* school (Prahalad and Hamel, 1990; Heene and Sanchez, 1997), on the other hand, argues that it is the competences (abilities) of the business and the distinctive way that it organizes its activities that determine its ability to outperform competitors. As with most controversies, we suggest that both schools of thought have their merits – both are partial explanations of the source of competitive advantage.

This chapter concentrates on developing an understanding of the major factors governing the level of performance of the business, namely its resources, competences – particularly its core competences – and its 'value-adding' activities.

After studying this chapter, students should be able to:

- explain the concepts of *core competences*, *competences* and *resources* and the relationships between them;
- explain the concept of the *value chain* and the value chain framework;
- explain the relationships between core competences and core activities;
- explain how the value chain framework 'works';
- explain how the configuration of value-adding activities can improve business performance;
- identify the potential benefits of collaboration with suppliers, distributors and customers.

Resources, competences and core competences

Definitions

The terms *competence* and *capability*, *core competence* and *distinctive capability* are often used interchangeably in textbooks on business strategy. Although some writers (Stalk *et al.*, 1992) have argued that there are significant differences between the terms *competence* and *capability*, we will use the terms to mean broadly the same things based upon the following definitions.

Competences

A *competence* is an attribute or collection of attributes possessed by all or most of the companies in an industry. Without such attributes a business cannot enter or survive in the industry. Competences develop from resources and embody skills, technology or 'know-how'. For example, in order to operate in the pharmaceuticals industry, it is necessary to possess both the ability to manufacture medicines (by using specially designed factory equipment) and, importantly, a detailed understanding of how medicines work on the human body. Every successful survivor in the industry possesses both of these areas of competence.

Core competences

A *core competence* or *distinctive capability* is an attribute, or collection of attributes, specific to a particular organization which enables it to produce above industry average performance. It arises from the way in which the organization has employed its competences and resources *more effectively* than its competitors. The result of a distinctive capability is an output that customers value more highly than those of competitors. It is based upon one or more of superior organizational knowledge, information, skills, technology, structure, relationships, networks and reputation.

Resources

A *resource* is an input employed in the activities of the business. Success rests in large part upon the efficiency by which the business converts its resources into outputs. Resources fall into four broad categories: human, financial, physical (buildings, equipment, stock, etc.) and intangible (e.g. 'know-how', patents, legal rights, brand names, registered designs, etc.).

Key concept

Competitive advantage

Competitive advantage is often seen as the overall purpose of business strategy. Some texts use the phrase *superior performance* to mean the same thing. Essentially, a business can be said to possess competitive advantage if it is able to return higher profits than its competitors. The higher profits means that it will be able to commit more retained profit to reinvestment in its strategy, thus maintaining its lead over its competitors in an industry. When this superiority is maintained successfully over time, we refer to it as a *sustainable* competitive advantage. Competitive advantage can be lost when management fails to reinvest the superior profits in such a way that the advantage is not maintained.

How core competences 'work'

Core competences tend to be both complex and intangible so that it is necessary to explore the nature of the resources and competences that underpin them before exploring the concept further (see Figure 2.1). The purpose of such analysis is to allow managers to identify which resources and competences act as the foundation of existing or potential core competences. It is extremely important to note that not all the competitors in an industry will possess core competences or distinctive capabilities (Kay, 1995). It is only those players that are producing above average performance that can be considered as possessing core competences. Those with only average or below average performance possess competences and resources (without which they could not compete in the industry at all) but not core competences (for further discussion of these concepts see Prahalad and Hamel, 1990; Kay, 1993; Heene and Sanchez, 1997; Petts, 1997).

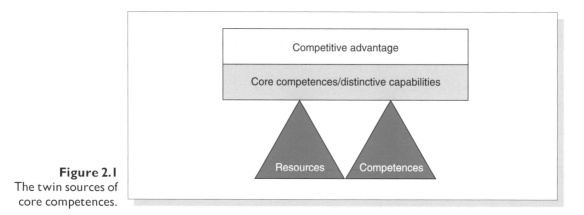

Figure 2.1
The twin sources of core competences.

Core competence (distinctive capability) = superior acquisition and employment of resources + superior development of 'general' competences

We will now consider these terms in more detail.

Resource analysis

Tangible and intangible resources

Resources can be either *tangible* or *intangible*. They are the inputs that enable an organization to carry out its activities. Tangible assets include stocks, materials, machinery, buildings, human resources, finance and so on. Intangible assets include skills, knowledge, brand names and goodwill, patent rights, etc. (see Coyne, 1986; Hall, 1992). Intangible resources are often produced within the organization, but tangibles are obtained from outside organizations. Such resources are obtained in resource markets in competition with businesses from within and outside the industry. Relationships with the suppliers of resources can form an important part of the organization's core competence, for example its ability to attract the most appropriately skilled human resources in the job market.

Analysing resources

When we analyse a company's resources as part of an internal analysis, several frameworks can be employed to provide a comprehensive review.

Analysis by category

Firstly, we might, for example, consider them by category: human, financial, physical or intangible. These resources are then evaluated quantitatively (how much or how many) and qualitatively (how effectively they are being employed). Much of this analysis is covered in Chapters 3–5. Physical resources such as buildings and machinery will typically be audited for capacity, utilization, age, condition, contribution to output and so on. Materials and stocks can be assessed on the basis of quality, reliability, availability, number of suppliers, delivery times and unit costs. Human resources are considered in terms of numbers, education, skills, training, experience, age, motivation, wage costs and productivity in relation to the needs of the organization.

Analysis by specificity

Secondly, we can analyse resources according to their *specificity*. Resources can be 'more' or 'less' specific. For example, skilled workers tend to have specialized and industry-specific knowledge and skills. Some technology, for example computer software, is for general (non-industry-specific) business use (e.g. word-processing, database and spreadsheet software). Other computer software applications, such as airline computer reservation systems, are written for highly specialized uses. Whereas non-specific resources tend to be more flexible and form the basis of competences, industry-specific resources are more likely to act as the foundations of core competences (e.g. the specialized knowledge of scientists in the chemical industry).

Analysis by performance

Thirdly, resources can be evaluated on the basis of how they contribute to internal and external *measures of performance*. Internal measures include their contribution to:

- business objectives and targets – financial, performance and output measures;
- historical comparisons – measures of performance over time (e.g. against previous years);
- business unit or divisional comparisons.

External measures can include:

- comparisons with competitors, particularly those who are industry leaders, those who are the closest competitors and are in its strategic grouping (see Chapter 5);
- comparisons with companies in other industries.

By employing these techniques of analysis, an organization is able to both internally and externally *benchmark* its performance as a stimulus to improving performance in the future. Performance, however, is based on more than resources, and competences must be similarly analysed and evaluated.

Competences

Competences are attributes, such as skills, knowledge, technology and relationships, that are common among the competitors in an industry. For example, all players in the pharmaceutical industry possess similar competences (basic abilities) in research and development, marketing, manufacturing and distribution. Competences are less tangible than resources and are consequently more difficult to evaluate.

They are more often developed internally but may be acquired externally or by collaboration with suppliers, distributors or customers.

Competences are distinguished from core competences by the fact that they do not produce superior performance and by the fact that they are not distinctive from the competences possessed by other companies in the industry. On the other hand, competences are essential for survival in a particular line of business. Competences also have the potential to be developed into core competences.

Core competences

Distinguishing core competences from general competences

Core competences are distinguished from competences in several ways:

- they are only possessed by those companies whose performance is superior to the industry average;
- they are unique to the company;
- they are more complex;
- they are difficult to emulate (copy);
- they relate to fulfilling customer needs;
- they add greater value than 'general' competences;
- they are often based on distinctive relationships with customers, distributors and suppliers;
- they are based upon superior organizational skills and knowledge.

In the motor industry, all manufacturers have the competences and resources required to build motor vehicles, but a company such as BMW has core competences in design, engine technology and marketing which act as the basis of its reputation for high-quality, high-performance motor cars. These core competences make it possible for BMW to charge premium prices for its products. In this way, core competences are the basis of a organization's competitive advantage.

Core competences and distinctive capabilities

Kay (1993) presented a slightly different explanation, arguing that competitive advantage is based upon what he termed *distinctive capability*. Distinctive capability can develop from reputation, architecture (internal and external relationships), innovation and strategic assets. Marks & Spencer's competitive advantage can be explained in terms of its reputation for quality, its special relationships with its suppliers and its customers. Marks & Spencer has very exacting but mutually profitable relationships with the businesses who supply its products. It demands high quality at reasonable cost, and flexibility in return for large volumes of business. Its relationship with customers is based upon its reputation for good service, refunds and exchanges of goods, and high-quality products. The end result is that it has a performance that is superior to most of its high street competitors.

Core competence arises from the unique and distinctive way that the organization builds, develops, integrates and deploys its resources and competences. An existing core competence can be evaluated for:

- *customer focus* – does it adequately focus on customer needs?
- *uniqueness* – can it be imitated by competitors and, if so, how easily?
- *flexibility* – can it be easily adapted if market or industry conditions change?
- *contribution to value* – to what extent does it add value to the product or service?
- *sustainability* – how long can its superiority be sustained over time?

Competences, as opposed to core competences, can also be judged against these criteria in order to evaluate their potential to form the basis upon which new core competences can be built.

Core competences can never be regarded as being permanent. The pace of change of technology and society are such that core competences must be constantly adapted and new ones cultivated. A good example of the need to adapt comes from an examination of IBM. In the 1980s, IBM had core competences in the design, production, marketing and sales of personal computers. The value that customers attached to these competences was lost in the late 1980s and early 1990s because competitors were able to match IBM's competences in design and production of personal computers and at a lower price. IBM had failed to adapt its core competences so that they became merely industry-wide competences. Its superiority was eroded because it failed to sustain its advantage.

Outcomes of the analyses

The aim of an analysis of resources, competences and core competences is, therefore, to:

- understand the nature and sources of particular core competences;
- identify the need for and methods of adaptation of existing core competences;
- identify the need for new core competence building;
- identify potential sources of core competence based on resources and competences;
- ensure that core competences remain focused on customer needs.

Resources, competences and core competences are obviously closely related to the ways in which a business organizes and performs its value-adding activities. It is therefore also necessary to analyse the way in which value-adding activities are configured and coordinated.

Key concepts

Competence leveraging and building

- *Competence leveraging* refers to the ability of a business to exploit its core competences in new markets, thus meeting new customer needs. It can also refer to the ability of the business to modify and improve existing core competences.
- *Competence building* takes place when the business builds new core competences, based upon its resources and competences. It is often necessary to build new competences alongside existing ones when entering new markets, as it is unlikely that existing competences will fully meet new customer needs.

Analysis of value-adding activities

What is value-adding?

Value chain analysis (Porter, 1985) seeks to provide an understanding of how much value an organization's activities add to its products and services compared to the costs of the resources used in their production. A given product can be produced by organizing activities in a number of different ways. Value chain analysis helps managers to understand how effectively and efficiently the activities of their organization are configured and coordinated. The acid test is how much value is added in the process of turning inputs into the outputs which are products in the form of goods and services. Value is measured in terms of the price that customers are willing to pay for the product.

Value added can be increased in two ways:

1 by changing customer perceptions of the product so that they are willing to pay a higher price for a product than for similar products produced by other businesses;
2 by reducing production costs below those of competitors.

Key concept

Value added

In simple terms, the value added to a good or service is the difference in the financial value of the finished product compared to the financial value of the inputs. As a sheet of metal passes through the various stages in car production, value is added such that a tonne of metal worth a few hundred pounds becomes a motor car worth several thousands of pounds. The rate at which value is added is dependent upon how well the operations process is managed. If the car manufacturer suffers a cost disadvantage by, say, holding a high level of stock or working with out-of-date machinery, then the value added over the process will be lower.

There are clear linkages between value-adding activities, core competences, competences and resources. Resources form the inputs to the organization's value-adding activities, while competences and core competences provide the skills and knowledge required to carry them out. The more that core competences can be integrated into value-adding activities, the greater will be the value added.

The value-adding process

Businesses can be regarded as systems that transform inputs (resources, materials, etc.) into outputs (goods and services). This is illustrated in Figure 2.2.

The activities inside the organization *add value* to the inputs. The value of the finished goods is equivalent to the price that a customer is willing to pay for the goods. The difference between the end value and the total costs is the *margin* (the quantity that accountants would refer to as the *profit margin* – before interest, taxation and extraordinary items).

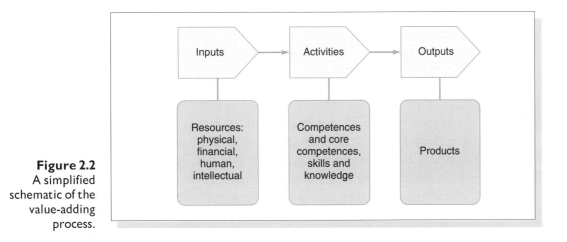

Figure 2.2
A simplified schematic of the value-adding process.

The value chain

The activities of the organization can be broken down into a sequence of activities known as the *value chain*, as described by Porter in 1985 (see Figure 2.3).

The activities within the chain may be classified into *primary* activities and *support* activities. *Primary activities* are those that *directly add value* to the final product. *Support activities* do not directly add value themselves but *indirectly add value* by supporting the effective execution of primary activities. Table 2.1 describes the primary and secondary activities.

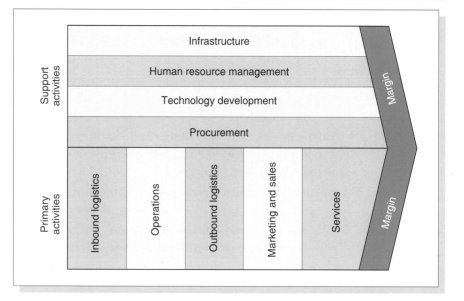

Figure 2.3
The value chain
(after Porter, 1985).

Table 2.1
A summary of the activities in the value chain

Primary activities	Inbound logistics	Receipt and storage of materials (inputs) Stock control and distribution of inputs
	Operations	Transformation of inputs into final product
	Outbound logistics	Storage and distribution of finished goods
	Sales and marketing	Making the product available to the market and persuading people to buy
	Service	Installation and after sales support
Support activities	Procurement	Purchasing of resources
	Technology development	Product, process and resource development
	Infrastructure	Planning, finance, information systems, management
	Human resource management	Recruitment, selection, training, reward and motivation

Analysis of the value chain

An organization's value chain links into the value chains of other organizations, particularly those of suppliers and distributors. This 'chain' of value chains is sometimes called the *value system* or *total supply chain*. Linkages with suppliers are known as *upstream* linkages, those with distributors and customers are *downstream* linkages.

Different types of organization will have very different value chains. For example, the value chain of Dixons, the electrical goods retailer, does not include the design and manufacture of the products it sells. Marks & Spencer's value chain does include some design but does not include manufacturing.

Similarly, not all of an organization's activities are of equal importance in adding value to its products. Those that are of greatest importance can be considered as *core activities* and are often closely associated to core competences. Thus, in a fashion house such as Calvin Klein, design activities are of the greatest importance in adding value and the organization's core competences are concentrated in this area.

Analysis of value-adding activities helps to identify where the most value is added and where there is potential to add greater value by changing the way in which activities are configured and by improving the way in which they are coordinated. It is important to note that an organization's value chain is not analysed in isolation but that it is considered in conjunction with its external linkages to suppliers, distributors and customers.

A value chain analysis would be expected to include:

- a breakdown of all the activities of the organization;
- identification of core activities and their relationships to core competences and current organizational strategies;
- identification of the effectiveness and efficiency of the individual activities;
- examination of *linkages* between activities for additional added value;
- identification of *blockages* that reduce the organization's competitive advantage.

A useful technique in value chain analysis involves comparison with the value chains of competitors to identify the benefits and drawbacks of alternative configurations.

The aim of value chain analysis is to identify ways in which the performance of the individual activities and the linkages between them can be improved. This may involve identification of improved configurations for activities or improved coordination of them. It is particularly important to consider the extent to which value chain activities support the current strategy of the organization. For example, if the current strategy is based upon high quality then the activities must be configured so as to ensure high-quality products. On the other hand, if the organization competes largely on the basis of price, then activities must be organized so as to minimize costs.

Core activities, non-core activities and outsourcing

An increasing trend in recent years has been for organizations to concentrate on core activities associated with core competences and to outsource activities that are not regarded as core to other organizations for whom the activities are core. This is why, for example, fashion houses concentrate on design and marketing, and outsource the production of their garments to businesses whose core activities are the manufacture of clothing. The combination of complementary core competences adds to the competitive advantage of all the collaborating companies. Value chain analysis should therefore also seek to identify where outsourcing might potentially add greater value than performing the activity in-house.

References and further reading

Coyne, K.P. (1986) Sustainable competitive advantage – what it is, what it isn't. *Business Horizons*, January–February, 54–61.

Hall, R. (1992) The strategic analysis of intangible resources. *Strategic Management Journal*, 13, 135–144.

Heene, A. and Sanchez, R. (1997) *Competence-Based Strategic Management*. London: John Wiley.

Kay, J. (1993) *Foundations of Corporate Success*. Oxford: Oxford University Press.

Kay, J. (1995) Learning to define the core business. *Financial Times*, 1 December.

Petts, N. (1997) Building growth on core competences – a practical approach. *Long Range Planning*, 30(4), 551–561.

Porter, M.E. (1980) *Competitive Strategy: Techniques for Analysing Industries and Competitors*. New York: Free Press.

Porter, M.E. (1985) *Competitive Advantage*. New York: Free Press.

Prahalad, C.K. and Hamel, G. (1990) The core competence of the corporation. *Harvard Business Review*, May–June.

Stalk, G., Evans, P. and Shulmann, L.E. (1992) Competing on capabilities: the new rules of corporate strategy. *Harvard Business Review*, March/April, 57–69.

Human resources and culture

As one of the four resource 'types' (along with physical, financial and intellectual resources), human resources are one of the key resource inputs to any organizational process. A thorough analysis of this resource is an important part of strategic analysis and this chapter explains the resource audit – one of the most widely used tools for this purpose.

Closely linked to human resources is the issue of an organization's culture. In this chapter, we define culture and then go on to explain its importance to an organization. The cultural web is discussed – a model used to explain the way that the features of culture determine the organization's paradigm. Finally, we discuss two cultural typologies.

After studying this chapter, students should be able to:

- define and explain the importance of human resources to an organization;
- explain the purpose of a human resource audit;
- describe what a human resource gap is;
- explain what a human resource audit contains and what it can be used for;
- describe human resource benchmarking;

■ explain what a critical success factor (CSF) is and how humans can be CSFs;

■ define culture and explain its determinants and why it is important;

■ explain the components of the cultural web and the nature of paradigms;

■ describe two typologies of cultural types.

Human resources

The importance of human resources

People are an important resource to most organizations. Decisions about the future strategy of the organization are made by people and strategies are implemented by people. The success or failure of a current strategy will depend not only on decisions made in the past but also on how those decisions are being implemented now by people employed by the organization. It is therefore important to ask questions about who, how and why people are doing what they are doing and what they should do in strategic implementation. In short, human resources add value, manage the business and can contribute to strategic success but, conversely, they can make spectacular errors that can be very costly to the organization.

An understanding of the capabilities of individuals and groups in terms of attitudes, abilities and skills, as well as an understanding of how individuals relate one to another, is an important part of the preparation and development of strategy. A key 'tool' in gaining an understanding of an organization's human resources is the human resource audit.

The human resource audit

The purpose of human resource audit

The human resource audit is an investigation into the size, skills, structure and all other issues surrounding those currently employed by the organization and its future human resource needs. The audit reviews the ability of the human resources to implement a chosen strategy or a range of strategic options.

Most organizations employ accountants to maintain a constant review of financial resources and, each year, limited companies subject themselves (by law) to a formal external financial audit. Human resources are another resource input and are equally, and in some contexts more, important than financial resources. An organization would be foolish to pursue a strategy without a thorough financial review, and the same is true of its human resources.

Once the audit has been completed, management should be able to answer the key question: Are the human resources in the organization a strength to be built on or a weakness that needs to be addressed? The information gained from a human resource audit provides an essential input into the evaluation of prospective future strategies and, in particular, how feasible each prospective strategy is and what 'gaps' exist in the human resource complement that need to be 'closed'.

Key concept

Human resource gaps

A 'gap' can occur in any area of human resource management. It rests upon a simple calculation:

Human resource gap = human resources necessary for the proposed strategy minus current state of the human resources

Gaps can occur in 'numbers' (i.e. head count) and/or in particular skills. In sectors such as banking, for example, skills gaps may be identified in particular computer languages. It may be that the audit reveals a deficit of 30 UNIX programmers – a negative gap. The task of the human resource department thus becomes to successfully appoint or retrain to gain the requisite number of skilled programmers.

'Positive gaps' may also be identified – surpluses of a particular type of employee. The human resource strategy thus becomes to put measures in place to dispose of the excess labour.

Gaps may be closed by recruitment, by retraining, by staff training and development, by redeployment, by redundancy, etc. Each of these solutions has financial and time implications.

The contents of a human resource audit

The contents of a human resource audit will vary from organization to organization depending on its size or geographic coverage (i.e. how decentralized it is). A typical audit checklist is as follows:

- the number of employees by a number of counting methods – the total number, by division, by location, by skill type, by grade or place in hierarchy, by age or length of service, by gender and by ethnic group;
- employee costs – usually measured by salary costs and 'add-ons' (e.g. national insurance, etc.);
- the organizational structure and the position of employees within the structure;
- recruitment and selection procedures and their effectiveness;
- the quality and effectiveness of training and development programmes used;
- the level of employee motivation and morale;
- the level of skills and capabilities present;
- the quality of employee or industrial relations between management and employees;
- the internal and external networks that employees in the organization have developed (and their effectiveness for various purposes);
- the monitoring of the effectiveness of existing human resource policies and control procedures.

Formal and informal human resource audits

The information provided by the audit can provide management with important information about the state of the organization's human resources. In some types of organization, regular audits are essential to success. For a professional soccer club or an orchestra, the state of the human resources is completely transparent and the audit occurs continually – although it may never be formally conducted. A football team that loses every match or an orchestra that sounds terrible will have obvious human resource skill deficits. A formal audit is hardly necessary in such a circumstance. In some other organization types, underperformance may be more difficult to detect and correct, however. A football goalkeeper making errors, for example, is a much more observable and transparent human resource deficit than an incompetent general practitioner. The goalkeeper is likely to be noticed by many thousands of fans whereas the GP's errors may persist for years before being noted.

Formal audits may be carried out by personnel specialists on a regular basis (say annually), or whenever management needs the information for the purposes of a strategic analysis. Practitioners in this area make the point that the simple following of 'lists', such as that outlined above, is only a starting point. As points of interest are raised, such as key skill deficiencies, then it is often a good idea to examine the reasons for the shortage as an integral part of the audit. Features of the labour market, for example, might explain shortages of some employee types.

The outcomes of a human resource audit

The problem of measurement

The various components of a human resource audit can sometimes present problems of measurement. We can measure entries such as employee costs, numbers, skills shortages or surpluses, etc. in numerical terms (either by head count or in monetary units). Industrial relations measures can partly be measured by such things as days lost through strikes, etc. How, though, might we measure staff morale or motivation? We might be able to say that staff morale is high or low, but any 'in-betweens' might be difficult to assign a value to in the same way as for, say, employee costs. The same problems arise with the levels of staff motivation and job satisfaction. It is also probably true in most organizations that large disparities exist between employees in respect of these intangibles. Some employees will be highly motivated and will enjoy good morale whereas others will not. It is for these reasons that a 'checklist' approach to human resource audit is rarely possible – it usually contains some subjective assessments of some parts of the audit.

Human resource benchmarking

The concept of benchmarking is one that we will encounter several times in this book. Essentially, benchmarking is a tool for comparing a feature of one organization with the same feature of another. It is particularly useful for comparison against the best in an industry for the feature in question. Followers of the best in the industry might then ask why the leader company has achieved the superior perfor-

mance (see our discussion of benchmarking in finance, Chapter 4, and in operations, Chapter 12).

The feature examined in a benchmarking analysis will depend upon what the organization needs to know. If, for example, a company identifies a negative gap in a key skill area which it has found difficult to close (say of good-quality graduates), a benchmark study will enable the company to find out about its competitors. If Company A is known to be able to attract the best graduates, then an examination of its human resource policies will enable other companies (competitors) to benchmark their own practices against it. It may be that Company A is identified as offering the best career-progression planning, the highest salaries or the best development opportunities. If this is found to be the case, then competitors will want to examine their own provision in these areas to see where they can be improved.

Lead companies may also be analysed for the ways in which they not only manage their internal human resources but also the ways in which they interact with external sources of labour. Many high-technology companies, for example, close skills gaps by making extensive use of contract workers or consultants. The ability to attract these 'mobile' workers can be just as important as attracting permanent employees.

Identifying human resources as critical success factors

As well as using a human resource audit to identify gaps, it can also be used to establish which, if any, employees or groups of employees are critical to strategic success. These are the people that the organization's success may have been built upon in the past and it is likely that the existing structures are centred around them.

In some organizations, critical success human resources may be found on the board of directors, giving strategic direction to the company as a whole. In others, they might be found in research, developing the new products upon which the future success will be built. Marketing people or operations management might also be critical in some businesses. It follows that a key part of the resulting human resource strategy will be to protect and retain such key people.

Key concept

Critical success factors

It is usually the case that there are one or more reasons why superior performers in an industry are in the positions that they are. These key reasons for success are called *critical success factors* (CSFs). Some companies have uniquely skilled employees, such as particularly important computer programmers or research scientists. In this case, the CSF is a human resource. In other businesses, the CSF might be a unique location, a brand image, an enviable reputation, a legally protected patent or licence, a unique production process or technology or any combination of these. This is not to say that other parts of the organization are unimportant, but merely that the CSF is *the* most important key cause of the success.

In terms of competitive strategy, the approach to a CSF is to defend it – in some cases at whatever cost it might take. This usually takes to form of 'locking it in' to ensure that the advantage is maintained or that competitors are prevented from gaining the same advantage.

Organizational culture

What is culture?

Culture is the organizational equivalent of a human's personality. One of the better definitions is that by Stacey (1996):

> The culture of any group of people is that set of beliefs, customs, practices and ways of thinking that they have come to share with each other through being and working together. It is a set of assumptions people simply accept without question as they interact with each other. At the visible level the culture of a group of people takes the form of ritual behaviour, symbols, myths, stories, sounds and artefacts.

In simpler language, culture can be explained in terms of the 'feel' of an organization or its 'character'. Definitions can be a bit inaccessible, but the importance of an organization's culture lies in the fact that it can be 'felt' whenever it is encountered. It is the way 'things are done' in a given setting.

Organizations are as individual as people and, in many ways, there are as many cultures as there are organizations – each one is unique. This is not to say, however, that we cannot identify common features between organizational cultures.

The determinants of culture

The reasons why an organization has a particular type of culture is as complicated a question as asking why a human has a particular personality. It has many possible influences, the net effect of which forges culture over a period of time. Any list would be necessarily incomplete, but the following are some of the most important:

- the philosophy of the organization's founders, especially if the organization is relatively young;
- the nature of the activities in the business and the character of the industry it competes in;
- the nature of the interpersonal relationships and the nature of industrial or employee relationships;
- the management style adopted and the types of control mechanism – for example, the extent to which management style is autocratic or democratic;
- the national or regional character of the areas in which the organization's activities are located; this in turn can affect the power distance, which also influences culture;
- the structure of the organization, particularly its 'height' and 'width' (see Chapter 10);
- the dependency the organization has on technology and the type of technology employed (the growth of e-mail, for example, has had an influence of the culture of some organizations).

Key concept

Power distance

This is a term attributed to Hickson and Pugh (1995). They use the term to describe "how removed subordinates feel from superiors in a social meaning of the word 'distance'. In a high power distance culture, inequality is accepted ... in a low power distance culture, inequalities and overt status symbols are minimized and subordinates expect to be consulted and to share decisions with approachable managers".

Why is culture important?

Culture is important because it can and does affect all aspects of an organization's activities. The metaphor of human personality may help us to understand this. Some people's personality means they are motivated, sharp, exciting to be with, etc. Others are dull, tedious, apathetic, risk-averse, etc. These personality features will affect all aspects of their lives.

The same is true of an organization's 'personality'. Culture is important for the following (not exhaustive) reasons; culture can have an influence on:

- employee motivation;
- the attractiveness of the organization as an employer and hence the rate of staff turnover;
- employee morale and 'goodwill';
- productivity and efficiency;
- the quality of work;
- the nature of the employee and industrial relations;
- the attitude of employees in the workplace;
- innovation and creativity.

The point to make after such a list is simply that culture is *very* important. It is essential that management understand the culture of the organization both in analysing strategic position and then in the implementation of strategy.

The cultural web

One of the most commonly used ways of making sense of an organization's culture is to use the cultural web (Johnson, 1992). It is a schematic representation of the elements of an organization's culture in such a way that we can see how each element influences the paradigm (Figure 3.1).

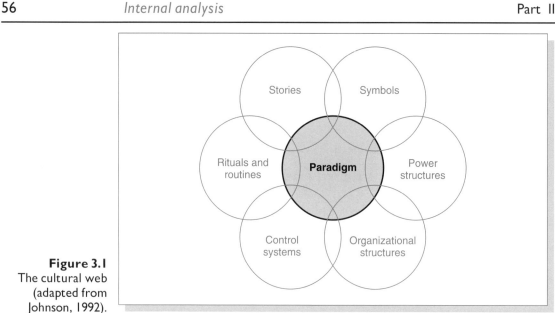

Figure 3.1
The cultural web
(adapted from
Johnson, 1992).

Paradigm

A paradigm is world view – a way of looking at the world. It is expressed in the assumptions that people make and in their deep-rooted beliefs. The paradigm of an organization or a national culture is important because it determines how it will behave in a given circumstance. Given a certain moral dilemma or similar choice, we might expect the paradigms of, for example, an orthodox Jew and an atheist to sometimes lead them to arrive at different conclusions. The things that cause one culture to adopt one paradigm and another culture to espouse a different one are set out in the cultural web.

The main elements of the web are described below.

Stories

Stories are those narratives that people within the organization talk to each other about, what they tell new recruits and outsiders about the organization. The stories typically recount events and people from the past and present – stories of famous victories and defeats. They tend to highlight what is considered important to the members of the organization.

Routines and rituals

Routines are the procedures for doing things within the organization. They are repeated on a regular basis to the extent that they are taken to be 'the way things are done'. Rituals have a longer timeframe and can be either formal and informal. Formal routines and rituals are a part of the organization's practice, such as the 'long service award' or the company Outward Bound course that work teams might go on from time to time. Informal routines and rituals might include the way that people behave at the annual Christmas party or the extent to which colleagues do (or do not) go for a drink together after work.

Symbols

Symbolic aspects of organizational life concern those things that symbolize something to some people: a certain level of promotion, the company car they drive, the position of their office, their job title. In some companies, these symbols have no apparent importance at all. In others, they matter a great deal. The way that employees respond to these symbols can tell us a great deal about the culture.

Structure

The structure of an organization can mean more than just those formal relationships that are shown on an organization diagram. Informal structures can also exist through interpersonal relationships that transcend the formal structures. Some organizations have highly developed informal structures, others do not.

Control systems

The way in which activities are controlled – whether 'tight' or 'loose' – is closely aligned to culture. This has a strong link to power distance and the nature of the activities that the organization is engaged in. Control systems, by definition, concern activity in which performance is gauged against a predetermined standard, and the methods of both standard-setting and monitoring performance vary significantly according to culture.

Power structures

The core assumptions that contribute to the paradigm are likely to be made by the most powerful management groupings in the organization. In some companies, this power resides in the research department, in others it will be the production people or those from another department. In some organizations, there may be arguments about what is important between one or more groupings.

How it works

Each component of the cultural web exerts its own influence upon the organization's paradigm. The paradigm describes the aggregate effects of all of the cultural influences on the way the members of the organization look at the world. This can apply to regions of the world just as it applies to organizations. People indigenous to one region of the world are often thought to have a different view of the world to the citizens of another. This difference is because of the influence that each component of the cultural web exerts on the national or regional paradigm.

We can also use the components of the cultural web to help us to understand a paradigm. In this case, we are using the six 'peripheral' factors as manifestations of, rather than contributors to, the paradigm. If, then, we want to understand the central beliefs of a company (its paradigm), we should examine the cultural web factors. By examining each one, just as we might examine the externalities of a human personality, we can gain clues as to the 'real personality' or culture that is at the centre (the paradigm).

Cultural typologies

A number of writers in organizational theory have attempted to group culture types together. The thinking behind such attempts at typology is that, if organizations can describe their cultures by type, this would help in strategic analysis. We will briefly consider two of these attempts.

Handy's culture types

Handy (1993) suggested that organizational cultures can be divided into four broad types: power cultures, role cultures, task cultures and person cultures.

Power cultures

This type of organization is dominated by either a very powerful individual or a dominant small group. It is typified by an organization that has grown as a result of entrepreneurial flair. Strategic decisions and many operational ones are made by the centre and few decisions are devolved to other managers. As the organization is dependent on the abilities and personality of the powerful individual, the ability of the organization to change in response to changes in the environment is sometimes limited by the centre. Power cultures are common in small entrepreneurial (owner-managed) companies and in some notable larger organizations with a charismatic leader.

Role cultures

This type of culture is found in many long-established organizations that have traditionally operated in stable environments. They tend to be very hierarchical and rely on established procedures, systems and precedent. They often respond slowly to change as it takes time for change to be recognized through the reporting mechanisms. Delays are also encountered in slow decision-making processes.

Role cultures are common in traditional bureaucracies such as the civil service, banks, insurance companies and in some newer business types such as call centres. The task of management in a role culture is to manage procedure. There is usually a high degree of decentralization, and the organization is run by rules and laid-down procedures. It is important, however, that this cultural classification is not viewed as inefficient or as a term of derision; it is a highly suitable cultural type for many organizations.

Task cultures

Task cultures are found in organizations engaged in activities of a non-repetitive nature, often high-value one-off tasks. Activities are normally based around flexible multi-disciplinary teams containing expertise in the major disciplines required to complete the project. Teams tend to be small but flexible and find change easy to identify and adjust to. Strategic planning tends to concentrate on the task in hand.

As their name suggests, task cultures can be found in organizations that are dedicated to a particular task. Consortia that work on large civil engineering projects may demonstrate task culture, as might missionary teams that work together on a medical project in the developing world.

Person cultures

Person cultures are those that exist primarily for the benefit of the members of the organization itself and, hence, they tend to be rare in commercial businesses. They can have a very different 'feel' to the other cultures as all members of the organization work for the benefits of themselves and the other members. They can be found in learned professional societies, in trades unions, in cooperatives, in some charities and in some religious organizations.

In reality, few organizations fit perfectly into just one classification and they may demonstrate elements of two or more cultures. Some diversified organizations may have divisions that fall into all the categories and the cultures may change over time. Many start as power cultures and then tend towards a role culture as their size increases.

Miles and Snow's culture types

Miles and Snow (1978) categorized cultures into four types, based on how they tend to react in strategic terms.

Defenders

These organizations tend to seek a competitive advantage in terms of targeting niche markets through cost reduction and specialization. They tend to operate in stable, mature markets and, as the name suggests, they favour defending their current market share by service improvements or further cost savings. Defenders therefore tend to be centralized, have rigid control systems and a hierarchical management structure that does not respond well to sudden change.

Prospectors

These organizations enjoy the challenge of developing and introducing new product to the market place. They actively seek out new markets for their products. These favoured strategies require it to constantly monitor the environment and be willing and able to respond quickly to changes that may occur. To that end, they are decentralized and flexible.

Analysers

These organizations are 'followers' and are conservative in nature. Steady growth through market penetration is the favoured option as this can be achieved without radical changes to structure. Moves into new markets and products only occur after extensive evaluation and market research. They learn from the mistakes of others and tend to balance power between the centre and divisions with complex control systems.

Reactors

Reactors are a bit like analysers in that they tend to follow rather than innovate. They differ from analysers in that they are less conservative and sometimes behave impulsively, having failed to fully consider the implications of their actions. These organizations may lack proper control systems and typically have a weak but dominant leader.

References and further reading

Campbell, A. and Goold, M. (1987) *Strategies and Style*. London: Basil Blackwell.

Campbell, A., Goold, M. and Alexander, M. (1994) *Corporate Level Strategy*. London: John Wiley.

Chandler, A. (1962) *Strategy and Structure*. Cambridge, MA: MIT Press.

Goold, M. (1996) Parenting strategies for the mature business. *Long Range Planning*, June, 395.

Handy, C.B. (1993) *Understanding Organisations*, Fourth Edition. London: Penguin.

Hickson D.J. and Pugh D.S. (1995). *Management Worldwide*. London: Penguin, p. 21.

Hofstede, G. (1980) *Culture and Organisations: Software of the Mind*. London: McGraw-Hill.

Johnson, G. (1992) Managing strategic change: strategy, culture and action. *Long Range Planning*, 25(1), 28–36.

Kay, J. (1993) *Foundations of Corporate Success*. Oxford: Oxford University Press.

Lynch, R. (1997) *Corporate Strategy*. London: Pitman.

Miles, R.E. and Snow, C.C. (1978) *Organisational Strategy, Structure and Process*. New York: McGraw-Hill.

Stacey, R. (1996) *Strategic Management and Organisational Dynamics, Second Edition*. London: Pitman.

Financial analysis and performance indicators

The ability to measure performance and make sense of an organization's financial situation is an important part of strategic analysis. In order to carry out a financial analysis of a company's situation or of an industry, it is necessary to understand some of the fundamentals of finance and its sources. This chapter begins with a discussion of the sources of corporate finance and then goes on to discuss the costs of the various types of capital. This information helps students to make sense of a company's financial structure before the tools of conventional financial analysis are discussed. The various 'tools' for financial analysis are introduced. Finally, the concept of benchmarking is explained and its use in analysis is discussed.

After studying this chapter, students should be able to:

- understand what is meant by financial analysis;
- identify the sources of funds available to companies and the relative advantages and disadvantages of each;
- assess a company's potential for further funding based on current position, future prospects and past performance;
- understand the cost and non-cost issues involved in raising and using various forms of capital;

■ understand the importance of the cost of capital;
■ understand the limitations of a company report and accounts as a source of data for financial analysis;
■ describe the major tools that can be used to analyse a company's financial position.

An introduction to financial analysis

The importance of finance

Most university business courses have some accounting and finance content. Readers may consequently be familiar with some of the content of this chapter and this will be to their advantage. This chapter takes material from the other units and develops it into the context of strategic analysis.

Money, or the lack of it, is central to the strategic development of all organizations, large or small. It is one of the key resource inputs and cannot be ignored. The most original strategies and the most complex plans for the future of a business are meaningless unless management has considered the financial position of the organization at the onset and during the period covered by the strategy. The ability of a company to finance both current and future strategies is central to any analysis of the company's position. A central theme to this chapter will be the ability of the company to finance current strategies – its ability to raise the funding required for future developments.

The success or failure of the organization is judged by its ability to meet its strategic objectives. The financial information (in the form of annual corporate reports) produced by companies provides a quantifiable means of assessing success. It is important to recognize, however, that other quantifiable information, such as efficiency and productivity data, and non-quantifiable data, such as the company's image, can also be used to make such judgements. In this chapter we will examine the value of information extracted from corporate reports as a source from which judgements can be made.

Corporate reports are, however, just one source of information about a company's financial state. Managers have a number of ways of gathering information about their own and competitors' finances and we will discuss these later in the chapter.

It is also important to bear in mind that financial performance is only one way of measuring success in strategy. Depending on the company's objectives, more immediate measures of success might include market share increase, enhancement of reputation, stock price improvement, reductions in complaints, improvement in the ability to attract a key resource input such as human resources, and several other things. It is thus short-termist and myopic to suggest that financial performance is the only measure of success. It is important, but not necessarily the most important measure at a given point in time.

Sources of corporate funding

Financial resources, as we have already learned, are an essential input to strategic development. Capital for development can be raised from several sources and these are summarized here.

Key concept

Capital

Accountants use the term capital to describe one particular type of 'money'. It is usually contrasted with revenue. *Revenue* is money that is earned through normal business transactions – through sales, rents or whatever the company does through its normal activities. Revenue is money that 'flows' through normal operations. *Capital* is money that is used to invest in the business – to buy new equipment, new capacity, extra factory space, etc. The investment of capital enables the business to expand and, through that expansion, to increase its revenue and profits in future years. Capital can be raised from shareholders, through retained profits, through rights issues, through loan capital or through the disposal of assets.

Share capital

In most limited companies, a sizeable proportion of capital is raised from shareholders (the financial owners of the company) in the form of share capital.

Historically, share capital has comprised the majority of capital for a limited company's start up and subsequent development. In return for their investment, shareholders receive a return in accordance with the company's performance in a given year in the form of a dividend.

The dividend per share is taken as an important measure, by shareholders, of the company's success in its chosen strategy. Shares also confer on their holders a right to vote on company resolutions at annual or extraordinary company meetings *pro rata* with the size of their holding. It follows, of course, that a shareholding in excess of 50% of voting shares confers total control over a company's strategy.

Under normal circumstances, share capital is considered to be permanent; it is not paid back by the company. It is thus unlike other forms of capital (e.g. loan capital). The shareholder's only 'payback' is in the form of dividends and through capital growth – an increase in the value of the shares. Shareholders who wish to divest their stock in a company must usually sell it via a stock exchange (in the case of shares in a public limited company) or through a private sale (in the case of a private company). In exceptional circumstances, some companies offer a 'buyback' of their own shares in order to increase the board's strategic control over the company.

Shareholders can be individuals or 'institutional shareholders'. Some individuals hold their personal share portfolio, but the vast majority of shares are held by institutional shareholders such as pension funds, life assurance companies and investment trusts. One large UK company, BOC Group plc, reported in 1999 that 92% of its ordinary share capital was held by institutional shareholders, with only 19 institutions holding these shares. This concentration of shareholding in the hands of a relatively small number of large investors is not untypical. The profile of shareholders, however, does vary between companies.

Key concepts

Share value and share volume

- *Share value* is the price of a given company's shares at a given point in time. Like any other commodity, its value is determined by the forces of supply and demand. Given that in normal circumstances the supply is fixed over the short to medium term, price is determined by how many people want to buy it. If the market has confidence in a company's prospects, demand for the share will rise and so, accordingly, will its price. If a company's prospects are considered poor, investors will sell the share, fewer investors will want to buy it and the price will fall.

■ *Share volume* is the number of shares issued by a company in total. This is usually determined at the foundation or flotation of a company, although rights issues and similar events can increase the share volume. It is generally true that larger companies have higher share volumes than smaller concerns.

Rights issue capital

From time to time, a company may seek to increase its capital for expansion or debt reduction by means of a *rights issue*. This is when a company issues new shares to the stock market, normally giving its own shareholders the first refusal *pro rata* with their current proportion of the company's share volume.

The decision to go for a rights issue may well be a strategic decision for management because it can impact on the ownership, and hence control, of the company. If existing shareholders do not exercise their right to buy, then it is likely that ownership will be diluted – i.e. shareholders will find that they own a lower percentage of share volume than they did prior to the rights issue.

Those shares not taken up by shareholders, who may be unable or unwilling to buy them, are normally covered by *underwriters* (institutional investors) at a price agreed in advance. Underwriting is an important technical feature of new share issues and as such is a cost in the process.

A variation on a rights issue is *placing*. A placing involves the selling of shares direct to a small number of investors, usually large financial institutions. This may be marginally cheaper (to the company) than a rights issue, but its major advantage is its flexibility in enabling new shareholders significant and possibly strategic holdings. Placings take place, for example, as a part of a joint venture agreement whereby the two companies exchange placed shareholdings as a sign of their mutual commitment to the alliance.

Retained profit as a source of capital

Shareholders provide other funds for development by agreeing *not* to receive all the company's profits in a given year. *Retained profit*, that element of operating profit not paid to shareholders in the form of dividend, is the most common method of funding strategic developments, particularly if the company is quite old in terms of years. By using this form of funding, organizations save on the costs involved in using alternatives such as fees to merchant banks, lawyers and accountants. It also means that management does not have to reveal or justify its strategies to others and risk its plans becoming known to competitors.

It should be recognized that retained profits do not constitute a loss to shareholders as such, because the value of the organization and consequently the share price is normally increased when these funds are used for reinvestment. It is, however, important that companies recognize the need to balance the proportion of profits distributed and retained in order to satisfy those shareholders who need a regular flow of funds themselves (e.g. insurance and pension companies).

Loan capital

An important consideration in the use of retained profits to fund corporate development is clearly the ability of the company to actually make a profit that can be, at least in part, distributed to shareholders as dividends. Although a company may make a profit from its normal activities after taxation, some profits will be required to meet the cost of other forms of *debt finance* or loans.

Debt finance is shown in the balance sheet under two headings:

1 creditors: amounts falling due within one year;
2 creditors: amounts falling due after more than one year.

The form of borrowing with most impact on strategic development is that falling due after more than one year – long-term debt. This can take a number of forms. In addition to the use of long-term bank loans, a company can use debentures, convertible loan stocks or corporate bonds.

Debt finance is normally for a set period of time and at a fixed or variable rate of interest. The interest must be paid every year, regardless of the level of profit (referred to as *servicing* the debt). The interest rate for this source is normally less than the cost of share capital (when the typical dividend payable on the shares is taken into account).

Comparing share capital and loan capital

Each type of capital described above has its pros and cons. Share capital has the advantage that the amount paid on the capital is dependent upon company results. A company can decide not to pay a dividend if profits are poor in any given year. Loan capital, by contrast, must be serviced regardless of results in much the same way that a mortgage on a house must be repaid regardless of other commitments.

Offsetting this advantage is the fact that share capital is permanent. As long as the company exists, it has an obligation to repay a dividend to its shareholders. Loan capital has the advantage to the company that it is time-limited. Servicing the capital is restricted to the term of the loan (like a mortgage on a house) and, when it is finally repaid in full, the business has no further obligation to the lender.

The fact that the repayment of debt finance takes precedence over dividends on shares means that shareholders bear an increased risk. If the company performs badly, their return on investment will be small or non-existent in a given year. Against this possibility, they usually expect to receive higher returns compared to providers of loan capital in the years when profits are good.

In practice, business profits can vary significantly over time. In some years, it is preferable to use loan capital, especially when interest rates are low and profits are high. In other years, when profits are lower and interest rates are higher, share capital works out cheaper. The fact that the benefits are so finely divided means that most companies opt to use an element of both. The relationship of debt capital to shareholder capital is referred to as the company's *gearing ratio*.

Gearing is an indication of how the company has arranged its capital structure. It can be expressed as either:

$$\frac{\text{Borrowed capital (i.e. debt)}}{\text{Total capital employed (i.e. borrowings plus shareholders' capital)}}$$

or:

$$\frac{\text{Borrowed capital (i.e. debt)}}{\text{Shareholders' capital (i.e. equity)}}$$

Both are usually expressed as percentages by simply multiplying the quotient by 100. It is not important which one is used unless we are comparing the gearing of two or more companies.

Other sources of capital

Although the foregoing are the most common mechanisms of raising capital for development, others are available in some circumstances.

One such method is to dispose of existing fixed assets. This can range from selling equipment or a factory to selling a subsidiary to a third party. Assets sales can offer the benefits of reducing liabilities (if the facility is loss-making) or of selling off non-core activities. The realizable price for the asset will depend on the timing of its sale.

Finally, marginal improvements in a company's capital situation can be achieved by improving the management of working capital. Over the course of a financial year, small savings can accumulate to significant proportions, increasing both profitability and capital for reinvestment. This can be achieved by:

- extending the time taken to pay creditors;
- getting debtors to pay sooner;
- controlling stocks more efficiently.

Key concept

Working capital

Working capital is the amount of money that a company has tied up in the normal operation of its business. Working capital comprises money tied up in:

- stocks;
- debtors (money owed to the business);
- creditors (money the company owes);
- cash or current bank deposits.

A company's objective is usually to minimize this figure.

Cost of capital

Definitions

Availability of capital (where to get it from) is one issue when examining a company's capital funding, but another equally important consideration is its cost. We learned above that providers of loans or share capital (equity) both require a return on their investment. Management therefore needs to know what return (profit) they need to make in order to meet the minimum requirements of capital providers. Failure to achieve this minimum will make the raising of future funds all the more difficult. The *cost of capital* can be seen as the minimum return required on the company's assets, which in turn may influence the objectives of the company.

At its simplest, the *cost of capital* can be viewed as the annual amount payable (as a percentage) against the principal amount of money. Most of us will be aware that the return payable on such things as loans varies between lenders and over time as interest rates and risk profiles vary. The cost of loans on a credit card, for example, is much higher than a mortgage loan (where the security against the loan is mainly responsible for the difference).

Costs of debt capital

The costs of debt capital are relatively easy to calculate as they tend to correspond closely to the prevailing rate of interest. If the loan is to be repaid at a fixed rate, the calculation is even more straightforward. It is generally the case that the rate of interest attached to a loan will be strongly influenced by the risk of default. Unsecured loans attract the highest rates whereas those that can be recovered by the sale of the asset against which the loan is taken out (such as a property) will attract a lower rate. The history of the business in dealing with lenders (its credit rating) will also be a factor.

Costs of share capital

Calculating the cost of share capital is slightly more complex as it contains more variables. Accounting academics have discussed at length what should and should not be included in this calculation and how each component should be weighted. Reasons for this complexity include the indefinite nature of the funding, the opportunity cost of undistributed profits and shareholders' expectations. In addition, some models try to include components for inflation, industry averages and attitudes towards risk.

At its simplest, the cost of share capital can be calculated as follows:

$$\text{Cost of share capital (equity) as a percentage} =$$

$$\frac{\text{Current net dividend per share}}{\text{Current market price of share}} \times 100 + \text{average percentage annual growth rate}$$

N.B. Dividend and share price must be expressed in the same units, e.g. pence.

Example

If the market price for shares was 400 p per share and the annual dividend was 20 p, and if growth in profits averaged 10% per annum, this gives:

$$\text{Cost of share capital} = \left(\frac{20}{400} \times 100\right) + 10\%$$
$$= 15\%$$

Models of capital costing

The CAPM model

The *capital asset pricing model* (CAPM) is a more complex but widely used model for calculating the cost of share capital:

$$\text{Cost of share capital} = (Ri + \beta Rm - Ri)$$

The model takes into account the competitor financial products available to potential investors. These range from the percentage return on virtually risk-free government bonds (Ri) to a component covering the average interest for the share (equity) markets overall (Rm). The final element of the model represents the company itself, or more correctly its position relative to the market overall. The β coefficient is a measure of the volatility of the company's financial returns.

The CAPM model does have a number of drawbacks which need to be recognized. First, the shares of the company need to be traded on a stock market. This means that the cost of equity in private companies cannot be calculated using this model. Second, the volatility of share prices in recent years causes problems in arriving at a date for 'acceptable' returns. The dynamic and complex nature of many industries and markets also suggest that historical data has limited value.

Example

CAPM model

Assume that risk-free government bonds were trading at 4% and the average return on the market was 10%. Assume also that the volatility of the company had been calculated at 1.1 (meaning that the shares fluctuated slightly more than the market average). Thus:

$$\text{Cost of share capital (equity)} = 4\% + 1.1(10\% - 4\%)$$
$$= 10.6\%$$

The WACC model

Whereas the CAPM model is used to calculate the cost of share capital, the *weighted average cost of capital* (WACC) can be used to determine the overall cost of funding to a company. The calculation of this information is relatively simple.

WACC = [(Proportion of loan finance) × (Cost of loan finance)] +
[(Proportion of shareholders' funds) × (Cost of shareholders' funds)]

Example

WACC model

Assume that a company had £30 million of loan capital and £70 million of equity funding, and that the cost of each type had been calculated as 5% and 15%, respectively. The calculation would be as follows:

Type of capital	Proportion	Cost (after tax)	Weighted cost
Loan finance	0.3	5%	1.5%
Shareholders funds	0.7	15%	10.5%
Total	1.0		12.0%

Why calculate the cost of capital?

The cost of capital is usually an important figure to calculate because, if it works out to be too high, the strategy that it is intended to fund may not be viable. Given that both debt and share capital attract servicing costs, the profit returns must exceed these servicing costs to the extent that the proposal is economically attractive.

If the projected returns on a strategic development (such as a new factory facility) are little more than the projected servicing costs, then management will have to make a judgement as to whether the investment is actually worth the risk.

The whole situation is rendered more complex if debt capital is obtained at a variable rate of interest. Interest rates can vary substantially throughout an economic cycle and depend upon such things as government inflation targets, the currency exchange value and the national rate of capital investment.

There are no guidelines as to the ideal capital structure – i.e. the balance between debt and equity finance. The optimal structure will vary from company to company, from industry to industry and from year to year. Some companies will calculate their WACC and include factors that are difficult to quantify, such as the degree of risk faced by the industry, trends in interest rates and even the cost and availability of funds to competitors.

Financial analysis

The basics

We would usually employ an analysis of a company's financial situation as part of an internal strategic analysis. We may wish to understand a company's finances in order to make an assessment of its 'health' or its readiness to undertake a phase of strategic development.

There are three areas of financial analysis:

1 longitudinal analysis (sometimes called trend analysis);
2 cross-sectional analysis (or comparison analysis);
3 ratio analysis.

A comprehensive analysis of a company's financial situation would normally involve an element of all three of these analyses. The one thing to bear in mind when looking at accounting statements is that they contain numbers in isolation. An accounting number on it own is just that – a number. In order to make any sense of it, we must compare it with other accounting numbers.

Longitudinal analysis

The simplest means of assessing any aspect of a company's finances is to compare the data for two or more years and see what has increased and what has decreased over that time period, and by how much. It goes without saying that the longer back in time we look, then the better idea we will get as to its current position in its historical context. Many company corporate reports provide a five- or ten-year record and this can help us in constructing a longitudinal analysis.

The easiest way to perform this analysis is conduct an initial scan of the figures to identify any major changes between the years. This involves simply looking along each line in turn and highlighting any larger than normal increases or decreases; for example, a scan along five years of stock figures from a balance sheet (indicated below) clearly indicates something happened in year 4. Not only did the figure more than double against year 3, it reverted to the 'normal' trend the following year.

Year	1	2	3	4	5
Stock	300	330	370	800	450

Anomalies such as these may need further investigation. Questions need to be asked, or rather answers found for the reasons for such an increase. The impact of the 'blip' on the year's performance must be assessed, as must its impact on current performance. Further investigation of the balance sheet or profit and loss account, together with any notes to the accounts, may provide some clues. It may be important to discover how such an increase was financed, why there was a need to carry such high levels of stock and the impact of such levels on suppliers and customers.

The initial scan may need to be followed by a more detailed analysis which calculates the year-on-year increase/decrease in percentage terms. It is sometimes helpful to plot trends on a graph against time. This can help to highlight changes at particular points in time.

The identification of trends, in terms of say turnover, costs or of some items of a balance sheet (such as stocks), can therefore be valuable in our financial analysis. Such trends should, however, be seen in their context. An organization operating in a static or slow growth market may judge a 1% year-on-year increase in turnover as a great success, whereas a company in a buoyant market would judge a 1% increase as a failure.

Cross-sectional analysis

Although longitudinal analysis helps us to assess performance against a historical trend, it tells us nothing of the company's performance against that of competitors or of companies in other industries. If we were, for example, to identify a strong sales growth of 10% a year in a longitudinal analysis of Company A's financial statements, we might be tempted to think that the company was performing well. If we were then to compare this company with one of its competitors, only to find that the industry average rate of growth was 15%, then we would wish to modify our initial assessment of Company A's performance.

Financial statements

One of the conditions placed upon limited companies is the requirement to file an audited annual report and accounts. There are five
compulsory components to this document as set out in the UK in the
Companies Act (1985 as amended): chairman's statement, auditor's
report, profit and loss statement, balance sheet and cash-flow statement. The accounting rules by which they are to be constructed are
prescribed in *financial reporting standards* to ensure that all companies
mean the same thing when they make an entry in one of the statements. When they are completed (following the end of the company's
financial year), they become publicly available. Each shareholder has
the right to receive a copy, and a copy is lodged at UK Companies
House in Cardiff or London (or Edinburgh if it is a Scottish company).

It is for the purposes of comparisons of this nature that cross-sectional analyses are important. As well as comparing accounting numbers such as turnover, it is often helpful to compare the ratios (see
next section) of two or more companies, such as return on sales or
one of the working capital ratios.

Ratio analysis

The third important tool in the analysis of company performance is
ratio analysis. A ratio is a comparison (by quotient) of two items from
the same set of accounts. Given that there are a lot of numbers in a set
of accounts, it will not come as a surprise to learn that a large number
of ratios can be drawn – some of which are more useful than others.

Ratio analysis is an area of some academic debate, and, accordingly,
the way in which ratios are expressed may vary between accounting
and strategy textbooks. What is important, therefore, is to employ a
consistent approach to ratio analysis, especially in longitudinal and
cross-sectional analyses.

For most purposes, we can divide ratios into five broad categories:

1 performance ratios;
2 efficiency ratios;
3 liquidity ratios;

    4 investors' ratios;

    5 financial structure ratios.

Performance ratios

As their name suggests, performance ratios test to see how well a company has turned its inputs into profits. This usually involves comparing *return* (PBIT, profit before interest and tax) against either turnover or against its capital. This is because the rates of tax and interest payable vary. Using profit after interest and tax would distort the performance figure because it would include an element of cost beyond the company's direct control (the rate of tax and the interest rate).

Return on capital employed is perhaps the most important and widely used measure of performance. It indicates the annual return being made compared to the funds invested. At its simplest, it is this figure that tests the gains of investing in a business as opposed to simply placing capital on return in a bank.

When an organization can break down its figures by divisions or subsidiaries, individual performance can be measured and decisions relating to continued ownership made.

Return on equity or *return on ordinary shareholders' funds* gives an indication of how effectively the share capital has been turned into profit (i.e. it does not take account of loan capital). This ratio should be used carefully as the capital structure of the company can affect the ratio.

Return on sales or *profit margin*, either net or gross, is a popular guide to the profitability of a company. This ratio assesses the profit made per £ sold. Return on sales tends to vary from industry to industry and between companies within an industry. Food retailers typically make between 5% and 12%, whereas companies in the pharmaceuticals sector rarely make less than 20%.

Examples

Performance ratios

Each ratio is expressed as a percentage by multiplying the ratio by 100.

$$\text{Return on capital employed } (\%) =$$

$$\frac{\begin{array}{c}\text{Profit before interest and tax}\\\text{(PBIT, from profit and loss account)}\end{array}}{\begin{array}{c}\text{Total capital employed}\\\text{(i.e. from one side of the balance sheet)}\end{array}} \times 100$$

$$\text{Return on shareholders' funds } (\%) =$$

$$\frac{\text{PBIT}}{\text{Shareholders' funds (from balance sheet)}} \times 100$$

$$\text{Return on sales } (\%) =$$

$$\frac{\text{PBIT}}{\text{Total sales (also called turnover or revenue)}} \times 100$$

$$\text{Gross margin } (\%) = \frac{\text{Gross profit}}{\text{Total sales}} \times 100$$

Note: *Gross profit* is the profit after direct costs (i.e. conversion costs) have been deducted from sales, but before indirect costs (i.e. administrative costs) are deducted. *Gross margin* is an indication of how effectively a company has managed its direct wages, energy and stocks.

Efficiency ratios

These ratios show how efficiently a company has used its assets to generate sales. We can use any one of a number of a company's inputs to test against sales or profits. Common efficiency ratios include *sales per employee* and *profit per employee*, both of which test the efficiency with which a company uses its labour inputs.

Key concept

Efficiency

The term efficiency is used in many ways – not just in accounting. We may speak of an efficient engine or the efficiency of a heating system in a house. Efficiency is a comparison of a systems output to its inputs with a view to testing how well the input has been turned into output. It follows that a more efficient system will produce more output for a given input than a less efficient one.

Efficiency can be expressed mathematically as a quotient:

$$\text{Efficiency } (\%) = \frac{\text{Work output}}{\text{Work input}} \times 100$$

Other commonly used efficiency ratios are *asset turnover* and a variant of this, *fixed asset turnover*. A high level of asset turnover indicates that the company is using its assets efficiently; conversely, a low level may indicate that the company is suffering from over-capacity. *Stock turnover* gives an indication of how well the company controls its stocks. A company that keeps stock moving will have a higher stock turnover than one that has piles of unsaleable or obsolete materials. Stock residence time has a cost implication and so a low stock turnover indicates inefficient and costly stock management.

Examples

Efficiency ratios

$$\text{Sales per employee } (£) = \frac{\text{Total sales (from profit and loss account)}}{\text{Number of employees (usually found in the notes to the accounts)}}$$

$$\text{Profit per employee } (£) = \frac{\text{PBIT}}{\text{Number of employees}}$$

$$\text{Stock turnover} = \frac{\text{Cost of sales (from profit and loss account)}}{\text{Value of stock (from balance sheet)}}$$

Stock turnover is measured in *times* – i.e. the number of times the total stock is turned over in a given year.

Liquidity ratios

These ratios test a company's ability to meet its short-term debts – an important thing to establish if there is reason to believe the company is in trouble. Essentially, they ask the question: Has the company enough available funds to pay what it owes?

The *current ratio* is the best known liquidity ratio. It is a measure of a company's total liabilities in comparison to its total assets and is thus calculated entirely from balance sheet figures. It is used to assess the company's ability to meet its liabilities by the use of its assets such as stock, debtors (receivables) and cash.

The *acid test ratio* is a variant of the current ratio and tests the company's ability to meet its short-term liabilities using its cash or 'near cash' assets. Many textbooks suggest that a ratio of 2:1 should be a target for this ratio and a target of 1:1 should be sought for the acid test ratio. These are simple guides and should not be taken as the norm for all industries. For example, many companies in the retail industry have few debtors and high stock turnover but still have creditors as a result of their current ratio being below 2:1.

Investors' ratios

This family of ratios tests for things that are important to a company's investors – usually its shareholders or potential shareholders. There are three ratios that are widely used.

Earnings per share (EPS) is calculated by dividing profit after interest and tax (called earnings) by the number of shares. It shows how much profit is attributable to each share. The *price/earnings ratio* (P/E) gives an indication of the stockmarket's confidence in a company's shares. It is the current market price of the company's ordinary shares divided by its EPS at the last year end and it follows, therefore, that the P/E varies with the share price. Broadly speaking, it is a way of showing how highly investors value the earnings a company produces. A high P/E ratio (where the price is high compared to the last declared EPS) usually indicates growth potential, whereas a low P/E suggests static profits. The P/E ratio for quoted companies is regularly published in the financial press.

Dividend yield is the third widely used investors' ratio. Potential shareholders often want to know what the most recent return on the share was in terms of percentage. Dividend yield is calculated by dividing the dividend per share at the last year end by the current price (and then multiplying by 100 to arrive at a percentage).

Examples

Investors' ratios

$$\text{Earnings per share (EPS)} = \frac{\text{Earnings (i.e. profit after interest and tax)}}{\text{Share volume}}$$

$$\text{Price/earnings ratio (P/E)} = \frac{\text{Price of share (as of 'today')}}{\text{EPS at most recent year end}}$$

$$\text{Dividend yield (\%)} = \frac{\text{Gross dividend per share}}{\text{Current price of share} \times 100}$$

Financial structure ratios

We encountered financial structure above, when we discussed the relative merits of loan and share capital. The way in which a company 'mixes' these forms of capital is referred to as its financial (or capital) structure.

The *gearing ratio* looks at the relationship between all the borrowings of the company (including short-term borrowings) and all the capital employed by the company. This provides a view of the extent to which borrowing forms part of the total capital base of the company and hence the risk associated with rising interest rates.

The *debt/equity ratio*, a variation on the gearing ratio, uses the shareholders' funds in the calculation rather than the total capital employed. This ratio provides a more direct comparison between the funds attributed to shareholders and the liability of the company to loan providers.

Examples

Financial structure ratios

$$\text{Gearing} = \frac{\text{Debt capital (typically borrowings due after one year)}}{\text{Debt capital plus shareholders' funds}}$$

$$\text{Debt/equity ratio} = \frac{\text{Debt capital (borrowings due after one year)}}{\text{Shareholders' funds}}$$

Limitations of financial information

For most purposes in strategic analysis, we can accept the proposition that the data we collect from a company's annual accounts is accurate and provides a truthful statement on its financial position. From time to time, however, we may need to qualify our analysis for one or more reasons.

First, although the financial statements are audited for accuracy, other parts of the annual report are not. If our financial analysis consists of an examination of the entire document and not just the accounting sections, then we would need to be aware of this. Additional disclosures made in corporate reports may serve a number of purposes. Some commentators have suggested that such disclosures may be something of a public relations and marketing exercise.

Second, we should remember that the financial information in a corporate report is historical, sometimes published months after the period described. Although this historical information can be used to judge past performance, it may have limited use in predicting future performance. The balance sheet shows the financial position at 'a moment in time' (at the year end). It does not (unlike the profit and loss account) summarize a full year's trading and things can sometimes change quickly after the year end.

In an attempt to avoid this potential problem, companies quoted on the Stock Exchange are required to produce interim reports, normally half-yearly and unaudited, which show their profit and turnover for that period. Quoted companies are also required to provide the Stock Exchange with information that may have a significant impact on its prospects, such as changes on the board of the company or anything that gives rise to a 'profits warning'.

Third, those who prepare a company's financial statements (the financial accountants) sometimes have cause to 'hide' bad news so as to avoid alarming the company's investors. It is possible to employ legal financial restructuring so as to make some figures appear better than perhaps they are. A year-on-year increase in the value of fixed assets, for example, may appear at first glance to be healthy, but it may be that the company has accumulated a high amount of debt to finance it. It is for this reason that we sometimes need to examine all parts of a company's financial statements to spot any countervailing bad news that has been obscured by the company in its reporting.

Other analysis tools

Although the majority of situations can be made sense of using the above 'tools', two other tools are sometimes useful; these are discussed here.

Financial benchmarking

Inter-company comparison or *benchmarking* is a variation on cross-sectional analysis. It usually involves an analysis of 'like' companies in the same industry, but it can occasionally be an inter-industry analysis.

In order to make the benchmarking analysis meaningful, the selection of a company should usually be guided by similarity with:

■ company size (i.e. the companies should be comparable in terms of turnover, market value or similar);
■ industry (in that the companies produce similar products);
■ market (i.e. the companies share a similar customer base).

In practice, sample selection for benchmarking study always involves some compromise because no two companies are directly comparable in all respects. Many companies, for example, operate in more than one industry and this may render problematic any comparisons with another company that operates in only one industry.

The practice of inter-company (cross-sectional) analysis using financial data has been undertaken by accountants for many years. Benchmarking, however, can be used to compare financial and, importantly, non-financial information between two or more companies.

Benchmarking is now used to compare the effectiveness of various processes, products and procedures against others. The objective is to identify where superior performance is found in whatever variable that is being used for comparison. Once the company with the highest performance is identified, the exercise becomes to explore the reasons behind the superior performance and to learn from the best practice.

The benchmarking process therefore involves decisions on:

■ what to benchmark (financial or non-financial data);
■ who to benchmark against (sample selection);
■ how to get the information;
■ how to analyse the information;
■ how to use the information.

The value of benchmarking is in identifying not only which company has the superior performance in a sector but also why this is the case. An analysis might, for example, show that Company X enjoys a return on sales that is significantly higher than that of the other companies in the sector. Company X thus occupies the profitability benchmark in the sector. The other companies may then wish to examine the practices within Company X that give rise to this level of performance.

For non-financial indicators, an analysis may highlight the fact that Company Y is able to attract the most well-qualified people within a key category of personnel (e.g. the best scientists or computer programmers). In this case, Company Y demonstrates the benchmark in successful recruitment. Other companies that are unable to attract the best personnel would usually wish to examine Company Y to see why it is so successful in this regard.

Common sizing of accounts

Common sizing of accounts is particularly useful in cross-sectional analyses, but can also be used to analyse the same company's accounts from year to year. If we were, for example, to examine the profit and loss accounts or balance sheets of two companies in the same industry, we may at first be unable to make sense of differences between the two. We can sometimes make sense of the two separate accounts by making the totals of both equal to 100 and then dividing each entry by the resultant quotient. A simplified example of common sizing of accounts is shown in Table 4.1.

Table 4.1
A simplified example of common sizing of accounts

	Company A		Company B	
	£m	Common size	£m	Common size
Sales	113.4	100	224.6	100
Cost of sales	65	57.32	112	49.87
Gross profit	48.4	42.68	112.6	50.13
Administrative costs	33.7	29.72	67	29.83
Operating profit	14.7	12.96	45.6	20.3

We can make comparisons between the cost structures of the two companies despite the fact that Company B has approximately twice the turnover of Company A. We can tell, for example, that, overall, Company B is better at controlling costs than Company A as evidenced by the fact that its operating profit is 20.3 compared to Company A's figure of 12.96 (both common-sized). We could draw comparable conclusions from other common sized components of the accounts.

References and further reading

Allen, D. (1997) *An Introduction to Strategic Financial Management*. London: CIMA/Kogan Page.

Department of Trade and Industry (1992) *Best Practice Benchmarking*. London: DTI.

Camp, R.C. (1994) *Business Process Benchmarking*. ASQC Quality Press.

Ellis, J. and Williams, D. (1993) *Corporate Strategy and Financial Analysis*. London: Pitman.

Franks, J.R. and Broyles, J.E. (1979) *Modern Managerial Finance*. Chichester: John Wiley.

Higson, C. (1995) *Business Finance*. Oxford: Butterworth-Heinemann.

Mott, G. (1991) *Management Accounting for Decision Makers*. London: Pitman.

CHAPTER 5

Products and markets

The way in which an organization relates to its markets is one of the most important aspects of competitive strategy. The idea of a market as a place where buyers and sellers come together can apply to both inputs and outputs. Product markets are those in which an organization competes for product sales; resource markets are those in which an organization competes for its resource inputs.

In this chapter, we discuss the key elements of this system: the nature of markets and the nature and importance of products. The way in which an organization configures itself in respect to these elements is crucial to the success of business strategy.

After studying this chapter, students should be able to:

- explain the term *market* and describe three ways by which markets can be defined;
- describe market segmentation and explain the ways in which markets can be segmented;
- describe three ways of approaching market segmentation;
- explain the term *product* and describe Kotler's five levels of product benefit;
- describe and criticize Copeland's product typology;
- understand the stages in, and uses of, the product life cycle;
- explain the concept of portfolio;

■ describe the composition and limitations of the Boston matrix;

■ explain how the GEC matrix works.

Ways of defining and understanding markets

Defining markets and market share

Economists refer to a market as a system comprising two 'sides'. The demand side comprises buyers or consumers of a product or resource; the supply side produces or manufactures the same.

In strategy, we often use the term slightly differently. By *market*, we usually mean a group of actual or potential customers with similar needs or wants (*the demand side*). We usually refer to *the supply side* as an industry.

The definition and boundaries of an organization's markets represent a key starting point for the formulation of strategy, and provide a basis for measuring competitive performance. The analysis and definition of markets will provide key information concerning threats and opportunities.

Market share is a measure of an organization's performance with regard to its ability to win and retain customers. It can be measured either by *volume* or by *value*. Volume measures concern the organization's share of units sold to the market (e.g. number of barrels of oil sold by an oil company in proportion to the total number of barrels sold). Value measures concern the sales turnover of one company in proportion to the total value of the market.

We can also define the boundaries of markets in different ways. If different companies define a market in different ways, it is not surprising that the sum of their claimed market share may add to more or less than 100%. The grocery market, for example, may mean different things to different companies. One might include just the English market for groceries, whereas another might measure it for the whole of the UK. It is clearly important, therefore, that market share measures are stated explicitly with the market boundaries clearly defined.

There are three ways in which markets are commonly defined:

■ definition based on product;
■ definition based on need satisfaction or function performed;
■ definition based on customer identity.

We will briefly examine each of these in turn.

Definition based on product

If someone working for an organization is asked what market they are in, a common reply will be to describe the products that are produced and/or sold. Thus, we would have examples such as 'consumer detergents' or 'industrial machinery'. If the product definition is wide, this type of definition is close to describing an industry. Since government economic statistics are often produced on this basis, markets defined in this way often have the advantage of ease of measurement.

A drawback of this approach is that it sometimes fails to take into account that a product may provide a range of different benefits, and the same need might be met by different products, often derived from completely different technology. This can lead to a failure to recognize threats that may come from a different industry altogether. Cinema and computer games appear to be entirely different products with different markets, but they both may compete for customers' discretionary income and time if they are considered as part of the 'leisure' market.

An advantage of a product-based definition of markets can be that economies of scale of production may be gained by the sharing of a particular production process. Taken to the extreme, this can lead to a view of a market as the market for the products that a company happens to make, even when they have little in common apart from a production process. An example of this would be a company using a plastic-moulding machine. If the company were to utilize the machine seven days a week, twenty-four hours a day, it would be efficient in production terms. However, if the range of products included golf tees, toys and components for the motor industry, the different end customers would make it very difficult to sell the products economically. It would have sacrificed marketing synergy for production efficiency, and an analysis of its customer base it would have to recognize that it operated in several markets.

Definition based on need satisfaction or function performed

The reason why consumers purchase a good or service is to gain *utility*. The concept of utility infers that, whenever a consumer makes a purchase, they make a cost–benefit calculation wherein they make the judgement that the benefit they will get from the product is worth more than the price paid.

This understanding enables the organization to understand its markets according to customers' perceptions.

Although the need satisfaction definition can lead to a more open-minded approach to the formulation of strategy, its weakness can be that very broad definitions can lead to a view of markets that does not allow a practical approach to decision-making. A cinema chain, for example, might define itself as being in the 'leisure' market, but it is probably wise for cinema companies also to consider threats and opportunities that might arise from television, bars, computer games, holidays, etc. Opportunities only arise from leisure activities that the company's competences would allow it to enter (see Chapter 2), and threats would come from activities that would be likely to substitute customers' business.

Key concept

Needs and wants

Whenever a customer makes a purchase decision, he or she expects to gain a benefit from the product purchased. This benefit satisfaction is usually expressed as a *need* or a *want*. The difference between the two is in the perception of the consumer – one customer's want is another's need.

The practical use of the distinction is in the price responsiveness of the product. Generally speaking, customers who need – or who believe they need – a product will be less price sensitive than those who merely want it. Hence, the greater the felt need, the more price inelastic the demand.

Definition based on customer identity

Groups of customers have requirements in common, and differ from other groups of customers. In this way, the *identity* of customers can be used to define markets. We could, for example, consider the 'office consumables market' a quite distinct market. The market might be for products as diverse as pencils, pens, envelopes, computer disks, etc., but the market could clearly be seen as being for things that offices in organizations need to buy on a regular basis.

In terms of strategy formulation, the advantage of this approach is that it allows accurate targeting of the customer, so that efficient use can be made of advertising, mail shots, personal selling, etc. Its main disadvantage is that, although marketing economies may be made, there is a risk that a number of different technologies need to be employed, so that it would be uneconomic to produce all the items required, and some or all of the products sold would have to be bought in. We can contrast this with the product definition approach in that, with this, some marketing may have to be subcontracted, whereas, with the customer identity approach, some manufacturing is likely to be outsourced.

Combined definition

In practice, most businesses serve several markets with a range of products. They will define their markets with a combination of the ways listed here and, to the extent that one or another approach is uppermost, the advantages and disadvantages that we have already encountered will apply. A key task for management at the strategic level is to produce combinations that gain synergistic benefits and that enable opportunities to be best chosen and exploited. In cases where changes in aspects of the technology of supply, or the characteristics of markets take place so that synergies previously achievable are no longer there, a case exists for restructuring an organization to divest itself of some activities and/or to acquire new ones.

In terms of working out competitive success in markets, a key concept is that of the *served market* – that part of a market that the company is in. It is on this basis that the measure of market share is most meaningful.

Market segmentation

Target marketing and market segmentation

Markets are rarely completely homogeneous. Within markets, there are groups of customers with requirements that are similar, and it is this similarity of needs and wants that distinguishes one market segment from another. These 'submarkets' are known as *market segments*. By considering the extent to which the segments should be treated differently from others, and which ones will be chosen to serve, organizations can identify target markets and gain a focus for their commercial activity.

This process of segmentation represents a powerful competitive tool. It is true to say that a business will prosper by giving the customer what the customer wants. Since not all customers are likely to want the same thing, then identifying subgroups and attending to their requirements more exactly is a way of gaining competitive advantage. We might say that it is better to be hated by half of potential customers and loved by the other half than to be quite liked by them all. The latter is a recipe for being everyone's second choice, and underlines the danger of placing too much reliance on averages in market research.

By identifying a specific market segment and concentrating marketing efforts at the segment, many organizations can build a mini-monopoly in the segment. Many organizations that have each identified a highly specific segment can each succeed and gain reasonable profits by configuring their internal activities to precisely meet the needs and wants of the customer group.

For the most part, we can assume that segments exist naturally in most markets, and it is up to organizations as to how to exploit the differences that exist in the submarkets. We do, however, have to recognize that activities of companies can also shape the segments to some extent. We could expect, for example, that men and women may buy differently. If, in those markets, suppliers offer and promote different products to men and women, then this tendency will be reinforced.

Three approaches to segment marketing

Three broad approaches are recognized with respect to the ways that an organization can approach marketing to market segments (or submarkets).

Undifferentiated marketing

The first approach in relating to segmentation is called *undifferentiated* marketing. This means that the organization denies that its total markets are segmented at all and relates to the market assuming that demand is homogeneous in nature. The economies of a standardized approach to marketing outweigh any advantages of segmenting the market.

Undifferentiated marketing is appropriate when the market the organization serves is genuinely homogeneous in nature. In Chapter 13 we will encounter this concept in the context of internationalization and globalization. Companies such as Coca Cola, Levi jeans and McDonald's employ this strategy successfully because demand for their products does not vary much from country to country. Organizations that adopt this approach have standard products, standard packaging and advertising, and these differ little or not at all between countries.

Differentiated marketing

Companies that adopt *differentiated* marketing recognize separate segments of the total market and treat each segment separately. Different segments need not always be different in every respect – it could be that some standard products can be promoted differently to different segments because of certain similarities or common characteristics. In other cases, the product will be substantially or completely different, and marketing to each segment will necessitate a distinctive approach to each one.

Concentrated marketing

An extreme form of differentiated marketing is *concentrated* marketing, where an organization's effort is focused on a single market segment. In return for giving up substantial parts of the market, an effort is made to specialize in just one niche, and so we may see this referred to as 'niche marketing'. This approach offers the advantage that the organization can gain a detailed and in-depth knowledge of its segment which, in turn, can enable an ever-improving match between the product and the customer requirement. The disadvantage relates to the extent to which the company may become dependent upon the one segment it serves. Any negative change in the demand pattern of the segment will leave the supplier vulnerable because of the narrowness of its market portfolio (see later in this chapter).

A company operating with a large product range in many markets will typically use a multi-focus strategy – a combination of the above.

Product positioning

Product positioning is the way in which a product or a brand is perceived in relation to preferences of segments of the market, and in relation to competitive products. Thus, in a particular alcoholic drinks market, attributes thought to be important by customers might be alcoholic strength (weak versus strong) and taste (bitter versus sweet). There may be groups of customers with preferences for any combinations of these attributes, and a range of competing products that by means of the products themselves and their advertising and promotion are seen to occupy a particular position. This can often be represented by a product positioning diagram, as shown in Figure 5.1. The oval shapes on the chart represent the preferences of a group of customers and the customers' perceptions of existing products are marked by a '×'.

If an organization finds a group of customers with a particular requirement for a combination not currently offered, it will literally have discovered a 'gap' in the market (see the 'gap' on the bottom right of the chart). More likely, it will have to make the best of subtle differences in position, since all major combinations may be filled.

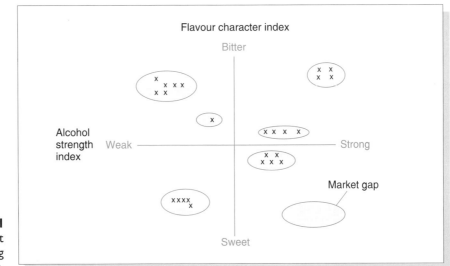

Figure 5.1
The product positioning framework.

Bases for segmentation

What is a segmentation base?

A segmentation base is a way of distinguishing one customer type from another. There are potentially limitless ways in which markets can be divided into segments, and the ultimate segment would be one customer. In practice, a number of criteria typically have to be met

before a base for dividing a market can be considered to be commercially viable. The major criteria for establishing market segments are:

- market size;
- identifiability of the segment;
- measurability of the segment;
- accessibility to the segment;
- buying behavioural characteristics of the segment.

We will briefly examine these criteria in turn.

Market size criteria

Smaller segments may allow more and more exact matching of customer requirements, but this comes at a cost as economies of scale of
marketing and manufacturing are lost. If an advertisement is produced, there will be fixed costs of production and design, whether
it is run once or several times. In production, separate tooling might
be required to produce different versions of a product. Companies
can reduce the cost by producing different versions of a product with
a large number of common components.

In the twenty-first century, some of the assumptions we have long
held that limit the smallest segments that can be economically
reached are likely to change. Flexible manufacturing technology is
reducing the minimum production runs that are economic for a separate product. In advertising, we are used to the concept of broad-
casting. In the future we shall have to become used to the concept
of 'narrowcasting', as a revolution in the media takes place. At present, if a company advertises on television, and its product is only of
interest to city dwellers, it is also unnecessarily paying to reach all the
rural viewers. Cable technology allows organizations to direct adverts
much more accurately at prospective customers. The same process is
taking place in mail shots: most mail shots can now be very accurately
aimed, and the Internet allows people to select what they want to see.
The result of this process will be that very great rewards will be available to organizations that can come up with sophisticated segmentation strategies, as opposed to straightforward old-style mass
marketing.

Identifiability of the segment

Ultimately, whatever base is being used for segmentation, we should
still be able to answer the question as to *who* is in the segment, even if

this is a bit indistinct. Otherwise, the organization will not be able to reach the segment effectively.

Measurability of the segment

If we cannot measure the size of the segment that using a particular base would create, then we would not be in a position to judge its potential. Any organization that adopts a marketing strategy without an accurate knowledge of the size of the market segment cannot be sure that it has the optimal level of information upon which to make important investment decisions.

Accessibility to the segment

Any market segment identified must obviously be reachable in an organization's marketing communications. However, in order for marketing communications to be cost-effective, they must be aimed at the target segment and not at others. This latter issue requires a careful examination of the media and how effectively each of the media reaches the target segment within cost constraints.

Buying behavioural characteristics of the segment

Even if all the other criteria can be met, it is pointless to divide a market up in a way that does not represent real or potential differences in buying behaviour. The whole point of market segmentation is to identify subgroups of a market that share commonalities such that their buying behaviour will be similar. If this is not the case for some reason, the exercise is useless.

Typical bases for segmentation of markets

In consumer markets (as distinct from industrial markets) we use the ways in which people naturally differ to divide markets up. The most commonly used 'people dividers' are:

1 demographic variables such as difference by age, stage of family life cycle, gender, income, occupation, education, race, religion;
2 geographic variables such as difference by country, region, type of housing/neighbourhood (geodemographic), etc.;
3 psychographic variables which exploit the lifestyle, personality or intelligence differences between people;

4   behavioural variables such as attitudes to brand loyalty, frequency of use (heavy or light usage), consumption occasion, etc.

Key concept

Demographic variables

In consumer markets, market segments are most commonly defined by using demographic variables. It is self-evident that people can be divided from each other in many ways and the more variables that are applied to a total market, the smaller and more homogeneous the segment becomes.

The most commonly used demographic variables are those that are readily identifiable. Differences such as sex, age, occupation, type of residence and stage of family life cycle are all easy to identify. Less easy – and therefore less usable – are differences such as religious affiliation, sexual orientation, political persuasion and musical preferences. It is unfortunate, then, that some of this latter category of variables are very powerful in respect of their ability to predict patterns of demand for some product types.

Products

Product definition

We can define a product as anything that is offered for sale. Hence, a product might be a physical good, a service or a mixture of both. A good is tangible and is something that can be owned. A service is something that is done on the buyer's behalf and is intangible in nature. Some products contain both a good and a service element, such as when we purchase hairdressing services from a barber or hairdresser (the service) who then also washes and blow-dries the hair using hair care products (such as shampoo – goods). The totality of the hairdressing product contains both goods and services.

Of value in product strategy is a consideration of how value might be added to the product from the point of view of the customer. To do this, it can be helpful to consider the product's features and benefits in a number of levels. Different approaches can give different numbers of levels. We shall consider here a five-level model (Kotler, 1997).

Kotler's five 'levels' of product benefit

Core and basic benefits

Kotler proposed at the most fundamental level the *core benefit* provided by the product. For a car, for example, this would be the ability to transport. Since all the products on the market will provide this benefit, this will rarely be the level on which companies compete. Added to the core benefit is the *basic product*, which would include everything that would be required to make the product practical in use. For the car, this might include the seats, appropriate controls, and legal safety equipment.

Expected, augmented and potential benefits

The next level is the *expected product*. Here we have all that the customer has come to expect in a product. In our example of a car, this might include a radio, comprehensive guarantee and certain levels of performance. The *augmented product* goes beyond the customer's expectations to provide something extra and desirable – for example, air conditioning and an on-board satellite navigation in a car. At the final level is the *potential product* – the product level that encompasses all that the product might ultimately become, but currently does not incorporate. The ownership of a certain car, for example, may confer on the owner a certain status in society, provide him or her with opportunities that would otherwise not present themselves or even assist in the attraction of a sexual partner.

Competition of augmented benefits

In mature markets, competition is normally at the augmented product level or above, and the basic product is taken for granted. What is in the expected product in one market may be in the augmented product in another. Air conditioning in a car might be a bonus in a temperate climate, but necessity in a tropical one. Thus, a car company that had gained a competitive advantage by superior reliability would lose that advantage once all cars had become reliable. It then has to be able to offer something else or face a lack of competitiveness. Over time, the augmented product becomes the expected product, so there has to be a continuous search for something extra to offer.

Augmentation adds to costs, and the company has to consider whether the customer will be willing to pay for the extra costs in the final price. Sometimes, after a period of rivalry in which competitors try to compete by adding more and more features and cost, a market segment emerges for a basic stripped-down low-cost version that just supplies the expected benefits.

Copeland's product typology and strategy

There is a commonly held view that different types of products need to be managed and brought to market in different ways. *Services*, for example, cannot be stored, must be consumed at the point of production, are intangible and it is difficult to judge their quality in advance. As a result of these factors, we might anticipate off-peak pricing offers, the need for supplier credibility and difficulties in advertising not experienced by physical products. *Industrial products* are less likely to be sold direct to the end user than consumer products, with advertising being relatively more important for consumer products and high-quality personal contact being relatively more important for industrial products (hence the use of sales representatives to speak directly to industrial buyers).

There have been a number of attempts to build on product characteristics to produce classification systems for products that will serve as a comprehensive guide. A system based on dividing consumer products into *convenience*, *shopping* and *speciality goods* (Copeland, 1923) has endured and is one of the most popular product classification systems used at the present time.

Convenience goods

Convenience goods are products whose purchase is relatively frequent, at low prices, and the customer sees little interest or risk in the purchase. Examples would include low-price confectionery, batteries, carbonated drinks. As a consequence, the customer will typically buy the product available in the most convenient outlet, and the supplier will have to make the product available in as many outlets as possible. Point-of-sale display and simple reminder advertising with little information content are likely to be important.

Shopping goods

In contrast, shopping goods are those that are typically more expensive, of more interest to the purchaser, and some risk is seen in the purchase. Examples would include cars, personal computers and cameras. The customer will typically 'shop around' to make comparisons and gather information. These goods do not, therefore, have to be available in all possible outlets, and promotional material will usually have a high information content. In some categories of shopping goods such as personal computers, customers can demonstrate a very high level of technical knowledge that assists them in their purchase and producers must usually satisfy customers on a technical level before a sale is made.

Speciality goods

Speciality goods are seen as products that are so differentiated from others, often carrying considerable prestige, that customers may insist on only one brand. High prices, high levels of service and restricted distribution would be appropriate. An example would be that of Hasselblad cameras, which dominate certain parts of the professional photography market. There is no need or benefit for the products to be available in every camera shop, but they would tend to appear in shops where customers would expect a high level of service and expertise.

Limitations of Copeland's framework

The use of classification systems is widely accepted by both managers and academic researchers. It is easy to show how they work in practice, and a multitude of examples can be produced to show how appropriate they are. A strong argument against their slavish adoption is that they can exhibit circular logic. In other words, we examine how a product is marketed, and on this basis assign it to a particular classification. We then use that to say how it *should* be marketed. This is a recipe for staying with the status quo, and companies adopting this practice, even if implicitly, will never lead with new product strategies. Over time, many products will gradually change from shopping goods to convenience goods. Thus, some watches will be speciality goods, some will be shopping goods and now the lowest priced watches on the market will effectively be convenience goods.

Changes in technology and customer taste or fashion may also create opportunities for things to be done differently, and there may always be part of a market that will respond to an approach that is different from the norm. Some organizations recognized that technology, in reducing transaction cost, could make telephone banking viable. Avon cosmetics was built on the basis that some customers would be prepared to buy cosmetics from people selling it on their doorsteps as opposed to buying in conventional retail outlets.

Product type may be a useful starting point to guide management thinking, but it is not a substitute for creativity and analysis.

The product life cycle

Uses of the product life cycle

The product life cycle concept is based on the analogy with living things, in that they all have a finite life. All products would be expected to have a finite life, whether it be long or short. The life cycle can operate at an individual product level, or a product type, or at a product class level, where arguably a market life cycle would be a more appropriate title. At individual product level, the product life cycle is a useful tool in product planning, so that a balance of products is kept in various stages of the life cycle.

At the product class level, we can use the product life cycle concept to analyse and predict competitive conditions and identify key issues for management. It is conventionally broken down into a number of stages as shown in Figure 5.2. We shall explore the key issues posed by the different stages.

The introduction stage

The introduction stage follows the product's development. It is consequently new to the market and will be bought by 'innovators' – a

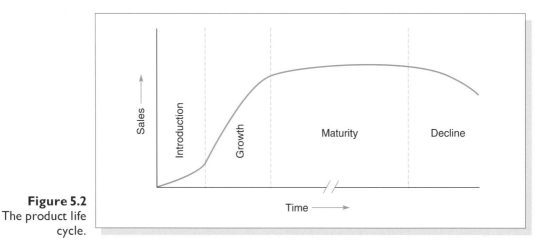

Figure 5.2
The product life cycle.

term used to describe a small proportion of the eventual market. The innovators may not be easy to identify in advance and there are likely to be high launch and marketing costs. Because production volumes are likely to be low (because it is still at a 'pilot' stage), the production cost per unit will be high.

The price elasticity of demand will strongly influence whether the product is introduced at a high 'skimming' price or a low 'penetration' price. Price skimming is appropriate when the product is known to have a price inelastic demand such as with new pharmaceuticals or defence equipment. Penetration is appropriate for products with a price elastic demand and when gaining market share is more important than making a fast recovery of development costs.

'Pioneer' companies (those who are first to the market with a particular product) are usually forced to sell the product idea in addition to an existing brand, and the early promotion may help competitors who enter the market later with 'me too' versions of the product idea.

Entering the market at an early stage is usually risky. Not only will the company be incurring a negative cash flow for a period, but many products fail at this stage. Against this risk is the prospect of increasing market share in the new product area faster than the 'me toos', such that the first product may become the industry standard in future years.

The growth stage

During the growth stage, sales for the market as a whole increase and new competitors typically enter to challenge the pioneer for some of the market share. The competitors may develop new market segments in an attempt to avoid direct competition with the established pioneering market leader.

The market becomes profitable and funds can be used to offset the development and launch costs. This is an important time to win market share since it is easier to win a disproportionate share of new customers than to get customers to switch brands later on. As new market segments emerge, key decisions will need to be made as to whether to follow them or stay with the original. It has been shown (Brown, 1991) that, in the electronic calculator market for example, demand was initially concentrated among scientists and engineers. Then businesses starting using them, then university students and finally the market reached its height when demand was found among schoolchildren. A pioneer wishing to stay in all these markets would have to make the brave decision to move out of organization-to-organization business into a mass consumer market.

The maturity stage

Maturity is reached when a high proportion of people who will eventually purchase a product have already purchased it once. This is likely to be the longest stage but, depending on the market, this could range from days or weeks to many decades or even centuries. It is important at this stage either to have achieved a high market share, or to dominate a special niche in the market. It can be expensive and risky to achieve large market share changes at this time, so some companies prefer to concentrate their competitive efforts on retaining existing customers and competing very hard for the small number of new customers appearing.

It has been pointed out that market shares among leading competitors are often very stable over extremely long periods of time (Mercer, 1993) and this may be used as a criticism of the product life cycle concept. However, over the time of maturity in the market, companies have to be vigilant in detecting change in the market, and be ready to modify or improve products and to undertake product repositioning if necessary.

The decline stage

It is part of product life cycle theory that all markets will eventually decline, and therefore companies have to be ready to move to new markets when decline is felt to be inevitable, or to be ready with strategies to extend the life cycle if this is felt to be feasible. Appropriate extension strategies could include developing new uses for the product, finding new users, and repositioning the product to gain a presence in the parts of the market that will remain after the rest of the market has gone. Even when markets have reached an advanced stage of decline, there may remain particular segments that can be profitable for organizations able to anticipate their existence and dominate them.

Companies that succeed in declining markets usually adopt a 'milking' strategy, wherein investment is kept to a minimum, and take up any market share that may be left by competitors that have left the market because of the decline. There is a certain recognition that death will come eventually and thus any revenues that can be made in the interim are something of a bonus.

Made simple

The human life cycle metaphor

The concept of life cycle does not just apply to products, it also applies to humans. Human beings undergo a life cycle that has a huge bearing, not just on our biological changes, but also on behaviour.

We undergo *introduction* when we are conceived and grow inside our mother. After birth, we begin to *grow* – a process that continues until, after puberty, we reach our full height and weight. Our *maturity* phase is the longest. For most people, this will last from our mid-teens until the time when our faculties begin to fail us – perhaps in our sixties or seventies. When we reach old age, we begin to *decline*. Our eyesight may begin to deteriorate, we slow down and we may lose some of our intellectual sharpness. Finally, when decline has run its course, life is no longer viable, and we *die*.

Criticisms of the product life cycle

The product life cycle appears to be both widely understood and used as a tool for strategic analysis and decision-making (Greenley and Bayus, 1993). Despite this, some important criticisms have been made. Although it is easy to go back into history and demonstrate all the features of the concept, it is hard to forecast the future and, in particular, it is hard to forecast turning points. Not to try to do so at all, however, would seem to avoid confronting hard strategic issues.

Another criticism is that life cycles may sometimes not be inevitable as dictated by the market, but created by the ineptitude of management. If management assumes that decline will come, they will take the decision to reduce investment and advertising in anticipation of the decline. Not surprisingly, decline does come, but sooner than it otherwise would have done had the investment not been withdrawn.

In a large-scale survey of UK companies, Hooley (1995) confirmed the existence of the familiar bell-shaped pattern of sales in many markets. The study, however, challenged the widely held view that profits would be low or negative in the early stages of the life cycle.

New product development

The importance of new products

Change in society, markets, economies and society has led to a shortening of life cycles, and this has intensified the need for most organizations to innovate in terms of the products they offer. New products can provide the mechanism whereby further growth can take place. Increasing competition, often itself coming from new or modified products, means that innovation is frequently not an option but a necessity.

'Newness' can vary from restyling or minor modification to producing products that are 'new to the world' and that lead to new markets. The higher the degree of newness, the more likely it is that major gains in sales and profits may be made, but, at the same time, the risks of incurring high costs and market failure are also increased. A single new product failure, if big enough, could bankrupt an organization. It is generally accepted that a very large proportion of new products fail, although precise quantification is impossible as many new products may be kept on the market despite not meeting their original objectives.

Organizations are faced with a dilemma in the management of new product development: new product development is essential, but is also fraught with risks. The successful management of the dilemma is often to produce a large number of new product ideas, most of which will never reach the market because they have been weeded out by an appropriate screening process.

New product idea generation

Ideas for new products can come from many sources. The greater the range of sources used, the more likely it is that a wide range and large number of new ideas will be produced (Sowrey, 1990).

Ideas from customers

For most organizations, the most important source of new ideas will be the customers. Obtaining ideas from customers is a good way of ensuring that ideas are produced that will produce products as a result of 'market pull'. This means that there will be a market for the products that result because they are specifically requested by the customers. Surveys and focus groups can help to produce ideas. The more straightforward approaches may give ideas for improvements, but more subtle approaches may reveal new needs.

Eric von Hippel (von Hippel, 1978) showed that a very successful approach for new ideas in industrial markets was to work with lead customers (respected, technically advanced buyers) to overcome their particular problems, and then to use the resulting new products to sell to other customers. Sometimes the products may require modification for the other customers at some cost, but the products then have unique value for these customers and the price inelasticity of demand (Coates and Robinson, 1995).

Ideas from research and development

R&D departments are useful at idea generation when a market opportunity has been identified but for which a solution has not yet been found. In this respect, R&D can lead to competitive advantage, as developments in the pharmaceuticals industry have proven on several occasions (e.g. the introduction of the anti-impotence drug Viagra by Pfizer Pharmaceuticals).

In some organizations, ideas emerge from R&D without a trigger from marketing intelligence. This is called 'technological push' and can sometimes lead to overspecified and high-cost products. At other times, technological push can result in a genuine breakthrough that marketing people can then 'run with'.

Other sources of ideas

It is impossible to construct a comprehensive list of sources of new products, but the following have proved to be useful in the past:

- advertising agencies (who sometimes have their 'finger on the pulse' of market requirements);
- consultants (who may carry out market research on a company's behalf);
- universities and other academic institutions;
- competitors (where an organization copies a competitive product);
- suppliers (who may have devised a way to use a component or material);

- employees, sometimes through 'employee idea' schemes;
- distributors and agents.

Screening

Once ideas for a new product have been generated, a company must then sift through them to develop only those with genuine potential – a process known as *screening*. As far as possible, the screening process has to attempt to avoid two potential types of errors: GO errors, where products are developed that ultimately fail or do not meet objectives, and DROP errors, where ideas are abandoned that would ultimately have succeeded. GO errors are recognizable, at least by the organization that makes them, but most DROP errors are unrecognized because the project has not gone ahead (unless of course a competitor makes a success of an idea that has been abandoned).

In practice, the screening process is normally multi-stage, with at least some kind of review at several points in the process. Since risks may be high, and organizational politics may play a part, it is usually recommended that, in at least one of the stages, a formal process is undergone in which the idea is evaluated against predetermined objective criteria.

Development

The stages in development will vary according to the nature of the product and the work required to develop a new version, but it is important to include stages of the screening process before activities that involve the commitment of large amounts of finance; also, it would not make sense to spend large amounts in developing a new product without producing evidence that there would be some demand for it. Stages in the process are typically as follows:

1 initial appraisal;
2 detailed business analysis and investment appraisal;
3 technical development;
4 market testing;
5 launch.

A traditional view of the development process is that one stage should precede another. With increasing competition, reducing time to market has become very important in many industries. To reduce the time to market, some of the activities may go on at the same time – sometimes known as *parallel processing*. This puts a premium on good communications in the company between functions such as technical R&D and marketing. To avoid the delays and complications that might be involved in handing a project from one function in the organization to another, multi-disciplinary teams known as *venture teams* may be created, and in some circumstances the team may be given the new product to manage when it is on the market. If such a team is created, it is likely that higher management will make the GO or DROP decision to avoid the risk of the bias of an enthusiastic but optimistic team taking over.

Product portfolio theory

What is a portfolio?

The notion of a portfolio exists in many areas of life, not just for products. Underpinning the concept is the need for a business to spread its opportunity and risk. A broad portfolio signifies that a business has a presence in a wide range of product and market sectors. Conversely, a narrow portfolio implies that the organization operates in only a few or even in one product or market sector.

A broad portfolio offers the advantage of robustness in that a downturn in one market will not threaten the whole company. Against this advantage is the problem of managing business interests that may be very different in nature and the company may be said to lack strategic focus. An organization operating with a very narrow portfolio (perhaps just one sector) can often concentrate wholeheartedly upon its sector, but it can become vulnerable if there is a downturn of demand in the one sector it serves.

The BCG matrix

The Boston Consulting Group matrix offers a way of examining and making sense of a company's portfolio of product and market interests. It is a way of viewing the entire product range to see a company's products as a collection of items in a similar way that a holder of shares in several companies might consider the decision on what to do with the shares.

One way of looking at the products in a portfolio is to consider each product in its position in the product life cycle and aim to have a balance of products in each stage. A more sophisticated approach is based on the idea that market share in mature markets is highly correlated with profitability, and that it is relatively less expensive and less risky to attempt to win a share in the growth stage of the market when there will be many new customers making a first purchase. This is the approach taken by the BCG matrix. It is used to analyse the product range with a view to aiding decisions on how the products should be treated in an internal strategic analysis. Figure 5.3 shows the essential features of the matrix.

The market share measure

The horizontal axis of the BCG matrix is based on a very particular measure of market share. That measure is share relative to the largest competitor. A product with a share of 20% of the market in which the next biggest competitor had a share of 10% would have a relative share of 2, whereas a product with a market share of 20% and the biggest competitor also had 20% would have a relative share of 1. The cut-off point between high and low share is 1, so high market share products in this analysis are market leaders. This arrangement of scale is sometimes described as being *logarithmic* in nature.

The market growth measure

The vertical axis of the BCG matrix is the rate of market growth, with the most relevant definition of the market being served. A popular point used to divide high and low growth in the market is 10% year-on-year growth, but we have found it useful in practical situations to

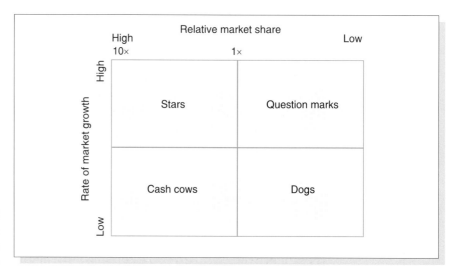

Figure 5.3
The Boston
Consulting Group
matrix.

use growth that is faster than the rate of growth in the economy as a whole, which, after inflation is usually between 1% and 2.5% a year.

Using the BCG matrix

Cash cows

A product with a high market share in a low growth market is normally both profitable and a generator of cash. Profits from this product can be used to support other products that are in their development phase. Standard strategy would be to manage conservatively, but to defend strongly against competitors. Such a product is called a *cash cow* because profits from the product can be 'milked' on an ongoing basis. This should not be used as a justification for neglect.

Dogs

A product that has a low market share in a low growth market is termed a *dog*, in that it is typically not very profitable. To cultivate the product to increase its market share would incur cost and risk, not least because the market it is in has a low rate of growth. Accordingly, once a dog has been identified as part of a portfolio, it is often discontinued or disposed of.

More creatively, opportunities might be found to differentiate the dog and obtain a strong position for it in a niche market. A small share product can be used to price aggressively against a very large competitor as it is expensive for the large competitor to follow suit.

The matrix does not have an intermediate market share category, but there are large numbers of products that have a large market share but are not market leaders. They may be the biggest profit earners for the companies that own them. They usually compete against the market leader at a disadvantage that is slight, but real. Management needs to make very efficient use of marketing expenditure for such products and to try to differentiate from the leader. They should not normally compete head on, especially on price, but attempt to make gains if the market changes in a way that the leader is slow to exploit.

Stars

Stars have a high share of a rapidly growing market and therefore rapidly growing sales. They may be the sales manager's dream, but they could be the accountant's nightmare, since they are likely to absorb large amounts of cash, even if they are highly profitable. It is often necessary to spend heavily on advertising and product improvements, so that, when the market slows, these products become cash cows. If market share is lost, the product will eventually become a dog when the market stops growing.

Question marks

Question marks are aptly named as they create a dilemma. They already have a foothold in a growing market but, if market share cannot be improved, they will become dogs. Resources need to be devoted to winning market share, which requires bravery for a product that may not yet have large sales, or the product may be sold to an organization in a better position to exploit the market.

Limitations of the BCG matrix

Accurate measurement and careful definition of the market are essential to avoid misdiagnosis when using the matrix. Critics, perhaps unfairly, point out that there are many relevant aspects relating to products that are not taken into account, but it was never claimed by the Boston Consulting Group that the process was a panacea and covered all aspects of strategy. Above all, the matrix helps to identify *which* products to push or drop, and *when*. It helps in the recognition of windows of opportunity, and is strong evidence against simple rules of thumb for allocating resources to products.

A composite portfolio model: the GEC matrix

The limitations of the BCG matrix have given rise to a number of other models that are intended to take a greater number of factors into account and to be more flexible in use. A leading example is the GEC matrix, developed by McKinsey and company in conjunction with the General Electric Company in the USA. It is mainly applied to strategic business units such as the subsidiaries of a holding company. The model rates *market attractiveness* as high, medium or low, and *competitive strength* as strong, medium or weak. Strategic business units are placed in the appropriate category and, although there is no automatic strategic prescription, the position is used to help devise an appropriate strategy.

Market attractiveness criteria will be set by the user, and could include factors such as market growth, profitability, strength of competition, entry/exit barriers, legal regulation, etc. Competitive strength could include technological capability, brand image, distribution channel links, production capability and financial strength. The flexibility to include as many variables as required is useful, but could lead to over-subjectivity. Most users of the model recommend that the variables be given a weighting to establish their relative importance which will, in turn, reduce the potential for bias. In practice, managers tend to be aware that the tool is likely to be used as a basis for resource allocation and, consequently, they may attempt to influence the analysis in the favour of their own product or strategic business unit. The analysis gives rise to a three-by-three matrix (Figure 5.4).

For products in cell A, the company would invest strongly, as this is potentially in an attractive strategic position, where distinctive competences can be harnessed to good opportunities. In B, the company could be aggressive and attempt to build strength in order to challenge, or it could build selectively. In C, there are real dilemmas, in that there is the difficulty of competing well against stronger competitors – most plausible options would be to divest, as the opportunity might be attractive to others, or to specialize around niches where some strength could be built. D would indicate investment and maintenance of competitive ability. E and F would indicate risk minimization and prudent choices for expansion. G and H would indicate management for earnings, whereas cell I would require divestment or minimizing investment.

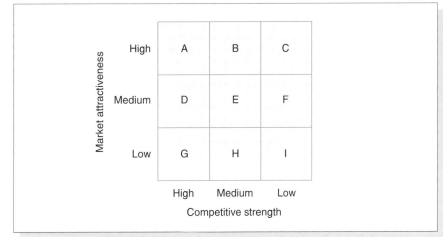

Figure 5.4
The GEC matrix.

Extreme care is required in the judgements that would place products or strategic business units into any one category, and the model does not take directly into account synergies between different products or business. The astute reader will recognize that the model represents a means of relating competences to the external environment and that it is also a means of taking SWOT a stage further.

References and further reading

Aaker, D.A. (1995) *Strategic Market Management*, Fourth Edition. New York: John Wiley.

Brown, R. (1991) The S-curves of innovation. *Journal of Marketing Management*, 7(2), 189–202.

Coates, N. and Robinson, H. (1995) Making industrial new product development market led. *Marketing Intelligence and Planning*, 13(6), 12–15.

Copeland, M.T. (1923) Relation of consumers' buying habits to marketing methods. *Harvard Business Review*, 1(April), 282–289.

Doyle, P. (1994) *Marketing Management and Strategy*. Englewood Cliffs: Prentice Hall.

Greenley, G.E. and Bayus, B.L. (1993) Marketing planning decision making in UK and US companies: an empirical comparative study. *Journal of Marketing Management*, 9, 155–172.

Hooley. G.J. (1995) The lifecycle concept revisited: aid or albatross? *Journal of Strategic Marketing*, 3, 23–39.

Jobber, D. (1995) *Principles and Practice of Marketing*. New York: McGraw-Hill.

Kotler, P. (1997) *Marketing Management Analysis, Planning, Implementation, and Control*, Ninth Edition. Englewood Cliffs: Prentice Hall International.

Lancaster, G. and Massingham, L. (1993) *Marketing Management*. London: McGraw-Hill.

Mercer, D. (1993) Death of the product life cycle. *Adman*, September, 15–19.

Sowrey, T. (1990) Idea generation: identifying the most useful techniques. *European Journal of Marketing*, 42(5), 20–29.

von Hippel, E. (1978) Successful industrial products from customer ideas. *Journal of Marketing*, 42(1), 39–49.

External analysis

The external environment is a bit like an onion. It comprises concentric strata of influences that can affect an organization. We considered the internal environment in Part II of the book. In this section, we look at the external environment.

The micro or 'near' environment is the sphere in which the organization interacts often – usually on a day-to-day basis. Any changes in the microenvironment can affect an organization very quickly and, sometimes, very dramatically.

In the case of most organizations, the microenvironment comprises influences from the competitive environment – its industry and markets. In Chapter 7, we discuss two models for making sense of this important strata of influence: Porter's five forces model and the resource- or core-competence-based model.

The macroenvironment contains a number of influences that affect not only an organization itself, but also the rest of the players in the industry. We introduce the SPENT framework to understand the forces at work in the macroenvironment.

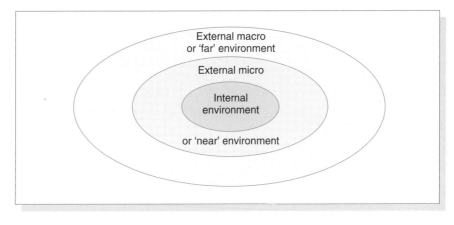

A schematic of the external environment.

Socio-demographic, political, economic, natural and technological influences are usually beyond an organization's ability to influence. Strategy usually therefore rests upon an organization's ability to cope with any changes in the macroenvironment. A key skill in strategic management is that of predicting changes in any of the SPENT influences and of accounting for potential changes in strategic formulation. We consider the macroenvironment in Chapter 6.

In Chapter 8, we introduce the strategic postures that organizations might adopt as a result of their external analyses. In this respect, Chapters 7 and 8 are naturally linked: Chapter 8 explains the implications of an organization's position in its microenvironment upon its competitive strategy.

Analysis of the macroenvironment

Introduction and chapter overview

Different textbooks tend to adopt their own mnemonic for external macroenvironmental analysis. Basic analysis includes analysis of the STEP (or PEST factors): socio-demographic, technological, economic and political factors. Other approaches, however, have attempted to include a category for the analysis of natural environmental factors. STEEP analysis, used in some books, has an extra 'E' for environmental analysis, but this book takes the view that 'E', in this context, is a bit confusing as the whole process is an analysis of the 'business environment'. Another approach – PESTLE or PESTEL analysis – includes the four PEST factors, the 'E' for natural environment and 'L' for legislative factors, although most books have taken the view (as does this text) that legislation is a political factor.

Hence, in an attempt to be complete while also avoiding confusion, this textbook suggests a new approach – SPENT analysis. It includes the four PEST or STEP factors plus 'N' for natural environmental factors. This chapter proceeds to consider how macroenvironmental analysis can be undertaken and then considers the content of the five SPENT factors.

After studying this chapter, students should be able to:

■ explain what is meant by the macroenvironment;
■ explain Ginter and Duncan's mechanisms of carrying out macroenvironmental analysis;
■ describe the components of each of the four SPENT influences;
■ describe how the SPENT factors are interlinked and interrelated.

The macroenvironment

What is the macroenvironment?

We refer to the macroenvironment as the broad environment outside of an organization's industry and markets. It is generally beyond the influence of the individual business but can have a significant impact on the microenvironment (industry and market) in which the business operates. The macroenvironment is sometimes referred to as the *far* or *remote* environment because it tends to exert forces from outside the organization's sphere of influence and the forces are usually beyond control.

Changes in the macroenvironment can be of immense importance to an organization; they tend to impact all organizations within an industry and sometimes also within the markets served by the industry. They can bring about the birth or death of an entire industry, they can make markets expand or contract, they can determine the level of competitiveness within an industry and many other things. It is therefore essential that managers are alert to actual and potential changes in the macroenvironment and that they anticipate the potential impacts on their industry and markets. Being able to predict changes and acting to take advantage of, or defend against, macroenvironmental changes can itself be a source of competitive advantage.

Conducting macroenvironmental analysis

Ginter and Duncan (1990) stated that macroenvironmental analysis involves:

- *scanning* the macroenvironment for warning signs and possible environmental changes that will affect the business;
- *monitoring* environments for specific trends and patterns;
- *forecasting* future directions of environmental changes;
- *assessing* current and future trends in terms of the effects such changes would have on the organization.

In their paper, Ginter and Duncan gave the example of the sportswear manufacturers Adidas and Converse. Converse failed to adequately analyse the macroenvironment and this, in turn, caused them to miss the opportunity of catering for the premium (upper-priced) segment of the running shoe market. Nike, on the other hand, more accurately predicted the strength of demand in the segment and exploited the market opportunities much more successfully (which partly explains why Nike is a better-known brand than Converse).

The same authors went on to identify the potential benefits of macroenvironmental analysis as:

- increasing managerial awareness of environmental changes;
- increasing understanding of the context in which industries and markets function;
- increasing understanding of multinational settings;
- improving resource allocation decisions;
- facilitating risk management;
- focusing attention on the primary influences on strategic change;
- acting as an early warning system, providing time to anticipate opportunities and threats and devise appropriate responses.

Limitations of macroenvironmental analysis

We should be careful to note that macroenvironmental analysis has its limitations and pitfalls. The macroenvironment can be extremely complex and at any one time there may be conflicting and contradictory changes taking place. The pace of change in many macroenvironmental situations is increasing and becoming more turbulent and unpredictable. This degree of uncertainty has, to some extent, cast some doubt over the value of carrying out a macroenvironmental analysis at all. By the time that an organization has come to terms with one major change in the macroenvironment, another change often occurs that requires even more attention and action.

Accordingly, those managers that are concerned with strategic analysis must:

■ be aware of the limitations and inaccuracies of macro-environmental analysis;

■ understand the complexity of the environment in which they operate and the sources of information on which the analysis is based;

■ carry out the analysis continuously (because it changes so frequently);

■ constantly seek to improve sources of information and techniques for its analysis;

■ use the information as one source of organizational learning (alongside other information gathering activities; see Chapters 7 and 15);

■ use the information to inform future strategy.

With these points in mind, macroenvironmental analysis is, nevertheless, a valuable mechanism for increasing the strategic awareness of managers.

SPENT analysis

Overview of the SPENT influences

The complexity of the macroenvironment makes it necessary to divide the forces at work into the five broad categories we have already encountered. It is important to remember that the five categories are partly inter-related and can interact with each other. In the process of SPENT analysis it is therefore important to explore and understand the relationships between the forces at work. It is equally important to identify the relative importance of the influences at work for the business, its industry and its markets. Finally, because of the uncertainty of the effects of macroenvironmental change on the microenvironment (see Chapter 7), it is essential that a range of possible outcomes of the changes are identified and considered. Techniques for such analysis are considered in a later section of this chapter.

Socio-demographic influences

Analysis of the social environment is concerned with understanding the potential impacts of society and social changes on a business, its industry and markets.

For most analyses, analysis of the social environment will require consideration of:

- *social culture* (values, attitudes and beliefs) – its impact on demand for products and services, attitudes to work, savings and investment, ecology, ethics, etc.;
- *demography* – the impact of the size and structure of the population on the workforce and patterns of demand;
- *social structure* – its impact on attitudes to work and certain products.

Social culture

The cultures of countries in which a business operates can be of particular importance. The culture of a country consists of the values, attitudes and beliefs of its people. These, in turn, will affect the way that they act and behave. There are important cultural differences between all countries. Culture can affect consumer tastes and preferences, attitudes to work, attitudes to education and training, attitudes to corruption and ethics, attitudes to credit, attitudes to the social role of a business in society and many other things. Even between similar countries or between regions of the same country, social culture can differ significantly in certain ways. Brewers, for example, are well aware of differences in 'drinking culture' across Europe: whereas the British, Germans, Irish and the Czechs prefer beer, the French, Italians and Spanish tend to prefer wine when relaxing with friends or on a night out. In some other countries, religious observance means that the majority don't drink alcohol at all.

Demography

Demographic trends are similarly important. Demography is the social science concerned with the charting of the size and structure of a population of people. The size of the population will obviously be a determinant of the size of the workforce and the potential size of markets. Just as important will be the structure of the population. The age structure will determine the size of particular segments and also the size of the working population. The size and structure of the population will constantly be changing and these changes will have an impact on industries and markets.

Social structure

Social structure is strongly linked to demography and refers to the ways in which the social groups in a population are organized. There are a number of ways of defining social structure such as by socio-demographic groupings, by age, sex, location, population density in different areas, etc. The social structure will affect people's lifestyles and expectations and so will strongly influence their attitudes to work and their demand for particular product types.

Some of the most important general changes in the social environment in recent years have been in people's attitudes to the natural environment (see Chapter 14). Increasing awareness of the problems caused by pollution and the exhaustion of non-renewable resources has caused businesses in many industries to rethink the way in which they produce their products and the composition of the products themselves. Similarly, changes in social structure (upward mobility), lifestyle (increased leisure) and demography (ageing populations in developed countries) have significantly altered many market and industry structures.

Political, governmental, legal and regulatory influences

The political environment is defined as that part of the macroenvironment that is under either the direct control or influence of the government and/or the state. 'Government', however, is a loosely defined term and can be considered at three 'levels':

- national level – the government of a particular country;
- subnational level – local government based at town halls, civic centres, etc. In some countries, some policy-making is devolved to regions, cantons, etc., such as (in the UK) in Scotland and Wales. Some federal countries, such as the USA, Germany and Switzerland, have relatively powerful 'local' (or state) policy-making bodies below national government level;
- supranational level – political bodies that exert influence upon several national governments. The European Union, NAFTA and the United Nations are examples of supranational political bodies.

Governments (at whatever level) have direct control or influence, to a greater or lesser extent, over:

- *Legislation and regulation* – this covers laws that influence employment, consumer protection, health and safety at work, contract and trading, trades unions, monopolies and mergers, tax, etc..
- *Economic policy* – particularly fiscal policy. Governments usually set policy concerning the levels of taxation and expenditure in the country.
- *Government-owned businesses* – nationalized industries. Some governments retain control over key strategic industries, and the way in which these are controlled can have 'knock-on' effects to other parts of the country.
- *Government international policy* – government intervention to influence exchange rates, international trade, etc.

The objectives that a government may have towards the regulation of business will depend in large part upon the political leaning of the governing party. Most governments have, however, sought to construct policy over a number of key areas of business activity:

- control of inflation (such as to improve international competitiveness);
- promotion of economic growth and investment;
- control of unemployment;
- stabilization of exchange rates;
- control of balance of payments;
- control of monopoly power, both by businesses and by trades unions;
- provision of public and merit goods like health, education, defence, etc.;
- control of pollution and environmental protection;
- redistribution of incomes (to varying degrees);
- consumer protection;
- regulation of working conditions;
- regulation of trade.

To varying degrees, all businesses will be affected by political influences. Accordingly, it is important for managers to monitor government policy to detect changes early so as to respond effectively.

Another important aspect of the political environment is *political risk* and its potential effects on business. Political risk is particularly important in international business. Although Europe and North America are comparatively politically stable, other parts of the world such as Eastern Europe, South America and parts of the

Middle East have undergone periods of political instability. It is therefore necessary to monitor closely the political situation in these areas when trading with them as the political risks are large. Even in more stable areas, political uncertainty can be higher at, for example, election times or when other political crises arise.

Economic influences

Analysis of the economic environment centres on changes in the macroeconomy and their effects on business and consumers. It is important to remember that, because governments intervene (to varying extents) in the operation of all countries' economies, many factors classed as political in this chapter will have important economic implications.

Broadly speaking, the regulation of a national economy is brought about by two key policy instruments: fiscal policy and monetary policy. These policy instruments, alongside influences from international markets, determine the economic climate in the country in which a business competes. From these, a number of other, vital economic indicators 'flow' and it is these that organizations experience – either for good or for ill.

Key concepts

Fiscal and monetary policy

- *Fiscal policy* is the regulation of the national economy through the management of government revenues and expenditures. Each fiscal year, a government raises so much in revenues (such as through taxation) and it spends another amount through its various departments (such as on health, education, defence, etc.). The government is able to influence the economic climate in a country by varying either or both of these sides of the fiscal equation.
- *Monetary policy* is the regulation of the national economy by varying the supply and price of money. Money supply concerns the volume of money (in its various forms) in the economy and the 'price' of money is the base rate which determines the interest rate that banks and other lenders charge for borrowings.

In the UK, the Chancellor of the Exchequer is in charge of fiscal policy; monetary policy is overseen by the Monetary Policy Committee of the Bank of England.

When the effects of fiscal and monetary pressure work themselves out in the economy, they can affect any or all of the following economic factors:

- economic growth rates (the year-to-year growth in the total size of a national economy, usually measured by gross domestic product);
- levels of income in the economy;
- levels of productivity (i.e. output per worker in the economy);
- wage levels and the rate of increase in wages;
- levels of inflation (i.e. the year-to-year rise in prices);
- levels of unemployment;
- balance of payments (a measure of the international competitiveness of one country's economy against its international competitor countries);
- exchange rates (the exchange value of one currency against another).

Economic growth, exchange rates, levels of income, inflation and unemployment will all affect people's ability to pay for products and services and hence affect levels and patterns of demand. Similarly, levels of productivity, wage levels, levels of inflation and exchange rates will affect costs of production and competitiveness. All of these indicators must be monitored in comparison with those faced by competitors abroad to provide indications of changes in international competitiveness.

Natural influences

The natural environment is able to exert a significant influence upon business in some situations although, for other businesses, it may have no apparent influence at all. As with socio-demographic, political and economic influences, the more widely spread a company's operations are, the more possible natural variables the company will need to be aware of. Although such events are natural, there is a debate as to the extent to which human activity has intensified their likelihood. In this context, natural events include earthquakes, landslides, avalanches, floods, tidal waves, deforestation, droughts, freezes, volcano eruption, etc. On a more day-to-day basis, the weather can determine demand for goods such as ice cream and clothes, and services such as travel.

There are two observations about natural events:

1 their impact upon business activity can be very powerful and, in almost all cases, the events are difficult to predict or avoid;
2 the risk of certain natural events occurring varies by geographical location.

Natural influences can occur on scales from very small to very large. A rainy spell may trigger an upturn in demand for umbrellas and waterproof boots, a sunny spell may stimulate demand for ice cream, sun-cream and shorts. A river in flood may cause damage to a handful of pubs, farms and other small businesses along its banks. The volcano eruption on the island of Montserrat in 1997 destroyed valuable property and the tourism industry on the island. On an even larger scale, earthquakes can destroy entire towns, kill tens of thousands of people and destroy all the businesses previously located in the unfortunate area in question. For businesses affected by natural impact, the effects can be very costly and far-reaching.

Technological influences

Analysis of the technological environment involves developing an understanding of the effects of changes in technology and their impact on all areas of an industry, its members and their activities, including:

- goods and services;
- production processes;
- information and communications;
- transport and distribution;
- society, politics and economics.

Changes in technology affect the products available to consumers and businesses, the quality of the products and their functionality. For example, the development of the microprocessor has made possible the development of many new products, including the personal computer, automatic washing machines and programmable video recorders. Production processes in many industries have been transformed and automated by computer-aided design and computer-aided manufacturing. This has speeded up design processes, transformed working practices and increased the efficiency of production.

Developments in information and communications technology, such as the development of personal computers, networks, satellite, cable and digital communications and the Internet, together with rapid advances in software, have all contributed to revolutionizing the way in which business is conducted in many industries. Activities are now better coordinated, research and development is speeded up and many businesses are much more flexible and responsive.

Similarly, changes in transport technology have revolutionized business and have changed societies and cultures. It is possible to transport materials, components and products with far greater speed and at much lower cost as a result of developments in road, rail, sea and air transport. These improvements in transport have also increased the amount of personal and business travel that people undertake. Increasing personal travel has had a significant influence on the patterns of consumption in many countries. For example, in the UK, patterns of food and alcohol consumption have altered dramatically. In the markets for alcoholic drinks, for example, continental lager consumption has increased, partly as a result of the increased mobility that modern transport systems have brought about.

Interestingly, it is in the technological environment that it is sometimes possible for large organizations to actually exert influence rather than be the recipients of it. IBM's role in the development of the personal computer, Philips' development of the compact disc, Microsoft's developments in operating systems and software are all examples of the impact of individual (albeit large) businesses on general levels of technology.

It is important to note, however, that not all technology is electronic. At is simplest, a technology is an innovation that in some way advances human understanding. In ancient Egypt, for example, the utilization of irrigation was a technology, as was the invention of the shaduf for transferring water from one location to another. The bow and arrow, the invention of gunpowder, the discovery of the forces at work in an arched bridge and innovations leading to the shaping of a modern motor car are all examples of technology. Chemists work with chemical technologies that lead to the development of new medicines, plastics, etc., engineers use different technologies to optimize the designs of everything from roads to buildings to aircraft.

As a consequence, it is important that organizations monitor changes in the technologies that can affect their operations or their markets. In most industries, organizations must be flexible and be ready to innovate and to adopt new technologies as they come along. The way in which (and the extent to which) organizations do or do not employ the latest technology can be an important determinant of its competitive advantage.

The relationships between the SPENT influences

The example of ecological concern

A temptation when carrying out a SPENT analysis is to think of each influence as separate when in fact they are often interlinked. Increasing concerns about ecology and 'green issues' provide a good example of this. In recent years there has been an important social trend which has changed people's attitudes towards the effects of products and production processes on the environment. Whereas twenty years ago most consumers showed little concern for the long-term effects of products and processes on the natural environment, today people are increasingly aware of the need to protect it. This has led to pressure on governments to introduce legislation and other measures to control pollution. The combined desire of consumers for products that are themselves environmentally friendly and which have been produced by 'green' methods has resulted in the realization by business that there are profits to be made by being environmentally friendly. This, in turn, has led to research and development aimed at designing products and processes that are less damaging to the environment. Among the numerous examples are aerosols that do not use CFCs, catalytic converters for automobile engines, unleaded fuel, reduced use of fuels that produce gases that damage the ozone layer and so on. The witnessing of real environmental incidents on television (i.e. natural macroenvironmental influences) serves to intensify concern about the natural environmental concerns and this, in turn, puts further, societal, pressure on businesses.

In this example, the effects of ecological issues (natural influences) on business combined with social factors (increased awareness of environmental issues) have impacted on political factors (legislation) and the three forces together have helped to stimulate technological change (products and processes that are less damaging to the environment). Accordingly, a macroenvironmental analysis should recognize the ways in which the five SPENT factors might be linked to each other.

By way of caution, however, it should be borne in mind that the SPENT framework is a 'prompt' to aid analysis and to ensure a disciplined approach to macroenvironmental analysis. The importance of the process is to identify issues that will have an impact on the organization and the industry. Categorizing them correctly between the factors is of secondary importance.

Using the SPENT analysis

How to carry out a SPENT analysis

Now that we know what the SPENT influences are and how they are inter-related, we turn to actually using the framework in strategic analysis. We generally think of the analysis as falling into four stages:

1 scanning and monitoring the macroenvironment for actual or potential changes in social, political, economic, natural and socio-demographic factors;
2 assessing the relevance and importance of the changes for the market, industry and business;
3 analysing each of the relevant changes in detail and the potential relationships between them;
4 assessing the potential impact of the changes on the market, industry and business.

What to analyse

When managers carry out a SPENT analysis as part of a strategic analysis (and the same is true of students examining a case study), they would normally examine how each factor might impact upon:

- *the industry in which the organization competes* – the effects of SPENT factors on the five competitive forces (buyer power, supplier power, threat of entry, threat of substitutes, competitive rivalry; see Chapter 7);
- *an organization's markets* – the effects of SPENT factors on product markets (e.g. market size, structure, segments, customer wants, etc.) and the resource markets in which organizations gain their inputs;
- *the internal parts of an organization* – the effects of SPENT factors on the organization's core competences, strategies, resources and value systems.

References and further reading

Chakravarthy, B. (1997) A new strategy framework for coping with turbulence. *Sloan Management Review*, Winter, 69–82.

Elenkov, D.E. (1997) Strategic uncertainty and environmental scanning: the case for institutional influences on scanning behaviour. *Strategic Management Journal*, 18(4), 287–302.

Fahey, L. and Narayanan, V.K. (1986) *Macroenvironmental Analysis for Strategic Management*. West Publishing.

Ginter, P. and Duncan, J. (1990) Macroenvironmental analysis. *Long Range Planning*, December.

Heene, A. and Sanchez, R. (1997) *Competence-Based Strategic Management*. John Wiley.

Helms, M.M. and Wright, P. (1992) External considerations: their influence on future strategic planning. *Management Decision*, 30(8), 4–11.

Levitt, T. (1983) The globalisation of markets. *Harvard Business Review*, May/June.

Makridakis, S. (1990) *Forecasting, Planning, and Strategy for the 21st Century*. New York: Free Press.

Mintzberg, H. (1991) *The Strategy Process: Concepts, Contexts, Cases*. Englewood Cliffs: Prentice Hall.

Sanchez, R. (1995) Strategic flexibility, firm organization, and managerial work in dynamic markets: a strategic options perspective. *Advances in Strategic Management*, 9, 251–291.

Sanchez, R. (1995) Strategic flexibility in product competition. *Strategic Management Journal* 16 (Summer), 135–159.

Stonehouse, G.H., Hamill, J. and Purdie, A. (1999) *Global and Transnational Business: Strategy and Management*. London: John Wiley.

Strebel, P. (1992) *Breakpoints*. Cambridge, MA: Harvard Business School Press.

Turner, I. (1996) Working with chaos. *Financial Times*, 4 October.

CHAPTER 7

Analysis of the competitive environment

An organization's external environment comprises two strata: the macroenvironment and the microenvironment. We considered the macroenvironment in Chapter 6 (using the SPENT framework); in this chapter, we turn to an analysis of the microenvironment.

The microenvironment comprises those influences that the organization experiences frequently. For most businesses, it concerns the industries in which they operate. Within this arena, businesses may compete with each other or, in some circumstances, collaboration may be more appropriate. We discuss two models for industry analysis in this chapter. Then we discuss the scope of collaborative behaviour, before considering the way in which competitors in an industry fall into strategic groups.

After studying this chapter, students should be able to:

- explain the importance of industry and market analysis;
- describe the construction and application of Porter's five forces framework;
- explain the limitations of Porter's five forces framework;
- define and distinguish between competitive and collaborative behaviour in industries;

- describe and explain the limitations of the resource-based model of industry analysis;
- define strategic groups and describe their usefulness in industry analysis.

Industries and markets

The importance of industry and market identification

Some strategic management texts wrongly use the terms *industry* and *market* interchangeably. Kay (1995) correctly pointed out that to confuse the two concepts can result in a flawed analysis of the competitive environment and, hence, in flawed strategy. Modern businesses (especially larger companies) may operate in more than one industry and in more than one market. Each industry and market will have its own distinctive structure and characteristics which will have particular implications for the formulation of business strategy. Kay (1993) also pointed out that a distinctive capability, or core competence, "becomes a competitive advantage only when it is applied in a market or markets". Industries are centred on the supply of a product whereas markets are concerned with demand. It is important, therefore, to understand and analyse both industries and markets to assist in the process of strategy selection.

Key concepts

Industry and market

- Industries *produce* goods and services – the supply side of the economic system.
- Markets *consume* goods and services that have been produced by industries – the demand side of the economic system.

The industry

It is sometimes difficult to define a particular industry precisely. Porter (1980) defined an industry as a group of businesses whose products are close substitutes, but this definition can be inadequate because some organizations and industries produce a range of products for different markets. Alternatively, organizations can be grouped according to the similarity of their production processes. Two major official classifications of industries, employing this means of grouping, are the *Standard Industrial Classification* (SIC) of economic activity in the UK and the *Nomenclature Générale des Activités Economiques dans les Communautés Européennes* (NACE) of the European Union. These classifications, mainly used by investors and stockmarkets, can be extended to define an industry as a group of businesses that share similar products, processes, technologies, competences, suppliers and distribution channels. Analysis of these features of an industry will inform the process of strategy formulation.

The competitors in a given industry may produce products for more than one market. For example, businesses in the 'white goods' industry produce both washing machines and refrigerators. The materials, technology, skills and processes employed in the manufacture of both products are very similar. The materials used are obtained from similar suppliers and the products are sold to consumers through the same distributors (e.g. the main electrical retail multiples). There is clearly, therefore, an identifiable 'white goods' industry. Yet both these products (washing machines and refrigerators) satisfy very different customer needs, are used for entirely different purposes and are therefore sold to separate markets. One make of washing machine competes with another, and one make of refrigerator competes with another.

Key concepts

Checklist of industry characteristics

The following are usually relevant when analysing an industry:

- location;
- location of support and resource markets for the industry;
- extent of concentration or fragmentation (i.e. industry structure);
- product types produced;
- levels of output, growth and life cycle position;
- ownership issues;
- the other activities of industry members.

The market

Whereas an industry is centred upon producers of a product (a good or service), a market is centred on customers and their requirements (needs and wants). A particular market consists of a group of customers with a specific set of requirements which may be satisfied by one or more products. Analysis of a market will therefore involve gaining an understanding of customers, their requirements, the products that satisfy those requirements, the organizations producing the products and the means by which customers obtain those products (distribution channels).

As well as selling their products in markets, businesses also obtain their resources (labour, materials, machinery, etc.) in markets – referred to as resource markets. Additionally, most businesses are interested in markets for substitute products and they will also be keen to investigate new markets for their products.

The relationship between a business, its industry and markets

Analysis of its industry and markets allows a business to:

■ identify other industries in which it may be able to deploy its core competences;
■ understand the nature of its customers and their needs;
■ identify new markets in which its core competences may be exploited (see Chapter 2 for a discussion of core competences);
■ identify threats from existing and potential competitors in its own and other industries;
■ understand markets from which it obtains its resources.

Analysis of the competitive environment (industry and market) is as important to the development of an organization's future strategy as is internal analysis (which was the subject of Part II of this book). The industry and market context will play an important role in shaping an organization's competences and core competences. The core competences of a business must continually be reviewed in relation to changing customer needs, competitors' competences and other market opportunities.

Industry analysis

What is industry analysis?

Industry analysis aims to establish the nature of the competition in an industry and the competitive position of a business with respect to its microenvironment. Industry dynamics, in turn, are affected by changes in the macroenvironment (see Chapter 6). For example, ageing populations in many developed countries have significantly affected the need to develop drugs suitable for treating the ailments of older people. There is a danger that industry analysis can be seen as a 'one-off' activity but, like all components of the strategic process, it should be undertaken on an ongoing basis. The industry analysis framework developed by Porter (1980) is the most widely used and is explained in this section.

Key concept

Micro- and macroenvironments

The most commonly used frameworks for analysing the external business environment distinguish between two levels or strata of environmental influence:

- *The micro (or near) environment* is that which immediately surrounds a business, the parts of which the business interacts with frequently and over which it may have some influence. For most purposes, we can identify competitors, suppliers and customers as comprising the main constituents of this strata of the environment.
- *The macro (or far) environment* comprises those influences that can affect the whole industry in which a business operates. The macroenvironment comprises influences arising from socio-demographic, political, economic, natural and technological factors. The nature of these factors normally means that individual businesses are unable to influence them – strategies must usually be formulated to cope with changes in the macroenvironment.

Porter's five forces model of industry analysis

Porter (1980) developed a framework for analysing the nature and extent of competition within an industry. He argued that there are five competitive forces which determine the nature of competition within an industry. Understanding the nature and strength of each of the five forces within an industry assists managers in developing the competitive strategy of their organization. The five forces are:

- the threat of new entrants to the industry;
- the threat of substitute products;
- the power of buyers or customers;
- the power of suppliers (to businesses in the industry);
- rivalry among businesses in the industry.

By determining the relative 'power' of each of these forces, an organization can identify how to position itself to take advantage of opportunities and overcome or circumvent threats. The strategy of an organization may then be designed to exploit the competitive forces at work within an industry.

When using Porter's framework (see Figure 7.1) it is important to identify which of the five forces are the key forces at work in an industry at any given point in time. In many cases, it transpires that one or more of the five forces prove to be 'key forces' and the strategic analysis must focus on these if it is to use the framework fruitfully. The dynamic nature of the competitive environment (meaning that it is constantly changing) means that the relative strength of the forces in a particular industry will change over time. It is therefore important that the five forces analysis is repeated on a regular basis so

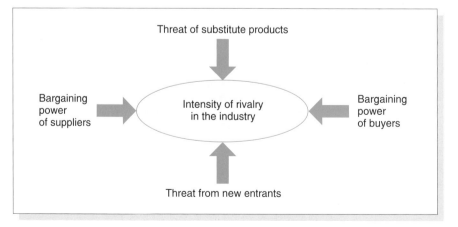

Figure 7.1
Porter's five forces framework (adapted from Porter, 1980).

as to detect such changes before competitors and allow an early adjustment of strategy. Before any conclusions can be drawn about the nature of competition within an industry each of the five forces must be analysed in detail.

We will now discuss each of the five forces in turn.

Force 1: The threat of new entrants to the industry

The threat of entry to an industry by new competitors depends upon the 'height' of a number of entry barriers. As a rule of thumb, the lower the entry barriers to an industry are, the more competitors will be players in the industry. Barriers to entry can take a number of forms.

The capital costs of entry

The size of the investment required by a business wishing to enter the industry will be an important determinant of the extent of the threat of new entrants. The higher the investment required, the less the threat from new entrants. The lower the required investment, the greater the threat.

Regulatory and legal constraints

Industry regulation varies. Some industries, such as energy, pharmaceuticals and defence equipment, are subject to a complex regulatory framework whereas others are less so. In some industries, regulation concerns health and safety, product handling and licences to operate, export, set up new facilities, etc. Each regulatory or legal permission or restriction is capable of acting as a barrier to entry.

Brand loyalty and customer switching costs

If the players in an industry produce differentiated products and customers are brand loyal, then potential new entrants will encounter resistance in trying to enter the industry. Brand loyalty will also be an important factor in increasing the costs for customers of switching to the products of new competitors.

Economies of scale available to existing competitors

If existing competitors are already obtaining substantial economies of scale, this will give them an advantage over new competitors who will not be able to match their lower unit costs of production.

Access to input and distribution channels

New competitors may find it difficult to gain access to channels of distribution, which will make it difficult to provide their products to customers or obtain the inputs required or find markets for their outputs.

The resistance offered by existing businesses

If existing competitors choose to resist strongly, it will make it difficult for new organizations to enter the industry. For example, if existing businesses are obtaining economies of scale, it will be possible for them to undercut the prices of new entrants because of their cost advantage. In some cases, existing competitors may make price cuts or increase marketing expenditure specifically to deter new entrants.

   If barriers to entry make it difficult for new competitors to enter the industry, this will limit the amount of competition within it. As a result, competitors within the industry will attempt to seek to strengthen the barriers to entry by cultivating brand loyalty, increasing the costs of entry and 'tying up' input and distribution channels as far as is possible.

Force 2: The threat of substitute products

A substitute can be regarded as something that meets the same needs as the product of the industry. For example, an individual wishing to cross the English channel can choose to travel by cross-channel ferry, by hovercraft or by the train service under the channel tunnel. These products all provide the benefit to the customer of crossing to France, despite the fact that the ferry and rail services are provided by different industries. The extent of the threat from a particular substitute will depend upon the following two factors.

The extent to which the price and performance of the substitute can match the industry's product

Close substitutes whose performance is comparable to the industry's product and whose price is similar will be a serious threat to an industry. The more indirect the substitute, the less likely will the price and performance be comparable.

The willingness of buyers to switch to the substitute

Buyers will be more willing to change suppliers from one industry if switching costs are low or if a competitor in another industry offers a product with a lower price or improved performance. This is also closely tied in with the extent to which customers are brand loyal. The more loyal customers are to one supplier's products (for whatever reason) then the threat from substitutes will be accordingly reduced.

Key concept

Switching costs

One of the key strategic manoeuvres in maintaining customer loyalty is to increase the cost – to the customer – of changing to a new supplier. If switching costs are high, then customers will have an economic disincentive to switch and hence will tend to stay with the existing supplier. For substitution of products within an industry, switching costs are usually very low. It costs nothing in money or effort, for example, to switch brands of coffee or washing powder.

For indirect substitutes (those provided by other industries), there are likely to be higher actual or perceived switching costs. If buyers have had to make an investment in order to accommodate one supplier's product, then switching may involve extra investment which would act as a disincentive to switch. Switching costs may be financial, but may also be expressed in terms of lower quality, reduced confidence in the competitor's product or poorer product performance.

Competitors in an industry will attempt to reduce the threat from substitute products by improving the performance of their products, by reducing costs and prices, and by differentiation.

Force 3: The bargaining power of buyers

The extent to which the buyers of a product exert power over an industry depends upon a number of factors. Broadly speaking, the more power that buyers exert, the lower will be the transaction price. This has obvious implications for the profitability of the supplier. The bargaining power of buyers will be influenced by the following factors.

The number of customers and the volume of their purchases

The fewer the buyers and the larger the volume of their purchases, the greater will be their bargaining power. A large number of buyers each acting largely independently of each other and buying only small quantities of a product will have comparatively weak power.

The number of businesses supplying the product and their size

If the industry in question is fairly concentrated and its members are large in comparison to the buyers, then buying power will tend to be reduced. The degree of concentration has the effect that a few suppliers will tend to reduce the bargaining power of buyers as choice and the ability to 'shop around' is reduced.

Switching costs and the availability of substitutes

If the cost of switching between substitutes is low, then customers (buyers) will be accordingly more powerful because of the inability of industry players to inflate their prices (which will be constrained by the price of the substitute products).

We should bear in mind that buyers are not necessarily those at the end of the supply chain. At each stage of a supply chain, the bargaining power of buyers will have a strong influence upon the prices charged and the industry structure.

In the supply chain for beer, for example, the buyers include consumers, wholesalers, supermarket chains, public houses and restaurants. The amount of power that each buyer exerts can differ substantially. Supermarket chains can exert far greater pressure on brewers than can individual consumers.

Force 4: The bargaining power of suppliers

Businesses must obtain the resources that they need to carry out their activities from resource suppliers. These resources fall into the four categories we have previously encountered: human, financial, physical and intellectual.

Resources are obtained in resource markets where prices are determined by the interaction between the businesses supplying a resource (suppliers) and the organizations from each of the industries using the particular resource in question. It is important to note that many resources are used by more than one industry. As a result, the bargaining power of suppliers will not be determined solely by their relationship with one industry but by their relationships with all of the industries that they serve.

The major factors determining the strength of suppliers are discussed below.

The uniqueness and scarcity of the resource that suppliers provide

If the resources provided to the industry are essential to it and have no close substitutes, then suppliers are likely to command significant power over the industry. If the resource can be easily substituted by other resources, its suppliers will have little power. It is for this reason, for example, that people with rare or exceptional skills can command higher salaries than lesser-skilled people.

The cost of switching to another resource

If the resource can be easily substituted, then switching costs will be low. If there is high labour turnover or low penalty clauses in debt rescheduling, then the power over suppliers of these resources will be increased.

How many other industries have a requirement for the resource

If suppliers provide a particular resource to several industries, they are less likely to be dependent upon one single industry. Thus, the more industries to which they supply a resource, the greater will be their bargaining power.

The number and size of the resource suppliers

If the number of organizations supplying a resource is small and there are a large number of buyers, then the greater will be their power over the organizations in that industry. If the suppliers are small and there are a large number of them, they will be comparatively weak, particularly if they are small in comparison to the organizations buying the resource from them. For example, most of Marks & Spencer's suppliers are relatively weak because they are small in comparison to the retailer. Marks & Spencer has a number of suppliers and is able to switch suppliers if necessary to gain lower input costs or higher quality.

In short, suppliers to an industry will be most powerful when:

- the resource that they supply is scarce;
- there are few substitutes for it;
- switching costs are high;
- they supply the resource to several industries;
- the suppliers themselves are large;
- the organizations in the industry buying the resource are small.

When the opposite conditions apply, suppliers will be weak.

Force 5: The intensity of rivalry among competitors in the industry

Businesses within an industry will compete with each other in a number of ways. Broadly speaking, competition can take place on either a price or a non-price basis.

Price competition involves businesses trying to undercut each other's prices; this will, in turn, be dependent upon their ability to reduce their costs of production. Non-price competition will take the form of branding, advertising, promotion, additional services to customers and product innovation. In some industries, competitive rivalry is fierce, whereas in others it is less intense or even genteel.

In Figure 7.1 we see that the other four forces point in towards this fifth force. This representation is intentionally to remind us that the strength of this force is largely dependent upon the contributions of the other four forces that 'feed' it. In particular, however, the intensity of competition in an industry will depend upon the following factors.

The height of entry barriers and the number and size of the competitors in the industry

If there are few, large competitors in the industry, it is likely that this is due to high entry barriers. Conversely, an industry of many, smaller competitors is likely to be the result of lower entry barriers. Competitive rivalry on both a price and a non-price basis will be higher in the industry comprising the more, and smaller, competitors.

The maturity of the industry

If the product is mature and the industry is subject to 'shake-out', then competition will be more intense (see discussion of this in Chapter 5).

The degree of brand loyalty of customers

If customers are loyal to brands, there is likely to be less competition and what competition there is will be non-price competition. If there is little brand loyalty then competition will be more intense.

The power of buyers and availability of substitutes

If buyers are strong and there are close substitutes available for the product, the degree of competitive rivalry will be greater.

A high degree of rivalry will usually compromise the potential profitability of an industry and will typically result in innovation which stimulates consumer demand for the products of the industry. In recent years, many industries have become more competitive.

The five forces framework and profitability: a summary

As has been discussed, a relationship can be established between a company's position in respect to the five forces and its potential profitability. Table 7.1 shows a summary of how the five forces can help to determine company and industry profitability.

Table 7.1
Porter's five forces and profitability – a summary

Force	Profitability will be higher if there is/are:	Profitability will be lower if there is/are:
Bargaining power of suppliers	Weak suppliers	Strong suppliers
Bargaining power of buyers	Weak buyers	Strong buyers
Threat of new entrants	High entry barriers	Low entry barriers
Threats from substitute products	Few possible substitutes	Many possible substitutes
Competitive rivalry	Little rivalry	Intense rivalry

Limitations of the five forces framework

Despite its obvious value as a tool for managers seeking to better understand the competitive environment, Porter's framework is subject to several important limitations. These are considered and then some suggestions are made for modifications to improve the value of the framework as an analytical tool. The major limitations of the framework are as follows.

It claims to assess industry profitability

Porter (1980) argued that the framework makes it possible to assess the potential profitability of a particular industry. Although there is some evidence to support this claim, there is also strong evidence to suggest that company-specific factors (such as individual competences) are more important to the profitability of individual businesses than industry factors (Rumelt, 1991).

It implies that the five forces apply equally to all competitors in an industry

In reality, the strength of the forces may differ from business to business. The framework implies that if, for example, supplier power is strong, this will apply to all the businesses in the industry. In fact, supplier power may differ from business to business in the industry. Larger businesses will face less of a threat from suppliers than will smaller ones. Similarly, businesses with strong brand names will be less susceptible to buyer power and substitutes than those with weaker brands.

It does not adequately cover product and resource markets

The concepts of buyer power and supplier power relate to the markets in which a business sells its products and obtains its resources. The conditions in both sets of markets are, however, rather more complex than Porter's framework implies (see Chapter 5).

It cannot be applied in isolation

Porter (1980) accepted that outcomes from applying the framework were only relevant while the macroenvironment remained constant. The continual move towards more complex and dynamic environments means that findings must be constantly reviewed.

It assumes that relationships with competitors, buyers and suppliers are adversarial

The five forces framework makes the implicit assumption that the goal of competitive strategy is to subjugate and gain ascendancy over suppliers and buyers. It also assumes that only by positioning itself favourably with regard to competitors can a company gain competitive advantage. In reality, relationships within industries are more complex than this suggests and, in many cases, players in an industry often see 'fair play' or 'give and take' as an important quality in all participants. Similarly, supplier and buyer relationships that may have lasted for decades are often more accurately described as partnerships – a more emollient and less-aggressive relationship than that implied by the five forces model.

Competitive and collaborative arenas

It is not always the case that businesses in an industry compete with each other; they might, from time to time, have reasons to collaborate with each other. Accordingly, in some 'arenas', businesses compete, whereas in others they may work together.

At the root of this understanding is the fact that organizations and industries are open systems – they interact with many environments. The 'arenas' in which an organization operates are the following.

- *Industry* – the industry within which the organization currently deploys its resources and competences in producing products.
- *Resource markets* – the markets from which the organization, its competitors and other industries obtain their resources.
- *Product markets* – markets in which the organization sells its products. These can be subdivided into markets for the organization's products, markets for substitute products, and new markets into which the organization may be considering entry.
- *Other industries* – where businesses possess similar competences to those of the organization. Such industries are important for two reasons. The first is that the business may be considering entry to them. The second is that the organizations in these industries are potential competitors who may enter the business's industry and markets.

Each of these arenas must be analysed as they directly affect an organization's competitive positioning and hence its chances of out-performing competitors. The competitive and collaborative arena framework builds upon Porter's five forces framework but explicitly recognizes that the competitive environment is divided into four separate but inter-related arenas.

A resource-based approach to environmental analysis

Limitations of existing frameworks of analysis

This chapter has so far concentrated on explaining the traditional strategic management frameworks employed in the analysis of the competitive environment. The resource-based approach to strategic management, which emphasizes the importance of core competence in achieving competitive advantage, employs a different approach to analysis of the competitive environment. There are several limitations to existing (traditional) frameworks:

- they do not sufficiently integrate external and internal analysis (Sanchez and Heene, 1997);
- they presuppose that businesses are naturally competitive and not collaborative in their behaviour;
- they tend to emphasize product markets rather than those from which organizations obtain their resources;
- they do not adequately recognize the fact that organizations themselves may alter their own competitive environments by their competence leveraging and building activities;
- they do not adequately recognize the fact that organizations currently outside a company's industry and market may pose a significant competitive threat if they possess similar core competences and distinctive capabilities;
- similarly, they do not recognize that the leveraging of existing competences and the building of new ones may enable businesses to compete outside their current competitive arenas.

The resource-based framework

A resource-based framework for analysis of the business and its competitive environment is shown in Figure 7.2. Analysis is divided into five inter-related areas:

1. the organization;
2. its industry;
3. product markets (existing markets, markets for substitutes, potential new markets);
4. resource markets;
5. other industries.

The significance of each area is considered below.

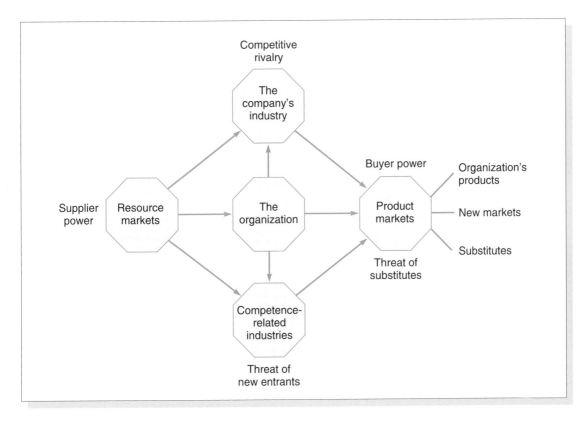

Figure 7.2
The resource-based model of strategy. (Note: competence-related industries are those in which businesses possess similar competences to those of competitors.)

The organization

'The organization' concerns the configuration of the internal value chain, its competences, resources and core competences, and is discussed in Part II of this book (in particular, in Chapter 2). In this context, we are particularly concerned with analysing the organization's value-adding capabilities and its backward and forward value chain linkages.

The organization's industry

The organization's industry consists of the business and a group of companies producing similar products, employing similar capabilities and technology.

Analysis of the industry therefore examines over time (for each player in the industry):

- the skills and competences of the competitors;
- the configuration of value-adding activities;
- the technologies employed;
- the number and relative size of competitors in the industry;
- the performance of competitors (particularly in financial terms);
- ease of entry to and exit from the industry;
- strategic groupings (see later in the chapter for a discussion of this concept).

This analysis will assist the organization in gaining greater understanding of its core competences, its major competitors and their core competences, and competitive and collaborative opportunities and threats.

Product markets

Product markets are those in which businesses deploy their competences and sell their products. A business may operate in one or more product markets. In addition, a business will be interested in understanding markets to which it is considering entry on the basis of its core competences and also markets for substitute products. Each of these markets will have its own characteristics and can be analysed in terms of:

- customer needs and motivations;
- unmet customer needs;

- market segments and their profitability;
- the number of competitors to the market and their relative market shares;
- the number of customers and their relative purchasing power;
- access to distribution channels;
- potential for collaboration with customers;
- ease of entry;
- potential for competence leveraging;
- need for new competence building.

Unless an organization's products are sold at a profit, the business will ultimately fail. Market-driven businesses that set out to meet existing customer needs, anticipate their currently unmet needs and actually seek to shape the needs of their customers are likely to be the most successful. For example, the Dutch electronics company Philips created a new customer need when it developed and launched the CD format for music and computer software.

Market subgroups

An important part of understanding the market is identifying subgroups within the market that share common needs. Such shared characteristics will cause specific customer groups to have different needs and to act and behave differently to other customer groups (or *segments*). Fundamentally, segmentation means subdividing the total market into customer subgroupings, each with their own distinctive attributes and needs. Customer groups are commonly segmented according to demographic variables (or 'people dividers') such as age, sex, occupation, socio-economic grouping, race, lifestyle, buying habits, geography (i.e. where they live), although other segmentation instruments are widely used (see Chapter 5). When customers are other businesses, they can be grouped by the nature of the business, organization type and their size. Each segment is then analysed for its size and potential profitability, for customer needs and for potential demand, based on ability and willingness to buy. Segmentation analysis assists in the formulation of strategy by identifying particular segments and consumer characteristics that can be targeted.

Customer motivations

Once market segments have been identified, they must be analysed to reveal the factors that influence customers to buy or not to buy products. It is particularly important to understand factors that affect customer motivations, such as sensitivity to price, sensitivity to quality and the extent of brand loyalty.

Differences in customer motivations between market segments can be illustrated by reference to the market for air travel. The market can be segmented into business and leisure travellers. Customers in each group have very different characteristics and needs. Business travellers are not particularly price-sensitive but are sensitive to standards of service, to scheduling and to availability of connections. Leisure travellers are generally much more price conscious than service conscious and are less sensitive to scheduling and connections. Market research has an important role to play in building understanding of customer needs so that they can be targeted by appropriate product or service features.

Potential new markets are those where the product or service bought by customers is based upon similar competences to those of the organization or where customer needs are similar to those of customers in a business's market. If conditions are favourable, the organization may consider using its current competences to enter new markets. Of course, it may also have to build new competences in order to be able to meet new customer needs.

Resource markets

Resource markets are those in which organizations obtain finance, human resources, materials, equipment, services, etc. It is evident that businesses will normally operate in several such markets, each with its own characteristics, depending upon the company-specific resources that are required. Resource markets can be analysed in terms of:

- resource requirements;
- number of actual and potential resource suppliers;
- size of suppliers;
- supplier capabilities and competences;
- potential for collaboration with resource suppliers;
- access by competitors to suppliers;
- the nature of the resource and the availability of substitutes.

By analysing each of its resource markets, the managers of a business can identify the extent of competition that they face from suppliers of resources, the competition that they face from other competitors using the same resources, and the potential for collaboration with suppliers (if appropriate).

Competence-related industries

Other industries containing businesses that possess similar competences and which often produce products that are substitutes for those of the business in question must also be analysed. This analysis is necessary for three reasons. First, the organization may face a threat from other competitors that possess similar competences and which may seek to enter its industry and markets. Second, the organization may be able to enter industries where competences are similar to those it already possesses. Third, the organization may be able to enter the markets currently served by competitors in the competence-related industry. Competence-related industries can be analysed for:

- key competences of the businesses in the industry;
- the number and size of the businesses in the industry;
- the threat from competitors in such industries who may leverage their competences to enter the markets of the business;
- opportunities for the business to leverage its existing competences and build new ones in order to enter competence-related industries and their markets;
- substitutability of the products of the industry for those of the business – i.e. how close the substitute product is to satisfying the same consumer demands as the business's product or service.

A summary of the resource-based model

The competence/resource-based model is more complex than the five forces framework but offers a more comprehensive analytical framework. It enables an organization to establish the extent of competition within its own industry and market. It also enables the organization to assess the threat of competition from competitors in industries where similar competences to their own are employed. Equally, based on this model, the organization is able to identify other markets that it may be able to enter by leveraging its existing competences and by adding new ones.

Once adapted, the framework enables managers to:

- understand the nature of competition within the industry and markets (both product and resource) in which they operate;
- understand the threat from competitors in other industries;
- understand potential opportunities in new industries and markets.

Strategic group and competitor analysis

What are strategic groups?

A business can rarely confine its analysis to the level of the industry and markets in which it operates. It must also pay particular attention to its closest competitors who are known as its strategic group (Porter, 1980). Strategic groups cannot be precisely defined but they consist of organizations possessing similar competences, serving customer needs in the same market segment and producing products or services of similar quality. Such analysis allows the managers of a business to compare its performance to that of its closest competitors in terms of profitability, market share, products, brands, customer loyalty, prices and so on. In this way managers are able to benchmark the performance of their organization against their closest rivals.

In the automotive industry, for example, we can observe a number of important strategic groupings. Although Lada and BMW are both motor manufacturers – and hence are technically competitors – they operate in quite different strategic groups. They are unlikely to appeal to the same customers, and their products, dealership networks, brand identities and prices are quite different. BMW's strategic group (that grouping of producers in the automotive industry that compete with each other directly) includes Lexus, Mercedes Benz, Jaguar and Audi.

Industry and market critical success factors

In any industry and its associated markets, there will be certain factors that are of fundamental importance to the success of the businesses operating within that competitive environment. These are known as critical success factors (CSFs; see the key concept in Chapter 3). Competitive analysis allows managers to identify CSFs. A business must ensure that its competences and core competences directly address these CSFs.

CSFs differ between individual industries and markets. In the pharmaceutical industry, CSFs will be in the areas of RD and production. CSFs will differ between the markets for drugs available over the counter and those available only on prescription. CSFs for the over-the-counter market will centre on advertising and linkages to retail pharmacy groups; those for the prescription market are likely to focus on clinical trials and linkages to governments and doctors. In this way pharmaceutical companies must develop competences that concentrate on the industry and market CSFs.

References and further reading

Aaker, D.A. (1992) *Strategic Market Management*. New York: John Wiley.

Abell, D.F. (1980) *Defining the Business: The Starting Point of Strategic Planning*. Englewood Cliffs: Prentice Hall.

Arthur, W.B. (1996) Increasing returns and the new world of business. *Harvard Business Review*, 74 (July-August).

Baden-Fuller, C. and Stopford, J. (1992) *Rejuvenating the Mature Business*. Oxford: Routledge.

Campbell, D.J. (1997) *Organizations and the Business Environment*. Oxford: Butterworth-Heinemann (see especially Chapter 20).

Chakravarthy, B. (1997) A new strategy framework for coping with turbulence. *Sloan Management Review*, Winter, 69–82.

D'Aveni, R.A. (1994) *Hypercompetition: Managing the Dynamics of Strategic Manoeuvring*. New York: Free Press.

Ginter, P. and Duncan, J. (1990) Macroenvironmental analysis. *Long Range Planning*, December.

Hamel, G. and Prahalad, C.K. (1989) Strategic intent. *Harvard Business Review*, 67(3).

Hamel, G. and Prahalad, C.K. (1994) *Competing for the Future*. Cambridge, MA: Harvard Business School Press.

Heene, A. and Sanchez, R. (1997) *Competence-Based Strategic Management*. New York: John Wiley.

Helms, M.M. and Wright, P. (1992) External considerations: their influence on future strategic planning. *Management Decision*, 30(8).

Kay, J. (1993) *Foundations of Corporate Success*. Oxford: Oxford University Press.

Kay, J. (1995) Learning to define the core business. *Financial Times*, 1 December.

Lindsay, W.K. and Rue, L.W. (1980) Impact of organization environment on the long range planning process. *Academy of Management Journal*, 23.

McGahan, A.M. and Porter, M.E. (1997) How much does industry matter, really? *Strategic Management Journal*, 18(summer special issue), 15–30.

McGahan, A.M. and Porter, M.E. (1997) The persistence of profitability: Comparing the market-structure and Chicago views. Manuscript. Harvard Business School.

Porter, M.E. (1979) How competitive forces shape strategy. *Harvard Business Review*, March/April.

Porter, M.E. (1980) *Competitive strategy: Techniques for Analysing Industries and Competitors*. New York: Free Press.

Porter, M.E. (1985) *Competitive Advantage*. New York: Free Press.

Prahalad, C.K. and Hamel, G. (1990) The core competence of the corporation. *Harvard Business Review*.

Rumelt, R.P. (1991) How much does industry matter? *Strategic Management Journal*, 12(3).

Simonian, H. (1996) Star parts for bit players. *Financial Times*, 28 October.

Strebel, P. (1992) *Breakpoints*. Cambridge, MA: Harvard Business School Press.

Turner, I. (1996) Working with chaos. *Financial Times*, 4 October.

CHAPTER 8

Competitive advantage: strategies, knowledge and core competences

The study of strategic management offers several explanations as to how competitive advantage can be achieved and sustained. This chapter focuses on the major explanations of competitive advantage: 'knowledge-based' strategy, competitive positioning and core competence.

The *knowledge-based* school suggests that competitive advantage arises from the creation and development of new knowledge through a process of organizational learning. The *competitive positioning* approach is based largely upon Porter's generic strategy framework (Porter, 1980, 1985). The *core-competence-* or *resource-based* approach explains competitive advantage in terms of the development and exploitation of an organization's core competences (see Chapter 2). These approaches can be seen as complementary and mutually enriching rather than mutually exclusive.

The chapter ends with a discussion of the general mechanisms that organizations employ to grow and develop in order to sustain and develop their competitive advantage. We use the Ansoff matrix as a starting point for this discussion.

Learning objectives

After studying this chapter, students should be able to:

- describe how knowledge management can lead to competitive advantage;
- explain the concept of competitive advantage;
- describe and evaluate Porter's generic strategy framework;
- explain the concept of hybrid strategy;
- explain the role of core competences and distinctive capabilities in building competitive advantage;
- explain the role of the value chain in linking core competences and generic strategies;
- identify the strategic growth options available to the business;
- identify where core competences and strategies can be exploited.

Sources of competitive advantage

Three schools of thought

The main goal of strategic management is to produce sustainable competitive advantage for a business. Competitive advantage can arise both from planned strategies and from opportunistic moves by the business – sometimes called emergent strategies. Competitive advantage is not easy to achieve and is even more difficult to sustain. Superior performance is built and sustained through continuous organizational learning and results in a constant process of new strategy development and improvement in the way in which business activities are carried out.

The rapid pace of technological, political, economic and social change, the increasing turbulence of the business environment, the growing sophistication of customer needs and the drastic shortening of product life cycles that typifies 'hypercompetition', all mean that competitive advantage is often contestable rather than sustainable. In other words, the search for strategies that produce and sustain superior performance over a long period of time has become increasingly difficult. Competitive advantage can only be developed and sustained through the creation of new business knowledge based upon continuous organizational learning.

In Chapter 1 of this book, we learned that the different strands of theory in strategic management offer several explanations and potential methods by which competitive advantage can be achieved. The 'competitive positioning' explanation is based largely upon Porter's five forces, generic strategy and value chain frameworks (Porter, 1980, 1985) which have been subsequently augmented by the concept of a hybrid strategy. For Porter, the first question to be answered was: In which industry should the business compete? Potential industry profitability, and hence attractiveness, was established through five forces analysis. Once the choice of industry was made, the organization then had to determine which generic strategy to pursue, and then to decide the optimum configuration of its value-adding activities to support the chosen generic strategy. The approach is essentially 'outside-in', with choices being initially concerned with which industry was likely to prove the most profitable.

The resource-based school (Rumelt, 1984, 1991; Prahalad and Hamel, 1990) emerged on the basis that competitive advantage results from the development and exploitation of core competences by individual businesses, whatever industry they are in. This theory is built upon the notion that certain firms outperform their competitors in the same industry. If this is the case, competitive advantage cannot be explained entirely by different industry conditions. The explanation for competitive advantage must rest, at least in part, within the firm itself. For this reason, the approach to strategy is best regarded as 'inside-out'.

The knowledge-based school suggests that competitive advantage arises from the creation and development of new knowledge through a process of organizational learning. Interestingly, the competitive positioning, core-competence- and knowledge-based approaches need not be viewed as mutually exclusive. Knowledge can be viewed as the basis of an organization's core competences and generic strategy. Equally, generic strategy can be viewed as being dependent upon a particular set of core competences underpinned by an appropriate configuration of value-adding activities. Porter argued that a generic strategy must be based upon an appropriate configuration of value-adding activities and, as was illustrated in Chapter 2, there are close relationships between key or core value-adding activities and core competences, which, in turn, are based upon strategic knowledge.

The development of a strategy will inevitably draw upon some analysis of the business, its objectives, its resources, competences, activities and its competitive environment. Even in the context of an emergent approach to strategy, managers still require an understanding of the business and the consequences of alternative courses of action.

This chapter provides tools that can be employed in developing our understanding of both current strategy and future strategic alternatives. The frameworks are first explored separately and then the linkages between them are developed. It is important to note that there is no universal prescription for building competitive advantage. Competitive advantage is, however, more likely to result from doing things differently from competitors and doing them better rather than from trying to emulate them. Hamel and Prahalad (1989) made a strong case that organizations should develop a 'strategic intent' to stretch their resources and competences to the limits in order to achieve superior performance. Similarly, superior performance is more likely to result from an informed approach to management based upon an understanding of the firm, the environment in which it operates and the strategic alternatives available to it. This chapter provides the basis of an informed approach to the development of corporate strategies.

Competitive and collaborative advantage

Competitive advantage will depend upon the ability of a firm to outperform its competitors. Sustainable competitive advantage requires that the firm outperform its rivals over a long period of time. Although there is no recipe or formula that can guarantee sustained superior performance, there are certain organizational behaviours that have been shown to make success more likely:

- *strategic intent* – constantly stretching the organization to its limits;
- *continuous improvement* – continually trying to improve products and services, relationships with customers and suppliers, and the way in which activities are organized and carried out;
- *doing things differently from competitors* – devising ways of doing business that are different from and better than the approaches adopted by competitors;
- *being customer oriented* – always seeking to meet customer needs;

- *building knowledge-based core competences and distinctive capabilities;*
- *developing clear and consistent strategies* that are understood by managers and by customers;
- *awareness of factors in the business environment*, potential changes and their likely implications for the business;
- *collaborating with other businesses and customers.*

Any strategy ought to take these factors into account as by doing so it is more likely that the strategy will be more difficult for competitors to emulate. Collaboration with suppliers, distributors and customers can be particularly important in building competitive advantage that is sustainable, as such collaboration can be particularly difficult for competitors to replicate.

Strategy: the frameworks

There are a number of frameworks that seek to explain the ways in which sustainable competitive advantage can be achieved, although these can all be understood in terms of the three schools of thought we encountered above. This chapter reviews the major frameworks, their strengths and weaknesses, and the relationships between them. The frameworks reviewed are:

- knowledge-based strategy;
- generic strategy;
- hybrid strategy;
- core competence/distinctive capability/resource-based strategy.

In all cases the organization will select a strategy from a range of possibilities and then configure and coordinate its value-adding activities in such a way as to support the chosen strategy.

Knowledge and competitive advantage

Organizational knowledge has been defined as "a shared collection of principles, facts, skills, and rules which inform organizational decision-making, behaviour and actions" (Stonehouse and Pemberton, 1999). If an organization possesses superior knowledge to its competitors then this can deliver core competences which, in turn, produce competitive advantage.

Knowledge can be either explicit or implicit. *Explicit knowledge* is knowledge whose meaning is clearly stated, details of which can be recorded and stored. *Tacit knowledge* (Demarest, 1997) is often unstated, based upon individual experience and is difficult to record and store. It is the knowledge of experts that is often difficult to record and store, but equally is difficult for competitors to imitate.

Various writers have attempted to categorize organizational knowledge. Sanchez (1996) suggested that "at least three categories of knowledge may exist within firms: know-how (practical knowledge), know-why (theoretical knowledge) and know-what (strategic knowledge)". Whitehill (1997) created the basis of a typology of knowledge, which included encoded (know-what), habitual (know-how), scientific (know-why) and so on. Again, as all organizations differ, it is impossible to be prescriptive, but businesses require knowledge of customers, products, processes, technology, competitors, the law, finance, etc.

Knowledge and organizational learning play a unique role in building and maintaining core competences. Core competences can be based upon knowledge of customers and their needs, knowledge of technology and how to employ it in distinctive ways, knowledge of products and processes, etc. Knowledge of the business environment, of competitors and their behaviour, of countries and their cultures can also assist in building competences that are both distinctive and superior to those of competitors. Knowledge acts as the foundation for competence building and leveraging. Microsoft's core competences are based upon the company's knowledge of how to build and market operating systems and software. Equally, Microsoft's competitive advantage is based upon a knowledge of computer hardware and networking, and a knowledge of the firms who produce those products. Microsoft has leveraged its competences in personal computer operating systems and software and also built new associated competences in order to build competitive advantage in computer networking and Internet software. Such competence building and leveraging is largely knowledge-based.

Michael Porter's generic strategies

Introduction

Perhaps the oldest and best known explanation of competitive advantage is given by Porter in his *generic strategy* framework. Although this framework has been increasingly called into question in recent years, it still provides useful insight into competitive behaviour. The framework and its limitations are considered in this section.

According to Porter (1985), competitive advantage arises from selection of the generic strategy that best fits the organization's competitive environment and then organizing value-adding activities to support the chosen strategy. There are three main alternatives:

- *differentiation* – creating a customer perception that a product is superior to that of competitors' products so that a premium price can be charged;
- *cost leadership* – being the lowest cost producer of a product so that above average profits are earned even though the price charged is not above average;
- *focus* – utilizing either a differentiation or cost leadership strategy in a narrow profile of market segments (possibly just one segment).

Porter's generic strategy framework

Porter argued that an organization must make two key decisions on its strategy:

1 Should the strategy be one of differentiation or cost leadership?
2 Should the scope of the strategy be broad or narrow?

In other words, the organization must decide whether to try to differentiate its products and sell them at a premium price or whether to gain competitive advantage by producing at a lower cost than its competitors. Higher profits can be made by adopting either approach. Secondly, it must decide whether to target the whole market with its chosen strategy or to target a specific segment or niche of the market. Figure 8.1 is drawn showing cost focus and differentiation as two ends or extremes of a continuum. This is because actual strategies can exist at, or anywhere between, the extremes. The same applies to the vertical direction. 'Broad' and 'narrow' are general extremes, where a broad strategy targets many markets and a disparate cross-section of customers, and a narrow scope of highly focused strategies may target a very small number of segments (possibly just one).

The point of the diagram is that it is best understood as a map. Companies in an industry can all be successful if they each choose

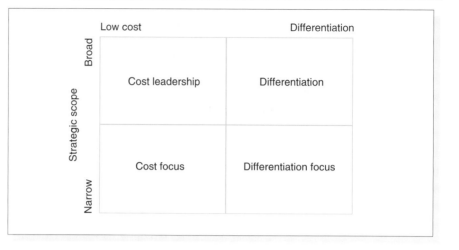

Figure 8.1
The generic
strategy framework
(adapted from
Porter, 1985).

different strategies. If, however, two or more competitors choose to compete in the same part of the map (i.e. adopting the same or similar generic strategy), competition will become intensified among those pursuing the same strategy. By plotting competitors on the map, we can get an idea of where the most intense competition will occur – i.e. in the area of the map containing the most competitors. Sections containing only one competitor will experience the least competition.

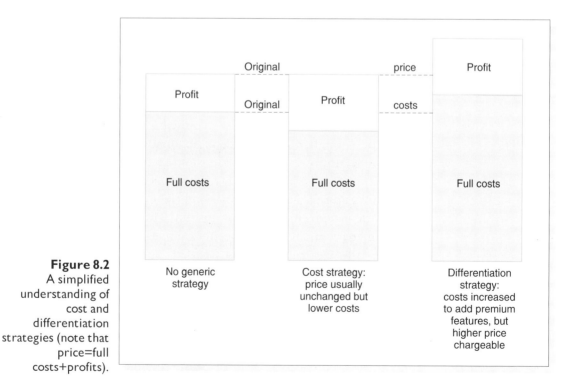

Figure 8.2
A simplified
understanding of
cost and
differentiation
strategies (note that
price=full
costs+profits).

Cost leadership strategy

A cost leadership strategy is based upon a business organizing and managing its value-adding activities so as to be the lowest cost producer of a product (a good or service) within an industry. There are several potential benefits of a cost leadership strategy:

- the business can earn higher profits by charging a price equal to, or even below, that of competitors because its unit costs are lower;
- it allows the business the possibility to increase both sales and market share by reducing the price to below that charged by competitors (assuming that the product's demand is price elastic in nature);
- it allows the business the possibility to enter a new market by charging a lower price than competitors;
- it can be particularly valuable in a market where consumers are price sensitive (see Figure 8.3);
- it creates an additional barrier to entry for organizations wishing to enter the industry.

Value chain analysis is central to identifying where cost savings can be made at various stages in the value chain and its internal and external linkages (see Chapter 2).

A successful cost leadership strategy is likely to rest upon a number of organizational features. Attainment of a position of cost leadership depends upon the arrangement of value chain activities so as to:

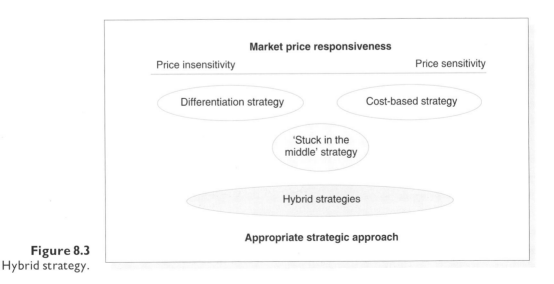

Figure 8.3
Hybrid strategy.

- reduce unit costs by copying rather than originating designs, using cheaper materials and other cheaper resources, producing products with 'no frills', reducing labour costs and increasing labour productivity;
- achieving economies of scale by high-volume sales, perhaps based on advertising and promotion, allowing high fixed costs of investment in modern technology to be spread over a high volume of output;
- using high-volume purchasing to obtain discounts for bulk buying of materials;
- locating activities in areas where costs are low or government help (e.g. grant support) is available;
- obtaining 'learning curve' economies (see the key concept in Chapter 13).

A cost leadership strategy, coupled to low price, is best employed in a market or segment where demand is price elastic – i.e. where volume is relatively responsive to price. Under such circumstances, sales and market share are likely to increase significantly, thus increasing economies of scale, reducing unit costs further and so generating above average profits.

Key concept

Price elasticity of demand

Economists use the term *price elasticity* to describe the extent to which the volume of demand for a product is dependent upon its price. The coefficient of elasticity is expressed in a simple equation:

$$Ep = \frac{\text{Percentage change in quantity}}{\text{Percentage change in price}}$$

The value of Ep (price elasticity) tells us the price responsiveness of the product's demand. If, for any given price change Ep is more than -1, it means that the change in price has brought about a higher proportionate change in volume sold. This relationship between price change and quantity is referred to as price elastic demand.

Demand is said to be price inelastic if the quantity change is proportionately smaller than the change in price (resulting in an Ep of less than -1). The larger the value of Ep, the more price elastic the demand; conversely, the nearer Ep is to 0, the more price inelastic the demand.

The price elasticity of demand (the value of Ep) is dependent upon the nature of the market's perception of a product. Products tend to be price elastic if the market sees a product as unnecessary but desirable. Products will have price inelastic demand if the customer perceives a *need* for a product rather than a *want* (such as the demand for most medicines, tobacco, etc.)

Alternatively, if a price similar to that of competitors is charged, accompanied by advertising to boost sales, similar results will be obtained.

Companies whose activities include high-volume standardized products are often cost leaders. The 'no frills' airlines are good examples. A 'basic' product is offered and costs per sale are minimized by such as online booking, faster aircraft turnaround between flights, no onboard 'free' food, etc.

Ryanair: a cost leader

An edited version of 'It's cheap but why not more cheerful?' by Tom Chesshyre (*The Times* (London), 2 January 2002). This is an edited summary of an interview with Michael O'Leary, chief executive of the Irish-based low-cost airline, Ryanair.

Michael O'Leary ... dashes to the counter of the Metro cafe at Stansted Airport – hub of the airline's operation in the UK – looking apologetic and glancing over anxiously at me as he makes his order.

You see, *The Times* travel desk receives more complaints about Ryanair than any other airline – regarding everything from delays, to poor in-flight service, to damaged luggage, to lengthy check-in queues. The Irish-based carrier, which has spearheaded the low-cost airline phenomenon in the past decade and which carried ten million passengers in the past year, crops up time and again in letters. A new complaint arrives [at *The Times*] virtually every week. Yet, as O'Leary is only too quick to point out, Ryanair rarely apologizes or tries to make up for these problems.

"Are we going to say sorry for our lack of customer service?" he asks rhetorically, putting down his cheese and ham croissant (after offering part of it, most un-Ryanairishly, to me). "Absolutely not. If a plane is cancelled will we put you up in a hotel overnight? Absolutely not. If a plane is delayed, will we give you a voucher for a restaurant? Absolutely not."

But isn't this a bit harsh, I ask. It can't just be a matter of saying "tough luck" if a flight is delayed – can it? Whatever happened to that old business maxim: the customer is always right? "Listen," he says bullishly. "Our customer service is about the most well-defined in the world. We guarantee to give you the lowest airfare. You get a safe flight. You get a normally on-time flight. That's the package. We don't and won't give you anything more on top of that." He pauses to take a sip of his tea – something passengers would have to pay for on-board Ryanair flights. You even have to shell out for a packet of peanuts or a glass of mineral water.

"Listen, we care for our customers in the most fundamental way possible: we don't screw them every time we fly them. [O'Leary, I soon realize, doesn't mince his words.] We care for our customers by giving them the cheapest airfares. I have no time for certain large airlines which say they care and then screw you for six or seven hundred quid almost every time you fly."

I'm getting the picture. But the fact is [*The Times*] still receives more complaints about Ryanair than any other airline. And many people are sick of the we've-got-the-cheapest-flights-so-grin-and-bear-it approach – as the Air Transport Users' Council (AUC), which monitors airline complaints, testifies. [The AUC says that] Ryanair is one of the worst offending airlines; that it seems to "stick two fingers up" at its disgruntled passengers; and that its delays record is poor for many European destinations.

Isn't it time Ryanair moved on a bit and stopped thinking about customers as cattle to be transported from A to B? Several [Ryanair customers] have complained about how difficult it is to talk to anyone at the airline when they have a problem. Frustrated customers say they have to make endless phone calls before finally getting through to an operator. Doesn't this seem as though Ryanair is treating them with disdain?

"Our position is simple," O'Leary says. "Generally speaking, we won't take any phone calls ... because they keep you on the bloody phone all day. We employ four people in our customer care department," he continues. "Every complaint must be put in writing and we undertake to respond to that complaint within 24 hours. Anyway, do you know what 70% of our complaints are about?" he says, sounding a bit aggrieved. "They're about people who want to make changes to what are clearly stated as being 'non-changeable, non-transferable and non-refundable' tickets." He adopts a 'complaining' voice, mimicking a customer: "I've changed my mind. My granny wasn't feeling well. I couldn't travel because I couldn't take time off work."

Aren't you being slightly cruel? "No ... because even if you can't change your ticket and you've got to buy a second one, you're still going to save money compared with buying a single ticket from the major airlines. Anyway, with our new system you can make some changes. If you pay 20 euros (£12.30) you can change the time of your flight, but not the name on the ticket."

Which is a start.

© Times Newspapers Limited (5 January 2002)

Differentiation strategy

A differentiation strategy is based upon persuading customers that a product is superior to that offered by competitors. Differentiation can be based on premium product features or simply upon creating consumer perceptions that a product is superior. The major benefits to a business of a successful differentiation strategy are:

- its products will command a premium price;
- demand for its product will be less price elastic than that for competitors products;
- above average profits can be earned;
- it creates an additional barrier to entry to new businesses wishing to enter the industry.

A business seeking to differentiate itself will organize its value chain activities to help create differentiated products and to create a perception among customers that these offerings are worth a higher price.

Differentiation can be achieved in several ways:

- by creating products that are superior to competitors by virtue of design, technology, performance, etc.;
- by offering superior after-sales service;
- by superior distribution channels, perhaps in prime locations (especially important in the retail sector);
- by creating a strong brand name through design, innovation, advertising, etc.;
- by distinctive or superior product packaging.

A differentiation strategy is likely to necessitate emphasis on innovation, design, research and development, awareness of particular customer needs and marketing. To say that differentiation is in the eyes of the customer is no exaggeration. It could be argued that it is often brand name or logo that distinguishes a product rather than real product superiority. For example, men's shirts bearing the logo of Ralph Lauren, Calvin Klein or Yves St Laurent command a price well above that of arguably very similar shirts which bear no logo. There is little empirical evidence of objectively better design or of better quality materials. Differentiation appears merely to be based on the fact that the designer's name is fashionable and that its products bear the logo.

A strategy like this is employed in order to reduce price elasticity of demand for the product so that its price can be raised above that of competitors without reducing sales volume. This, in turn will generate above average profits when measured against sales (i.e. return on sales).

Focus strategy

A focus strategy is aimed at a segment of the market for a product rather than at the whole market or many markets. A particular group of customers is identified on the basis of age, income, lifestyle, sex, geographic location, some other distinguishing segmental characteristic or a combination of these. Within the segment a business then employs either a cost leadership or a differentiation strategy.

The major benefits of a focus strategy are:

- it requires a lower investment in resources compared to a strategy aimed at an entire market or many markets;
- it allows specialization and greater knowledge of the segment being served;
- it makes entry to a new market less costly and more simple.

A focus strategy will require:

- identification of a suitable target customer group which forms a distinct market segment;
- identification of the specific needs of that group;
- establishing that the segment is sufficiently large to sustain the business;
- establishing the extent of competition within the segment;
- production of products to meet the specific needs of that group;
- deciding whether to operate a differentiation or cost leadership strategy within the market segment.

An example of a business that pursues a focus strategy is Ferrari, which targets the market for high-performance sports cars (a relatively small number of customers in relation to the total market for cars). Ferrari, unlike Toyota or Fiat, does not produce family saloons, minis, 'off-road' vehicles or 'people carriers'. It produces only high-performance cars. Its strategy is clearly one of differentiation based on design, superior performance and its Grand Prix record, which allows it to charge a price well above that of its competitors.

Many businesses use a focus strategy to enter a market before broadening their activities into other related segments.

Criticisms of Porter's generic strategy framework

A critical evaluation of the framework

In recent years Porter's generic strategy framework has been the target of increasing criticism (see, for example, Johnson and Scholes, 1993, 1997 (especially the *strategy clock* model); Cronshaw *et al.*, 1990; Miller, 1992; Mintzberg, 1991). The main objections to Porter's model are described below.

A business can apparently employ a successful hybrid strategy without being "stuck in the middle"

Porter argued that a business must choose between a differentiation and cost leadership strategy. To be "stuck in the middle" between the two, he argued, will result in suboptimal performance because of the company's competitive exposure to companies employing all other of the four generic strategy types. There is plenty of evidence to suggest, however, that some companies with lower than industry-average costs can nevertheless sell their products on the basis of differentiation. A good example of this is Nissan, the Japanese motor manufacturer, whose unit costs are among the lowest in the industry but whose prices are comparable to or above the average. It is able to charge a premium price because customers perceive its products to be reliable and as having a high level of specification as standard. A business like Nissan can thus be regarded as having a *hybrid strategy* which combines elements of differentiation, with price and cost competitiveness (see Figure 8.3, p. 161). A successful hybrid strategy will be based upon a conscious decision by senior mangers to combine differentiation with price and cost control. Under such circumstances a business can be successful. When a business slips into the situation unconsciously it can still be regarded as being 'stuck in the middle' but is less likely to be successful.

Cost leadership does not, in and of itself, sell products

Buying decisions are made upon the basis of desirable product features or upon the price, not on the basis of the unit cost itself. This criticism is less valid if a company competes in an industry on the basis of price.

Differentiation strategies can be used to increase sales volumes rather than to charge a premium price

Porter's work does not consider the possibility that a business employing a differentiation strategy might choose not to charge a premium price, but rather to increase sales and market share by foregoing the premium price for an introductory period. This criticism, however, does not fundamentally undermine Porter's thinking.

Price can sometimes be used to differentiate

The model does not consider the possibility that price may be used to differentiate a product. Mintzberg (1991) argued that price, along with image, support, quality and design, can be used as the basis of differentiation.

A 'generic' strategy cannot give competitive advantage

It is evident that in order to outperform competitors a business must do things better than and differently to its competitors. The word 'generic' could be construed to imply that Porter is arguing that there are general recipes by which competitive advantage can be achieved. This, however, is not the case. Porter's model is merely a framework by which competitive strategies can be grouped to assist in understanding and analysis.

The resource/competence-based strategy has arguably superseded the generic strategy framework

The resource-based approach argues that it is the core competences of the individual business that confer competitive advantage, and not generic strategies. In fact, the two approaches do not preclude each other. The relationships between the two approaches are discussed in a later section of this chapter.

Despite these criticisms, Porter's work can, in modified form, constitute the basis of a useful framework for categorizing and understanding sources of competitive advantage. The idea of a hybrid strategy is discussed below.

Hybrid strategies

There is a body of evidence that suggests that successful strategy can be based upon a hybrid (a mixture) of differentiation, price and cost control (see Figure 8.3, p. 161). The hybrid strategy framework developed here is based upon the following assumptions:

- strategy can employ a combination of differentiation, price and cost control;
- differentiation can be used as the basis for charging a premium price or in order to increase sales and/or market share;
- there are clear linkages between core competences, strategy and value-adding activities;
- the framework is not intended as a recipe for competitive advantage, rather as way of grouping different strategies.

The extent of differentiation, price and cost control will depend upon the nature of the market in which the business is operating. In markets where consumers show a preference for quality, the emphasis will be less on price and costs, whereas in markets where demand is price sensitive the emphasis will be on keeping both prices and costs as low as possible. Of course, organizations may also seek to shape customer attitudes by advertising and promotion so as to modify market conditions.

Competence-based competitive advantage

The generic strategy model is not the only one that seeks to provide an explanation of the sources of competitive advantage. The *competence-* or *resource-based model* emphasizes that competitive edge stems from attributes of an organization known as *competences* or *capabilities* which distinguish it from its competitors, allowing it to outperform them (see Chapter 2).

Core competence and distinctive capabilities

Chapter 2 explained the ways in which internal analysis makes it possible to better understand core competences by a process of deconstructing them into the component resources and competences that act as their foundation. This chapter builds upon this analysis to explore the ways in which existing competences can be extended and new ones cultivated. It goes on to examine how and where these core competences can be exploited so as to acquire and sustain competitive advantage. Much of the recent attention to the concept of core competence is based upon the work of Hamel and Prahalad (1989, 1990) and Stalk *et al.* (1992), who advocated the idea of competing on the basis of capabilities. Similarly, Kay (1993) advanced the idea that competitive advantage is based upon distinctive capability.

Core competences

Perhaps the best known explanation of core competence is that provided by Prahalad and Hamel (1990):

> Core competencies are the collective learning of the organization, especially how to co-ordinate diverse production skills and integrate multiple streams of technologies.

Prahalad and Hamel specified three tests to be applied in the identification and development of core competence. A core competence should:

1 equip a business with the ability to enter and successfully compete in several markets;
2 add greater perceived customer value to the business's products than that perceived in competitor's products;
3 be difficult for competitors to imitate.

According to Prahalad and Hamel, there are many examples of core competence resulting in competitive advantage. Philips' development of optical media, including the laser disc, has led to a whole range of new hi-fi and information technology products. Honda's engine technology has led to advantage in car, motor cycle, lawn mower and generator businesses. Canon's expertise in optics, imaging and micro-processor controls has given access to diverse markets, including those for copiers, laser printers, cameras and image scanners.

Prahalad and Hamel argued that competitive advantage is likely in practice to be based upon no more than five or six competences. These competences will allow management to produce new and unanticipated products, and to be responsive to changing opportunities because of production skills and the harnessing of technology. Given the turbulent business environment in many industries, such adaptability is essential if competitive advantage is to be built and sustained.

Distinctive capabilities

Kay (1993) took the concept of capability, initially identified by Stalk *et al.* (1992), to develop a framework that explains competitive advantage in terms of what he defines as *distinctive capability* (see also Chapter 2). This idea of distinctive capability has much in common with that of core competence in that it views competitive advantage as being dependent upon unique attributes of a particular business and its products.

According to Kay (1993), distinctive capability results from one or more of the following sources.

- *Architecture* – the unique network of internal and external relationships of a business which produces superior performance. These can be unique relationships with suppliers, distributors or customers which competitors do not possess. Equally, the unique relationships may be internal to the business and based upon the way that it organizes its activities in the value chain.
- *Reputation* – this stems from several sources, including superior product quality, characteristics, design, service, etc.
- *Innovation* – the ability of the business to get ahead and stay ahead of competitors depends upon its success in researching, designing, developing and marketing new products. Equally it depends upon the ability of the business to improve the design and organization of its value-adding activities.
- *Strategic assets* – businesses can also obtain competitive advantage from assets such as natural monopoly, patents, copyrights, which restrict competition.

Core competence, distinctive capability and competitive advantage

So what do the concepts of core competence and distinctive capability add to our understanding of competitive advantage? First, they provide us with insight into how a business can build attributes which can deliver superior performance. Second, they inform the process of determining where such competence and capabilities can be exploited.

The process of building new core competences or extending existing ones must take into account the following considerations:

- *Customer perceptions* – competences, capabilities and products must be perceived by customers as being better value for money that those of competitors. The business's reputation can be particularly important in this regard.
- *Uniqueness* – core competences must be unique to the business and must be difficult for competitors to emulate. Similarly there must be no close substitutes for these competences.
- *Continuous improvement* – core competences, goods and services must be continuously upgraded to stay ahead of competitors. Product and process innovation are particularly important.
- *Collaboration* – competitive advantage can result from the business's unique network of relationships with suppliers, distributors, customers and even competitors. There is the potential for 'multiplier effects' resulting from separate businesses' complementary core competences being combined together.
- *Organizational knowledge* – competences must be based upon organizational knowledge and learning. Managers must improve the processes by which the organization learns, builds and manages its knowledge. Knowledge is, today, potentially the greatest source of added value.

Core competence, generic strategy and the value chain: a synthesis

How the different approaches 'agree'

It has been argued (see, for example, Heene and Sanchez, 1997) that the resource or competence-based approach is largely incompatible with the competitive positioning or generic strategy approach advocated by Porter (1980, 1985). Mintzberg *et al.* (1995), however, made the case that the two approaches are in many respects complementary rather than mutually contradictory. Perhaps the best way of illustrating the linkages between the approaches is through the value chain of the organization.

As competitive advantage is based upon the unique approach of the individual business to its environment, it is not possible to identify a one-for-all prescription that will guarantee superior performance in all situations. Both the competitive positioning and the resource-based approach, however, provide frameworks that allow broad sources of competitive advantage to be categorized for the purposes of analysis and development of future strategy. A differentiation strategy, for example, will be likely to be dependent upon core competences in areas of the value chain such as design, marketing and service. Similarly a cost- or price-based strategy may well require core competences in value chain activities such as operations (production), procurement and, perhaps, marketing. It is much less likely that a cost leader will have core competences based on design and service. Possible relationships between core competences, generic strategies and the value chain are shown in Table 8.1.

Where to exploit core competences and strategies

As core competences and business strategies are developed, it is necessary to decide where they should be exploited. Core competences and strategies can be targeted on existing customers in existing markets or it may be possible to target new customers in existing markets. Alternatively, it may be possible to target new customers in new markets. These markets may be related to markets currently served by the organization or they may be unrelated markets. The organization may also consider employing its competences in a new industry. These decisions, on where to deploy core competences, are concerned with determining the '*strategic direction*' of the business. Once this decision has been made, then decisions must be made on the *methods* to be employed in following the chosen strategic direction.

The process of exploiting existing core competences in new markets is known as competence leveraging. In order to enter new mar-

Table 8.1

Core competences, generic strategies and the value chain

Value chain activity	Areas of competence associated with differentiation strategies	Areas of competence associated with cost/price-based strategies
Primary activities		
Inbound logistics	Control of quality of materials	Strict control of the cost of materials Tendency to buy larger volumes of standard inputs
Operations	Control of quality of output, raising standards	Lowering production costs and achieving high-volume production
Marketing and sales	Sales (and customer relations) on the basis of quality technology, performance, reputation, outlets, etc.	Achieving high-volume sales through advertising and promotion
Outbound logistics	Ensuring efficient distribution	Maintaining low distribution costs
Service	Adding to product value by high quality and differentiated service	Minimal service to keep costs low
Support activities		
The business's infrastructure	Emphasis on quality	Emphasis on efficiency and cost reduction
Human resource development	Training to create a culture and skills that emphasize quality, customer service, product development	Training to reduce costs
Technology development	Developing new products, improving product quality, improving product performance, improving customer service	Reducing production costs and increasing efficiency
Procurement	Obtaining high-quality resources and materials	Obtaining low-cost resources and materials

kets it is often necessary for the organization to build new core competences, alongside the existing core competences that are being leveraged, so as to satisfy new customer needs. Identification of customer needs to be served by core competences is based upon analysis of the organization's competitive environment using the resource-based framework developed in Chapter 2. The remainder of this chapter considers the alternative strategic directions that an organization can pursue and the methods that can be employed in following these strategic directions.

Strategic directions

Igor Ansoff's product–market framework

The most commonly used model for analysing the possible strategic directions that an organization can follow is the Ansoff matrix shown in Figure 8.4. This matrix shows potential areas where core competences and generic strategies can be deployed. There are four broad alternatives:

- *market penetration* – increasing market share in existing markets utilizing existing products;
- *market development* – entering new markets and segments using existing products;
- *product development* – developing new products to serve existing markets;
- *diversification* – developing new products to serve new markets.

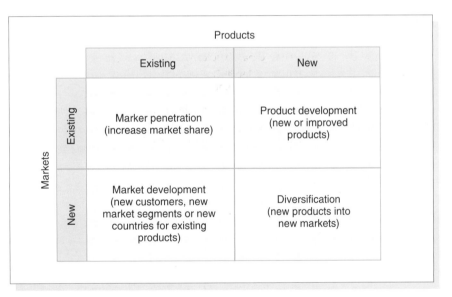

Figure 8.4
The Ansoff matrix (growth vector components) (adapted from Ansoff, 1987).

Market penetration

The main aim of a market penetration strategy is to increase market share using existing products within existing markets. This may involve taking steps to enhance existing core competences or building new ones. Such competence development may be intended to improve service or quality so as to enhance the reputation of the organization and differentiate it from its competitors. Equally, competence development may be centred on improving efficiency so as to reduce costs below those of competitors.

Mature or declining markets are more difficult to penetrate than those that are still in the growth phase. In the case of a declining market, the organization may also consider the possibility of *withdrawal* so as to redeploy resources to more lucrative markets (see the discussion of disposals and withdrawals in Chapter 11).

When a business's current market shows signs of saturation, it may wish to consider alternative directions for development.

Market development

Market development is based upon entry to new markets or to new segments of existing markets while employing existing products. Entering new markets is likely to be based upon leveraging existing competences but may also require the development of new competences (see the key concept in Chapter 2 for a definition of leveraging). Entering new segments of existing markets may require the development of new competences that serve the particular need of customers in these segments.

Internationalization and globalization are commonly used examples of market development. It is likely that an organization will need to build new competences when entering international markets to deal with linguistic, cultural, logistical and other potential problems.

The major risk of market development is that it centres on entry to markets of which the business may have only limited experience.

Product development

Product development centres on the development of new products for existing markets. As with the previous two growth directions, the intention is to attract new customers, retain existing ones and to increase market share. Providing new products will be based upon exploiting existing competences but may also require that new competences are built (such as in product research).

Product development offers the advantage to a business of dealing with customer needs of which it has some experience because they are within its existing market. In a world of shortening product life cycles, product development has become an essential form of strategic development for many organizations.

Diversification

Diversification is business growth through new products and new markets. It is an appropriate option when current markets are saturated or when products are reaching the end of their life cycle. It can produce important synergies and can also help to spread risk by broadening the product and market portfolio. Diversification can take two main forms depending upon just *how different* the products and markets are to existing ones.

Related diversification is said to have occurred when the products and/or markets share some degree of commonality with existing ones. This 'closeness' can reduce the risk of diversification. In practice, related diversification usually means growth into similar industries, or forward or backward in a business's existing supply chain.

Unrelated diversification is growth into product and market areas that are completely new and with which the business shares no commonality at all. It is sometimes referred to as *conglomerate* diversification.

Strategic development and risk

There are risks associated with all forms of strategic development. The risks are smallest when development is largely based upon existing core competences and when it takes place in existing markets. The risks are greatest when development requires entry to unrelated markets. Whether or not the risks are worth taking will depend upon the current position of the business and the state of its markets and products. Entry to new markets, whether related or unrelated, will depend upon the business's assessment of the opportunities in new markets compared to opportunities in its existing markets.

References and further reading

Ansoff, I. (1987) *Corporate Strategy*. London: Penguin.

Cravens, D.W., Greenley, G., Piercy, N.F. and Slater S. (1997) Integrating contemporary strategic management perspectives. *Long Range Planning*, 30(4), 493–506.

Cronshaw, M., Davis, E. and Kay, J. (1990) On being stuck in the middle or good food costs less at Sainsbury's. Working paper. Centre for Business Strategy, London School of Business.

Demarest, M. (1997) Understanding knowledge management. *Long Range Planning*, 30(3), 374–384.

Grant, R.M. (1991) The resource based theory of competitive advantage: implications for strategy formulation. *California Management Review*, 33(spring), 114–135.

Hall, R. (1992) The strategic analysis of intangible resources. *Strategic Management Journal*, 13, 135–144.

Hamel, G. and Prahalad, C.K. (1989) Strategic intent. *Harvard Business Review*, 67(3).

Hamel, G. and Prahalad, C.K. (1994) *Competing for the Future*. Cambridge, MA: Harvard Business School Press.

Heene, A. and Sanchez, R. (eds) (1997) *Competence-Based Strategic Management*. New York: John Wiley.

Johnson, G. and Scholes, K. (1997) *Exploring Corporate Strategy*. Hemel Hempstead: Prentice Hall.

Kay, J. (1993) *Foundations of Corporate Success*. Oxford: Oxford University Press.

Kay, J. (1995) Learning to define the core business. *Financial Times*, 1 December.

Miller, D. (1992) The generic strategy trap. *Journal of Business Strategy*, 13(1), 37–42.

Mintzberg, H. (1991) *The Strategy Process: Concepts, Contexts, Cases*. Englewood Cliffs: Prentice Hall.

Mintzberg, H., Quinn, J.B. and Ghoshal, S. (1995) *The Strategy Process: Concepts, Contexts and Cases*, European Edition. Englewood Cliffs: Prentice Hall.

Porter, M.E. (1980) *Competitive Strategy: Techniques for Analysing Industries and Competitors*. New York: Free Press.

Porter, M.E. (1985) *Competitive Advantage*. New York: Free Press.

Prahalad, C.K. and Hamel, G. (1990) The core competence of the corporation. *Harvard Business Review*, May–June.

Rumelt, R.P. (1984) Towards a strategic theory of the firm. In: Lamb, R.B. (ed.), *Competitive Strategic Management*. Englewood Cliffs: Prentice Hall.

Rumelt, R. (1991) How much does industry matter? *Strategic Management Journal*, March.

Stalk, G., Evans, P. and Shulmann, L.E. (1992) Competing on capabilities: the new rules of corporate strategy. *Harvard Business Review*, March/April, 57–69.

Stonehouse, G.H. and Pemberton, J. (1999) Learning and knowledge management in the intelligent organisation. *Participation and Empowerment: An International Journal*, 7(5), 131–144.

Whitehill, M. (1997) Knowledge-based strategy to deliver sustained competitive advantage. *Long Range Planning*, 30(4), 621–627.

PART IV

Strategic implementation and management

The process of strategic implementation begins by taking the information gained from the strategic analysis. This information is then used as an input to the process of selecting the most appropriate strategic option. A model for this stage is discussed in Chapter 9 and a number of tools are described to assist in the process.

Once the most appropriate strategic option has been selected, an organization must consider a number of issues relating to actually putting the proposed strategy into action.

First, implementation involves reconfiguring the organization's resource base. Does it have the inputs it needs in terms of finance, employees, physical inputs (e.g. stocks, land, buildings, etc.) and intellectual assets (e.g. legal permissions) to carry the strategy out? If not, these will need to be obtained. Resources held in excess of those required for the strategy will be disposed of (Chapter 10).

Second, the organization will need to bring its structure and culture into such a position that they facilitate a successful outcome. It may be that structure and culture are (to begin with) not entirely appropriate. In such a situation, the organization's management will need to make any requisite changes (Chapter 10).

Third, the implementation of strategy usually involves some internal changes – say of its culture, structure, systems or resources. The management of internal change can be the greatest management challenge in the strategic process and we address this matter in Chapter 10.

Fourth, implementation sometimes involves planning for growth or decline in the size of the business. Some strategies involve growth, and this can be achieved through either internal or external development or, occasionally, through joint ventures. These, and planning for a reduction in size, are discussed in Chapter 11.

Fifth, successful implementation sometimes involves a significant change in the organization's approach to its customers. This brings into focus the issue of product quality. The operations function and the quality of output it produces is of strategic importance and is often a key area of consideration in strategic implementation (Chapter 12).

Sixth, one of the most important strategic issues that has a bearing upon business success is the extent to which the business is internationalized. In some markets, such as those for petrochemicals, pharmaceuticals, air travel, banking and professional education, this is among the most important considerations. We consider international strategy in Chapter 13.

Seven, strategic implementation increasingly necessitates a thorough investigation of how the strategy will impact upon the organization's internal and external stakeholders. The social impact of a business's activities (i.e. of its strategy) is sometimes a matter that requires detailed examination during implementation. We consider the social and ethical role of businesses in Chapter 14.

Finally, it is important to understand that the fact that a strategy is being undertaken doesn't mean that the organization's environment is not changing. It may be that there have been some changes in the internal or external environment since the previous strategic analysis was undertaken. Some of these changes may mean that the strategy currently being implemented is no longer appropriate. It is for this reason that the strategic process is ongoing – it never ends. At every stage of implementation, the business needs to continually re-evaluate its environments. Changes in any of these may necessitate a revision of the strategic selection and, accordingly, a modification of the process of implementation.

CHAPTER 9

Evaluation and selection of strategies

Introduction and chapter overview

Important decisions are never easy. In order to ensure that we make the right choice in any given situation, we must first be in possession of all relevant information. This is the purpose of the strategic analysis stage – to ensure that the management of a business is fully aware of the internal strengths and weaknesses, and of the external opportunities and threats.

The next stage in making an important decision is to be aware of *all* the options available. The most obvious choice is not necessarily the right one. Following the generation of options, the next stage is to evaluate each option using consistently applied criteria. The purpose of evaluation is to ensure that all options are assessed with equal thoroughness. Finally, strategic selection involves actually making a decision based upon the evaluation of the options.

This chapter considers each of these stages in turn.

Learning objectives

After studying this chapter, students should be able to:

- describe the nature of strategic options;
- explain the key areas that strategic decisions concern;
- describe the four criteria that are applied to strategic options;

- understand the financial tools that can be used to evaluate strategic options;
- understand a number of other tools that can be used to evaluate strategic options;
- explain the limitations of an emergent approach to strategy when it comes to strategic evaluation and selection.

Identifying strategic options

The nature of strategic options

At the start of this chapter, we must remind ourselves of what makes a decision *strategic* in nature as opposed to one that is *operational*. We encountered these terms in Chapter 1 in the context of the nature of strategic objectives.

Strategic decisions are taken at the highest level of an organization. They concern decisions on how the whole organization will be positioned with respect to its product and resource markets, its competitors and its macro influences. Accordingly, the options at the strategic level are those that offer solutions to the 'big questions' in this regard.

Operational decisions are those that are concerned with how the internal parts of the organization should be configured and managed so that they best achieve the strategic objectives.

The 'big questions' that are considered in strategic selection usually concern three major areas, all of which are discussed in detail elsewhere in this book:

1 decisions on products and markets (see Chapter 5);
2 decisions on generic strategy and scope (see Chapter 8);
3 decisions on growth and development options (see Chapter 11).

In most cases, a business will need to make continual decision on all of these matters. We should not lose sight of the fact that the strategic process is just that – a process. Strategic selection is no more of a 'once for all' activity than either strategic analysis or strategic implementation and management. For organizations that exist in rapidly changing environments, decisions on strategic options will be required on a continual basis, hence the importance of ensuring we have a good grasp of the issues that are discussed in this chapter.

Product and market decisions

The questions over *which products* and *which markets* are extremely important because they can determine not only the levels of profitability, but also the survival of the business itself.

There are a number of product and market decisions to be made.

Product and market categories

First, decisions must be made about the categories of products that the business will offer. We encountered the major product classifications in Chapter 5, particularly those distinctions between:

- goods and/or services;
- consumer and/or industrial products;
- convenience, shopping and speciality products (Copeland, 1923).

For markets, the business will have to reach decisions on geographic coverage, international exposure and the benefits and risks that attend such options (see Chapter 13).

Product features

Second, decisions must be made on the features that the product will possess. The mix of product benefits that a product will possess will not only strongly affect costs, but also the position that the product will assume in the market. We encountered Kotler's (1997) five 'levels' of product features (or 'benefits') in Chapter 5, and the inclusion or 'leaving out' of any of these will have a strong bearing upon any proposed strategy.

Product and market portfolios

Third, product and market decisions must include a consideration of portfolio. The extent to which the products and markets are focused or spread can be very important. A broad portfolio (presence in many product market sectors) offers the advantages of the ability to withstand a downturn in one sector and to exploit opportunities that arise in any of the areas in which the business operates. Conversely, a narrow portfolio enables the organization's management to be more focused and to develop expertise in its narrower field of operation.

Life cycle considerations

The final consideration to be made for products and markets concerns their life cycle positions. It is perhaps intuitively obvious to say that products or markets that are approaching late maturity or are in decline should be of particular concern, but there is also a need to produce new products or develop new markets on an ongoing basis.

Generic strategy decisions

Decisions over the organization's generic strategy are important not only because they define the organization's competitive position, but also because they will determine the way that the internal value chain activities are configured (see Chapter 2 and Chapter 8).

If the company elects to pursue a differentiation strategy, for example, the implications of this will be felt in all parts of the organization. The culture and structure will need to be configured in such a way that they support the generic strategy and the product features and quality will also reflect this (see Chapter 12). Similarly, the way in which the organization configures its resource base will need to support the strategy.

The same issues will be considered if a cost-driven strategy is chosen, although the way in which the internal activities are configured will be somewhat different.

Growth and development decisions

Unless the strategy choices include a 'no change' option, it is likely that strategy will involve a change in the company's size. This may be a 'grow smaller' element, such as when the company has a presence in a declining market, but most growth strategies are 'grow bigger' in nature.

Two types of decisions are taken in this regard. The first decisions concern the generic growth direction that the organization will pursue (see Chapter 8). These strategies arise from Igor Ansoff's (Ansoff, 1987) framework and should not be confused with Porter's generic strategies (Porter, 1985). The second set of decisions concern the mechanism that the company will employ to pursue its generic growth strategy (see Chapter 11).

Ansoff's generic growth strategies concern whether growth will involve new or existing markets and products. The growth mechanisms can be either internal (organic) or external. Each growth option has its own benefits and risks and the strategy evaluation and selection stage will usually involve a full analysis of these.

Applying evaluation criteria

When considering which course of action to pursue, it is normally the case that a number of options present themselves to an organization's top management. In order to ensure that each option is fairly and equally assessed, a number of criteria are applied.

For each option, four criteria are applied: questions to ask of each option. In order to 'pass', the option must usually receive an affirmative answer to each one. The four criteria are:

1 Is the strategic option *suitable*?
2 Is the strategic option *feasible*?
3 Is the strategic option *acceptable*?
4 Will the strategic option enable the organization to *achieve competitive advantage*?

Suitability criteria

A strategic option is suitable if it will enable the organization to actually achieve its strategic objectives. If it will in any way fall short of achieving these objectives, there is no point in pursuing it and the option should be discarded.

To give a simple example, the option of driving south out of Paris would be an unsuitable one if my objective was to reach London. If, however, one option was to drive north or even in a northerly direction, then we could accept the option as being suitable. Similarly, if an organization's objective is to spread its market portfolio by gaining a presence in foreign markets, then the option of increasing the company's investment in its domestic home would clearly be unsuitable.

Feasibility criteria

A strategic option is feasible if it is possible. When evaluating options using this criterion, it is likely that the options will be feasible to varying degrees. Some will be completely unfeasible, others 'might be' feasible and others are definitely so.

The extent to which an option is suitable will depend in large part upon the resource base that the organization has. A deficit in any of the key resource areas (physical resources, financial, human and intellectual) will present a problem at this stage of evaluation. If an option requires capital that is unavailable, human skills that are difficult to buy in, land or equipment that is equally difficult to obtain or a scarce intellectual resource, then it is likely to fail the feasibility criteria.

Acceptability criteria

A strategic option is acceptable if those who must agree to the strategy accept the option. This raises an obvious question: Who are those who agree that the option is acceptable?

We encountered the concept of stakeholders in Chapter 1 and we shall return to it in more detail in Chapter 14. The extent to which stakeholders can exert influence upon an organization's strategic decision-making rests upon the two variables, power and interest (see Chapter 1). Stakeholders that have the highest combination of both the ability to influence (power) and the willingness to influence (interest) will have the most *effective* influence. Where two or more stakeholder groups have comparable influence, the possibility of conflict over acceptability will be heightened. In most cases, the board of directors will be the most influential stakeholder.

Competitive advantage criteria

We learned in Chapter 1 that one of the key objectives in strategy is to create competitive advantage. This criterion asks a simple question of any strategic option: What is the point of pursuing an option if it isn't going to result in superior performance (compared to competitors) or higher than average profitability? In other words, a strategic option would fail this test if it was likely only to result in the business being 'ordinary' or average with regard to the industry norm.

This is particularly important when considering product options. For example, if a new product option is forecast to receive an uncertain reception from the market, we might well ask what is the point of the launch at all. It would be unlikely to result in competitive advantage for the business.

Financial tools for evaluation

In the evaluation and selection stage, a number of 'tools' are available to managers that may assist in deciding upon the most appropriate option. Not all of them will be appropriate in every circumstance and some are more widely used than others. They are used to explore the implications of the options so that the decisions that are made are based upon the best possible information.

Accountants are usually very involved in strategic evaluation and selection because of their expertise in understanding the financial implications of the possible courses of action. There are two major areas of financial analysis:

- cash-flow forecasting;
- investment appraisal.

Cash-flow forecasting

One of the most straightforward financial tools is cash-flow analysis – sometimes called funds-flow analysis. Essentially, it involves a forecast of the expected income from an option, of the costs that will be incurred and, from this, the forecast net cash inflows or outflows. For most options, the forecast will be broken down into monthly 'chunks' and a profit and loss statement will be constructed for each month. If the same procedure is carried out for each option, the most favourable can be identified.

Investment appraisal

An investment, at its simplest, is some money put up for a project in the expectation that it will enable more money to be made in the future. The questions surrounding investment appraisal concern *how much* will the organization make against each investment option.

There is a strong time element to investment appraisal techniques because the returns on the investment may remain for several years or even decades. It is for this reason that a factor is often built into the calculation to account for inflation.

The first and most obvious thing that accountants want to know about any investment is the *payback period*. This is the time taken to repay the investment – the shorter the better. If, for example, an investment of £1000 is expected to increase profits by £100 a month, then the payback period will be ten months.

In practice, payback periods are rarely this short and it is this fact that makes investment appraisal calculations a bit more complicated. When the effects of inflation are taken into account, the returns on an investment can be eroded over time. Consequently, accountants include a factor to account for the effects of inflation, usually on a 'best-guess' basis.

Limitations of the financial tools

The limitations of the financial tools rest in the problem of the unpredictability of the future. We learned in Chapters 6 and 7 that the macro- and microenvironments can change – sometimes rapidly. Accordingly, the actual returns that an organization makes on an investment may not always be what was expected.

A similar limitation applies to forecasting the level of inflation for net present value calculations. In the major First World economies such as those in Western Europe, North America, Japan and Australia, the level of inflation has historically been relatively stable at between 2% and 10%, with an occasional 'shock' such as in the mid-1970s when in the UK it reached 24%. In other parts of the world, however, problems with the supply of goods and the value of currency can lead to much higher inflation levels – sometimes exceeding 1000% a year. A presumption of low and stable inflation will therefore tend to encourage investment rather than high and unpredictable inflation.

Other tools for evaluation

Financial evaluation of strategic options is very important, but for most organizations other tools can also provide useful information. These may require financial information as an input and so they should be seen not as 'instead of' financial analyses, but 'as well as'. They enrich the information enabling management to select the best strategic option.

Cost–benefit analysis

Cost–benefit analysis applies to almost every area of life, not just strategic evaluation and selection. Each option will have a cost associated with it and will be expected to return certain benefits. If both of these can be quantified in financial terms, then the cost–benefit calculation will be relatively straightforward. The problems is that this is rarely the case.

The costs of pursuing one particular option will have a number of elements. Any financial investment costs will be easily quantifiable.

Against this, the cost of not pursuing the next best option needs to be taken into account – the opportunity cost. There may also be a number of social and environmental costs which are much harder to attach a value to.

The same problems apply to the benefits. In addition to financial benefits, an organization may also take into account social benefits and others such as improved reputation or improved service. Intangible benefits are very difficult to attach a value to for a cost-benefit analysis as they can take a long time to work through in increased financial performance.

Key concept

Social costs and benefits

All organizations have an impact upon the societies that are in their locality or that are affected by their products or activities. Although the term *social* is a bit nebulous, it is generally taken to mean the effect on the conditions of employment, social well-being, health, chemical emissions, pollution, aesthetic appearance (e.g. 'eyesores'), charitable societies, etc.

A strategic option will have an element of social cost and social benefit. We would describe a social cost as a deterioration in any of the above: an increase in unemployment, higher levels of emissions, pollution, declining salaries, etc. Conversely, a social benefit will result in an improvement in the conditions of society: increasing employment, cleaner industry, better working conditions, etc.

Impact analysis

When a strategic option may be reasonably expected to have far-reaching consequences in either social or financial terms, an impact study may be appropriate. Essentially, this involves asking the question: If this option goes ahead, what will its impact be upon . . .?

The thing that might be impacted upon will depend upon the particular circumstances of the option. For a proposed development of a new nuclear power station, for example, the impact study would typically take into account the development's implications for local employment, local tourism, heath risk to employees and local residents, the reputation and appearance of the town or region, local flora and fauna, and some other things.

In many cases, an impact study will be an intrinsic part of the cost–benefit calculation, and it suffers from the same limitations – that of evaluating the true value of each thing that may be impacted.

'What if?' and sensitivity analysis

The uncertainties of the future, as we have seen, makes any prediction inexact. Although an organization can never be certain of any sequence of future events, 'what if?' analysis and its variant, sensitivity analysis, can give an idea of how the outcome would affected by a number of possible disruptions.

The development of computerized applications such as spreadsheets has made this activity easier than it used to be. A financial model on a spreadsheet that makes a number of assumptions such as revenue projections, cost forecasts, inflation rate, etc., can be modified to instantly show the effect of, say, a 10% increase in costs or a higher-than-expected rate of inflation. This is designed to show how sensitive the cash flow is to its assumptions – hence the name.

Qualitative variables can also be analysed. If an option has a high dependency upon the availability of a key raw material or the oversight of a key manager, a 'what if?' study will show the effect that the loss or reduction in the key input would have.

Strategic evaluation in emergent strategies

In Chapter 1, we encountered the idea that business strategies can be either deliberate (or prescriptive) or emergent (we return to this concept in more detail in Chapter 15). This is to say that some strategies are planned in advance, often following a rational sequence of events – prescriptive strategies. Others are not planned in this way and are said to be emergent – they result from an organization's management following a consistent pattern of behaviour.

This distinction is important when it comes to strategic evaluation. Companies that employ the deliberate model are likely to use the criteria and the tools above, whereas those that prefer the emergent model are very unlikely to do so explicitly. This is not to say, however, that the analytical process cannot form a part of an intelligent manager's intuitive thinking.

It is here that one of the potential limitations of emergent strategy becomes apparent. If an organization follows a deliberate process with its systematic and sequential events, then it can be more certain that all possible options have been identified and evaluated before the most appropriate one is selected. An intuitive emergent approach that relies upon patterns of behaviour cannot be certain that the best option is taken in all times of decision. It might get it right – but it might not.

References and further reading

Ansoff, I. (1987) *Corporate Strategy*. London: Penguin.

Copeland, M.T. (1923) Relation of consumers' buying habits to marketing methods. *Harvard Business Review*, 1(April), 282–289.

Kotler, P. (1997) *Marketing Management Analysis, Planning, Implementation, and Control*, Ninth Edition. Englewood Cliffs: Prentice Hall International.

Porter, M.E. (1985) *Competitive Advantage*. New York: Free Press.

CHAPTER 10

Strategic implementation

Introduction and chapter overview

Strategic implementation is all about what issues are considered to be necessary for the successful execution of strategy. In a prescriptive strategic process, strategic implementation would be carried out only after a company has gathered sufficient information on its internal and external environments (this being the purpose of strategic analysis) and after it has undertaken the process of strategy evaluation and selection (see Chapter 9).

In order to successfully carry out a strategy, a company must consider several key areas. First, it must establish how the strategy will be resourced. Second, it should ask itself how well its current culture, structure and internal systems are able to meet the challenges of the strategy. Changes in any or all of these may become necessary. Finally, most strategies necessitate some degree of internal change and this process of change will need to be managed. This chapter discusses each of these matters in turn.

Learning objectives

After studying this chapter, students should be able to:

- describe where implementation fits into the strategic process;
- describe the role of resource planning in strategic implementation;
- explain how and why corporate culture plays an important part in implementation;

- understand the link between structure and strategy;
- describe the essentials of change management.

Implementation and the strategic process

Most people intuitively understand that a lot of information is required before any big decision is made. We wouldn't buy a house without a thorough survey and we would normally find out something about a company before we accepted a job with it. In the same way, a business would be risking a great deal if it were to pursue a strategic option without first carrying out a detailed analysis of its internal and external environments.

Successful strategy selection and implementation relies upon the information obtained in the strategic analysis. It is important that the company is aware of its internal strengths and weaknesses and its external opportunities and threats. Without being 'armed' with this information, the company cannot be certain that the chosen strategy would be the correct choice. The process leading to implementation is shown in Figure 10.1.

In order to successfully carry out (implement) a strategy, an organization will need to work out how to resource it. This means how it will obtain the requisite finance, human resources (usually in the form of appropriately skilled employees) and the plant, equipment and buildings. It should also reconfigure its culture and structure to 'fit' the proposed strategy. Finally, strategic implementation often means change inside the organization in order to achieve the required objectives. Change management is thus the third area to be considered in strategic implementation. This chapter will briefly consider each of these issues.

In chapter 1, we reviewed Mintzberg's (1985) division of strategy into deliberate and emergent. This is relevant to implementation in that some strategies are implemented in intentional and sequential ways whereas others (emergent strategies) tend to be implemented in an incremental way. Whereas deliberate strategies are often planned in detail, emergent strategies may be implemented on a more *ad hoc* basis, typically with much shorter timescales and with a more flexible approach.

The implementation stage in the process often sees a shift in responsibility, from the strategic level down to divisional or functional managers. This transfer may also act as a barrier to the implementa-

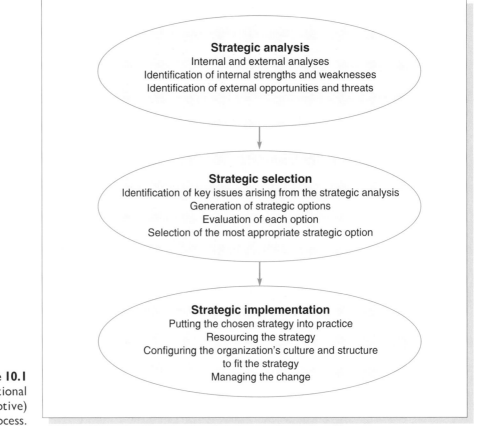

Figure 10.1
The linear-rational
(prescriptive)
strategic process.

tion of the desired strategy as responsibility is shifting from the few to the many. Each new implementer may have slightly different interpretations of what is required of them, thus creating an uneven application of the strategy and strategic 'drift'. These distortions are further exaggerated if the implementers are working in different units of an organization and in different locations.

Alexander (1985) identified inadequate planning and communication as two major obstacles to the successful implementation of strategies. The lack of support at the implementation stage from those responsible for developing the strategy was also identified as a major problem. Other writers in the field have found similar problems. Many failed strategies have done so because of a failure to taken account of internal issues such as information systems, organizational structure and the inability of the company's culture to adapt.

Resources and implementation

Resources: the key inputs

In the same way that people and animals need the inputs of air, food, warmth, etc., so also organizations need inputs in order to function normally. Economics textbooks would refer to these inputs as the *factors of production*. They fall into four broad categories:

1 physical resources (land, buildings, plant, equipment, etc.);
2 financial resources (investment capital – share, loan, debenture, bond capital, etc. – required for development and expansion);
3 human resources (obtaining the requisite number of appropriately skilled employees, agents, contractors, etc.);
4 intellectual or 'intangible' resources (non-physical inputs that may be necessary in some industries, such as databases, legal permissions, brand or design registration, contacts, etc.; see Hall, 1992).

In most industries, competitors must obtain resource inputs in competitive markets. This means that they must compete with other businesses for the best people, the cheapest and adequate finance, the best locations for development, etc. All of these inputs have a cost attached to them and so careful planning for resource requirement is usually a key calculation in strategic implementation.

Matching strategy with resources

Once a strategic option has been settled upon (in the strategic selection stage), management attention turns to evaluating the resource implications of the strategy. The extent to which the resource base needs to be adjusted will, of course, depend upon the degree of change that the proposed strategy entails.

Broadly speaking, resource planning falls into three categories (Johnson and Scholes, 1998).

First, some strategies, particularly those that are not particularly ambitious, require *few changes* in the resource base. They may require, for example, a *slight* increase in financing to fund modest expansion or the recruitment or retraining of a small number of new employees to meet a skill shortage in one or two areas. Conversely, of course, a 'few changes' strategy may require the disposal of some assets or a slight reduction in the human resource base.

Second, some strategies require an *increase* in the resource base in order to facilitate a more substantial programme of growth. This usually entails two things: an internal reallocation of resources and the purchasing of fresh resource inputs from external suppliers. Internal reallocation entails reducing resource employment in one area of the business and moving it across to where it is needed, say by redeploying human resources or by selling some equipment to reinvest the money in the area of growth. New resources (from outside the organization) are obtained through the usual channels: the job market, the real estate market, the financial markets and so on.

Third, some strategies involve a *reduction* in the resource base in order to successfully manage decline in one or more areas of the business. If an organization finds, after a resource audit, that it has too many resources (say too many employees, too much land, etc.) then measures are put in place to carry out some reduction. Excess capital or physical resources can often be successfully reinvested in business areas that are in more buoyant markets while excess human resources must usually be made redundant.

Key concept

Resource audit

An audit process can be used to make assessments of any or all of the resource inputs. In Chapter 3, we encountered the human resource audit, but the same procedures can be employed to audit financial, physical or intellectual resources.

The nature of audit of any kind (including resource audits) is the purposeful checking or testing of whatever is being audited. Resources are audited (or purposefully checked) for:

- *sufficiency* (is there enough for the purpose);
- *adequacy* (is the condition, location, state or quality of the resource adequate for the purpose);
- *availability* (are the required resources available at the time and in the quantities required).

An audit of an organization's land and buildings (examples of physical resources) might take the form of assessing whether the floor area is *sufficient* for current needs and any planned expansion. This might be followed by an evaluation of its *adequacy* – its location relative to customers, etc., and its condition. Finally, if more is required or if development of the land or buildings is needed, *availability* is examined, either of additional property or of permissions for development.

Developing and controlling resources

In order to meet the resource requirements of a proposed strategy, resources are developed and then controlled to ensure they meet the needs of the strategy.

Financial planning

Financial planning takes the form of financing the proposed strategy (see Chapter 4 for a more detailed discussion of these issues). *Capital budgeting* concerns projecting the capital needs of a strategy. This is usually a relatively straightforward operation as costs can normally be forecast with some accuracy. Once the capital requirements are known, a plan is put in place to finance any shortfall. Whereas some strategies can be financed from retained profits (depending upon how much retained profit the company has on its balance sheet), others are financed from external sources such as share (rights) issues, debt capital or the issuing of corporate bonds or debentures. The pros and cons of these approaches to financing are discussed in Chapter 4.

Human resource planning

Human resource planning (see Chapter 3) involves projecting the human capital required for the successful execution of the proposed strategy. It would typically take the form of forecasts of both the *numbers* of people required and the types of *skills and abilities* that will be in demand. If a shortfall in either of these is identified, the 'gap' will be filled by either training or appointing. Training, retraining and staff development are designed to close the skills gap by developing existing employees; appointing new employees is appropriate if human resources needs cannot be met internally.

Physical resource planning

Physical resource planning is slightly more complex than financial and human resource planning. The reason for this is that so many inputs fall into this category. We include in this category land, buildings, location, plant, equipment and raw material stock.

Some physical resources are more easily obtained than others. Most stock, plant and equipment is relatively easily obtained, unless the requirement is very specialized. More problematic is obtaining location, land and buildings. Businesses that have requirements for key locations and buildings of particular specificity expose themselves to the possibility of having to settle for second best if they are unable to effectively compete in these particular resource markets.

One industry that exemplifies competition for physical resources is retailing. The location of a retail outlet will often be a key determinant in the success of the business. Successfully competing with other retailers for prime locations and the best buildings will consequently be of paramount importance, especially when these locations are in short supply (which they are in the best parts of most high streets).

Intellectual resource planning

Intellectual resources – inputs that cannot be seen and touched – can be the most important resource inputs of all (see Chapter 2). Some proposed strategies have a requirement for a legal permission, a database (say of key customers in a certain market segment), a patent registration or something similar.

It is the possession (or not) of key intellectual resources that often determines the success of strategy. Some business operations require a legal licence or permission, examples of these being energy production, defence equipment, pharmaceuticals and construction. Others rely upon a particular information input such as a database, superior market knowledge or superior technical knowledge. We will return to the theme of organizational learning in Chapter 15.

Culture and implementation

Culture suitability

We encountered the concept of culture in Chapter 3. Strategic implementation usually involves making an assessment of the suitability of a culture to undertake the strategy. In the same way that human personalities differ in their readiness to undertake certain courses of action, so also some organizational 'personalities' differ.

In the context of implementation, culture is usually analysed for its suitability. If we consider human personalities, we can readily appreciate that they are not equally suitable for all jobs or tasks.

Some people, for example, have a personality that is ready to embrace a new challenge and who take to change with vigour and excitement. Other people prefer things not to change and have a more conservative nature. These two personality types highlight the suitability contrasts that can exist.

In Chapter 3 we encountered two typologies of corporate culture. Handy (1993) identified four types of culture: power, role, task and person. Miles and Snow (1978) also identified four culture types by their reaction tendency, and this is probably the more useful typology in this context.

Miles and Snow's typology and cultural postures

Miles and Snow's (1978) typology divided culture types according to how they approach strategy. These distinctions are important as they tell us how each culture type will react to different strategic options.

A review of the Miles and Snow categories

Defender cultures are suitable for organizations that exist in relatively well-defined market areas and where improving the position in existing markets is the most appropriate strategic option (e.g. market penetration). The culture would feel uncomfortable with having to develop new markets or diversification. The values resident within defender cultures work well if markets are stable and relatively mature.

Prospector cultures, in contrast to defenders, are continually seeking out new product and market opportunities. Accordingly, they often create change and uncertainty. The cultural norms within such organizations are consequently more able to develop new markets and products.

Analyser cultures exhibit features of both defenders and prospectors. They have developed a culture that is able to accommodate both stability (which defenders like) and instability (which prospectors have learned to adjust to). The culture can be formal in some circumstances and flexible and 'organic' in others.

Reactor cultures can sometimes lack strategic focus and are consequently sometimes accused of being 'blown around' by changes in their environments. They do not innovate and tend to emulate the successes of competitors.

The purpose of examining Miles and Snow's typology

It is evident that the ability of cultures to undertake different strategic courses of action varies. It is likely, for example, that defender cultures and those like them would be less able to undertake a programme of radical change than, say, those that exhibit prospector characteristics.

The difference between *what is* and *what is required* for a strategy is one of the most important aspect of strategic implementation. The gap between the two presents a challenge to management in respect of either changing the culture or compromising on strategic objectives such that cultural change is required to a lesser extent. We will return to the nature of change – including cultural change – later in this chapter.

Structure and implementation

What is structure?

Organizational structure refers to the 'shape' of the business. The importance of structure to strategic success is intuitively easy to grasp by using the structure of a human body as a metaphor. Some people are naturally large and may be a tad overweight, whereas others are smaller, lithe and fit. The skeletal and muscle structure of people is a major determinant of their suitability for certain activities. People who are large and overweight are less suitable for ballet dancing but are more suitable as sumo wrestlers. Conversely, smaller and fitter people are better at running, rowing and competitive horse-racing.

Organizational structures tend to be described in terms of their 'height', their 'width' and their complexity. A fourth, related, way of describing organizational structures is according to their method of division.

The 'height' of structures

Height refers to the number of layers that exist within the structure. It is perhaps intuitively obvious that larger organizations are higher than smaller ones. The guide to how high an organizational structure should be depends upon the complexity of the tasks that a proposed strategy entails. A small, single-site manufacturer will typically be involved in competing in one industry, sometimes with a single product type. This scenario is much less complex than a multinational chemical company that competes in many national markets, in several product types and with a high dependence on research and legal compliance.

Essentially, height facilitates the engagement of specialist managers in the middle of an organization who can oversee and direct the many activities that some large organizations are involved in. Not all organizations have this requirement and it would be more appropriate for such organizations to have a flatter structure (see Figure 10.2).

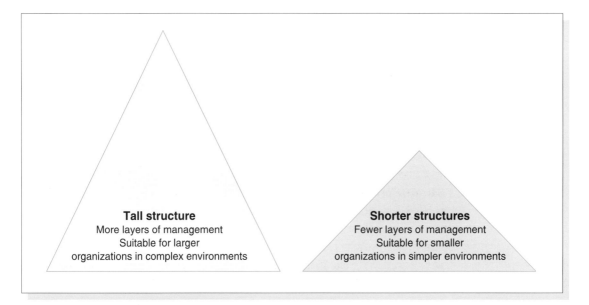

Tall structure
More layers of management
Suitable for larger
organizations in complex environments

Shorter structures
Fewer layers of management
Suitable for smaller
organizations in simpler environments

Figure 10.2
The height and width of organizations.

Key concept

Tall and short structures

■ *Tall structures*, involving more layers of specialist managers, enable the organization to coordinate a wider range of activities across different product and market sectors. It is more difficult for senior management to control and is obviously more expensive in terms of management overhead.

■ *Shorter structures* involve few management layers and are suitable for smaller organizations that are engaged in few products or market structures. They are cheaper to operate and facilitate a greater degree of senior management control.

The 'width' of structures

The 'width' of organizational structures refers to the extent to which the organization is centralized or decentralized. A decentralized organizational structure is one in which the centre elects to devolve some degree of decision-making power to other parts of the organization. A centralized organization is one in which little or no power is devolved from the centre. In practice, a continuum exists between the two extremes along which the varying extents of decentralization can be visualized (see Figure 10.3).

As with the height of structures, there is a trade-off between the costs and benefits of width. The advantages of centralization are mainly concerned with the ability of the centre to maintain tighter direct control over the activities of the organization. This is usually more appropriate when the organization is smaller and engages in few product or market segments. Some degree of decentralization is advantageous when the organization operates in a number of markets and specialized local knowledge is an important determinant of overall success.

Complexity of structure

The complexity of structure is usually taken to mean the extent to which the organization observes formal hierarchy in its reporting

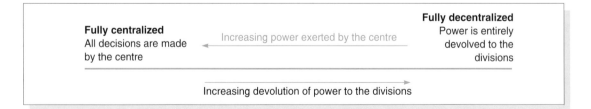

Figure 10.3
The centralization–decentralization continuum.

relationships. Strict hierarchy is not always an appropriate form of organization, especially when it cannot be automatically assumed that seniority guarantees superior management skill.

In some contexts, formal hierarchy is entirely appropriate in implementing strategy. In others, however, allowing employees to act with some degree of independence can in fact enable the organization to be more efficient. The use of matrix structures, for example, can result in the organization being able to carry out many more tasks than a formal hierarchical structure can. Many companies go 'halfway' in this regard by seconding employees into special task forces or cross-functional teams that are not part of the hierarchical structure and which act semi-independently.

Methods of divisionalization

The fourth and final way of understanding how structure fits into strategic implementation is by considering how the parts of the organization are to be divided. As with all the other matters to be considered in structure, the method of division is entirely dependent upon the context of the company and its strategic position. It is a case of establishing the most appropriate divisional structure to meet the objectives of the proposed strategy.

Divisions are based upon the grouping together of people with a shared specialism. By acting together within their specialism, it is argued that synergies can be obtained both within and between divisions. There are four common methods of divisionalization:

1 by functional specialism (typically operations, human resources management, marketing, finance, R&D);
2 by geographic concentration (where divisions are regionally located and have specialized knowledge of local market conditions);
3 by product specialism (where divisions, usually within multi-product companies, have detailed knowledge of their particular product area);
4 by customer focus (where the company orientates itself by divisions dedicated to serving particular customer types – for example, retail customers, industrial customers, etc.).

Managing the changes in implementation

The need for change

At its simplest, strategy is all about change. In this chapter, we have encountered the importance of an organization's resource base, its culture and its structure. In order to bring about strategic repositioning (say in respect to products and markets), all of these may need to be changed.

Different organizations exhibit differing attitudes to change. We can draw a parallel here with different types of people. Some people are very conservative and configure their lives so as to minimize change. Such people will generally fear change and resist it. Other people seem to get bored easily and are always looking for new challenges, new jobs, and so on. Organizations reflect this spectrum of attitudes. It is here that we encounter the concept of *inertia*.

Inertia: identifying barriers to change

Inertia is a term borrowed from physics. It refers to the force that needs to be exerted on a body to overcome its state in relation to its motion. If a body is stationary (i.e. at rest), we need to exert a force upon it to make it move. The size and shape of the body will have a large bearing upon its bearing – compare the inertia of a football to that of a train.

In the same way, different organizations present management with varying degrees of inertia. Some are easy to change and others are much more reluctant. The willingness to change may depend upon the culture of the organization, its size, its existing structure, its product and/or market positioning and even its age (i.e. how long it has existed in its present form).

For most purposes, we can say that resistance to change on the part of employees can be caused by one or more of the following attitudes.

First, it may be that those affected by the change *lack an understanding* of the details. They may not have had the reasons for the change explained to them or they may not be aware of how they will be personally affected. This particular barrier can normally be overcome relatively easily by management taking the requisite measures to close the information gap.

Second, there may be a *lack of trust* on the part of employees with respect to management.

Third, employee inertia may be based upon *fear* – particularly with respect to their personal position or their social relationships. Those affected by the change may fear that the proposed changes will adversely affect their place in the structure or the relationships they enjoy in the organization.

Finally, some inertia is driven by *uncertainty* about the future. Attitudes to uncertainty vary significantly between people, with some showing a much more adverse reaction to it than others.

Kurt Lewin's three-step model of understanding change

Lewin (1947) suggested that organizational change could be understood in terms of three consecutive processes: unfreezing, moving and then refreezing.

Unfreezing

Unfreezing involves introducing measures that will enable employees to abandon their current practices or cultural norms in preparation for the change. In many organizations, nothing has changed for many years and unfreezing is necessary as a 'shaking-up' phase. The impetus for unfreezing can come from either inside or outside the organization itself. Changing market conditions, for example, sometimes give employees warning that change will be imminent. A particular market crisis may precipitate the expectation among employees that change must happen as a result. Internally, a management shake-up, a profit warning or talk of restructuring may bring about similar expectations.

Moving to the new level

Moving to the new level involves bringing about the requisite change itself. The time period given over to this phase varies widely. Structural change can usually be brought about relatively quickly. Changes in internal systems sometimes take longer (such as the introduction of new quality or information systems), and changing culture can take years.

Refreezing

Refreezing is necessary to 'lock in' the changes and to prevent the organization from going back to its old ways. Again, we would usually take cultural changes to require more 'cementing in' than some other changes and some resolve might be required on the part of senior management.

Step and incremental change

The pace at which change happens can usually be divided into one of two categories: step and incremental (see Figure 10.4). There are two factors that determine which is the most appropriate (Quinn and Voyer, 1998):

1 How urgent the need for change is. A market crisis will typically bring about an urgent need for rapid change whereas preparing for the introduction of a new legal regulation in five years' time will usually allow change to be brought about more slowly and perhaps more painlessly.
2 How much inertia is resident within the organization's culture. The time taken to unfreeze the inertia in some organizations will necessarily take longer than in others.

Step change offers the advantage of 'getting it over with'. It enables the organization to respond quickly to changes in its environment and hence enable it to conform with new conditions without lagging behind. Its disadvantages include the 'pain' factor: it may require some coercion or force on the part of management, which in turn may damage employee–management relationships.

Incremental changes offer the advantage of a step-by-step approach to change. For organizations with high inertia, incremental change enables management to gain acceptance before and during the change process; consequently, it tends to be more inclusive. The process is divided into a number of distinct phases and there may be

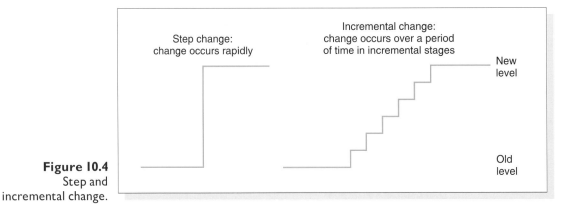

Figure 10.4
Step and
incremental change.

periods of 'rest' between the phases. It would be an inappropriate technique to use in situations of rapid environmental change.

Models for managing change

The process of actually managing strategic change brings us to consider a number of managerial approaches and their appropriateness in various contexts. Writers in this area have tended towards two complementary approaches:

- the managerialist approach;
- the change agent approach.

The managerialist approaches

Some writers have suggested that change can be successfully managed by employing a range of managerial practices. We can conceive of this approach as an 'if this doesn't work, try this' mechanism.

Most academics and managers have agreed that the process should begin with *education* and *communication*. The purpose of this is to inform those (usually internal) stakeholders who will be affected by the change. The message communicated will usually contain an explanation of the reasons for the change and an overview of its timescale and extent. In some organizational contexts, this procedure alone will be sufficient to overcome inertia and get the change process underway. In others, this will not be enough.

The next step will thus be to progress to *negotiation* and *participation*. Affected stakeholders will be invited to contribute to the process and to participate in its execution. It is thus hoped, by this process, that employees will be 'on board' – that they will feel some sense of ownership of the change. Some managers may introduce some degree of manipulation (of employees) in this stage, possibly by appealing to the emotional responses of employees or by over- or under-stating the reality of the changes in the environment.

Finally, if all else has failed to bring about the willing participation of the employees, management may be able to introduce some degree of *coercion*. This tactic is far from being appropriate in all contexts, but, where it is possible, it can be used to significant effect. Coercion is the practice of forcing through change by exploiting the power asymmetry between executive management and 'rank and file' employees. It is usually only used as a last resort as it can have a very negative effect on management–employee relationships after the change.

The change agent approach

Some texts refer to this approach as the 'champion of change' model. It is a change process that is managed from start to finish by a single individual. The individual (or change agent) may be key manager within the organization or he may be brought in as a consultant for the duration of the process.

The change agent approach offers a number of advantages.

First, it provides a focus for the change in the form of a tangible person who becomes the personification of the process. A 'walking symbol' of change can act as a stimulus to change and can ensure that complacency is avoided.

Second, in many cases, the change agent will be engaged because he is an expert in his field. He may have overseen the same change process in many other organizations and so is well-acquainted with the usual problems and how to solve them.

Third, the appointment of a change agent sometimes means that senior management time need not be fully occupied with the change process. The responsibility for the change is delegated to the change agent and management thus gain the normal advantages of delegation. Accordingly, senior management are freed up to concentrate on developing future strategy.

References and further reading

Alexander, L.D. (1985) Successfully implementing strategic decisions. *Long Range Planning*, 18(3).

Hall, R. (1992) The strategic analysis of intangible resources. *Strategic Management Journal*, 13, 135–144.

Handy, C.B. (1993) *Understanding Organisations*, Fourth Edition. London: Penguin.

Johnson, G. (1987) *Strategic Change and the Management Process*. Oxford: Blackwell.

Johnson, G. and Scholes, K. (1998) *Exploring Corporate Strategy*, Fifth Edition. Hemel Hempstead: Prentice Hall.

Lewin, K. (1947) Frontiers in group dynamics. Part II-B: Feedback problems of social diagnosis and action. *Human Relations*, 1, 147–153.

Lewin, K. (1951) *Field Theory in Social Science*. New York: Harper.

Miles, R.E. and Snow, C.C. (1978) *Organisational Strategy, Structure and Process*. New York: McGraw-Hill.

Mintzberg, H. (1987) Five Ps for strategy. *California Management Review*, Fall. Reprinted in Mintzberg, H., Quinn, J. B. and Ghoshal, S. (1998) *The Strategy Process: Revised European Edition*. Hemel Hempstead: Prentice Hall.

Mintzberg, H. (1990) The design school: reconsidering the basic premises of strategic management. *Strategic Management Journal*, March.

Mintzberg, H. and Waters, J.A. (1985) Of strategies deliberate and emergent. *Strategic Management Journal*, 6.

Moss Kanter, R. (1989) *The Change Masters: Innovation and Entrepreneurship in the American Corporation*. Englewood Cliffs, NJ: Simon & Schuster.

Pettigrew, A.M. (1988) *The Management of Strategic Change*. Oxford: Blackwell.

Quinn, J.B. (1980) Managing strategic change. *Sloan Management Review*, Summer, 3–20.

Quinn, J.B. (1980) *Strategies for Change*. Homewood: Irwin.

Quinn, J.B. and Voyer, J. (1998) Logical incrementalism: managing strategy formation. In: Mintzberg, H., Quinn, J.B. and Ghoshal, S. (eds), *The Strategy Process*. Englewood Cliffs: Prentice Hall.

Schein, E.H. (1985) *Organisational Culture and Leadership*. San Francisco: Jossey-Bass.

Stacey, R.D. (1993) *Strategic Management and Organisational Dynamics*. London: Pitman.

Williamson, O. (1975) *Markets and Hierarchies*. New York: Free Press.

11

Strategic development: directions and mechanisms

The decision as to which method of strategic development to adopt is critical to the success of competitive strategy. We encountered the idea of growth as one of the main business objectives in Chapter 1. Chapter 8 discussed the theory of development strategies and their contribution in achieving growth objectives. The theories developed in these earlier chapters underpin much of the discussion undertaken here. The variety of methods used for development will be considered, together with a critical appraisal of the success or failure of these methods.

The chapter briefly considers the directions of business growth and then proceeds to examine each of the mechanisms. Internal (or organic) growth is explored and the chapter then discusses the various mechanisms of external development, focusing particularly on mergers and acquisitions. Empirical research findings are presented that call into question the success of some of these approaches. The recent trend in collaborative arrangements such as the strategic alliance is discussed and, finally, the chapter looks at 'downsizing' strategies such as demerger.

After studying this chapter, students should be able to:

■ describe the general directions of business growth;

- define and distinguish between internal and external business growth;
- describe the various types of merger and acquisition;
- explain the motivations behind mergers and acquisitions and the reasons why they succeed or fail;
- describe what a strategic alliance is and why organizations enter into them;
- explain what is meant by a disposal and describe why organizations pursue this pathway;
- understand the regulatory and legal frameworks that influence business growth.

Directions of growth

Generic directions and mechanisms

Before we proceed in the rest of this chapter to review the mechanisms of business growth, it is worth taking a moment to examine the directions that growth can take. In Chapter 8 we encountered the Ansoff matrix. This is useful for examining the generic direction of growth (not to be confused with Porter's generic strategies) – i.e. the extent to which the strategy relies on new and existing products and markets. However, it is possible to pursue each of Ansoff's directions in a number of ways.

Growth can be within the same industry or in a different industry. The former is typically referred to as *related* whereas the latter is *unrelated*, but these characterizations are often less than useful because the division of growth directions into only two types is an oversimplification. When it comes to risk and the chances of success of a given growth strategy, the most important element is often the extent to which competences exist within the business that can be leveraged in the new setting, whether it is in a new industry or the same one.

Unrelated development

With this reservation in mind, it is nevertheless possible to classify directions into types for ease of understanding. Unrelated developments (which are usually classified as diversification in the Ansoff matrix) – those in which a different industry is entered – can be classified according to *how different* the 'new' industry's activities are compared to the existing one. If it is possible to exploit existing competences in the new industry, the chances of success are increased (such as with similarities in technology, marketing, design concept or similar). We can refer to this type of unrelated development as *concentric*. If, however, the new industry entered does not enable any existing competences to be leveraged and/or there are no common links between new and existing, the risk is higher. This is referred to as a *conglomerate* development. Conglomerated companies are therefore those containing a broad range of business interests, many of which have no apparent link to each other.

Related development

Most growth and development, however, occurs within the areas in which a business is most acquainted – its micro or near environment. Within this setting, growth can occur in two ways: vertically or horizontally.

Vertical growth is development of a business into a different stage of the supply chain of which it is a part. Backward vertical development is movement towards a supplier of resources used by the business. This might be an attempt to secure supply of a key resource or to gain a cost advantage over competitors by 'locking in' a supplier. Conversely, forward vertical development is growth towards the next stage in the supply chain by gaining an interest in a buyer of

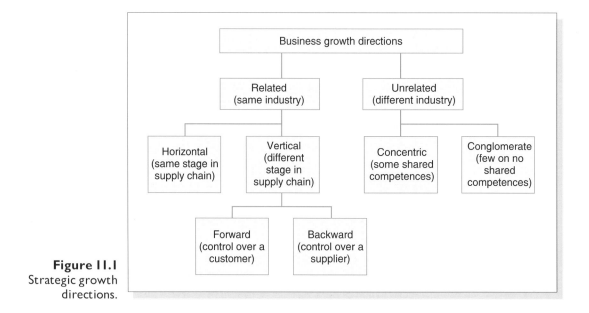

Figure 11.1
Strategic growth
directions.

the company's outputs. In both cases, the strategic logic is to secure a foothold in the same supply chain to guarantee supply or distribution.

Horizontal development is a move resulting in higher market share within the same markets. The acquisition of, or merger with, a competitor would be one way of achieving this, for example. The strategic logic behind horizontal development is typically to gain leverage or market power over suppliers or buyers. Higher volume generally confers greater scale economies in purchasing whereas larger product market share confers greater pricing power over customers.

In the remainder if this chapter, we will examine the mechanisms of how these directions can be pursued.

Organic (internal) growth

The most common mechanism of growth

Organic growth is the most straightforward mechanism of business growth. Most companies have used internal growth as their main method of growth at some time, and so its 'popularity' is obvious. The essential feature of organic growth is the reinvestment of previous years' profits in the same business that generated the profit. By increasing capacity (by, say, the purchase of enlarged premises or more machines), the business takes on more employees to cope with the extra demand. In so doing, turnover increases and so does the capital (balance sheet) value of the business.

Organic growth is common during the early stages of corporate development as companies build markets and develop new products. However, large companies may use it alongside external growth to consolidate market position. The development of a new supermarket outlet is an example of internal growth. Earlier years' profits are channelled into the development and the company benefits from the increased market share and increased turnover.

Organic growth offers the advantage that is it usually a lower-risk option than external growth. The fact that the increase in capacity remains fully under the control of the existing management means that the risks of dealing with other companies is avoided. Core competencies can usually be exploited and existing expertise can be capitalized upon.

On the other hand, organic growth is usually a slower mechanism compared to external growth. The 'bolting on' of a new company by external growth is a faster route to growth than gradual growth by internal means. Some large companies have reached their present size largely through successful year-on-year organic growth.

Internal growth

Internal growth is expansion by means of the reinvestment of previous years' profits and loan capital in the same business that generated the profits. This results in increased capacity, increased employment and, ultimately, increased turnover.

- *Advantages* – lower risk, within existing area of expertise, avoids high exposure to costs of alternative growth mechanisms (e.g. by debt servicing).
- *Disadvantages* – slower than external growth, little scope for diversification, relies upon the skills of existing management in the business.

External mechanisms of growth: mergers and acquisitions (M&As)

Definitions

It is difficult to open the business press without encountering details of a proposed or progressing merger or acquisition. The term *merger* is, however, sometimes replaced in such text with the word *takeover* or by *acquisition*. The same news story may use all three terms as though the words meant the same thing. For the purposes of a strategy text such as this, it is important to clarify the main terms that are generally used in connection with this process.

In a *merger* the shareholders of the organizations come together, normally willingly, to share the resources of the enlarged (merged) organization, with shareholders from both sides of the merger becoming shareholders in the new organization.

An *acquisition* is a joining of unequal partners, with one organization buying and subsuming the other party. In such a transaction the shareholders of the target organization (the smaller one) cease to be owners of the enlarged organization unless payment to the shareholders is paid partly in shares in the acquiring company. The shares in the smaller company are bought by the larger.

A *takeover* is technically the same as an acquisition, but the term is often taken to mean that the approach of the larger acquiring company is unwelcome from the point of view of the smaller target company. The term *hostile takeover* describes an offer for the shares of a target public limited company which the target's directors reject. If the shareholders then accept the offer (despite the recommendation of the directors), then the hostile takeover goes ahead.

Whichever of these routes is taken, the result is a larger and more financially powerful company. The word *integration* is the collective term used to describe these growth mechanisms.

A brief history of M&As

The popularity of M&As has changed over time. The early 1970s, late 1980s and mid to late 1990s were all periods of high levels of M&A activity. In addition to the general state of the macroeconomy as an explanation for such period of increased M&A activity, it is also probably true that increased business internationalization has contributed to a general increase over time. The reconfiguration of some new technology-based industries and more laissez-faire government attitudes towards industry structure are also strong influences.

Key concept

Combined market value

All public limited companies have a market value. Market value equals the number of shares on the stock market (the *share volume*) multiplied by the share price. It is taken to be a good indicator of the value of a company because it accounts for the company's asset value plus the 'goodwill' that the market attaches to the share. It follows that the combined market value of a merger or acquisition is the two companies' values added together. It is an indication of what the company will be valued at after the integration goes ahead.

Although the M&A process is a well-used mechanism in strategic development, recent history has shown that UK-based companies have used it rather more than those based in mainland Europe. Only in the USA have companies used the mechanism to a similar extent. However, recent figures show increased M&A activity in the global economy generally as companies feel the need to increase in size to become more internationally competitive.

One of the consequences of M&A activity is that many of the well-known 'names' of yesteryear have disappeared, while some of today's best known companies are relatively young in their current form. GlaxoSmithKline plc, the leader in the world pharmaceutical industry, came about through the merger of Glaxo Wellcome and SmithKline Beecham in the late 1990s. Similarly Diageo, the giant food and drinks company, was formed by the merger between Guinness and Grand Metropolitan (hence becoming the 'beer and Burger King' company).

A common misunderstanding surrounding the integration process is that two organizations always come together in their entirety. In practice, many integrations are the result of one organization joining with a divested *part* of another. That is to say that one company has made a strategic decision to withdraw from an industry or market and, in an attempt to maximize the value of the resources it no longer wants (i.e. an unwanted part of the previous company structure), it sells them to another company. The reasons why companies demerge and sell subsidiaries in non-core elements is addressed later in this chapter.

Explanations and motivations for M&As

There are a number of potential reasons for pursuing an external growth strategy. We have already encountered the overall objective of growth, but growth is seldom a stand-alone objective. The question is: Why is growth a desired objective? These motivations can be summarized as follows:

- to *increase market share* in order to increase pricing power in an industry;
- to *enter a new market*, possibly to offset the effects of decline in current markets or to broaden market portfolio;
- to *reduce competition*, possibly by purchasing a competitor;
- to *gain control of valuable brand names* or pieces of intellectual property such as patents;

- to gain preferential *access to distribution channels* (to gain resource inputs on preferential terms or to secure important supplies) by purchasing a supplier;
- to *broaden product range* in order to exploit more market opportunities and to spread risk;
- to *develop new products* for the market faster than internal R&D could do;
- to *gain access to new production or information technologies* in order to reduce costs, increase quality or increase product differentiation;
- to *gain economies of scale*, such as by increasing purchasing power so that inputs can be purchased at lower unit cost;
- to *make productive use of spare or under-used resources*, such as finance that is sitting on deposit in a bank;
- to '*asset strip*' – the practice of breaking up an acquired company and recovering more than the price paid by selling the parts separately;
- to *enhance corporate reputation* (appropriate if the existing company name has been associated with an alleged misdemeanour).

The precise nature of the integration selected will depend upon the specific objectives being pursued. If, for example, market share is the most important objective, then it is likely that a company will seek a suitable horizontal integration. On the other hand, a vertical integration would be more appropriate if supply or distribution concerns are uppermost amongst a company's threats.

External growth is usually expensive and it therefore has significant financial resource implications, not to mention a sizeable legal bill. Accordingly, it is entered into for specific strategic purposes that cannot be served through the normal progression of organic development.

Synergy: the main objective of M&As

Over-riding all other purposes served by integration is that of synergy. Synergy refers to the benefits that can be gained when organizations join forces rather than work apart. An integration can be said to be synergistic when the *whole is greater than the sum of the parts*. More popularly, synergy can be expressed as 2 + 2 = 5. If the integration is to achieve synergy, the 'new' company must perform more efficiently than either of the two parties were they to have remained separate.

On a simple level, we can conceptualize synergy using a human example. When two people work *together* performing a task such as lifting heavy logs onto a lorry, they can achieve far more work than two people lifting logs separately. A rally team of two enables the team to win a race if they work together with one driving and one navigating. If the two were to work separately, then each person would have to drive and navigate at the same time.

Synergy is measured in terms of increased added value. Kay (1993) made the point that: "Value is added, and only added, [in an integration] if distinctive capabilities or strategic assets are exploited more effectively. A merger adds no value if all that is acquired is a distinctive capability which is already fully exploited, as the price paid will reflect the competitive advantage held". Accordingly, integrations that do not enable the 'new' organization to produce higher profits or consolidate a stronger market position are usually deemed to have been relatively unsuccessful. The next section describes why failures sometimes occur.

Potential problems with M&As: why do they sometimes go wrong?

The fact that M&As are undoubtedly popular as methods of business growth may lead us to believe that they are always successful. In practice, this is not always true. A number of studies have analysed the performance of companies after integrations and the findings are not very encouraging (see, for example, Kay, 1993; Porter, 1985; Ravenscraft and Scherer, 1987).

These studies found that many corporate 'marriages' failed to work and ended in divorce. Of those that did survive, Kay (1993) found that when profitability before and after the integration was compared, a 'nil to negative effect' was achieved.

The main failure factors

There are a number of reasons why integrations do not work. We can summarize these 'failure factors' under six headings:

1 *lack of research* into the circumstances of the target company (and hence incomplete knowledge); failure in this regard can result in some nasty surprises after the integration;
2 *cultural incompatibility* between the two parties;
3 *lack of communication* within and between the two parties;

4   *loss of key personnel* in the target company after the integration;

5   *paying too much for the acquired company* and hence over-exposing the acquiring company to financial risk;

6   *assuming that growth in a target company's market will continue indefinitely* – market trends can fall as well as rise.

Government policy and integrations

Government policy on mergers may have contributed to some integration failures. Corporate growth can be restricted by government (which in the UK is represented by the Competition Commission), as companies are only allowed to establish a certain market share. In the UK an integration that would result in the new organization controlling over 25% of the market is generally subject to scrutiny by the Competition Commission and often results in such a merger being blocked. Being prevented from expanding in a related area may force some companies to take the more risky route of diversification (acquiring a company making different products in different markets).

Success factors for M&As

History has shown that M&As work best when the initiator company follows a number of 'rules'. They are designed to offset the failure factors we identified above.

First, success depends upon the *identification of a suitable 'target' candidate* with whom to merge or acquire. The emphasis on the word *suitable* is expanded upon below.

Second, a preparation for an approach should involve a detailed evaluation of the target company's *competitive position*. This would typically comprise a survey of its profitability, its market share, its product portfolio, its competitiveness in resource markets and so on.

Third, consideration should be given to the *compatibility of the two companies' management styles and culture*. Because integrations often involve the merging of the two boards of directors, it is usually important that the directors from the two companies are able to work together. In addition, the cultures, if not identical in character, should be able to be brought together successfully.

Fourth, there should be the possibility of a successful marriage between the two *corporate structures* (see the discussion of this in Chapter 10). If one is, for example, very tall and centralized and the other is shorter and decentralized, problems may occur in attempting to bring the two together.

Fifth, if the target company has key personnel (say a key manager or a distinctive research capability resident within a number of uniquely qualified scientists), then measures should be taken to ensure that these *key people are retained after the integration*. This can often be achieved by holding contractual talks with such people before the integration goes ahead.

Finally, the initiating company should ensure that the *price paid for the target* (or the valuation of its shares) *is realistic*. A key calculation of any investment is the return made on it; this is usually measured as the profit before interest and tax divided by the price paid for it. It follows that the return on investment (as a percentage) will depend upon the price paid for the target company. The valuation of a company is a complex accounting calculation which depends the balance sheet value, the prospects and performance of the company and the value of its intangible assets (e.g. its brands, patents, etc.).

Porter (1987) identified three criteria for success in mergers and acquisitions. 'Attractiveness' describes the likelihood of making above average profits in the target company's industry or industry segment. This can be seen as an objective test of the industries future prospects. The 'cost of entry' describes the overall cost of the merger or acquisition and includes the major capital sum (for the target's shares) plus additional and sometimes hidden costs such as payments to advisors (e.g. merchant banks and legal people) and the indirect or invisible costs such as management time and integration costs. Third, 'competitive advantage' asks whether synergistic gains actually exist between the two companies.

External growth without M&As: strategic alliances

What are strategic alliances?

The term *strategic alliance* is used to describe a range of collaborative arrangements between two or more organizations. These agreements can vary from a very formalized agreement, which could see the creation of a new jointly owned limited company, to an informal arrangement for a short-term project.

The legal structure of the organization is not a barrier to cooperation. In recent years, for example, many government departments and quangos have entered into partnerships with public companies such as through the UK government's Private Finance Initiative. In the private sector, public limited companies have also employed this approach to further their particular strategic objectives such as when BT and Securicor got together in a highly formalized agreement to form Cellnet, the mobile phone company. The channel tunnel, in common with other large construction projects, was built by a consortium of several companies working together for the duration of the project.

Strategic alliances can therefore assume a number of different forms depending upon the structure, the mechanism of decision-making, the nature of the capital commitment and apportionment of profit. Some exist for a particular project only and are short-term in timescale whereas others are more permanent. The choice of arrangement will depend upon the specific objectives that the participants have at the time.

Types of strategic alliance

Focused and complex alliances

The degree of involvement between the joint venture partners can range between the focused and the complex.

Focused alliances are those that tend to focus on collaboration at one or possibly two stages of the value chain. They may, for example, purchase as one in order to exert greater buying power on a supplier. Others may collaborate on product distribution or on technology.

More complex alliances are those that involve cooperation over a wide range of activities on the value chain. The relationship that existed between 1979 and 1994 between Honda from Japan and the British Rover Group was a complex alliance. Although the two companies remained legally separate, they cooperated in all of the primary value-adding activities, including product design.

Consortia

The term *consortium* is often used when referring to an alliance that involves more than two organizations. Consortia are often created for time-limited projects such as civil engineering or construction developments. The channel tunnel was constructed by a number of construction companies in a consortium that was called Trans Manche Link (TML). TML was dissolved upon the completion of the project.

Camelot, the UK National Lottery operator, is another example of a consortium.

The form of alliance chosen by the parties will depend upon several factors. The complexity of the alliance will depend upon the objectives that the two parties are pursuing. Alliance partners tend to seek cooperation on the minimum number of areas that are needed in order to avoid over-exposure to the risk of one of the parties leaving abruptly or 'finding out too much'. The selection of partners for a consortium will depend upon matching the resource and skill requirement of the project with those organizations that are willing to contribute to the effort. Organizations with previous experience of projects of the type proposed will obviously be among the most in demand as consortium participants.

Motivations for forming strategic alliances

International competitive pressures

One of the major drivers towards the use of strategic alliances in corporate development is the growth in international market development. As organizations seek out new markets for their products, many recognize that they have skills or knowledge deficiencies where an in-depth knowledge of a foreign market is required. The need to develop local knowledge is increased if overseas production (with an overseas alliance partner) is being considered to meet market demands. While local knowledge can be hired (say through a local importing agent), it is often quicker and more reliable to seek assistance from an already established producing organization of the host country. It should also be noted that a legal requirement of many countries is that foreign organizations must have host partners before they can trade, making a joint venture an essential method of development.

Capital pooling

Although the globalization of markets may have encouraged some organizations into considering the use of alliances, there are other factors that have encouraged companies to develop them further within national boundaries. The high capital requirements of many projects, in terms of both set-up costs, ongoing running cost and delays in profit generation, together with high levels of risk generally generated by such delays are reasons for considering the use of alliances. The desire to gain economies of scale in areas such as research and development and the desire to secure access to markets are other reasons why companies choose alliances.

Successful alliances

The success of an alliance is attributed to a number of factors, some of which are similar to the factors present in a successful integration. Faulkner (1995) suggested the following critical success factors:

- complementary skills and capabilities of the partners;
- the degree of overlap between the parties' markets be kept to a minimum;
- a high level of autonomy, with strong leadership and commitment from the parent organizations (if appropriate);
- the need to build up trust and not to depend solely on the contractual framework of the relationship;
- recognizing that the two partners may have different cultures.

Researchers in this area have noted that alliances seem to work best when the partners are from related industries (or the same industry) or when the objective of the alliance is the development of a new geographical region. Success is further enhanced when the parties are of a similar size and are as equally committed (in resource terms) to the alliance. Strict adherence to the initial objectives of the alliance can often limit its success, as modification of the original purpose may become necessary if the business environment changes. There is thus a need to continually reappraise the parameters of the agreement.

Brouthers *et al.* (1993) advanced a more succinct version of Faulkner's success factors in the '3 Cs' of successful alliances. The two parties should have:

- complementary skills;
- compatible goals;
- cooperative cultures.

Disposals

What are disposals?

We should not assume that business strategies are always designed to cause business growth. There are times when organizations may wish to become smaller. As with growth strategy, size reduction can be achieved by organic reduction (by winding down production of a product area), by divestment (the opposite of acquisition) or by demerger (the opposite of merger).

Demergers and divestments (which together are referred to as *disposals*) involve taking part of a company and selling it off as a 'self-contained' unit with its own management, structure and employees in place. The unit may then be sold on to a single buyer (for whom it will be an acquisition) or it may be floated on the stock market as a public limited company.

Reasons for disposal

There are a number of reasons why a company may elect to dispose of a part of its structure. The most prominent reasons include:

1 under-performance of the part in question (e.g. poor profitability), possibly due to negative synergy;
2 a change in the strategic focus of the organization in which the candidate for disposal is no longer required;
3 the medium- to long-term prospects for the disposal candidate are poor;
4 the disposal candidate is an unwanted acquisition (or an unwanted subsidiary of an acquired company that is otherwise wanted);
5 the need to raise capital from the disposal to reinvest in core areas or to increase liquidity in the selling company;
6 the belief that the disposal candidate would be more productive if it were removed from the seller's structure;
7 in some circumstances, disposal may be used as a tactic to deflect a hostile takeover bid, particularly if the predatory company is primarily interested in acquiring the company to gain control over the disposal candidate;
8 as part of a programme of 'asset stripping' – the process of breaking a company up into its parts and selling them off for a sum greater than that paid for the whole.

Shareholders and disposals

The most common method of corporate disposal is a 'private' transaction between two companies, which is intended to be of benefit to both parties. The seller gains the funds from the transaction and is able to focus on its core areas. The buyer gains the product and market presence of the disposal which, in turn, will be to its strategic advantage.

Disposals are designed to create synergy to the shareholders in the same way as integrations. We should not lose sight of the fact that business organizations are owned by shareholders and it is the role of company directors (as the shareholders' agents) to act in such a way that shareholder wealth is maximized. If this can be achieved by breaking a part of the company off, then this option will be pursued.

The value of disposals to shareholders can be illustrated by an example where a demerger was successful. As part of a strategic review in ICI plc in the early 1990s (the British chemical multinational), the main board made the decision to focus on its core areas of speciality chemicals. This necessarily meant that parts of the company that did not fit into the realigned structure would be disposed of. Some parts, especially the bulk intermediates plants, were divested to competitors for whom the bulk business was within their core.

What was previously ICI pharmaceuticals division was not divested – the board decided that it should be demerged. The division was made into a stand-alone company, Zeneca plc, which was floated on the stock exchange, with the proceeds from the flotation going to benefit the shareholders of ICI. The stock market welcomed the flotation of Zeneca as, it believed, it could now compete in the competitive pharmaceuticals industry without the 'encumbrance' of being a part of a widely diversified chemical group (ICI). In the months following the demerger, the value of ICI shares increased by over 75% and Zeneca's share price increased by some 400%.

Other methods of disposal

In addition to divestments and demergers, two other disposal methods are noteworthy.

Equity carve-outs

Equity carve-outs are similar to demergers insofar as the spin-off company is floated on the stock exchange. However, in this form of disposal, the selling company retains a shareholding in the disposal, with the balance of shares being offered to the stock market. In this respect, equity carve-outs can be seen as a semi-disposal: part of the disposal is kept, but not as a wholly owned subsidiary. The decision of the Thomson Corporation of Canada to float the Thomson travel group in 1998 is an example of such a policy. In this case the Thomson family retained 20% of the new company's equity in order to gain an ongoing return on the stock, albeit without strategic control over the company.

Management buy-outs

A management buy-out (MBO) is said to have occurred when a company which a parent company wishes to dispose of is sold to its current management. MBOs are often a mutually satisfactory outcome when the disposal candidate is unwanted by its parent but when it has the possibility of being run successfully when the existing management have the requisite commitment and skills.

The advantages of MBOs can be summarized as follows:

1   The selling parent successfully disposes of its non-core business and receives a suitable price for it which it can then reinvest in its main areas of activity.
2   The divested organization benefits from committed managers (who become its owners). When the management team finds itself personally in debt as a result of the buy-out (having had to find the money for the purchase), their motivation and commitment tends to be maximized. In some MBOs, some of the capital for the purchase is provided by venture capital companies.
3   If part of the MBO capital is met by the company's existing employees, the organization benefits from the commitment of people who have part-ownership, and who therefore share in the company's success through dividends on shares and through growth in the share price.

The regulatory framework of external growth

The purpose of regulation

Most governments have taken the view that there is some need to put in place a regulatory framework for external business growth because of the implications for competition in markets. There is a careful balance to be struck in this regard. Governments are usually keen to encourage business activity in their countries because of their beneficial effects upon employment, tax revenues, exports and standard of living. At the same time, it is generally true that, the larger organizations become, the more difficult it is for smaller competitors to make headway against them in terms of pricing and market share. Regulation is therefore a matter of some discretion.

National and supranational regulators

In the UK, regulation arises from two sources: from the national level and from the European level. They have in common two areas of concern: company size and, more specifically, market share.

European Union regulation

Since Britain joined the European Community in 1973, it has been subject to EU regulations and directives. European competition regulations are provided for in The Treaty of Rome, 1957 (the primary legislation of the EU), in the form of two 'articles' that regulate integration between companies resident within two or more EU states. Both articles are designed to stimulate competition between companies in member states. They can be used by authorities within the EU to influence the behaviour of businesses that may seek to enter into integrations that may reduce competition in a market. One of these, Article 86, refers particularly to mergers and acquisitions.

Article 86 is designed to prohibit the abuse of a dominant market position (i.e. a high market share). It does not prohibit monopoly as such, but seeks to ensure that large businesses do not use their power against consumer and competitor interests. This indirectly acts against large companies seeking to acquire a high market share by integration.

The administrative part of the EU – the European Commission – has the responsibility to implement Article 86. It can prohibit mergers or acquisitions that result in a combined national market share of 25% or when the combined turnover in EU markets exceeds a certain financial figure (which at 1998 was ECU 250 million). On a more operational level, the way that integrations are conducted is also regulated. Rules are in place regarding the transparency of approach (i.e. how it should be announced) and how shareholders should be informed of proposed integrations.

Integrations in the UK

Integrations between companies based in the UK are subject to possible scrutiny by the Office of Fair Trading (OFT) and the

Competition Commission (CC). Their activity is governed by two major pieces of British legislation: the Fair Trading Act, 1973 and, to a lesser extent, the Competition Act, 1998.

The Fair Trading Act, 1973 targets three areas in pursuit of maintaining healthy levels of competition in markets:

1 monopoly practices;
2 restrictive practices;
3 mergers and acquisitions.

Under its provisions to review mergers and acquisition, this Act allows the Government's regulatory bodies to review an integration if the combined market share exceeds 25%. In this regard, it is in agreement with Article 86.

The OFT and the CC

The two bodies in the UK that exist to regulate integrations activity are provided for under the terms of the Acts of Parliament mentioned above. Both act independently of the Government under the instruction of the Secretary of State for Trade and Industry and exist in the legal form of quangos.

The Office of Fair Trading

The OFT was established in 1973 and is headed by the Director General of Fair Trading (DGFT) – an individual charged with, among other things, the enforcement of the terms of the Fair Trading Act. The OFT is also required to act as a central bureau which collects and publishes information on competition and anti-competitive practices in the UK.

The DGFT has six broad areas of responsibility. The first and most important of these is to collect information on business activities that are potentially harmful to competition or the public interest, including mergers and acquisitions (the DGFT has the power to refer cases to other authorities for review).

In this regard, the OFT is able to review an integration when:

- two or more enterprises cease to be distinct;
- at least one of them is a UK or UK-controlled company;
- there is a combined market share of 25% or assets to the value of £70 million.

In applying the above criteria, the following factors need to be taken into account by the DGFT:

- the extent of competition within the UK in respect to the market in question;
- the level of efficiency of the companies intending to integrate;
- the impact the proposed integration will have on employment in both a national and a regional context;
- the competitive position of UK companies on an international basis;
- the national strategic interest (rarely an important factor);
- the implications of the method of financing used to fund the merger (particularly in respect to the welfare of shareholders or the banking sector);
- the probability that a weak partner will be turned round by the acquirer.

The Competition Commission

The role of the CC (formerly known as the Monopolies and Mergers Commission) is to look into proposed mergers and acquisitions when instructed so to do by the OFT or by the Secretary of State for Trade and Industry. It is headed by a full-time chairman to whom three part-time deputy chairmen report. This team then draws upon the expertise of specialist members from a range of backgrounds, including business, finance, academia and trades unions. All of the members, including the chairman, are appointed by the Secretary of State.

The CC is unable to act on its own initiative, and its recommendations after an investigation are advisory only. The Secretary of State may elect to adopt or reject its findings.

The Commission describes itself having ". . . two distinct functions. On its reporting side the Commission has taken on the former MMC role of carrying out inquiries into matters referred to it by the other UK competition authorities concerning monopolies, mergers and the economic regulation of utility companies. Secondly, the newly established Appeal Tribunals hear appeals against decisions of the Director General of Fair Trading and the Regulators of utilities in respect of infringements of the prohibitions contained in the Act concerning anti-competitive agreements and abuse of a dominant position."

References and further reading

Ansoff, H. (1987) *Corporate Strategy*. London: Penguin.

Bishop, M. and Kay, J. (1993) *European Mergers and Merger Policy*. Oxford: Oxford University Press.

Brouthers, K.D., Brouthers, L.E. and Wilkinson, T.J. (1993) Strategic alliances: choose your partners. *Long Range Planning*, 28(3), 18–25.

Faulkner, D. (1995) *Strategic Alliances: Cooperating to Compete*. New York: McGraw-Hill.

Firth, M. (1991) Corporate takeovers, stockholder returns and executive rewards. *Managerial and Decision Economics*, 12.

Franks, J. and Harris, R. (1989) Shareholders wealth effects of corporate takeover: the UK experience 1955–85. *Journal of Financial Economics*, 23.

Geroski, P.A. and Vlassopoulos, A. (1990) Recent patterns of European merger activity. *Business Strategy Review*, Summer.

Glaister, K.W. and Buckley, P. (1994) UK international joint ventures: an analysis of patterns of activity and distribution. *British Journal of Management*, 5.

Grundy, T. (1996) Strategy, acquisition and value. *European Management Journal*, 14(2).

Haspeslagh, P. and Jemison, D. (1991) *Managing Acquisitions: Creating Value Through Corporate Renewal*. New York: Free Press.

Kay, J. (1993) *Foundations of Corporate Success*. Oxford: Oxford University Press.

Kitching, J. (1974) Why acquisitions are abortive. *Management Today*, November.

Meeks, G. (1977) *Disappointing Marriage: A study of the Gains from Mergers*. Cambridge: Cambridge University Press.

Porter, M.E. (1980) *Competitive Strategy*. New York: Free Press.

Porter, M.E. (1985) *Competitive Advantage*. New York: Free Press.

Porter, M.E. (1987) From competitive advantage to corporate strategy. *Harvard Business Review*, May/June.

Ravenscraft, D.J. and Scherer, F.M. (1987) *Mergers, Sell-offs and Economic Efficiency*. Washington, DC: Brooking Institution.

Shleifer, A. and Vishny, R. (1986) Large shareholders and corporate control. *Journal of Political Economy*, 94, 461–488.

Shleifer, A. and Vishny, R., (1991) Takeovers in the '60s and the '80s: evidence and implications. *Strategic Management Journal*, 12.

Sudarsanam, P.S. (1995) *The Essence of Mergers and Acquisitions*. Englewood Cliffs: Prentice Hall.

Walsh, J. and Ellwood, J. (1991) Mergers, acquisitions and the pruning of managerial deadwood. *Strategic Management Journal*, 12.

CHAPTER 12

Quality, operations, performance and benchmarking

Introduction and chapter overview

The strategic development of many companies has been marked by a recognition that good quality in operations can contribute significantly to competitive advantage. One approach in particular (total quality management or TQM) is seen by many companies as an important part of this operational emphasis, especially for those that aim to be 'world class' organizations. In order to recognize the importance of quality, each of the world's major industrialized nations has its own quality award. These awards act as an important strategic tool and can assist in an organization's product and market positioning.

In this chapter we explain how this emphasis on quality management has come about and explore the main features demonstrated by those organizations that have successfully adopted a TQM philosophy. Key features of the quality award frameworks are also discussed. Finally, the chapter explains the various types of operational benchmarking in common use and the benefits that each has to offer.

After studying this chapter, students should be able to:

- describe the main order-winning factors for business;
- define quality and total quality management;
- explain how TQM evolved;
- explain the main principles of TQM;
- discuss the role of quality awards and prize schemes including the EFQM excellence model;
- describe and distinguish between *enablers* and *results* elements of the excellence model;
- describe how such self-assessment frameworks are used and say what benefits they can bring to businesses;
- distinguish between the different types of benchmarking and explain the benefits of each.

Operational performance in 'winning' organizations

The strategic performance objectives

If we were to examine the strategic planning process for any highly successful company, we would find a set of key planning decisions. These decisions begin with goal-setting – what the organization hopes to achieve. This then leads on to policy decisions – the organizational rules by which people should behave when going about their work. In turn, these lead to operational and process planning decisions – how the work will be carried out. Traditional financial and marketing goals are clearly important, but for many world-class organizations a focus on customer-driven quality and operational performance is essential to business success.

Successful organizations share a number of important objectives with respect to these customer-driven quality and operational performance aspects of the value chain. The key to success in the most important part of the value-adding process can be expressed in simple terms:

- *Do the right things right* – i.e. provide the goods or services that the customer wants, without mistakes. This means providing the product that the customer wants, right first-time, every time.

- Do things *quickly*, giving the fastest possible turn around for a customer, from placing an order to receiving the ordered products.
- Be *reliable*, which is providing the customer with products or services on time and keeping any delivery promises made.
- Be *flexible* and responsive to change – to be able to deal with unexpected circumstances, or simply to deal with changes in customer requirements.
- Be *cheap* – providing products or services at competitive prices while still maintaining a profit. Or, in the case of non-profit-making businesses, giving best-value performance.

Key concept

Operations and operations strategy

The operations function of an organization is at the centre of the value-adding process. It should not be confused with the 'operational level' as distinct from the 'strategic level' (see Chapter 1).

The operations function is that part of the organization that produces the output for which the organization is known. For a motor manufacturing company, the operations function comprises the chain of events from buying in the sheet steel to driving the finished car out of the factory. For a hospital, the operations function comprises the clinical departments, both medical and surgical, which are staffed by nurses, doctors and other paramedic employees.

It should be distinguished from all of the other parts of the organization that do not directly add value, such as personnel and finance.

An operations strategy, like a human resource strategy or a marketing strategy, is a course of action put in train at the operational level (see Chapter 1) to help achieve an organization's corporate-level strategies.

The customer's influence on quality and performance

The most important set of factors that impact on any organization's operations strategy are those set by the customers. The purpose of any operations function is to manage the value-adding activities inside the business in such a way that customer requirements are met in full.

What 'matters' to the customer will, of course, vary from market to market. For each element of product that is of concern to a customer, organizations will have an internal response that facilitates the satisfaction of the customer concerned. The most successful businesses are those that can most effectively configure their operations to meet customer requirements.

The various areas of focus for an organization when developing competitive strategy are listed in Table 12.1. It is notable from this list just how important quality and customer focus become in the overall strategic focus. The quality of products (goods and services) can be seen to extend from the original design, to on-time delivery, reliability in service through to after-sales service. This is what we mean by customer-driven quality.

Quality begins with the quality of product design. Do the specifications achieve what the customer wants? Does the company fully understand the customer's needs and requirements? Quality extends into the manufacturing or service processes. Can the company deliver the products at the right price? The efficiency of work processes and the competences of employees need to be such that products can be made cost-effectively and consistently to design specifications. Have all wasteful processes – those that do not add value – been eliminated? In the case of service operations, the customer is often in face-to-face contact with the employee providing the service. The customer

Table 12.1

Factors affecting customer-driven quality and the operating performance characteristics of an organization

What matters to customers in selecting a product purchase	How a business responds to the customer demands
Low price (value for money)	Producing efficiently at low or reasonable unit cost
High-quality products	Building quality into processes and products
Fast delivery	Short manufacturing lead times, ex-finished goods stock (see key concept – types of stock) or fast distribution
Product and service reliability	Building reliability into products and delivering dependable service
Innovation (using leading-edge technologies)	Keeping abreast of latest developments and emphasizing R&D
Wide product choice	Flexibility to change and wide product mix
Responsive to changes in customer requirements	Flexibility in volume and delivery, quick response times to change

should be made to feel confident that the service is speedy, professional, efficient and provides value for money.

Product reliability is another important issue. From the customer's perspective, product reliability is measured by the product's functional performance and so the product must perform as expected. Continuous good functional performance over time is also important. The product must continue performing throughout what the customer considers to be a reasonable life-expectancy. Reliable fast delivery of products or off-the-shelf availability of consumer products is also a major consideration. Can the company meet the delivery lead time requirements? Does it do so reliably and consistently? In the case of service industries, the service provided is less tangible than physical products and therefore it is often the customer's perception of the reliability and timeliness of the service provided that is important.

For many businesses 'what really matters for customers' can be seen to extend beyond the above issues. Customer-driven quality often requires innovation and the use of leading-edge technologies. Such innovation can be applied to materials and product design, or even to the manufacturing processes or the way services and facilities are provided.

Key concept

Types of stock

Stocks are the physical goods that are bought in, converted and then sold to customers in a manufacturing or assembly business. There are three types of stock, depending upon where they are along the production process:

- *Raw materials* or purchased parts are stocks in their 'raw' state. Raw materials are those goods that are purchased, before they undergo any processing within the manufacturing process.
- *Work-in-progress* is the name given to stocks that are actually being worked on in the manufacturing process.
- *Finished goods* are those stocks that have passed through the process and are ready for distribution to the customers.

The list in Table 12.1 is useful as a starting point to identifying the wide-ranging issues that must be addressed by manufacturing and service sector organizations in the quest to become leaders in their own markets. Many 'winning' organizations – those that have a competitive advantage in their industry – have arrived at the conclusion that one area of concern in operations is more important than any other – quality.

Quality

What is quality?

A number of academics and practitioners have attempted to provide a coherent definition of quality. The fact that there are so many definitions is testimony to the fact that it is a complicated matter upon which to agree.

For a common product such as a car, we might think of quality as referring to reliability, build, safety features, etc. For a service such as plastering a wall, we would probably arrive at a different set of things to describe a 'quality' job, such as the finish of the surface, the flushness of the edges and the extent to which it is even. It is the fact that the quality criteria vary from product to product that makes it difficult to agree on a definition.

Some of the most noted thinkers in the field have described quality in respect to 'excellence', or more accurately, 'perceived excellence'. Although quality means many things to different people, in general we can consider quality as meeting customer needs or expectations. In Table 12.2, we summarize some of the most widely used definitions.

Table 12.2
Some definitions of quality

Quality 'guru'	Definition of quality
Deming	Quality should be aimed at meeting the needs of the consumer, present and future
Juran	Quality is fitness for the purpose for which the product is intended
Crosby	Quality is conformance to requirements (either customer requirements or the specification predetermined for it)
Oakland	Quality is meeting customer requirements

The quality 'gurus'

A quality guru is someone who has been recognized for his contribution to the management of quality within business and whose messages have led to major change in the way organizations operate. A number of people are highly regarded as major contributors in the field of quality management. The major thinkers in the area are described in Table 12.3.

Historical perspective of quality

Quality has been an issue for as long as business has been carried out. For traditional crafts such as blacksmiths, tailors, innkeepers, etc., it was the craftsmen themselves who were responsible for the price, delivery and degree of quality of their wares and services. Reputations were established on the quality of workmanship, which in turn led to more demand for their skills and higher levels of profitability and prosperity for the individual. The more successful 'masters' recruited apprentices and employed other tradesmen. Quality was assured informally and depended on the pride that each individual had in his or her own work. In Europe, crafts guilds were established which aimed to ensure that adequate training was given and that apprentices 'qualified' only when they were demonstrably capable of producing adequate standards of workmanship. Much of this pride in workmanship was lost during the industrial revolution in the late eighteenth century with the introduction of machinery and high-volume manufacturing. However, large-scale production methods brought about a need to ensure consistent reproduction of parts, manufactured to exacting specifications and so the concept of *quality control* was born.

In the early 1900s, Frederick W. Taylor introduced his ideas on scientific management. His methodology was to separate the planning (thinking) function from the physical work elements in production. By breaking down each job into smaller elements of work, he was able to train workers to perform simple mechanical tasks that comprised only a part of the total production process. High-volume repeatability allowed gains in speed and efficiency, and this in turn led to cheaper products. Quality-control techniques enabled specially trained inspec-

Table 12.3
The quality 'gurus'

Quality 'guru'	Main messages
W. Edwards Deming	Sometimes referred to as 'the father of TQM', Deming believed that bad management was responsible for more than 90% of quality problems. He argued that quality improvement is achieved by continuous reduction in process variation using *statistical process control* and employee involvement. Later, Deming developed his 'System of Profound Knowledge' in which he stressed the need for the organizations to operate as a coherent system with everybody working together towards the overall aims. Good quality relies in large part upon an understanding of the nature of variation (statistical theory), careful planning and prediction based on experience. Finally, he stressed the importance of psychology, recognizing the relationships of extrinsic and extrinsic motivation factors in the workplace.
Joseph M. Juran	Juran proposed a general management approach with human elements. He believed that less than 20% quality problems are due to the workers themselves. He defines quality as 'fitness for use'. Juran recommended a project approach to improvements by setting targets, planning to achieve targets set, assigning responsibility and rewarding results achieved.
Arman V. Feigenbaum	Proposed a systematic approach involving every employee and all functions. He emphasized the need for 'quality-mindedness' through employee participation. Made the point that expenditure on prevention costs would lead to an overall reduction in product failure costs.
Kaoru Ishikawa	Stressed the importance of statistical methods, using his 'seven tools of quality' for problem-solving. Also recognized for his contributions to the company-wide quality-control movement, involving all staff at all levels through quality circles.

tors to test finished components against a predetermined specification. This enabled defective parts to be identified and then removed or re-worked before they reached the customer.

The modern quality movement

The modern quality movement began in the 1950s. The demand for goods and merchandise saw Western industrial nations producing

Genichi Taguchi	Developed the 'quality loss function' concerned with the optimization of products and processes prior to manufacture. His methods can be applied in the design phase of products or systems, or in production to optimize process variables.
Shigeo Shingo	Shingo introduced a practical approach to achieve zero defects. With careful design of products and tooling systems, he eliminated the need for sample inspection, through his system of mistake proofing known as 'Poka-Yoke'. He is also acknowledged for his work on fast tooling changeovers. Commonly known as SMED (single minute exchange of dies), this is one of the most important contributions to just-in-time operating systems.
Philip B. Crosby	Crosby's 14-step approach to quality improvement sets out to achieve conformance to requirements through prevention not inspection. Believing that 'quality is free' and 'zero defects' should be the target, Crosby rejected statistically acceptable levels of quality. He believed in a 'top-down' approach to quality management and proposed his four absolutes of quality: quality is defined as conformance to requirements; a system of prevention not appraisal; performance standard should be zero defects; the measurement of quality should be the financial cost of non-conformance.
Tom Peters	Peters' early work stressed the importance of visible leadership and encouraged MBWA (management by walking about), giving managers the opportunity to listen and solve problems through face-to-face contact with workers. His later work focused on customer orientation and he stressed that managers need to be 'obsessed' with quality, never accepting shoddy goods. He recognized that everyone needs to be trained in quality tools and supported the use of cross-functional teams. He believed that organizations should overcome complacency by creating 'endless Hawthorne effects' (after the work of Elton Mayo) through the generation of new goals and environments. He also stressed the importance of the role of suppliers and customers in the quest for improvement.

higher volumes of product with a resulting decline in quality. In Japan, during the rebuilding of its industrial base after the 1939–45 war, help was given through a number of management consultants. In particular, the work of Dr W. Edwards Deming and Dr Joseph Juran led the Japanese to completely review the accepted views on quality management.

Statistical quality-control techniques were introduced to reduce variation in the production processes. Much emphasis was placed on the way that quality was managed, rather than simply concentrating on only the technical issues. The focus shifted from one of quality inspection to one of preventing quality problems. Management began educating and involving all employees to look for ways to improve product quality and work methods. The Japanese developed a new culture of continuous improvement in which everyone was encouraged to believe that they had two jobs – doing the work and improving the work. They called this approach *kaizen*.

This new manufacturing philosophy gradually evolved and led to the Japanese domination in manufacturing industries by the late 1970s. During the 1980s, the rest of the world awoke to this transformation and the TQM movement was born.

Key concept

Kaizen

Kaizen is a culturally embedded concept of continual improvement pioneered in Japanese companies. It concentrates on small gradual changes involving all employees in every area of business. According to Imai (1986), it is "the single most important concept in Japanese management – the key to Japanese competitive success". Kaizen is process-oriented change, involving operators continuously searching for better ways to do their job.

Some companies use 'kaizen teams' who take responsibility for identifying opportunities for improvement. Typically, ideas for change will be investigated, tested and measured by the team. Any saving in job cycle time, even though it may only amount to a few seconds, will be introduced as the new standard method of production. Staff are encouraged to participate in kaizen teams and are given full training in problem-solving tools and techniques.

The kaizen process begins with examination of the work processes and operating practices, continuously looking for improvement opportunities. It is important that every employee strives for improvement and so an acceptance of kaizen by the organizational culture is an important element. Employees are empowered to experiment and make incremental changes and are sometimes provided with their own limited budgets for doing so. It is important that kaizen activities are actively supported by management who will usually provide additional resources if required, perhaps when ideas for change are complex, requiring technical expertise, extra finance or help in other ways.

Total quality management

What is TQM?

Today, TQM is an holistic approach, which provides awareness of the customer–supplier relationship and continuous improvement effort in all departments and functions. There has been much written on the subject of TQM, and the philosophy means many things to different people.

Some have used an external customer focus, aiming to ensure employee awareness of customer needs and an elimination of faulty goods or services. Others have focused on the tools of quality such as brainstorming, statistical tools, control charts, etc., to encourage problem-solving and a right-first-time attitude. Many have used teamwork and 'empowerment' in an effort to develop a 'quality' culture, to improve staff motivation and an ongoing cycle of quality improvement.

There are as many approaches to TQM as there are consultants selling their own formula for success, but whatever the approach the following features of TQM are usually present:

- it is strongly led by senior management;
- it is customer-oriented;
- it recognizes internal customers in the value chain and external customers;
- it represents a fundamental change away from *controlling* bad quality to *preventing* bad quality from happening – it *causes* good quality;
- it encourages a right-first-time approach to all activities;
- everybody is made responsible for quality;
- there is an emphasis on kaizen;
- training and quality 'tools' are introduced in support of the quality regime;
- employees are encouraged to look for ways for improving quality in their own areas, such as by process 'tightening';
- the introduction of measurement systems to eliminate and control waste.

Waste

Waste describes any activity in an operations process that is not value-adding. It costs money but does not create value commensurate with its cost.

Examples include:

- process inefficiency (say as a result of bad design);
- any process that does not add value – e.g. unnecessary inspection activities or materials handing activities (say from station to station in the process);
- any stock that is not actually being processed (and to which value is therefore not being added); this includes all raw materials, all finished goods and any work-in-progress that is queuing between production stages;
- stocks that have failed a quality test, either in-process or at final quality control;
- machine 'down-time' – i.e. production time lost through machines not being operable for any reason such as breakdown, or through tooling up or tooling down between batches;
- the time and stock involved in producing unsold or unsaleable stocks.

Oakland's model for TQM

A number of frameworks for TQM have been developed. The earliest were proposed by academics trying to explain and rationalize the TQM concepts, to facilitate implementation by managers in industry. Many business consultants followed with their own ideas and a proliferation of TQM models ensued.

Oakland's framework

Professor John Oakland developed a relatively simple framework, which usefully described the main features of TQM (see Figure 12.1). According to Oakland (1993): "[TQM is] an approach to

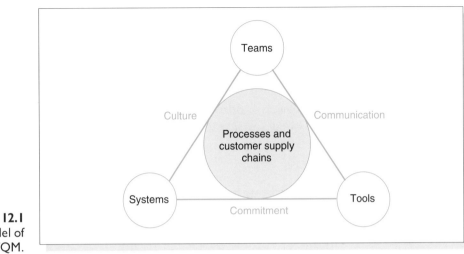

Figure 12.1
Oakland's model of
TQM.

improving the competitiveness, effectiveness and flexibility of a whole organization''.

The role of processes

At the heart of Oakland's model are processes and customer supplier chains in order to recognize the importance of meeting customer requirements. The term *customer* does not refer just to the end customer; it also recognizes that all organizations have chains of internal customers and suppliers. For example, in a manufacturing plant, raw materials are received into stores from suppliers, they are then fed into the first production process. Here the materials are worked on in some way and then passed on to the next department (the next internal customer) where they are worked again. At each stage value is added until the final product is sold to the external customer. Each operator in the chain is therefore both a customer and a supplier, with each having the responsibility of meeting their respective customer's requirements. Failing to do so at any stage results in inferior quality and a need to correct or rework the work-in-process stock or the finished goods. At every stage, the work process and the skills of the operator must be capable of doing the job correctly to the designed specification.

Quality systems

To achieve consistency in work processes a company must be organized so that the required standards are known and understood by all employees. This requires management systems to plan, monitor and control all activities. For many organizations, this is achieved by setting out objectives through a quality 'policy' and the use of a fully documented quality system such as ISO 9000. Using such a system ensures a consistent level of quality, which in turn promotes customer confidence. In addition, such systems help the organization to manage internal and external operations in a cost-effective and efficient way.

Tools and techniques of quality

The quality system provides a framework for recording and dealing with quality problems. However, simply asking staff to take responsibility for solving their own quality problems is usually not enough. Employees often must be trained and educated so that they can identify problems and deal with them effectively. Many organizations now train staff in basic problem-solving tools and other quality techniques, encouraging them to become proactive in quality improvement activities.

Teams and the organization

Clear lines of authority and responsibility are important in most organizational structures (see Chapter 10). Just as important, however, is the need to ensure that departments and functions do not become so compartmentalized that barriers develop. In most modern manufacturing and service companies, work processes are complex in nature and are often beyond the control of any one individual. A team approach, therefore, offers a number of advantages.

The use of teams allows more complex problems to be solved because it brings together different skills and expertise. Interdepartmental teams can resolve issues that cross over functional boundaries and will also help reduce problems of internal politics. Teamworking can also help develop skills and knowledge and it is often more satisfying for the individuals involved – improving morale, participation and decision-making.

Commitment, culture and communication

Achieving right-first-time quality requires a dedicated, well-motivated and loyal workforce who have been educated and trained to do the job properly. This requires leadership, policy-setting, careful planning and the provision of appropriate resources at every level in the company. Senior managers must demonstrate their own commitment, and the 'quality message' must be communicated and understood by everyone in the organization. Development of a TQM culture usually takes many years and must be demonstrated from senior management level down through the whole organization.

Quality awards and assessment frameworks

Recognition for quality

The realization that quality is a key determinant of the competitive position of a business has brought about a number of methods of recognition. Accordingly, every First World economy has its own government-sponsored award to recognize those organizations that have achieved high quality and to stimulate others to follow the same path. These frameworks are all based on the philosophy of TQM and have much in common. The high profile and publicity gained by the winners of these internationally recognized awards give organizations significant marketing opportunities. Three of the major frameworks in use today are the Deming Prize (Japan), the Malcolm Baldrige Award (USA) and the EFQM European Quality Award.

These frameworks have continued to evolve and are now becoming adopted by countries worldwide in similar forms. The primary use of the frameworks is as a self-assessment tool by which companies can critically review their own activities against a comprehensive set of criteria. Typically an organization prepares a detailed written submission of strengths and weaknesses for all aspects of its operations and business performance. For the best companies (those that demonstrate the highest levels of achievement), the submission can be used to judge them for the award. More importantly, and for most organizations, any weaknesses they have identified can be prioritized and developed into an action plan for business improvement.

The Deming Prize has several categories, including prizes for individuals, small companies and factories. Hundreds of companies apply for the Deming Prize each year. Each applicant must submit a detailed account of quality practices and methods and from these submissions a short-list of companies is selected for site visits and assessment. The Malcolm Baldrige Award, named after a former Secretary of

Commerce, was designed to operate in a similar manner to the Deming Prize. Since 1988, 41 companies have received the Baldrige Award. The award is given in manufacturing, service, small business, education and health care. It has the specific aim of improving the competitiveness and performance of organizations by promoting performance excellence, recognizing achievements and publicizing their successful strategies. Promotion of successful strategies in this way guides other organizations to observe and learn from them through benchmarking. It is the third of the awards mentioned above that we will consider it more detail – the EFQM model.

The EFQM excellence model

Following the success of the Deming Prize and the Malcolm Baldrige Award, fourteen leading European organizations, supported by the European Commission, formed the Brussels-based European Foundation for Quality Management (EFQM) in 1988. By 2001, membership of the EFQM had grown to over 850 member organizations from across Europe and in most sectors of commercial and not-for-profit activity. The mission of the EFQM is to promote self-assessment as key process to drive business improvement. The model, now known as the EFQM excellence model, is shown in Figure 12.2.

The EFQM excellence model is based on the following premise: "Excellent results with respect to performance, through leadership driving policy and strategy, people, partnerships, resources and processes" (EFQM, 2001). Excellence is defined by EFQM as outstanding

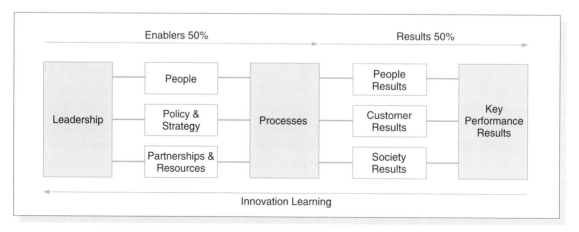

Figure 12.2
The EFQM excellence model.

practice in managing the organization and achieving results, and is based on a set of eight fundamental concepts.

The excellence model contains nine elements, each of which contains a number of subcriteria: five *enablers*, so called because they refer to *how* the organization sets up to do business; and four *results* elements, which refer to *what* the organization achieves by following the model. The self-assessment model can be used by all types and size of organization. Published guidelines are specifically written by the EFQM.

The EFQM excellence model offers a rigorous and structured self-assessment approach to business improvements based on hard facts. Careful assessment against each criterion allows an organization to calculate an overall score from a total possible 1000 points. This score can then be viewed as a benchmark for comparisons with other organizations. Award-winning organizations achieve scores of around 700 points.

One of the most powerful attractions of the model is its use as a self-assessment diagnostic tool. This forms the basis for a company-wide plan of improvement activities, which can be prioritized to yield best results. Improvements can be measured and revisited year after year to observe progress. Benchmarking both internally and externally provides a powerful method of setting realistic improvement targets, and is referred to constantly within the model. Because of its importance, benchmarking will be discussed in more detail later in this chapter.

The enabler criteria

The first five criteria of the EFQM excellence model are devoted to examining how the organization sets itself out to manufacture goods or provide services to customers.

Leadership

This first element looks for visible demonstration of commitment to excellence by all managers within the organization. Managers must develop the mission, vision and be 'role model' leaders, of a culture of excellence. They should define priorities, provide the resources and ensure the management system is developed, implemented and continuously improved. They should also be involved with customers and suppliers promoting partnerships and joint improvement 'win-win' activities.

Policy and strategy

Policy and strategy for any company must be based on comprehensive and relevant information (this being the purpose of strategic analysis). It is important to understand customers' needs and to exploit, as far as possible, the strengths of suppliers. To ensure competitiveness, the organization needs to review performance and use benchmarking to compare with best practice, the competition and other best-in-class organizations.

People

The knowledge, competencies and capabilities of the employees must be identified, managed and developed. The organization should encourage individual and team participation in improvement activities and empower staff to take action.

Partnerships and resources

This refers to all of the resources employed by the company, other than the human resources already covered above. These include the external partnerships, financial resources, information resources, suppliers and materials, buildings, plant and equipment, technology and intellectual property. The company must demonstrate how it manages and exploits its resources to gain competitive advantage.

Processes

Each key process must be systematically designed, measured and managed to established standards (e.g. ISO 9000). Constantly striving to be more competitive requires regular reviews of processes and actual performance levels. Excellent companies talk to their customers and suppliers, and proactively involve them in the design of products and services. The use of *best practice benchmarking* helps identify innovation and new technologies and leads to improvements (see later in this chapter).

The results criteria

The remaining four criteria of the EFQM excellence model examine what the organization is actually achieving. This is with regard to customer results, people results, society results and key performance results. To achieve a high score, a company must have strongly positive trends over at least five years in business results and profitability. Measures must also be in place showing strong satisfaction trends from all stakeholders – i.e. customers, suppliers, employees and the wider community.

Benchmarking

What is benchmarking?

One of the key features established within any of the above frameworks is the importance of *benchmarking*. Superior performers in most industries regularly review themselves against the competition and other best-in-class companies to remain at the top. A report, *Fit for the Future*, published by the Confederation of British Industry (CBI) in 1997 examined the strengths of UK companies. The report concluded: "The most powerful process any company can adopt and which delivers immediate, measurable and sustainable productivity improvements is the transfer of best practice."

This is the key to successful benchmarking – for an organization to analyse its own performance and then compare performance in several areas against competitors. If, for example, one competitor in an industry enjoys a lower rate of waste or higher quality than others, questions can be asked as to what the superior company has done to bring about the superior performance. By using benchmarking in this way, 'best practice' procedures can be emulated and performance improved in the lower performers.

Successful benchmarking usually rests upon the premise that competitors in an industry are willing, to some extent, to share, collaborate or make information available upon their performance and processes. The happy result of successful benchmarking is that all participants in an industry have improved quality performance, so improving customer satisfaction with the industry's products.

Types of benchmarking

In recent years, the interest in benchmarking has grown. What started out as a relatively simple concept has become increasingly complicated. Benchmarking has proved to be a profitable source of income for management consultants who have developed and published many different approaches and methodologies. For any organization just beginning to benchmark, reading the literature will confirm that there are many types of benchmarking in existence. Where do they start? Which form of benchmarking is best?

In this section we will consider the different types under three broad headings: metric, diagnostic and process benchmarking. A simple way is to view them along a continuum, as shown in Figure 12.3.

We can see from Figure 12.3 that there is an increase in effort, resources and costs as we move from metric benchmarking through to full process benchmarking. At the lower end, metric benchmarking can provide an indication of relative performance and perhaps identify leading competitors, but it is unlikely to yield any real ideas on how to change. At best it will only help define performance gaps.

Moving up, diagnostic benchmarking requires a little more effort but in return will identify areas of strength and more detail on areas of weakness for the organization. Done correctly, it will also help prioritize which processes should be targeted for improvement activities.

Process benchmarking requires considerably more resource, effort and time, but organizations successfully completing the process will be rewarded with many benefits of transferred best practice.

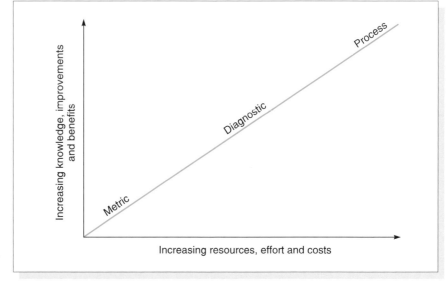

Figure 12.3
Types of
benchmarking.

Metric benchmarking

Many organizations, both in manufacturing and in service-based sectors, use metric benchmarking as a means of direct comparison, both internally and externally, with other organizations. Metrics are performance indicators used as comparative measures. There are many published forms of metric data from which simple comparisons can be drawn – for example, league tables such as those published by government agencies or public sector organizations such as (in the UK) the NHS. Another example is the university league tables published by the *Financial Times*. In the manufacturing sector, examples include the publication of *Manufacturing Winners* by the DTI (1995) or the *Management Today*/Cranfield University Britain's Best Factories Award.

Metric benchmarking is often used by companies to make inter-site comparisons using key performance indicators such as product costs, staffing levels, resources per unit produced, waste or rework levels, stock turnover rates, etc. They are useful provided that each site is measured in the same way using like-for-like comparisons. Perhaps the biggest disadvantage of metric benchmarking is that, even when it shows a performance gap between two companies, it does not explain how better performance can be achieved.

Diagnostic benchmarking

Made in Europe, a report written by IBM consultants and London Business School (Hanson *et al.*, 1994), introduced an approach that measures and compares businesses on world-class scales. The tool used, PROBE (PROmoting Business Excellence), led the way to what is now referred to as diagnostic benchmarking.

This study compared hundreds of manufacturing organizations across Europe, examining the relationship between practice and performance. The research found that good practice correlated strongly with performance. The tool has been followed by a number of similar instruments, some of which have been designed for particular industry sectors. Examples of such tools include *Learning Probe*, developed for use by the Further Education sector, and *Probe for Healthcare*, for use in NHS organizations.

Researchers in Newcastle Business School at the University of Northumbria developed one such instrument, called PILOT[1]. It was a questionnaire-based survey instrument based on PROBE, which asked around 50 questions on practice and performance measures,

---

[1]PILOT is a benchmarking survey tool developed by Newcastle Business School as part of the Regional Competitiveness Project – a three-year project (1996–98), 50% funded through European Regional Development Fund and led by the Northern Development Company.

suitable for both manufacturing and service sector organizations. On completion of the questionnaire, the participating organizations received feedback showing them how they compared against other organizations in the area. Like the PROBE analysis, the PILOT study found that good practice correlated strongly with business performance.

Process benchmarking

By far the most involved form of benchmarking, process benchmarking is where the most substantial benefits can be found. The focus is on any key business process that has been identified as an area for improvement.

Fundamental to the success of process benchmarking is the recognition that many organizations have functions that use generically similar business processes regardless of sector or industry type. Thus, one main advantage of process benchmarking is that businesses need not restrict themselves to observing practices in companies that are considered direct competition. Most business organizations, for example, issue invoices, collect payables (debts), appoint new people, etc., and these types of 'generic' activities can be benchmarked regardless of industry.

Benchmarking activities can be widened to include partners from different sectors and this can enable completely new ways of working to be identified. This can lead to significant improvements in operating efficiency across industrial sectors.

Process benchmarking can be divided into four stages.

1   Understanding the nature and complexity of the business processes that are to be benchmarked. This requires careful process-mapping and measurement of process metrics.
2   Identifying potential and willing benchmarking partners – not always a straightforward task as some corporate cultures resist 'opening up' to outside organizations.
3   Data collection and measurement. It is important to ensure that processes are compared on a like-with-like basis.
4   Implementation of change and transfer of best practice for a given process. This is not always easy because cultural, demographic or technological barriers may present unforeseen problems.

References and further reading

CBI (1997) How competitive is British manufacturing? [foreword]. *Fit for the Future*. London: Confederation of British Industry.

DTI (1995) *Manufacturing Winners*. DTI, TEC National Council and Department of Employment Group.

EFQM (2001) *Introducing Excellence*. Brussels: European Foundation for Quality Management.

Hanson, P., Voss, C., Blackmon, K. and Oak, B. (1994) *Made in Europe: A Four Nations Best Practice Study*. London: IBM Consultancy Group and London Business School.

Imai, M. (1986) *Kaizen: The Key to Japan's Competitive Success*. New York: McGraw-Hill.

Oakland, J.S. (1993) *Total Quality Management*, Second Edition. Oxford: Butterworth-Heinemann.

International and global strategies

Introduction and chapter overview

One of the most important considerations in the implementation of strategy is the extent to which the organization's activities are spread across geographical regions. Some businesses are entirely domestically based, others operate in many countries and yet others operate in almost all regions of the world. This chapter is concerned with a discussion of the key issues surrounding the *why* and *how* questions: Why do organizations expand in this way and how do they go about it? The *why* questions are covered in a discussion of the factors that drive increased internationalization. The *how* questions are answered in a discussion of the market entry options.

Learning objectives

After studying this chapter, students should be able to:

■ define and distinguish between internationalization and globalization;

■ explain the factors that drive globalization;

■ describe and demonstrate the application of Yip's framework for analysing the extent of globalization in an industry and market;

■ explain the major global strategy alternatives;
■ describe the modes of international market entry.

Internationalization and globalization

What is the difference?

Business has been international since the days of the ancient Egyptians, Phoenicians and Greeks. Merchants travelled the known world to sell products manufactured in their home country and to return with products from other countries. Initially, international business simply took the form of exporting and importing. The term *international* describes any business that carries out some of its activities across national boundaries.

Globalization, on the other hand, is more than simply internationalization. A large multinational company is not necessarily a global business. In order for a business to become global in its operations, we would usually expect a number of important characteristics to be in place.

First, global organizations take advantage of the increasing trend towards a convergence of customer needs and wants across international borders (e.g. for fast foods, soft drinks, consumer electronics, etc.; see Levitt, 1983).

Second, global organizations compete in industries that are globalized. In some sectors, successful competition necessitates a presence in almost every part of the world in order to effectively compete in its global market.

Third, global organizations can – and do – locate their value-adding activities in those places in the world where the greatest competitive advantages can be made. This might mean, for example, shifting production to a low-cost region or moving design to a country with skilled labour in the key skill area.

Finally, global organizations are able to integrate and coordinate their international activities between countries. The mentality of 'home base, foreign interests' that has been so prevalent among traditional multinational companies is eroded in the culture of global businesses. They have learned to effectively manage and control the various parts of the business across national borders and despite local cultural differences.

The development of an organization's global strategy, therefore, will be concerned with global competences, global marketing and global configuration and coordination of its value-adding activities (see discussion of value-adding in Chapter 2).

Key concepts

Multinational and transnational companies

Both multinational and transnational companies share the feature that they are usually large and they have direct investments in one or more foreign countries. The foreign investments may be part-shareholdings, but are more usually wholly owned subsidiaries.

The difference is in the degree to which the foreign investments are coordinated. We tend to think of a *transnational company* as one that has a high degree of coordination in its international interests. It will usually have a strategic centre which manages the global operation such that all parts act in accordance with a centrally managed strategic purpose.

The term *multinational company* is usually taken to mean an international company whose foreign interests are not coordinated from a strategic centre.

Globalization of markets and industries

Levitt and market homogenization

It was Levitt (1983) who first argued that changes in technology, societies, economies and politics are producing a 'global village'. By this he meant that consumer needs in many previously separate national markets were becoming increasingly similar throughout the world. Developments in transport have not only made it easier to move products and materials between countries but they have also resulted in a huge increase in the amount that people travel around the world. Such travel educates people to the products available in other countries and, on their return home, they often wish to have access to products and services from overseas. This trend has been reinforced by changes in information technology, particularly those related to cinema and television, which have been important in some aspects of cultural convergence. The development of the WTO (World Trade Organization) and its predecessor, GATT (the General Agreement on Tariffs and Trade), has resulted in huge reductions in the barriers to trade between countries since the Second World War. Rising income levels throughout many parts of the world have also given economic impetus to the development of global markets.

It is not only markets that are in many cases becoming more global. Industries are also becoming more global. The value chains of businesses in many industries span the globe. In the case of the fashion house Yves Saint Laurent, design and marketing are concentrated in France, whereas products are mainly manufactured in the Far East. Organizations concentrate certain of their activities in locations where they hope to obtain cost, quality or other advantages. Other activities, such as distribution, are also often dispersed around the world. The way in which a business configures its activities across national borders can be an important source of competitive advantage. The spread of an organization's value-adding activities around the world also means that there are important advantages to be gained from effective integration and coordination of activities.

Porter and multi-domesticity

Porter (1990) argued that industries can be either global or *multi-domestic*. Multi-domestic industries are those in which competition in each nation is essentially independent. He gave the example of consumer banking, where a bank's domestic reputation and resources in one nation have tended to have little effect on its success in other countries. The international banking industry is, Porter argued, essentially a collection of domestic industries.

Global industries are those in which competition is global. The consumer electronics industry is a good example, where companies such as Philips, Sony and Panasonic compete in almost all countries of the world. The implication would appear to be that businesses should adopt a global strategy in global industries and a multi-local strategy in multi-domestic markets. Yet the situation is not so simple as this. Even markets such as consumer banking are becoming more global.

It is also the case that the degree of globalization of an industry or market may not be uniform. In other words, some aspects of an industry or market may be indicative of globalization whereas others may be indicative of localization. The degree of globalization of an industry can be assessed using Yip's globalization driver framework (Yip, 1992). This is a more useful framework than Porter's because it makes it possible to evaluate both the overall degree of globalization of an industry and which features of the industry are more or less global in nature.

Globalization drivers

Yip's framework

Yip (1992) argued that it is not simply the case that industries are 'global' or 'not global', rather that they can be global in some respects and not in others. Yip's globalization driver framework makes it possible to identify which aspects of an industry are global and which aspects differ locally. Analysis using this framework can play an important role in shaping the global strategy of a business. A global strategy, according to Yip, will be global in many respects but may also include features that are locally oriented.

Yip argued that: "To achieve the benefits of globalization, the managers of a worldwide business need to recognize when industry conditions provide the opportunity to use global strategy levers."

Yip identified four drivers (Figure 13.1) which determine the nature and extent of globalization in an industry. These are:

- market drivers;
- cost drivers;
- government drivers;
- competitive drivers.

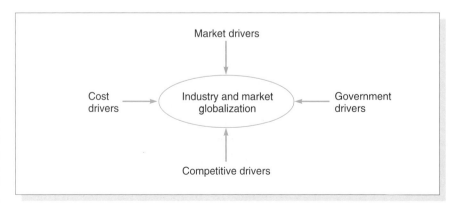

Figure 13.1
A framework describing drivers for internationalization (adapted from Yip, 1992).

Table 13.1 shows a breakdown of the globalization drivers. We will consider each of these drivers in turn.

Table 13.1
A summary of the globalization drivers

Market globalization drivers	Cost globalization drivers
▪ common customer needs ▪ global customers ▪ global distribution channels ▪ transferable marketing techniques ▪ presence in lead countries	▪ global scale economies ▪ steep experience curve effect ▪ sourcing efficiencies ▪ favourable logistics ▪ differences in country costs (including exchange rates) ▪ high product development costs ▪ rapidly changing technology
Government globalization drivers	Competitive globalization drivers
▪ favourable trade policies ▪ compatible technical standards ▪ common marketing regulations ▪ government-owned competitors and customers ▪ host government concerns	▪ high exports and imports ▪ competitors from different continents ▪ interdependence of countries ▪ competitors globalized

Market globalization drivers

The degree of globalization of a market will depend upon the extent to which there are common customer needs, global customers, global distribution channels, transferable marketing and lead countries. It is not simply a case of a market being global or not global. Managers must seek to establish which, if any, aspects of their market are global.

Common customer needs

Probably the single most important market globalization driver is the extent to which customers in different countries share the same need or want for a product. The extent of shared need will depend upon cultural, economic, climatic, legal and other similarities and differences. There are numerous examples of markets where customer needs are becoming more similar. Examples include motor vehicles, soft drinks, fast food, consumer electronics and computers. The importance of McDonald's, Burger King and Pizza Hut in fast food, of Coca Cola and Pepsi Cola in soft drinks and of Sony and Panasonic in consumer electronics serves to illustrate converging customer needs in certain markets. Levitt (1983) referred to this similarity of tastes and preference as increasing *market homogenization* – all markets demanding the same products, regardless of their domestic culture and traditional preferences.

Global customers and channels

Global customers purchase products or services in a coordinated way from the best global sources. Yip identifies two types of global customers:

1 *National global customers* – customers who seek the best suppliers in the world and then use the product or service in one country; for example, national defence purchasers who try to source the highest specification weapons and other military hardware from around the world for use by the domestic armed forces.
2 *Multinational global customers* – they similarly seek the best suppliers in the world but then use the product or service obtained in many countries; for example, transnational corporations source components for their products globally to ensure optimal quality standards.

Examples of markets with global customers include automobile components, advertising (advertising agencies) and electronics. Nissan, for example, manufacture motor cars in a number of different locations around the world including Japan, the UK and Spain, but source many components for all of these locations globally. Businesses serving global customers must "be present in all the customers' major markets" (Yip, 1992).

Alongside global customers there are sometimes global, or more often regional, distribution channels which serve the global customers. Global customers and channels will contribute towards the development of a global market.

Transferable marketing

Transferable marketing describes the extent to which elements of the marketing mix, such as brand names and promotions, can be used globally without local adaptations. Clearly, when adaptation is not required it is indicative of a global market. In this way brands such as McDonald's, Coca Cola and Nike are used globally. Yet advertising for Nike can be both global and locally adapted according to the popularity of different sports in different parts of the world. If marketing is transferable it will favour a global market.

Lead countries

When, as Porter (1990) found, there are certain countries which lead in particular industries, then it becomes critical for global competitors to participate in these lead countries in order to be exposed to the sources of innovation. Lead countries are those that are ahead in product and/or process innovation in their industry. These lead countries help to produce global standards and hence global industries and markets. Japan, for example, has leadership in the consumer electronics industry and leads developments within it, whereas the USA is the lead country in microcomputer and Internet software.

Cost globalization drivers

The potential to reduce costs by global configuration of value-adding activities is an important spur towards the globalization of certain industries. If there are substantial cost advantages to be obtained then an industry will tend to be global.

Global-scale economies

When an organization serves a global market, it is able to gain much greater economies of scale than if it serves only domestic or regional markets. Similarly, serving global markets also gives considerable potential for economies of scope. Thus, businesses such as Procter and Gamble and Unilever who produce household products such as detergents gain huge economies of scope in research, product development and marketing.

Key concepts

Economies of scale and scope

- *Economies of scale* describe the benefits that are gained when increasing volume results in lower unit costs. Although economies of scale can arise in all parts of the value chain, it is probably best understood by illustrating it using purchasing as an example. An individual purchasing one single item will pay more *per item* than a large company buying many of the same item. It is said that the purchaser who is able to purchase in bulk (because of the size and structure of the buyer) enjoys scale economies over smaller organizations who buy in at lower volumes.

- *Economy of scope* is a concept that describes the benefits that can arise in one product or market area as a result of activity in another. For example, research into material properties for the benefit of the NASA space programme (one area of scope) has resulted in advances in other areas such as fabrics, non-stick pans and coatings for aircraft. Organizations who invest heavily in R&D (such as pharmaceutical companies) are among those who are always seeking economies of scope – seeking to use breakthroughs in one area to benefit another.

Steep experience curve effect

When there is a steep learning curve in production and marketing, businesses serving global markets will tend to obtain the greatest benefits. In many high-tech and service industries there are steep learning curves, yielding the greatest benefits to global businesses.

Key concept

Learning curve

The idea of the learning curve (see Figure 13.2) has been used in many areas of life – not just in business. It describes the rate at which an individual or an organization learns to perform a particular task. The gradient of the beginning of the curve is referred to as its 'steepness' and is the most important part. The steeper this first part, the quicker the task is being learned. The general shape of a learning curve is described as *exponential* because the gradient usually decreases along its length as the time taken to perform the task decreases as those performing the task become more accomplished at it.

When a lecturer sits down to mark a batch of exam papers, he must first familiarize himself with the questions and the answers that are expected. Having done that, the first paper will take the longest of all to mark. When the lecturer has internalized all of the questions and

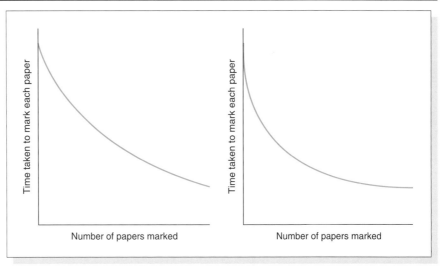

Figure 13.2
Learning curves. A
shallow learning
curve (left)
indicates a slow
learner; a steep
learning curve
(right) indicates a
fast learner.

answers, the time taken to mark each paper will reduce until the last few papers take the shortest time of all.

Sourcing efficiencies

If there are efficiency gains to be made by centralized sourcing carried out globally then this will drive an industry towards globalization. Businesses such as those in sports apparel and fashion clothing benefit from global sourcing to obtain lowest prices and highest quality standards.

Favourable logistics

If transportation costs comprise a relatively high proportion of sales value, there will be every incentive to concentrate production in a few, large facilities. If transport costs are relatively small, such as with consumer electronic goods, production can be located in several (or many) locations which are chosen on the basis of other cost criteria such as land or labour costs.

Differences in country costs

Production costs (materials, labour, etc.) vary from country to country, which, like favourable logistics, can stimulate globalization. Thus, countries with lower production costs will tend to attract businesses to locate activities in the country. Many Asian countries have been chosen as centres for production because of their favourable cost conditions. Although countries such as Thailand have suffered in some respects because of the devaluation of their currency in 1997–98, from the point of view of being chosen as centres for production they have benefited.

Rapidly changing technology and high product development costs

Product life cycles are shortening as the pace of technological change increases. At the same time R&D costs are increasing in many industries. Such product development costs can only be recouped by high sales in global markets. Domestic markets simply do not yield the volumes of sales required to cover high R&D costs. Thus industries such as pharmaceuticals and automobiles face very rapidly changing technology and hypercompetition, together with high development costs. As a consequence, they must operate in global markets so as to ensure the volumes of sales necessary to recoup these costs.

Government globalization drivers

Since the Second World War many governments have taken individual and collective action to reduce barriers to global trade.

Favourable trade policies

The World Trade Organization (WTO) and its predecessor, the General Agreement on Tariffs and Trade (GATT), have done much to reduce barriers to trade which have, in the past, hindered globalization of many industries. Although there are still significant barriers to trade in certain areas, the movement towards freedom of trade has been substantial, thereby favouring globalization. The growth of customs unions and 'single markets' such as the European Union and the North American Free Trade Area (NAFTA) have also made an important contribution in this regard.

Compatible technical standards and common marketing regulations

Many of the differences in technical standards between countries which hindered globalization in the past have been reduced. For example, telecommunications standards, which have traditionally differed between countries, are increasingly being superseded by international standards. Similarly, standards are converging in the pharmaceutical, airline and computing industries which makes it easier to produce globally accepted products.

There remain important differences in advertising regulations between countries, with the UK regulations among the strictest. Generally, however, these differences are being eroded and this is expected to favour greater globalization.

Government-owned competitors and customers

Government-owned competitors, which often enjoy state subsidies, can act as a stimulus to globalization as they frequently compete with other global competitors, thus being forced to become more efficient and global market oriented. On the other hand, government-owned customers tend to favour domestic suppliers, which can act as a barrier to globalization. The privatization of many state-owned businesses in many European countries has reduced this barrier to globalization.

Host government concerns

The attitudes and policies of host government concerns can either hinder or favour globalization. In certain circumstances, host governments may favour the entry of global businesses into domestic industries and markets, which will assist globalization. For example, the UK government has, in recent years, done much to attract inward investment by Japanese and Korean companies. The more governments that espouse such policies, the greater will be globalization of an industry. In other cases, host governments will seek to protect industries that they see as strategically important and will attempt to prevent foreign businesses from entry.

Competitive globalization drivers

The greater the strength of the competitive drivers, the greater will be the tendency for an industry to globalize. Global competition in an industry will become more intense when:

- there is a high level of import and export activity between countries;
- the competitors in the industry are widely spread (they will often be on different continents);
- the economies of the countries involved are interdependent;
- competitors in the industry are already globalized.

High exports and imports

The higher the level of exports and imports of products and services, the greater will be the pressure for globalization of an industry.

Competitors from different continents

The more countries that are represented in an industry and the more widely spread they are, the greater the likelihood of globalization.

Interdependence of countries

If national economies are already relatively interdependent, then this will act as a stimulus for increased globalization. Such interdependence may arise through, for example, multiple trading links in other industries, through being a part of a single market or through being in a shared political alliance.

Competitors globalized

If a competitor is already globalized and employing a global strategy, there will be pressure on other businesses in the industry to globalize as well. Globalization in the automotive industry is high because of the pressure on organizations to compete globally. An automobile manufacturer will struggle to survive if it only serves domestic markets.

Using the globalization driver framework

Yip's globalization driver framework provides an extremely useful tool for analysing the degree of globalization of an industry or market. Equally, it makes possible an understanding of which particular aspects of an industry or market are global and which aspects are localized. Each of the drivers must be analysed for the industry and market under consideration and the results of the analysis will play an important role in assisting managers to form the global strategy of their organization. The results will help to determine which features of the strategy are globally standardized and which features are locally adapted.

There are several models that explain the basis of global strategy. This chapter explains the frameworks developed by Porter (1986a,b, 1990) and Yip (1992). Porter focuses on adapting the generic strategy framework to global conditions and the role of configuration and coordination of value-adding activities in securing global competitive advantage. Yip develops the concept of 'total global strategy' based upon his globalization driver framework.

Although these are the models considered in this chapter, interested readers should consider reading the work of Bartlett and Ghoshal (1987, 1989), Prahalad and Hamel (1986) and Stonehouse *et al.* (2000).

Porter's global generic strategies

We learned in Chapter 8 that Porter (1980) argued that competitive advantage rests upon a business selecting and adopting one of the three generic strategies (differentiation, cost leadership or focus) to modify the five competitive forces in its favour in order to earn higher profits than the industry average. In 1986, Porter extended the generic strategy framework to global business. The model suggests that a business operating in international markets has five strategy alternatives (Figure 13.2). The five strategic postures are defined according to their position with respect to two intersecting continua: the extent to which the industry is globalized or country-centred (horizontal axis), and the breadth of the segments served by the competitors in an industry (vertical axis), which, put simply, means the number of different customer groups that are served by an industry.

The five strategic postures are:

1 *Global cost leadership* – the business seeks to be the lowest cost producer of a product globally. Globalization provides the opportunity for high-volume sales and greater economies of scale and scope than domestic competitors.
2 *Global differentiation* – the business seeks to differentiate products and services globally, often on the basis of a global brand name.
3 *Global segmentation* – this is the global variant of a focus strategy in which a single market segment is targeted on a worldwide basis employing either cost leadership or differentiation.
4 *Protected markets* – a business that identifies national markets where its particular business is favoured or protected by the host government.

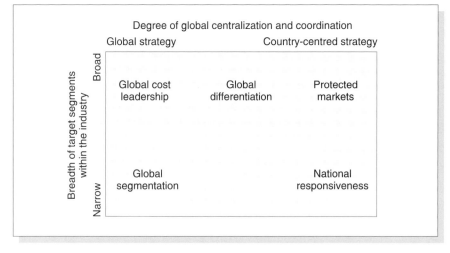

Figure 13.3
Porter's global
strategy framework
(adapted from
Porter, 1986).

5 *National responsiveness* – the business adapts its strategy to meet the distinctive needs of local markets (i.e. not a global strategy). Suitable for purely domestic businesses.

The model suffers from flaws similar to those discussed in Chapter 8 relating to the generic strategy framework. As in the case of the conventional understanding of generic strategy, it is possible for a business to pursue a hybrid international strategy. Nissan, for example, concentrates both on cost control and also on ensuring that it differentiates its products on the basis of their reliability.

Porter's global strategy: configuration and coordination of internal activities

One of Porter's most important contributions to understanding global strategy is his work on the global value chain (1986, 1990). Porter makes the case that global competitive advantage depends upon configuring and coordinating the activities of a business in a unique way on a worldwide basis. To put it another way, competitive advantage results from the global scope of an organization's activities and the effectiveness with which it coordinates them. Porter (1986, 1990) argues that global competitive advantage depends upon two sets of decisions:

1 *Configuration of value-adding activities* – managers must decide in which nations they will carry out each of the activities in the value chain of their business. Configuration can be broad (involving many countries) or narrow (few or one countries).

2 *Coordination of value-adding activities* – managers must decide the most effective way of coordinating the value-adding activities that are carried out in different parts of the world.

Configuration and coordination present four broad alternatives, as illustrated in Figure 13.4. In the case of configuration, an organization can choose to disperse its activities to a range of locations around the world, or it may choose to concentrate key activities in locations that present certain advantages. Many businesses concentrate the manufacture of their products in countries where costs are low but skill levels are good. Many clothing manufacturers manufacture their products in the Far East where labour costs are low but tailoring standards are high. An organization can decide to coordinate its worldwide activities or to manage them locally in each part of the world. The latter approach misses the opportunity for global management economies of scale. For Porter, the 'purest global strategy' is when an organization concentrates key activities in locations giving competitive advantages and coordinates activities on a global basis. In the long term, according to Porter, organizations should move towards 'purest global strategy' as far as is practicable.

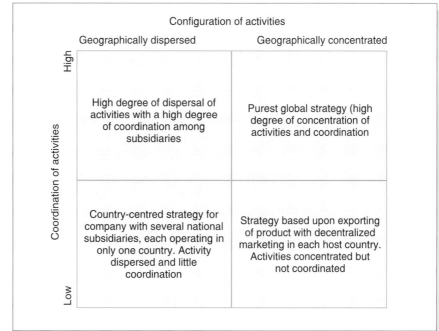

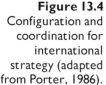

Figure 13.4
Configuration and coordination for international strategy (adapted from Porter, 1986).

'Total' global strategy

Yip's stages in total global strategy

Yip (1992) argued that successful global strategy must be based upon a comprehensive globalization analysis of the drivers we encountered above. Managers of a global business must, he contended, evaluate the globalization drivers for their industry and market and must formulate their global strategy on the basis of this analysis. If, for example, they find that customer demand is largely homogeneous for their product, then they can produce a largely standardized product for sale throughout the world. If, on the other hand, they find that there are few cost advantages to global concentration of manufacturing because of unfavourable logistics or adverse economies of scale, they may choose to disperse their manufacturing activities around the world to be close to their customers in different parts of the world. Thus, the 'total global strategy' of an organization can be a mix of standardization and local adaptation as market and industry conditions dictate.

Yip went on to identify three stages in developing a 'total global strategy':

1 *Developing a core strategy* – this will, in effect, involve building core competences and a generic or hybrid strategy which can potentially give global competitive advantage (see Chapter 8).
2 *Internationalizing the core strategy* – this will be the stage at which the core competences and generic strategy are introduced to international markets and when the organization begins to situate its value-adding activities in locations where competitive advantages such as low cost and access to materials or skills are available. This will include choice of which markets the business will enter and the means by which it will enter them.
3 *Globalizing the international strategy* – this stage is based upon coordinating and integrating the core competences and strategy on a global basis. It will also include deciding which elements of the strategy are to be standardized and which are to be locally adapted on the basis of the strength of the globalization drivers in the industry and market.

Key strategic decisions

Once a business has developed core competences and strategies that can potentially be exploited globally, the decisions must be made as to where and how to employ them. Initial moves into overseas markets will involve market development as such markets and segments can be regarded as new to the business. The initial market development may then be followed by product development and, perhaps, diversification (see Chapter 8).

When a business enters international and global markets it will be necessary to build new competences alongside those that have brought about domestic competitive advantage. These new competences could well be in the areas of global sourcing and logistics, and global management.

The globalization of a business does not happen overnight. It may well involve entry to key countries with the largest markets first, followed by entry to less important countries later. In the initial stages of globalization the key decisions are usually as follows:

1   which countries are to be entered first;
2   in which countries are value-adding activities to be located;
3   which market development strategies are to be employed to gain entry to chosen overseas markets.

Market entry decisions

Decision criteria

The decision as to which countries and markets are to be entered first will be based upon a number of important factors:

■ *The potential size of the market* – is the market for the product in the country likely to be significant? This will, in turn, be determined by the factors following.
■ *Economic factors* – are income levels adequate to ensure that significant numbers of people are likely to be able to afford the product?
■ *Cultural and linguistic factors* – is the culture of the country likely to favour acceptance of the product to be offered?
■ *Political factors* – what are the factors that may limit entry to markets in the host country?
■ *Technological factors* – are levels of technology adequate to support provision of the product in the host market and are technological standards compatible?

To begin with, a business will choose to enter markets in those countries where the above conditions are most favourable.

Location of value-adding activities

Managers must determine within which countries they will locate key value-adding activities of their business. They will seek to gain cost, skill and resource advantages. In other words, they will attempt to locate activities in countries where there are production advantages to be gained.

Such advantages depend upon:

- *wage levels* – low wage levels will assist in low production costs;
- *skill levels* – there must be suitably skilled labour available;
- *availability of materials* – suitable materials must be accessible;
- *infrastructure* – transport and communications must be favourable to the logistics of the business.

The existence of these conditions within a country will, in turn, depend upon:

- *economic factors* – level of economic development, wage levels, exchange rate conditions;
- *social factors* – attitudes to work, levels of education and training;
- *political factors* - legislation favouring investment, etc.;
- *technological factors* – levels of technology and transport and communications infrastructure of the country.

Market development methods

Once decisions have been made as to which countries' markets are to be entered and where value-adding activities are to be located, the task for management becomes the determination of which method of development to employ to enter another country. Broadly speaking, a business can choose either internal or external methods for development of overseas markets (see Chapter 11). Internal methods are usually slower, but tend to entail lower risk. External methods involve the business developing relationships with other businesses. Internal methods of development include direct exporting, overseas manufacturing, local assembly and establishing overseas subsidiaries. External methods include joint ventures and alliances, mergers and acquisitions, franchising and licensing. The choice of method will depend upon a number of factors:

- the size of the investment required or the amount of investment capital available;
- knowledge of the country to be entered and potential risk involved (e.g. risk of political instability);
- revenue and cash flow forecasts and expectations;
- operating cost considerations;
- control considerations (some investment options will have implications for the parent company to control activity in the host country).

Internal development methods

Internal methods are based upon the organization exploiting its own resources and competences and involve the organization carrying out some of its activities overseas. This may be exporting its products or setting up some form of production facilities abroad. The advantages of internal methods of development are that they maximize future revenue from sales abroad and they make possible a high degree of control over overseas activities. On the other hand, they can involve significant risk if knowledge of the host country and its markets is limited, and they may require considerable direct investment from the business.

The major internal methods of development overseas are direct exporting and development of an overseas facility.

Direct exporting

Direct exporting is the transfer of goods (or services) across national borders from the home production facility. Such exporting may simply be shipping a product or, as sales increase, a sales offices may be set up overseas. Exporting, at its simplest, is the marketing abroad of a product made in an organization's home country.

To avoid some of the pitfalls of direct exporting (e.g. lack of local knowledge and access to distribution channels), many exporting businesses make use of local agents or distribute their products through locally based retailers (known as a *piggyback* distribution arrangement).

Overseas production or assembly

Organizations may choose to manufacture or assemble their product overseas. There are a number of reasons for direct investment.

Transport costs for the finished product may be so high as to discourage exporting, or the business wishes to take advantage of local cost advantages. In some industries, direct investment may be an appropriate option to circumvent import restrictions put in place by host governments.

Internal development may involve establishing a foreign subsidiary of the business. This is the case when it is favourable for the parent company to have total control of its overseas operations, decision-making and profits. Such a subsidiary may carry out the full range of activities of the parent business or it may be only a manufacturing or marketing subsidiary.

External development methods

External methods of development involve the organization entering into relationships with businesses in a host country. External development methods can take the form of alliances or joint ventures, mergers or acquisitions, or franchises (see Chapter 11 for a discussion of these topics). Such methods have the advantages of providing local knowledge – potentially reducing risks – and reducing investment costs (except in the case of mergers or acquisitions). The major disadvantages (again except in the case of mergers and acquisitions) are reduced revenues and reduced control of activities as optimal income is traded off against the advantage of lower financial exposure.

International alliances and joint ventures

Alliances and joint ventures allow a business to draw upon the skills, local knowledge, resources and competences of a locally based company. They reduce the risks of entry to overseas markets by providing local knowledge and they help reduce investment costs. The Honda–Rover alliance (1979–94) provided Rover with access to Honda's technology and reputation and gave Honda access to the European market via Rover's inside knowledge and production facilities (see the Honda–Rover case study in Part V of this book).

International mergers and acquisitions

A business may use mergers or acquisitions to enter overseas markets. Such mergers and acquisitions give a business access to the knowledge, resources and competences of a business based in the host country, thus reducing some of the risks of market entry.

International franchising and licensing

A franchise is an arrangement under which a franchiser supplies a franchisee with a tried-and-tested brand name, products and expertise in return for the payment of a proportion of profits or sales. The major advantage to the franchiser is that the risk, investment and operating costs of entering overseas markets are reduced considerably. At the same time, the franchisee can contribute their local knowledge at the same time also benefiting from the lower risks associated with an established business idea. Much of Burger King's expansion overseas has come through franchise development.

Licensing is similar to franchising buts involves a producer transferring certain rights to a licensee for the sole use in a host country of its established brand, recipe, registered design or similar piece of intellectual property. The licensee pays the licensor a royalty for the use of the intellectual property and, as with franchising, gains from the established market position of the brand. Licensing is widely used in brewing and in some scientific industries.

References and further reading

Bartlett, C. and Ghoshal, S. (1987) Managing across borders: new organisational responses. *Sloan Management Review*, Fall, 45–53.

Bartlett, C. and Ghoshal, S. (1989) *Managing Across Borders: The Transnational Solution*. Cambridge, MA: Harvard Business School Press.

Douglas, S.P. and Wind, Y. (1987) The myth of globalisation. *Columbia Journal of World Business*, Winter, 19–29.

Doz, Y. (1986) *Strategic Management in Multinational Companies*. Pergamon Press.

Hamel, G. and Prahalad, C.K. (1985) Do you really have a global strategy. *Harvard Business Review*, July/August.

Heene, A. and Sanchez, R. (eds) (1997) *Competence-Based Strategic Management*. New York: John Wiley.

Henzler, H. and Rall, W. (1986) Facing up to the globalisation challenge. *McKinsey Quarterly*, Winter.

Levitt, T. (1983) The globalisation of markets. *Harvard Business Review*, May/June.

Mintzberg, H., Quinn, J.B. and Ghoshal, S. (1995) *The Strategy Process: Concepts, Contexts and Cases*, European Edition. Englewood Cliffs, NJ: Prentice Hall.

Porter, M.E. (1980) *Competitive Strategy: Techniques for Analysing Industries and Competitors*. New York: Free Press.

Porter, M.E. (1985) *Competitive Advantage*. New York: Free Press.

Porter, M.E. (1986a) *Competition in Global Business*. Cambridge, MA: Harvard University Press.

Porter, M.E. (1986b) Changing patterns of international competition. *California Management Review*, 28(2), 9–40.

Porter, M.E. (1990) *The Competitive Advantage of Nations*. New York: Free Press.

Prahalad, C.K. and Doz, Y.L. (1986) *The Multinational Mission: Balancing Local Demands and Global Vision*. New York: Free Press.

Prahalad, C.K. and Hamel, G. (1990) The core competence of the corporation. *Harvard Business Review*, 79–91.

Stonehouse, G., Hamill, J., Campbell, D.J. and Purdie, A. (2000) Global and Transnational Business Management and Strategy. Chichester: John Wiley.

Yip, G.S. (1992) *Total Global Strategy: Managing for Worldwide Competitive Advantage*. Englewood Cliffs, NJ: Prentice Hall.

Social responsibility and business ethics

Business ethics is one of the most argued-about areas of business research. Almost every possible position is reflected in the literature. This chapter aims to set out an impartial discussion of the subject, beginning with an introduction to the issues surrounding the debate about the relationships between business and society. The stockholder and stakeholder positions are discussed. The stakeholder position is presented as a kind of social contract and the ways in which stake-holders are classified are discussed. The debate is explored further using Donaldson and Preston's (1995) framework for understanding the stakeholder debate. The nature of stakeholder concerns is presented and the strategic postures that businesses can adopt with regard to social concerns are outlined. Finally, some of the ways in which businesses attempt to discharge social responsibility are discussed.

After studying this chapter, students should be able to:

- understand the stockholder and stakeholder positions as descriptors of business relationship to society;
- describe the ways in which stakeholders have been classified;
- describe the instrumental and normative approaches to the stakeholder relationship;

- explain the environmental and ethical concerns of stake-holders;
- describe the strategic postures that businesses can adopt in respect to social issues;
- discuss the mechanisms by which businesses discharge their social responsibilities.

Business and its relationship to society

Introduction

Any regular reader of the news will be aware of a trend over recent years towards an increasing awareness of the behaviour of business with respect to what have become known as 'ethical' or 'social' issues. Alleged 'bad' behaviour such as irresponsible environmental behaviour, the way in which employees are treated, suspect product safety and responses to accidents such as oil spills are often reported and discussed in some depth in the press and on television.

Events such as these raise an important strategic question: What is the precise nature of a business's relationship to society? The traditional 'economic theory of the firm' posits the notion that businesses exist primarily to make profits for their owners. Some writers in this field have taken the view that the only moral behaviour of business is that which is dedicated to maximizing profits for its shareholders (see, for example, Friedman, 1970). Others have adopted the diametrically opposite position – that businesses have a moral obligation to those constituencies from which they directly or indirectly benefit (see, for example, Clarkson, 1995; Evan and Freeman, 1993; Freeman, 1994). This area of argument has been called the stakeholder–stockholder debate.

The stockholder position

The stockholder position on business's responsibility to society argues that businesses exist primarily for their owners (usually shareholders). Accordingly, any business behaviour that renders profit performance suboptimal is not only theft from shareholders but will also, eventually, lead to a level of business performance that will harm all of the stakeholders (including employees, suppliers, etc.).

In what has become a well-known article, the Nobel Laureate Professor Milton Friedman contended in 1970 that "the moral obligation of business is to increase its profits". Friedman argued that the one and only obligation of company directors (who are the legal agents of shareholders' financial interests) is to act in such a way as to maximize the financial rate of return on the owners' shares. The capitalist system upon which the Western economies is based rests in large part upon the presupposition that investments made in shares (e.g. in pension funds, unit trusts, etc.) will perform well. The profitable performance of shares lies in an increase in the share's value and in the rate of dividend per share – objectives that can only be served by financial profits.

Proponents of stockholder theory argue that, because the only moral duty of directors is to maximize shareholders' wealth, then the activities of business beyond profit-making are actually no concern of other stakeholders. The intellectual pedigree of this view of social responsibility can be traced back over two hundred years.

The classical economic philosophy of Adam Smith (Smith, 1776) concerns the maximization of benefit to society through the economic mechanism whereby all individuals and businesses act freely in their own economic best interests. Smith's 'invisible hand' principle shows how, when each individual and business is free of external influence to make economic decisions, then ultimately everybody in society will benefit. Profitable business stimulates both economic growth in the macroeconomy and increased employment. Increased rates of employment, in turn, stimulate spending power in the economy, and hence businesses further increase their profits. If this virtuous cycle can be maintained, then society becomes prosperous and the net effect is very positive.

The stakeholder position

The stakeholder position posits that organizations, like individual people, are citizens of society. Citizenship carries with it certain *rights* – from which we benefit – but also certain *obligations*. Evidently, we enjoy the benefits of society, such as civil peace, freedom under the rule of law, the right to own and enjoy our property and so on. In return, we accept our obligations – both legal and social. Legally, we collectively agree to obey the law, to pay our taxes and to respect civil authority. Socially, most of us accept that society works best when we accord each other certain basic civilities. We apologize when we bump into somebody in a corridor, we sympathize with and comfort those going through hard times and we celebrate with each other when one of us gets good news.

In other words, there is a reciprocation package. If we wish to continue to enjoy the benefits of citizenship, then we must, in exchange, also accept our responsibilities. Turning to business, it is obvious that businesses enjoy certain benefits from society. They gain finance capital and employees from society and they rely on the continuing support of customers, local communities, suppliers and others. The stakeholder view of the business–society relationship argues that, because businesses benefit from the goodwill of society, they owe certain duties in return.

The implications of this proposition are far-reaching. In essence, stakeholder theory argues that shareholders are neither the sole owners of a business nor the sole beneficiaries of its activities. Although shareholders are undeniably one stakeholder group, they are far from being the only group who expect to benefit from business activity and, accordingly, are just one of those groups who have a legitimate right to influence a company's strategic objectives.

One way of conceptualizing stakeholder theory is as a *social contract*. Under a social contract, social institutions (such as governments or businesses) can only continue to enjoy social legitimacy if they continually modify their policies and activities to accord with societal opinion. We can readily appreciate that this must be the case for a democratically elected government as political parties seeking office offer policies that they feel will accord with the electorate's aspirations. If, during a government's term of office, policy objectives diverge from those of the electorate, the probability that they will be removed from office at the next election is increased.

Key concept

Social contract

Social contract theory posits the notion that any social institution exists alongside its constituencies via a social contract. The concept is a very old one, but successive thinkers since the seventeenth century have modified our understanding of it. The English philosophers Thomas Hobbes (1588–1679) and John Locke (1632–1704) developed the theory to explain the relationship between a government and the people over which it governs. In the twentieth century, the theory was modified to help to explain the relationship between powerful business organizations and the stakeholders that they can influence (see, for example, Rawls, 1971; Donaldson, 1982).

The essence of the theory is one of reciprocal responsibility. The constituency agrees to accept the authority of the powerful institution and the institution agrees to act in the best interests of its constituencies. If either party breaks the terms of the contract, then, it is argued, the nature of the contract is destroyed.

With respect to the business–stakeholder relationship, a social contract is said to exist between a powerful business organization and those groups in society upon which it relies. The stakeholders (in effect) agree to support the activities of the organization (say as employees, customers, etc.) as long as the organization acts in a manner that is acceptable to the stakeholders.

The problem is, of course, that businesses are not subject to election by their constituents. Accordingly, according to social contract theory, businesses act in such a way as to accord with their stakeholders' concerns. There are a number of ways in which organizations demonstrate their policies to stakeholders and we will return to this theme later.

Ways of classifying stakeholders

We encountered the idea of stakeholders in Chapter 1, where we learned that a stakeholder was 'Any group or individual who can affect or [be] affected by the achievement of an organization's objectives' (Freeman, 1984, p. 46).

However, given the broad range of parties that are included in most definitions of 'stakeholder', there are bound to be difficulties in formulating strategy if all stakeholder opinions are to be treated with equal weight. Who could honestly argue, for example, that the owner of a local bar should or does have the same influence over strategy as the chief executive or a majority shareholder? It seems, therefore, that not all stakeholders are equal. A number of ways of classifying stakeholders have been advanced and these are examined in the next part of the chapter.

Criteria for distinguishing between stakeholders

In addition to the power–interest map (which we encountered in Chapter 1), other writers in the literature have attempted to classify stakeholders according to criteria based on how stakeholders relate to the organization's activities.

Narrow and wide stakeholders

Evan and Freeman (1993) classified stakeholders as *narrow* and *wide*, where the criterion for selection into each category is the extent to which stakeholders are affected by the organization's policies and strategies. Narrow stakeholders (those that are the most affected by the organization's policies) will usually include shareholders, management, employees, suppliers and customers that are dependent on the organization's output. Wider stakeholders (those less affected) may typically include government, less-dependent customers, the wider community (as opposed to local communities) and other peripheral groups. The Evans and Freeman model may lead us to conclude that an organization has a higher degree of responsibility and accountability to its narrower stakeholders. It may be excused for paying less attention to the concerns of its wider stakeholders.

Primary and secondary stakeholders

Clarkson (1995) drew a distinction between *primary* and *secondary* stakeholders. According to Clarkson: 'A primary stakeholder group is one without whose continuing participation the corporation cannot survive as a going concern'. Hence, whereas Evans and Freeman view stakeholders as *being* (or not being) *influenced* by an organization, Clarkson sees the important distinction as being between those that do *influence* an organization and those that do not. For most organizations, primary stakeholders (those most vital to an organization) will include government (through its tax and legislative influence), customers and suppliers. Secondary stakeholders (those without whose 'continuing participation' the company can probably still exist) will therefore include communities and, in some cases, the management of the organization itself.

Active and passive stakeholders

Mahoney (1994) divided stakeholders into those that are *active* and those that are *passive*. Active stakeholders are those that seek to participate in the organization's activities. These stakeholders may or may not be actually a part of the organization's formal structure. Management and employees obviously fall into this active category, but some parties from outside an organization may also fall into this category such as regulators (in the case of UK privatized utilities) and environmental pressure groups. Passive stakeholders, in contrast, are those that do not normally seek to participate in an organization's policy-making. This is not to say that passive stakeholders are any less interested or any less powerful, but they do not seek to take an active part in the organization's strategy. Passive stakeholders will normally include most shareholders, government and local communities.

Descriptions of the organization–stakeholder relationship

Donaldson and Preston's framework

Whatever model of stakeholder model one finds most appealing, we turn now to the question as to *why* organizations do or do not take account of stakeholder concerns in their strategy formulation and implementation. A parallel can be drawn between the ways in which organizations view their stakeholders and the ways in which individual people consider (or do not consider) the views of other people. Some people are concerned about others' opinions of them, whereas other people seem to have little or no regard for others' concerns. Furthermore, the reasons *why* individuals care about others' concerns will also vary.

In attempting to address this issue, Donaldson and Preston (1995) drew a distinction between two motivations describing *why* organizations accede to stakeholder concerns. They describe these two contrasting motivations as the *instrumental* and the *normative*.

The instrumental view of stakeholders

The *instrumental* view of stakeholder relations posits that organizations take stakeholder opinions into account only insofar as they are consistent with other, more important, economic objectives (e.g. profit maximization). Accordingly, it may be that a business modifies its objectives in the light of environmental concerns *but only* because acquiescence to stakeholder opinion is the best way of optimizing profit or achieving other business success. If the loyalty or commitment of an important primary or active stakeholder group is threatened, it is likely that the organization will modify its objectives because not to do so would threaten to reduce its economic performance (e.g. profitability). It follows from the instrumental stakeholder approach that an organization's values are guided by its stakeholders' opinions – it may not have any inherent moral values of its own except for the over-riding profit motive.

The normative view of stakeholders

The *normative* view of stakeholder theory differs from the instrumental view because it describes not *what is*, but what *should be*. The most commonly cited moral framework used in describing that which *should be* is derived from the philosophy of the German ethical thinker Immanuel Kant (1724–1804). Kant's moral philosophy centred around the notion of civil duties which, Kant argued, are important in maintaining and increasing the net good in society. Kantian ethics are in part based upon the notion that we each have a moral duty to each other in respect of taking account of each others' concerns and opinions. Not to do so will result in the atrophy of social cohesion and will ultimately lead to everybody being (morally and possibly economically) worse off.

Extending this argument to stakeholder theory, the normative view argues that organizations should accommodate stakeholder concerns, not because of what the organization can 'get out of it' for its own profit, but because it observes its moral duty to each stakeholder. The normative view sees stakeholders as ends in themselves and not as merely instrumental in the achievement of other ends.

Stakeholder concerns

The social concerns of stakeholders

We now turn to the issues that are most frequently raised as being areas of concern. The most frequently mentioned stakeholder concerns can be divided into two broad and interconnected categories:

1 concerns over the organization's attitude towards the *natural environment*;

2 concerns over the *ethical behaviour* of organizations.

The framework (or taxonomy) in Table 14.1 describes how these broad categories are linked and subdivided.

All of the areas in Table 14.1 (environmental and ethical concerns) are matters for which organizations are (according to stakeholder theory proponents) accountable. Given that different stakeholders have raised these matters as being of concern, then all of them are part of the portfolio of issues for which organizations are, in part, responsible to society.

Table 14.1

A taxonomy of concern

Key area	Subsidiary concerns	Examples of personal opinion areas
Environmental concern	Concern over the state of natural resources	▪ Energy resources and conservation ▪ Mineral resources and conservation ▪ Extinction and over-fishing
	Concern over the way in which business activities affect environmental pollution	▪ Global warming ('greenhouse' effect) ▪ Ozone layer depletion ▪ Health concerns (e.g. skin cancer, asthma) ▪ Industrial emissions (e.g. into rivers, etc.) ▪ Rubbish and waste (including land-fill, nuclear, etc.) ▪ 'Acid' rain (from coal power station emissions)
Ethical concern	Concern arising over the asymmetric nature of markets	▪ Third World debt and its repayment terms (to First World banks) ▪ 'Fair-trade' between rich First World companies and poorer Third World producers ▪ Multinational companies alleged 'exploitation' of weaker Third World economies
	Concern arising over the business's alleged responsibility to society	▪ Community involvement ▪ Marketing practices (e.g. corporate sponsorships and advertising) ▪ Animal 'cruelty' issues ▪ Product health and safety ▪ Compensation and reparations (e.g. drugs, oil spills)
	Concern arising from the internal and industry activities of the business	▪ Employment practices (e.g. employment rate of minorities, disabled people, women, etc.) ▪ Health and safety in the workplace (over and above the legal minimum) ▪ Treatment of suppliers, customers and other stakeholders (e.g. days taken to pay smaller creditors)

Strategic postures in social responsibility

The term *social responsibility* describes the persuasion that organizations are not free to act as though the above concerns did not exist. However, it is evident that not all organizations espouse the same attitudes with respect to social and environmental concern. Four general degrees of responsiveness of organizations have been identified:

- socially obstructive;
- socially obligative;
- socially responsive;
- socially contributive.

Socially obstructive organizations

Some businesses are actively *socially obstructive*. This description can be applied to organizations that actively resist any pressures or attempts to modify pure business objectives in the light of social concern. Such organizations may resist attempts to make them abide even to the minimum legal standards of behaviour – behaviour which may be followed by denial and an attempt to keep 'interfering' bodies out of their business. Some have argued that tobacco manufacturers fall into this category as, in order to protect their sales of cigarettes, they may effectively deny that tobacco causes as much harm as some health professionals have suggested may be the case. Such companies would presumably argue that it would not be in their strategic interests to respond to stakeholder concerns.

Socially obligative organizations

Some businesses observe no more than their minimum *social obligations*. This description can be applied to organizations that are prepared to abide by whatever restrictions are placed upon them by governments – in other words, the legal minimum. They are unwilling to give credence to any pressure or lobby groups that, in the opinion of the organization, do not have any statutory influence over them.

Socially responsive organizations

The third group are those that are *socially responsive*. These organizations submit to minimum legal standards for corporate behaviour towards society and the environment, but go further than socially obligative organizations. The difference is that socially responsive organizations will do more to address people's concerns if pressurized to do so by stakeholders such as pressure groups.

Socially contributive organizations

The final group are those organizations that seek to make a *social contribution*. This description can be applied to organizations that willingly do all they reasonably can to extend their social and environmental involvement. In this sense, such organizations seek to make a positive contribution to the communities they serve, to help protect the natural environment and to avoid any unethical business practices. Some social contributive organizations may exist primarily for the purpose of promoting social responsibility and ethical business practice.

Mechanisms of social responsibility discharge

Given the extent to which organizations vary in their postures towards social responsibility, it is not surprising that a range of mechanisms have been adopted to express such responsibility. Essentially, this section is concerned with answering the question: How do organizations express their concerns over social issues?

The answer is that there are a number of mechanisms by which organizations discharge their responsibility to society (or their alleged responsibility). The most frequently adopted mechanisms are:

- modification of mission statement or other explicit declaration;
- adopting prescriptive codes of conduct;
- issuing publicly available reports on the social impact of business activity or including social information in regular corporate reports;
- issuing a separate social audit of the organization in addition to the mandatory financial statements.

We will consider these matters briefly in turn.

Modified mission statements

Some organizations publish a mission statement as a vehicle by which stakeholders can be informed about what the most important strategic objectives of the enterprise are. Accordingly, it can generally be assumed that, if an issue is mentioned specifically in a mission statement, then the organization considers it to be of strategic importance. Hence, a mention of a social or ethical concern in the statement is a good indication to stakeholders that the issue is to be given very high prominence.

One enthusiastic adopter of this mechanism is Body Shop plc, the retailer of 'cruelty-free' cosmetics and health products. Its mission statement begins with the words "to dedicate our business to the pursuit of social and environmental change", and continues, "to passionately campaign for the protection of the environment, human and civil rights, and against animal testing within the cosmetics and toiletries industry".

Body Shop's explicit statement is, however, rare. Most adopters of revised mission statements are much less direct. They may, for example, contain a clause on being fair to employees, to pay its suppliers on time or to make a contribution (albeit undefined) to the community.

Ethical 'codes of conduct'

Some organizations go a step further than modifying their mission statement by issuing a code of business ethics. This is a document that codifies how the organization intends to act towards its stakeholders. Many of the UK's largest companies have issued such a document, including British Airways, Barclays and Lloyds Banks, Whitbread, British Aerospace, Phillips Petroleum and United Biscuits. The Institute of Business Ethics in London is a body promoting, among other things, such codes of ethics. Its patrons include senior religious leaders in the UK, including the Archbishop of Canterbury and the Chief Rabbi, and its council includes some leading business people. The Institute recommends that organizations issue statements with respect to ethical practice regarding:

- relations with customers;
- relations with shareholders and other investors;
- relations with employees;
- relations with suppliers;
- relations with the government and the local community;
- the environment;
- taxation;
- relations with competitors;

- issues relating to international business;
- behaviour in relation to mergers and take-overs;
- ethical issues concerning directors and managers;
- compliance and verification.

Corporate social reporting

Social reporting is the practice wherein a company voluntarily informs its stakeholders of its behaviour with respect to ethical and social concerns. The point here is that organizations have no legal obligations to make such disclosures, but they nevertheless do. The disclosures may be of a social or environmental nature and, it has been argued, are designed to legitimize the organization's behaviour in the eyes of potentially critical stakeholders (see, for example, Guthrie and Parker, 1989; Gray *et al.*, 1995).

Social reporting disclosures can be carried in a number of company-produced documents. The practice is more established among larger companies, which have more complex stakeholder relationships than smaller ones. Although the annual report remains the primary vehicle for social disclosure for most companies, some companies produce separate environmental or social reports (see next section). These are non-mandatory documents that set out in more detail how the company has behaved with respect to environmental or social concerns over the past year.

Social accounts

As with other forms of social disclosure, the production of social accounts is entirely voluntary. Social accounts are designed to report on the company's impacts (through its activities) on each of its social constituencies. Accordingly, those who prepare these statements must go to some length to find out and, if possible, quantify the extent to which the company has benefited or detracted its stakeholders.

In order to add credibility to the social accounts, some companies have them independently audited in the same manner as their financial statements are. Audits have tended to be carried out by specialized consultancy groups, but the larger financial auditors are gradually picking up on social audit as demand for the service grows.

Social accounts are, however, relatively new to the world of business ethics. Early adopters included several alternative trading organizations (ATOs – businesses which exist to pursue ethical purposes such as 'fair' Third World trade), but growth in the practice is expected among more mainstream businesses.

References and further reading

Campbell, D.J. (1997) *Organisations and the Business Environment.* Oxford: Butterworth-Heinemann.

Clarkson, M.B.E. (1995) A stakeholder framework for analysing and evaluating corporate social performance. *Academy of Management Review*, 20(1), 92–117.

Donaldson, T. (1982) *Corporate Morality.* Englewood Cliffs, NJ: Prentice Hall.

Donaldson, T. and Preston, L.E. (1995) The stakeholder theory of the corporation: concepts, evidence and implications. *Academy of Management Review*, 20(1), 65–91.

Evan, W.M. and Freeman, R.E. (1993) A stakeholder theory of the modern corporation: kantian capitalism. In: Cryssides, G.D. and Kaler, J.H. (eds), *An Introduction to Business Ethics.* Englewood Cliffs: Prentice Hall, 254–266.

Freeman, R.E. (1984) *Strategic Management: A Stakeholder Approach.* Boston: Pitman.

Freeman, R.E. (1994) The politics of stakeholder theory: some future directions. *Business Ethics Quarterly*, 4(4), 409–421.

Friedman, M. (1970) The social responsibility of business is to increase its profits. *New York Times Magazine*, 13 September, 7–13.

Gray, R., Kouhy, R. and Lavers, S. (1995) Corporate social and environmental reporting. A review of the literature and a longitudinal study of UK disclosures. *Accounting, Auditing and Accountability Journal*, 8(2), 47–77.

Guthrie, J.E. and Parker, L.D. (1989) Corporate social reporting: a rebuttal of legitimacy theory. *Accounting and Business Research*, 9(76), 343–352.

Mahoney, J. (1994) Stakeholder responsibilities: turning the ethical tables. *Business Ethics – A European Review*, 3(4), 212–218.

Rawls, J. (1971) *A Theory of Justice.* Cambridge, MA: Harvard University Press.

Smith, A. (1776) *An Inquiry into the Nature and Causes of The Wealth of Nations* (Glasgow Edition, 2 vols, 1982). Glasgow: Liberty Fund.

CHAPTER 15

Strategic management: present and future trends

Strategic management is comparatively young discipline, if indeed it can be called a discipline when it is in fact a multi- and inter-disciplinary field of study. Strategists draw heavily upon disciplines as diverse as organization theory and behaviour, human resource management, economics, accounting and finance, and marketing, as well as attempting to formulate their own theories and analytical frameworks. The future of strategic management will undoubtedly be longer than its past. For this reason, the theories, tools and techniques employed in strategic management are in many cases far from being fully formulated. The subject will continue to evolve and the sophistication of its methods and methodology will develop and improve over time.

At the heart of strategic management is the desire to explain why certain businesses achieve competitive advantage through superior performance. The view in the 1980s was that competitive advantage was based upon the competitive positioning of the organization in its environment based upon highly systematic planning (Argenti, 1965; Porter, 1980, 1985). In the 1990s, this view was challenged by strate- gists who believed that, in a turbulent business environment, strategy could be developed incrementally and that competitive advantage depended upon the ability of the business to build core competences that cannot be easily replicated by competitors (Prahalad and Hamel, 1990, 1994; Heene and Sanchez, 1997; Kay, 1993). This chapter, intended to be a summary of the book, serves the dual purpose of identifying the origins of strategic management before considering recent developments that will shape its future.

Learning objectives

After studying this chapter, students should be able to:

- outline the development of strategic management as an academic discipline;
- explain and explore the planned/prescriptive approach to strategic management;
- explain and explore the emergent/incremental approach to strategic management;
- explain and explore the competitive positioning approach to strategic management;
- explain and explore the resource/core competence approach to strategic management;
- identify likely developments in strategic management – namely, collaborative advantage and knowledge management.

Themes in strategic management

The 'big' controversies

The developing nature of strategy as a coherent academic discipline is reflected in two related debates revolving around what constitutes the most appropriate approach to strategic management (see Figure 15.1). There is some disagreement among strategists as to the best way of understanding the determinants of competitive advantage. Some writers advocate an approach to strategic management that is *planned* or *prescriptive* (sometimes called *deliberate*), whereas others argue that it is better to evolve strategy incrementally (the *emergent* approach to strategy; see the key concept in Chapter 1)). A parallel debate centres upon whether competitive advantage stems primarily from the competitive position of the business in its industry or from business-specific core competences. These themes are explored in the following sections of this chapter.

The debate surrounding the development of strategic management can be summarized under two broad headings:

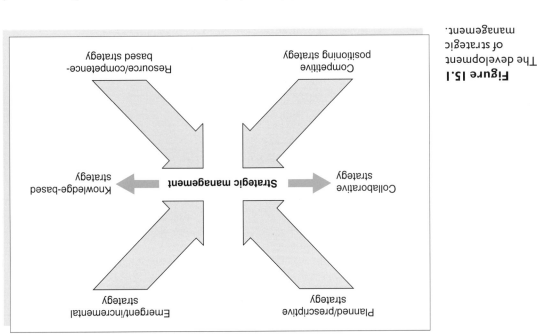

Figure 15.1
The development
of strategic
management.

1 the planned/prescriptive versus emergent/incremental controversy;

2 the competitive positioning versus resource/core-competence-based strategy controversy.

We discussed the first of these debates in Chapter 1 and the second in Chapter 7. Here, we summarize the main features of these approaches and briefly explore their advantages and disadvantages (see Table 15.1). The arguments are discussed below.

The prescriptive versus emergent strategy debate

Planned or prescriptive strategy

The planned or prescriptive approach views the formulation and implementation of strategic management as a logical, rational and systematic process. After analysis of the business and its environment, strategists must set well-defined corporate and business objectives, formulate, select and implement strategies that will allow objectives to be achieved. Such an approach has been criticized on the grounds that there is often a major discrepancy between planned and realized strategies (Mintzberg, 1987). It is also argued that the increasing turbulence and chaos of the business environment makes highly pre-scriptive planning a nonsense. Rigid plans prevent the flexibility

Table 15.1

Approaches to strategic management

Approach	Theory	Advantages	Criticisms
Prescriptive or planning strategy	▪ Strategic management is a highly formalized planning process ▪ Business objectives are set and strategies are formulated and implemented to achieve them	▪ Clear objectives provide a focus for the business ▪ Objectives can be translated into targets against which performance can be measured and monitored ▪ Resources can be allocated to specific objectives and efficiency can be judged ▪ The approach is logical and rational	▪ There are often major discrepancies between planned and realized strategy ▪ Rigid planning in a dynamic and turbulent business environment can be unproductive ▪ Prescriptions can stifle creativity ▪ Rigid adherence to plans may mean missed business opportunities
Emergent or incremental strategy	▪ Strategy emerges and develops incrementally over time in the absence of rigid planning	▪ Emergent strategy increases flexibility in a turbulent environment, allowing the business to respond to threats and exploit opportunities ▪ Changing stakeholder interactions can mean that strategy is often, of necessity, emergent	▪ There is a danger of 'strategic drift' as objectives lack clarity ▪ It is more difficult to evaluate performance as targets are less well defined
Competitive positioning approach to strategy	▪ Competitive advantage results from an organization's position with respect to its industry ▪ The business analyses the competitive strength of the forces in its industry and selects an appropriate generic strategy. The business configures its value-adding activities to support this generic strategy ▪ The approach to strategy is 'outside-in'	▪ Well-developed analytical frameworks such as Porter's five forces, value chain and generic strategies ▪ Structured approach helps to simplify the complexity of business and the business environment ▪ Good for identifying opportunities and threats in the environment	▪ Neglects the importance of business-specific competences as opposed to industry-wide factors ▪ Some of the analytical frameworks (e.g. generic strategies) have been widely criticized
Resource- or competence-based approach to strategy	▪ Organizations must identify and build core competences or distinctive capabilities that can be leveraged in a number of markets ▪ The approach to strategy is 'inside-out'	▪ The approach emphasizes the importance of the individual business in acquiring competitive advantage ▪ Strategic intent, vision and creativity are emphasized	▪ Analytical frameworks are in their infancy and are currently poorly developed ▪ The importance of the environment in determining competitive advantage is under-estimated

that is required in an environment of volatile change. Being over-prescriptive, it is argued, also stifles the creativity that often underpins successful strategy.

On the other hand, it is argued that systematic planning makes it possible to organize complex activities and information, unite business objectives, set targets against which performance can be evaluated and generally increases the degree of control that can be exercised over the operation of the business. The planned or prescriptive approach is often linked to the *competitive positioning* approach (see later in this chapter).

Emergent or incremental strategy

The emergent or incremental view of strategy adopts the position that strategy must be evolved incrementally over time. This view is based upon the premise that businesses are complex social organizations operating in rapidly changing environments. Under such circumstances, strategy will tend to evolve as a result of the interaction between stakeholder groups and between the business and its environment. It is argued that an emergent approach has the advantages of increased organizational flexibility. It can form a basis in organizational learning and can provide an internal culture in which managers can think and act creatively rather than have to act within the rigid framework of deliberate strategy. The danger is that an emergent approach may result in a lack of purpose in strategy and it can make it difficult to evaluate performance (because if an organization has no explicit objective, performance against it cannot be measured). To counter the criticisms of emergent strategy, Quinn (1978) and Quinn and Voyer (1994) see a role for some planning in the context of emergent strategy, advocating 'purposeful incrementalism'. This approach places a strong emphasis on *organizational learning* (see later in this chapter).

The competitive positioning versus resource/core competence debate

Competitive positioning

This school of thought dominated strategic management in the 1980s and still had considerable significance in the 1990s. Although the approach was widely criticized in the 1990s, the analytical frameworks devised by Porter in the 1980s (Porter 1980, 1985) are still widely used by both managers and academics. The major strength of the approach lies in the ready applicability of these frameworks to the analysis of the business and its environment. The approach to strategy is essentially 'outside-in' (McKiernan, 1997), to establish a competitive position for the business in its environment which results in it out-performing its rivals.

In terms of procedure, the process of analysing competitive position begins with the *free forces framework*. This is used to analyse the nature of competition in the organization's industry. This is followed by selection of the appropriate *generic strategy* together with *value chain analysis* to ensure that the business configures its value-adding activities in such a way as to support a strategy based on either differentiation or cost leadership.

In the 1990s, this approach was criticized for its over-emphasis of the role of the *industry* in determining profitability and its underestimation of the importance of the individual business (Rumelt, 1991). Porter's frameworks have also been criticized as being too static, although Porter argues that they must be applied repeatedly to take account of the dynamism of the environment. The reality is that, without Porter's work, strategic management would be devoid of many of its most practical and applicable analytical tools.

Resource- or core-competence-based strategy

The 1990s witnessed the rise of what is known as *resource-* or *core-competence-based* strategic management (Prahalad and Hamel, 1990; Heene and Sanchez, 1997; Kay, 1993). The major difference to the competitive positioning approach is that the importance of the individual business in achieving competitive advantage is emphasized rather than the industry. The approach is therefore 'inside-out'. Although this approach came to prominence in the 1990s, its origins lie in the work of Penrose (1959), who emphasized the importance of the business and its resources in determining its performance. Interest in the approach was revived by Prahalad and Hamel's 1990 work 'The core competence of the corporation'. A core competence is some combination of resources, skills, knowledge and technology that distinguishes an organization from its competitors in the eyes of customers. This distinctiveness results in competitive advantage.

The approach also emphasizes organizational learning, knowledge management and collaborative business networks as sources of competitive advantage (Sanchez and Heene, 1997; Demarest, 1997).

The resource/core competence approach has focused the search for competitive advantage on the individual business, but its critics argue that it lacks the well-developed analytical frameworks of the competitive positioning school and, perhaps, understates the potential importance of the business environment in determining success or failure.

Towards an integrated approach to strategy

Similarities and differences between the approaches

The prescriptive and competitive positioning approaches are often seen as related to each other because they both adopt a highly structured view of strategic management. Similarly, the emergent and competence-based approaches are often linked to each other because of their shared focus on organizational knowledge and learning.

On the other hand, the prescriptive and emergent approaches are often presented as being diametrically opposed, as are the competitive positioning and competence-based approaches. The reality is that the approaches are in many ways complementary as they present different perspectives of the same situation.

Mintzberg *et al.* (1995) argue that the competence-based and competitive positioning approaches ought be seen as ''complementary, representing two different forms of analysis both of which must be brought to bear for improving the quality of strategic thinking and analysis''. Similarly, Quinn and Voyer (1994) recognize that within logical incrementalism 'formal planning techniques do serve some essential functions'.

Acknowledging the contribution of each approach

The point is that each approach has its merits. By acknowledging the contribution of each approach, managers can arrive at an enriched method of understanding the complex area of strategic management. The contribution of each approach to an integrated understanding can be summarized as follows:

- ■ *planned/prescriptive* – a degree of planning is necessary to provide focus for the strategy of the organization and to assist in the evaluation of performance;
- ■ *emergent/incremental* – plans must always be flexible to allow organizations to learn and adapt to changes in the environment;
- ■ *competitive positioning* – emphasizes the importance of the environment and provides useful tools for analysing the business in the context of its industry;
- ■ *resource/competence-based* – focuses on the importance of the business and assists in identifying company-specific sources of competitive advantage.

Accordingly, we suggest that strategy must be both inward- and outward-looking, planned and emergent. By adopting this synthesis, a broader understanding of competitive advantage can be gained.

The future of strategic management thinking

This book has discussed the 'state of the art' in strategic thinking at the time of publication. In attempting to predict the areas that will focus the minds of academics in the near future, two central areas of interest are prominent: *collaborative advantage* and *knowledge management*.

Collaboration and competitive behaviour in industries

In recent years, considerable research and theorization has focused on the extent to which collaboration between businesses (as opposed to competition) may contribute towards the attainment of competitive advantage (Contractor and Lorange, 1988; Hamel *et al.*, 1989; Quinn *et al.*, 1990; Reeve, 1990; Davidow and Malone, 1992; Heene and Sanchez, 1997).

Collaboration in non-core activities

The competence-based approach suggests that businesses should concentrate upon developing core competences so as to achieve competitive advantage. Any activities that are not seen as core can be outsourced to other organizations for whom those activities are core. Most networks centre on a focal business whose strategy drives the operation of the network. Quinn *et al.* (1990) suggest that such are the changes in service technologies that they now "provide sufficient scale economies, flexibility, efficiency and specialization potentials that outside vendors [sellers] can supply many important corporate functions at greatly enhanced value and lower cost. Thus many of those functions should be outsourced."

Rather than abandoning control to outside vendors it is sometimes best to form some sort of alliance or network with them. Collaborative networks potentially provide several advantages by:

- allowing businesses to concentrate on their core competences and core activities;
- allowing businesses to pool core competences, thus creating synergy between them;
- reducing bureaucracy and allowing flatter organizational structures;
- increasing efficiency and reducing costs;
- improving flexibility and responsiveness;
- making it difficult for competitors to imitate.

The formation of a collaborative network will involve:

- identification of the core competences of the organization;
- identification and focus upon activities that are critical to the core competence of the organization and outsourcing those that are not;
- achieving the internal and external linkages in the value/ supply chain that are necessary for effective coordination of activities and which enhance responsiveness.

Collaboration can be:

- *horizontal* – partners are at the same stage of the value system and are often competitors;
- *vertical* – partners are at different stages of the value system (this includes collaboration with suppliers, distributors and customers).

Collaboration can provide benefits, including the linking of core competences (of the two parties in the relationship), access to resources and technology, risk reduction, greater control over supplies, betters access to customers and reduced competition. Collaboration, however, can create problems, which include conflicting objectives between the participating businesses, cultural differences, changing requirements among the partners and coordination and integration problems.

Virtual organizations

Developments in information and communications technology (ICT) have greatly increased the potential for collaboration between businesses by making it much easier to integrate and coordinate network activities. These changes in technology have made possible the development of 'virtual' organizations. A virtual organization is a network of linked businesses that coordinate and integrate their activities so effectively that they give the appearance of a single business organization.

There is considerable potential for such virtual organizations to enhance competitive advantage. ICT linkages greatly increase flexibility and efficiency, and make it difficult for competitors to replicate the activities of the network. Linkages to suppliers and customers are greatly improved, as are flows of the information required for strategic decision-taking. The net result is that the virtual corporation is more flexible, more responsive and better able than its non-virtual rivals to compete on the bases of time and customer satisfaction.

Organizational learning and knowledge management

Closely related to the rational/logical approaches to strategy (such as the prescriptive and competitive positioning schools of thought) is the notion that organizations must continually learn both about themselves and their environment. At the same time – and here this point is in agreement with the core competence approach – it is widely acknowledged that organizational knowledge underpins many core competences. Accordingly, organizational learning and knowledge management have been the subject of considerable recent research and theorization (see, for example, Argyris, 1992; Grant, 1997; Demarest, 1997). Grant (1997) argues that "the knowledge-based view represents a confluence of a number of streams of research, the most prominent being 'resource-based theory' and 'epistemology'".

Explicit and implicit knowledge

Organizational learning and knowledge management are concerned with the creation, development and dissemination of knowledge within an organization. This 'knowledge' can be either explicit or implicit.

- *Explicit knowledge* is knowledge whose meaning is clearly stated, details of which can be recorded and stored (e.g. important formulations, procedures, ways of acting, etc.).
- *Implicit or tacit knowledge* (Demarest, 1997) is often unstated, based upon individual experience and difficult to record and store. Implicit knowledge is often a vital source of core competence and competitive advantage as it is most difficult for competitors to emulate (e.g. experience in a given sector, an understanding of a particular technology or the multiple contact networks that have been built up over many years by managers and sales people).

Both forms of knowledge begin as individual knowledge but, to substantially improve performance, they must be transformed into organizational knowledge. This is a particularly difficult transformation for implicit knowledge. It is the role of knowledge management to ensure that individual learning becomes organizational learning.

Types of organizational learning

Argyris (1978, 1992) argued that organizations must develop 'double loop learning'. In other words, learning is not just a case of learning how to solve an immediate problem but must also aim at developing principles that will inform and determine future behaviour. It must also result in the ability to generalize from specific learning. Such learning takes place when individual solutions are reached and then generalized to apply in other circumstances.

Senge (1990) identified two types of learning found in leading organizations: 'adaptive learning' and 'generative learning'. Adaptive learning centres on changing in response to developments in the business environment. Such adaptation is often necessary for business survival. Generative learning is, on the other hand, about building new competences or identifying or creating opportunities for leveraging existing competences in new competitive arenas. For example, Marks & Spencer's entry into financial services was based upon leveraging its existing competences in retailing and adding new competences, based upon learning about the nature of financial services, initially through its store card operations.

The keys to successful knowledge management

Knowledge management incorporates organizational learning, but it is also concerned with the management of existing stocks of knowledge. Effective knowledge management must overcome:

- barriers to learning and knowledge creation;
- difficulties in storing and sharing knowledge (particularly tacit knowledge);
- difficulties in valuing and measuring knowledge (based on Demarest, 1997).

Knowledge management is, therefore, primarily concerned with the creation of new knowledge, storage and sharing of knowledge and the control of knowledge. Knowledge management is an important element in building core competences that must be distinctive and difficult to imitate.

The often intangible nature of knowledge tends to make it distinctive and difficult to copy. In the case of a company such as Microsoft, it is evident that its core competences are largely knowledge-based. Quinn (1992) argued that "most successful enterprises today can be considered intelligent enterprises" as they focus on building knowledge-based core competences. Similarly, Grant (1997) pointed out that "companies such as Dow Chemical, Anderson Consulting, Polaroid and Skania are developing corporate-wide systems to track, access, exploit and create organizational knowledge". Within such organizations, questioning and creativity are encouraged, as are trust, teamwork and sharing. At the same time, they have created infrastructures that support learning, that assist in the storage and controlled diffusion of knowledge and which coordinate its application in creating and supporting core competences.

There is some way to go in understanding the role of knowledge and its management in strategy. It is likely that significant developments will take place in this area in the new millennium.

References and further reading

Ansoff, I. (1987) *Corporate Strategy*. London: Penguin.
Argenti, J. (1965) *Corporate Planning*. Allen and Unwin.
Argyris, C. (1977) Double loop learning in organisations. *Harvard Business Review*, September–October, 115–125.
Argyris, C. (1992) *On Organisational Learning*. London: Blackwell.

Argyris, C. and Schon, D. (1978) *Organisation Learning: A Theory of Action Perspective*. Reading: Addison Wesley.

Contractor, F. and Lorange, P. (1988) Why should firms co-operate? In: *Co-operative Strategies in International Business*. Lexington Books.

Cravens, D.W., Greenley, G., Piercy, N.F. and Slater, S. (1997) Integrating contemporary strategic management perspectives. *Long Range Planning*, 30(4), 493–506.

Davidow, W.H. and Malone, M.S. (1992) *Structuring and Revitalizing the Corporation for the 21st Century: The Virtual Corporation*. London: Harper Business.

Demarest, M. (1997) Understanding knowledge management. *Long Range Planning*, 30(3), 374–384.

Grant, R.M. (1991) The resource based theory of competitive advantage: implications for strategy formulation. *California Management Review*, 33 (Spring), 114–135.

Grant, R.M. (1997) The knowledge-based view of the firm: implications for management practice. *Long Range Planning*, 30(3), 450–454.

Hamel, G. and Prahalad, C.K. (1989) Strategic intent. *Harvard Business Review*, 67(3).

Hamel, G. and Prahalad, C.K. (1994) *Competing for the Future*. Cambridge, MA: Harvard Business School Press.

Hamel, G., Doz, Y. and Prahalad, C.K. (1989) Collaborate with your competitors and win. *Harvard Business Review*, January–February.

Heene, A. and Sanchez, R. (eds) (1997) *Competence-Based Strategic Management*. London: John Wiley.

Heracleous, L. (1998) Strategic thinking or strategic planning. *Long Range Planning*, 30(3).

Kay, J. (1993) *Foundations of Corporate Success*. Oxford: Oxford University Press.

Kay, J. (1995) Learning to define the core business. *Financial Times*, 1 December.

McKiernan, P. (1997) Strategy past, strategy futures. *Long Range Planning*, 30(5).

Mintzberg, H. (1987) Crafting strategy. *Harvard Business Review*, July–August.

Mintzberg, H. (1991) *The Strategy Process: Concepts, Contexts, Cases*. Englewood Cliffs: Prentice Hall.

Mintzberg, H., Quinn, J.B. and Ghoshal, S. (1995) *The Strategy Process: Concepts, Contexts and Cases*, European Edition. Englewood Cliffs: Prentice Hall.

Penrose, E. (1959) *The Theory of the Growth of the Firm*. Oxford: Oxford University Press.

Porter, M.E. (1980) *Competitive Strategy: Techniques for Analysing Industries and Competitors*. New York: Free Press.

Porter, M.E. (1985) *Competitive Advantage*. New York: Free Press.

Prahalad, C.K. and Hamel, G. (1990) The core competence of the corporation. *Harvard Business Review*, 79–91.

Quinn, J.B. (1978) Strategic change: logical incrementalism. *Sloan Management Review*, Fall.

Quinn, J.B. (1992) *The Intelligent Enterprise: A Knowledge and Service-Based Paradigm for Industry*. New York: Free Press.

Quinn, J.B. and Voyer, J. (1994) *The Strategy Process*. Englewood Cliffs: Prentice Hall.

Quinn, J.B., Dooley, T. and Paquette, P., (1990) Technology in Services: Rethinking Strategic Focus, *Sloan Management Review*, Winter.

Reve, T. (1990) The firm as a nexus of internal and external contracts. In: Aoki, M., Gustafsson, M. and Williamson, O.E. (eds), *The Firm as a Nexus of Treaties*. London: Sage.

Rumelt, R. (1991) How much does industry matter? *Strategic Management Journal*, March.

Sanchez, R. and Heene, A. (eds) (1997) *Strategic Learning and Knowledge Management*. New York: Wiley.

Senge, P. (1990) Building learning organisations. *Sloan Management Review*, Fall.

Case studies

Learning outcomes grid

Case	Author (by the book authors unless stated)	Industry and market	Objectives and stakeholders	Internal analysis	Generic strategy and value chain	External analysis: SPENT	External analysis: five-forces, etc.	Ethics	Mergers, acquisitions and joint ventures	Implementation	Ansoff and growth	Levels of strategy	International
Pilkington and its float glass innovation			✓					✓					
The UK decorative paint industry							✓						
Ben Jerry's Homemade Ice Cream Inc.								✓					
Who owns Newcastle United?			✓										
Food retailing in the UK	*Tony Purdie	✓				✓	✓						
Derwent Valley Foods Limited	*Morgan Howe			✓	✓								
Kwik Save Group plc				✓	✓							✓	
Kwik Save: Somerfield	*Tony Purdie								✓			✓	
The UK outbound tour operations industry	Nigel Evans					✓	✓						
MyTravel plc (formerly Airtours)	Nigel Evans	✓		✓	✓	✓	✓					✓	
Honda–Rover: how successful was it?									✓				
Amazon.com	Colin Combe			✓	✓					✓			
Strategic alliances in the airline industry	Nigel Evans					✓			✓				✓
The Gulf War (1990–91)			✓							✓		✓	

*Additional material by named author. All authors are members of the faculty at Newcastle Business School

Suggested case questions

Case	Learning outcomes	Sample questions
Pilkington and its float glass innovation	Ethics	1 Identify the options open to Pilkington when it developed the float glass innovation. 2 Which option would conventional competitive strategy theory have prescribed? 3 What factors were relevant to Pilkington in arriving at its decision? 4 Do you think Pilkington was right in the decision it made? Explain your answer.
Pilkington and its float glass innovation	Objectives and stakeholders	1 Identify the stakeholders in Pilkington. 2 What were the company's objectives and how did they change over time? 3 Which stakeholders have been most influential in objective-setting during Pilkington's history and what were their motives and aspirations for the company.
The UK decorative paint industry	External microenvironmental analysis (five forces)	1 Identify the main industry characteristics. 2 Perform an industry analysis on the UK decorative paint industry using the five-forces framework. 3 Comment on industry performance using the financial data at the end of the case. 4 To what extent does this data confirm or contradict your conclusions from the industry analysis?
Ben & Jerry's Homemade Ice Cream Inc.	Ethics	1 Identify the stakeholders that Ben & Jerry's and Häagen Dazs had in common at the time of the controversy. 2 Which of Donaldson and Preston's view of stakeholders did Häagen Dazs have at the time of the confrontation? Provide evidence from the case for your answer. 3 Which of Donaldson and Preston's view of stakeholders did Ben & Jerry's have in the case? Provide evidence from the case for your answer. 4 Comment upon the ethical behaviour of the two 'sides' of the Pillsbury dough boy campaign. Which side, if either, was right?

Who owns Newcastle United?	Objectives and stakeholders	1 Identify from the case the key stakeholders in Newcastle United plc. 2 Construct a power–interest matrix for the key stakeholders in the company at: (a) the beginning of the case (before the story broke); (b) after the story broke; and (c) after the World Cup. Show how the key stakeholders moved on the map during the case. 3 Comment on who owns Newcastle United.
Food retailing in the UK	Industry and markets	1 Describe the main industry and market characteristics. 2 How have the industry and market changed over recent years? 3 What factors have helped to bring about change in the industry and market structures?
Food retailing in the UK	External analysis: SPENT	1 Identify from the case the SPENT factors affecting the food retailing industry. 2 Which of the SPENT factors are the most important to the industry?
Food retailing in the UK	External analysis: five forces	1 Use the information in the case to construct a five-forces analysis of the food retailing industry. 2 From the five-forces analysis, comment on the expected performance of players in the industry. 3 Use the financial data in Appendix 8 to comment on the performance of competitors in the industry.
Derwent Valley Foods Limited	Generic strategy and internal analysis	1 Using evidence from the case, identify the company's generic strategy. 2 Describe the internal activities that support the generic strategy. 3 How successful has the generic strategy been?
Kwik Save Group plc (A)	Generic strategy and internal analysis	1 Using evidence from the case, identify the company's generic strategy. 2 Describe the internal activities that support the generic strategy. 3 Use information from the case to comment on the success of the generic strategy.
Kwik Save Group plc (A)	Value chain	1 Use the information in the case to construct a value chain analysis of Kwik Save. 2 Comment on the effectiveness of any outsourced activities and any forward or backward linkages. 3 Comment on how the configuration of value chain activities supports the generic strategy.
Kwik Save Group plc (A)	Ansoff and growth	1 Use Ansoff's matrix to describe the growth directions used by Kwik Save. 2 Which mechanisms of growth did Kwik Save employ? 3 Comment on the success of the growth strategies.

Kwik Save (B): Somerfield	Mergers and acquisitions	1 Explain the industry and characteristics that were relevant to Somerfield in its deliberations. 2 Explain the strategic motivations for Kwik Save to enter into the merger. 3 Why did Somerfield find Kwik Save attractive? 4 Describe the expected synergies. How realistic were they? 5 Comment on the extent to which the merger was successful.
Kwik Save (B): Somerfield	Ansoff and growth	1 Identify, using the Ansoff matrix, the strategic directions that Somerfield adopted over the period of the case. 2 Which mechanisms of growth did the company adopt?
The UK outbound tour operations industry	External analysis: SPENT	1 Identify the SPENT factors that have affected the tour operations industry over the period of the case. 2 Which factors have been the most important in shaping strategy?
The UK outbound tour operations industry	External analysis: five-forces and industry analysis	1 Identify the components of the supply chain that includes the tour-operations industry. 2 Conduct a five-forces analysis of the tour-operations industry. 3 Comment on the intensity of rivalry in the industry.
MyTravel plc (formerly Airtours)	Industry and markets	1 Which industry or industries does MyTravel compete in? 2 Which markets does it serve? 3 Identify the key characteristics of the industry and market.
MyTravel plc (formerly Airtours)	Internal analysis	1 Use a range of appropriate frameworks to carry out an internal analysis of MyTravel (formerly Airtours). 2 Use the information generated in the internal analysis to comment on the company's strengths and weaknesses.
MyTravel plc (formerly Airtours)	Generic strategy and value chain	1 Identify the generic strategy or strategies that MyTravel (formerly Airtours) has adopted. 2 Use the value chain model to show how internal activities have been configured to support the generic strategy.
MyTravel plc (formerly Airtours)	External analysis: SPENT analysis	1 Conduct a SPENT analysis of the company. 2 Which of the SPENT factors identified are particular opportunities for the company and which are particular threats?
MyTravel plc (formerly Airtours)	External analysis: five forces	1 Use the five-forces framework to analyse the strategic position of the company. 2 Describe the level of rivalry within the industries of which MyTravel is a part.

MyTravel plc (formerly Airtours)	Ansoff and growth	1 During the course of the case, the company undertook a number of growth measures. Identify the major moves in terms of the Ansoff matrix. 2 Which mechanisms of growth did the company employ?
Honda–Rover: how successful was it?	Mergers and acquisitions	1 Explain the logic behind the multiple mergers that occurred in the 1950s and 1960s to bring the BL Group into existence. 2 What advantages did Rover Group gain from the alliance with Honda? 3 What advantages did Honda gain? 4 Suggest reasons why both parties entered into the alliance warily at first. 5 How might Honda have avoided the disappointment of seeing the alliance dissolved in 1994? 6 Suggest reasons why the Land Rover Discovery was badged as a Honda for sale in Japan and not sold as a Rover product. 7 Discuss the extent to which the alliance was a success for both parties.
Amazon.com	Internal analysis	1 Use a range of appropriate frameworks to carry out an internal analysis of Amazon.com. 2 Use the information generated in the internal analysis to comment on the company's strengths and weaknesses.
Amazon.com	Generic strategy and value chain	1 Identify Amazon's generic strategy. 2 Use the value chain model to show how internal activities have been configured to support the generic strategy.
Amazon.com	Implementation	1 Identify the resources that Amazon has used in the implementation of its strategy. 2 Which of these has been the most strategically important. 3 Comment on the culture and structure of Amazon, and their appropriateness for the chosen strategy.
Strategic alliances in the airline industry	External analysis: SPENT analysis	1 From the case, identify the SPENT factors that have influenced the airline industry. 2 Which of the SPENT factors have encouraged alliance development and which have discouraged alliances?
Strategic alliances in the airline industry	Mergers, acquisitions and joint ventures	1 Why do airlines seek to develop alliances? 2 Explain the sources of synergy in airline alliances. 3 What types of alliances are employed in the airline industry (simple/complex)? 4 Comment on the success of airline alliances.
Strategic alliances in the airline industry	International	1 Why are some airline alliances international? 2 Which factors have stimulated the development of international alliances?

The Gulf War (1990–91)	Objectives and stakeholders	1 Identify the key stakeholders in the case scenario. 2 In what ways did each key stakeholder contribute to the formulation of the strategic objectives? 3 Who ultimately set the strategic objectives and what were they? 4 Describe the resource inputs that were employed in the implementation of the strategy. 5 Which of Mintzberg's five Ps best describes the strategy followed by the allies in the Gulf War?
The Gulf War (1990–91)	Implementation	1 Describe the resources needed to execute the chosen strategy for the Gulf War. 2 Comment on the extent to which the strategy was successful.
The Gulf War (1990–91)	Levels of strategy	1 What were the strategic objectives? 2 What were the operational objectives? 3 Who was responsible for formulating the operational part of the strategy? 4 Discuss the extent to which the operational objectives were congruent with the strategic objectives?

Pilkington and its float glass innovation

A brief history of the company

Pilkington plc began life in 1826 in the Lancashire town of St Helens. It became Pilkington Brothers in 1849 as the business passed wholly into the hands of the Pilkington family. The company assumed limited company status in 1894. The Pilkington family, paternalistic in nature, imprinted its culture on the company, and the fact that it remained a private company until 1970 meant that the family retained full control over strategy for most of its history. Its reputation as a socially responsible company owed much to the family ownership.

As one of the earliest movers in the glass mass-production industry, Pilkington enjoyed market dominance throughout the second half of the nineteenth century. Its dominant position in the UK was supported by substantial exports to Europe and to the USA – one of the earliest companies to enjoy export success on this scale. Its success subsequently led to its expansion both in the UK and overseas. By the 1930s, Pilkington had established several overseas operations to manufacture sheet glass and safety glass. By the 1950s, the company was manufacturing in Argentina, Australia, Brazil, Canada, New Zealand and South Africa – an international company with a dominant position in Europe.

Pilkington's reputation as a socially responsible company was founded upon its relationships with its employees and the local community. In the early days of the company, it was a pioneer in the creation of employee pension funds and hospital facilities (for employees). Retired employees received vegetable seeds and coal, bereavement counselling, transport for day trips, 'meals on wheels' and other benefits.

Its loyalty to its employees was also high. The Community of St Helens' Trust was a charitable foundation established by the company to help the community cope with a downsizing of the size of the workforce. From 15,000 in 1970, the workforce was reduced to 8000 by 1986. The Trust was set up to provide finance and small business start-up support for former employees lost in the downsizing. By 1987, the Trust had helped to launch 500 small firms and over 6000 jobs in the St Helens area, some of which became Pilkington suppliers.

In other areas, Pilkington was active in community initiatives. It was a founder member of Business in the Community and the Per Cent Club (a body of large companies committed to making annual charitable donations of 0.5% of pre-tax profits). Overseas, it helped to endow educational projects, including the creation and funding of a community school in a Third World country.

Glass production

Since the 1830s, glass had been produced by the 'brown cylinder process' – a process by which sheet glass (mainly for window panes) was made by rolling heated thermoplastic glass between two cylinders (rather like an old-style wringer). The process was improved in the 1890s by innovations brought over from the USA, and the need for higher-performance glass for the new mass-production motor industry also acted as a stimulus for some innovation. However, the essentials of the process remained more-or-less unchanged until the middle of the twentieth century. It was, until that time, the industry standard method, employed by all players in the industry.

The problems with the cylinder process techniques were twofold. First, it was relatively slow and labour-intensive. Second, it was difficult to make the glass absolutely flat due to imperfections in the rollers and other parts of the heating and cooling process. Accordingly, the glass suffered from problems in finish – looking through it did not give a completely clear view. Some older houses still contain imperfect glass produced by the cylinder method.

The float glass breakthrough

In the 1950s, Pilkington made a technological breakthrough that was to have a far-reaching influence upon the industry. Technical manager Alistair Pilkington conceived the idea of forming a ribbon of glass by floating the melted raw materials at high temperature over a bath of molten tin. This 'float glass' process promised to offer two key advantages. First, it would produce plate glass that was guaranteed to be flat on the bottom and on the top, thus providing a much superior product quality than was possible under the cylinder process, despite its many refinements over the years. This quality rested upon the physical properties of liquids – they always find their own level. Because molten tin is liquid, the bottom of the glass sheet would be flat, and, because the glass would be liquid when introduced to the molten tin, it would set, over a temperature gradient, to a flat surface (the 'top' of the glass plate ribbon). Second, the volumes that could be produced by the process would be much larger than was possible using the roller processes. This, in turn, would create substantial cost advantages for Pilkington over its competitors.

The company decided to commit a substantial amount of investment capital into turning the idea into a producible product on a mass scale. Because the company was, at the time, a private limited company, it was able to keep the whole thing secret (public companies usually disclose details of their major research themes in order to stimulate investor interest). By 1959, the product was ready to be launched.

Implications of the innovation

From the time the idea was first mentioned, the board of Pilkington Brothers realized its potential implications. If Pilkington were to go into full-scale production without disclosing the technology to competitors, it would have the potential to give the company an unassailable competitive advantage – perfect quality glass at lower cost than all other competitors in the global industry.

The company's chairman at the time, Lord Pilkington, later recalled the tone of the Board's deliberations:

A great deal was said about ethics: that it was not our job to deliberately deny existing glass competitors the opportunity of living in competition with us. I don't think we were short-sighted or rapacious. There was a great deal of investment worldwide in plate [i.e. the cylinder process], and people needed to have time to write off this plant or convert over. The alternative was chaotic disruption of a great industry.

Lord Pilkington was referring to the Board's choices. If it were to set up its float glass production facility *and* keep it a secret, it could wipe out the rest of the industry within a few months. Customers would have no incentive to buy from competitors producing inferior products at higher prices, and Pilkington would be able to satisfy global demand with its superior high-volume product at lower prices.

The other alternative was to patent the technology. This would make the process available to competitors, thus allowing them to survive. In exchange for use of the patent (and the technology), Pilkington would receive substantial licensed royalty payments from competitors, thus providing return on the investment incurred in development and enabling the company to extend its competitive advantage by investing in other areas.

The company's record of its own history recounts the story:

Pilkington decided on a policy of licensing the process to existing major glass manufacturers. At the same time the company encouraged its licensees to assist in the further development of float by granting them free use of any improvements they might make on condition these were also made available to Pilkington itself. The first float licence was granted, to PPG [Pittsburgh Plate Glass], in 1962. Others quickly followed. Pilkington stopped making polished plate glass [made by the cylinder method] in 1967 and others soon followed suit.

Earnings from the royalties amounted to £400 million over the twenty years in which the patent was in effect. By the late 1970s, the float glass method had become the standard industry production technique and perfect glass at low cost was the norm, thanks to Alistair Pilkington's innovation almost thirty years earlier.

Meanwhile, Pilkington Brothers floated on the UK stock exchange in 1970. By the time the patent for the float glass innovation expired, Pilkington's competitors had used the technology to consolidate their own positions and some of them emerged as strong competitors.

The BTR take-over attempt

In 1986, the British industrial company BTR plc attempted a hostile takeover of Pilkington plc. In order to convince Pilkington shareholders to sell up, BTR made a pointed criticism of Pilkington's strategy with regard to the float glass innovation. Its offer to shareholders asked why Pilkington had chosen to license its flat glass breakthrough technology 'for short term gain at the cost of long term ownership and the eventual creation of self-inflicted competition'.

Pilkington replied on two fronts. In order to address BTR's criticism, it made the commercial case for patenting the technology (referring to the £400 million in royalty payments). Then, in the 1987 annual report, having defeated the BTR bid, the Chairman's statement included the following remarks:

> Our ability to demonstrate that it was possible to achieve world leadership in an industry, while maintaining that important balance between the interests of our shareholders, employees and the wider community, was a powerful and convincing defence [against the BTR bid]. Throughout the bid we were able to rely on the wholehearted support of our employees. This support gathered momentum and widened to all the communities in which we work. I cannot recall a similar bid where such universal support was generated by a target company.

The UK decorative paint industry

The UK has one of the longest-established paint industries in the world, with a history that can be traced back well over a century. Since the mid-1980s, the UK has been able to boast the largest paint producer in the world (ICI Paints Division), and some of the most significant research in paint and associated technology has been undertaken by companies in the UK. The UK industry has total annual sales of approximately £2 billion, which makes it (in terms of aggregate turnover) about the same size as the crisps and snacks industry or the UK-based film industry.

There are several types of paint produced in the UK in addition to the familiar brush- or roller-applied decorative paints. The majority of paint production falls into four main user categories: decorative, industrial, automotive (including original equipment manufacturing (OEM)) and 'specialist' coatings products. This case study is particularly concerned with the decorative paint industry, whose products provide the benefits of obscuring a substrate (such as a wall), providing weather protection and providing a pleasing finish in a range of colours and finishes.

The number of competitors within the industry has varied according to the general buoyancy of the economy as a whole. As a mature product, sales of paint closely reflect the overall rate of national economic growth. In the mid-1980s, the number of UK producers peaked at over 330, but this number reduced to around 250 during the recession between 1991 and 1993 due to falling demand from industry, local authorities, the DIY sector and construction companies. Between 1993 and 2000, the number of paint companies increased again as the general demand in the economy increased. Decorative paint producers are keenly aware of the need to keep prices as low as possible because, in addition to consumers having a choice of many different paint producers, the major benefits of decorative paint can be met using several alternative materials.

Although the industry contains a small number of relatively large producers (notably the two largest – ICI Paints Division and SigmaKalon), the majority of competitors are small to medium in size, varying from as few as five employees to as many as 500. Leigh's Paints of Bolton, for example, is one of the largest with 350 employees, whereas a typical 'small' producer is Caledonia Paints Ltd in Glasgow where the proprietor both produces and distributes the product using a small production facility and a van that has been equipped to carry cans of paint to a limited number of local buyers.

The technology contained in the majority of paint products is relatively straightforward. Most conventional paints (including all decorative gloss and emulsion paints) are manufactured by a process called *high-speed dispersion*, which involves stirring the 'ingredients' together at very high rotational speed until the requisite level of consistency is achieved. High-speed dispersion machines are rather like large kitchen mixers and can be purchased, reconditioned, for as little as £5000. The formulations ('recipes') for most simple paints can be readily obtained from suppliers of raw materials who have a vested interest in ensuring that paint manufacturers have ready-to-use formulations for successful paint production.

The paint industry is a part of the broader chemical industry. As such, producers are subject to the same health, safety and emissions legislation as other parts of the chemicals sector such as petrochemicals. This has presented a number of challenges to paint companies over recent years. Two such hurdles have been the COSHH Regulations, 1989, which significantly tightened materials handling rules in the workplace, and the Environmental Protection Act, 1990, which increased restrictions on environmental malpractices, including emissions of harmful substances into the environment. In common with other companies in the chemical industry, many competitors have seen the apparent advantage of pursuing international standards accreditation and these (ISO 9000 quality standard and ISO 14000 environmental standard) have consumed significant amounts of management time. Some of the larger paint buyers have made it a condition of supply that all paint suppliers should be accredited with ISO 9000.

Concentration has significantly increased over recent years among the key volume buyers of decorative paints. Whereas, in the early

1970s, decorative paint was retailed largely through small independent DIY stores, the expansion of the DIY 'sheds' has meant that buyers are now able to purchase in much higher volumes and competition among manufacturers has intensified for shelf space As these 'sheds' have become larger and fewer in number (through mergers, acquisitions and some withdrawals from the retailing of DIY products), competition among paint producers has become even more intensified. Concentration has also increased, although to a lesser extent among the trade buyers such as painting contractors and construction companies.

The basic ingredients of paint fall into three chemical categories. Resins (also called *binders* or *vehicles*) are typically synthetic polymers that bind together other components and also provide the mechanism by which the paint sticks to a substrate and provides weatherability. Because most binders are derived from oil products, the costs to paint manufacturers are, in part, dependent upon the market rate for crude oil. The second category – pigments and extenders – are typically dry powders that are dispersed into the vehicle and provide colour, opacity and some chemical properties such as anti-corrosiveness. These compounds are also subject to variable market prices according to the relative volumes of market supply. The pigment that is used most is titanium dioxide – a white pigment that adds colour to almost all white and light-coloured paints (to which additional tints are added). Titanium dioxide results from the processing of a titanium ore which, like all ores, is subject to price variations according to its abundance (or scarcity) and availability. Titanium dioxide production is highly concentrated – four large producers control most of the world output. Third, most paints contain a solvent (usually an organic oil-derived compound) that makes the paint 'wet' and which evaporates when the paint is applied. Most of these components require production on a large scale and are consequently made by large chemical intermediate manufacturers, many of which are chemical multinationals (e.g. Exxon, Bayer, Total Oil, Shell, etc.) for whom paint components comprise a relatively small proportion of their output. Like binders, much of the content of solvents is oil-derived. Accordingly, the prices charged to paint companies for solvents are largely a function of the price of oil (which, in turn, depends upon the production volumes of oil on the world market).

Competition among players in the decorative paint industry has become increasingly intense as the number of competitors has increased and the concentration among buyers has forced producers to cut prices and provide enhanced service to the DIY 'sheds' to gain shelf space in DIY superstores at the expense of other producers. It is likely that the more successful companies in the future will be those that can control costs most effectively and/or persuade paint users of the distinctiveness or quality of their products to gain brand loyalty.

Financial results for a selection of competitors in the UK industry are shown in Table 1.

Table 1
Selected results for UK-based decorative paint companies for year ending 2000 (includes international and export sales)

Company	Total sales	Trading profit (PBIT)
ICI Paints Division	£2152 million	£177 million
SigmaKalon	1640 million euros	110.8 million euros
Humbrol	£14.374 million	£0.571 million
Akzo Nobel Decorative Paints	£203.4 million	£6.994 million
Coates Brothers	£137.8 million	£5.749 million
Manders	£37.2 million	£0.107 million
Valspar	£28.0 million	£0.834 million
Trimite	£27.6 million	£0.554 million

Ben & Jerry's Homemade Ice Cream Inc.

'A new corporate concept of linked prosperity'

The beginning

Ben Cohen and Jerry Greenfield became friends at school in the late 1960s in Burlington, Vermont, in the north-eastern USA. Their reputation as the two 'odd' eccentrics at school led them to form a strong friendship that would last for many decades.

When they left school, both Ben and Jerry became 'hippies' – social drop-outs who lived an alternative and unconventional lifestyle. They each grew their hair and a beard and, together with their dog, Malcolm, they moved in together as flatmates. One of the interests they shared was food and, as they discussed various ways of making a living, they concluded that the two most exciting areas of fast food at the time were bagels and ice cream.

Having established that the equipment needed to bake bagels would cost $40,000, the two men enrolled on an ice-cream-making correspondence course for the cost of $5 each.

In 1978, having developed some basic ice cream recipes, Ben and Jerry set up a shop in a renovated petrol station in Burlington with a capital investment of $12,000 ($4000 of which was borrowed). From the outset, Ben and Jerry wanted to produce a premium product and the fact that it was made from 'fresh Vermont milk and cream' was stressed. The outlet was called Ben & Jerry's Homemade Ice Cream and, to give the shop a unique and welcoming character, they employed a piano player to play blues in the background.

Initially, the shop was a success among Burlington locals, many of whom had known the men when they were growing up. The staff that Ben and Jerry employed were encouraged to take the same 'hippy-ish' view of business activity as the owners ('every day was a party'), but the major competitive advantage arose from the uniqueness of the product. Whereas the majority of ice cream products were traditionally flavoured, Ben and Jerry introduced unusual flavours, with 'chunks' of fruit, chocolate, nuts, toffee and similar sweets to make the textures more interesting. 'Chunky' ice cream became the prominent feature of the new organization's image.

During the summer of 1978, customer numbers grew as the reputation of the shop and the ice cream grew. It was when the winter set in at the end of the year that the troubles began. Over-the-counter ice cream sales dried up and Ben and Jerry realized they would have to find other outlets for their products if they were to avoid bankruptcy.

They persuaded a number of local grocers in Vermont to stock the product in one pint tubs, but it soon transpired that a broader customer base would be needed. Having approached a number of national supermarket chains, Ben Cohen learned that the size of the business, not to mention his appearance and attitude to business, made the buyers reluctant to take stock from him. He was advised that he ought to seek to sell the ice cream to large independent ice cream distributors in neighbouring states who would then sell the product on to the major retail multiples. It was then that Ben and Jerry encountered a problem.

The Pillsbury confrontation

Ben approached the Dari-Farms corporation with a view to have it distribute Ben & Jerry's ice cream throughout New England. Dennis Silva, the company vice president agreed to take some Ben & Jerry's stock despite Ben's unconventional approach to business. In order to increase distribution further, Ben also approached Paul's Distributors, whose chairman, Chuck Green, also agreed to act as a Ben & Jerry distributor.

The market leader in the super-premium ice cream segment at the time was Häagen Dazs, which was then owned by the large US-based Pillsbury Corporation. Pillsbury turned over $4 billion a year and had extensive food interests in addition to Häagen Dazs, including Green Giant (vegetables) and Burger King, the fast-food outlet.

Kevin Hurley, president of the Häagen Dazs subsidiary of Pillsbury, was the son-in-law of the company's founder, Reuben Matthus. Matthus had started Häagen Dazs in 1959 in New York. He came up with the Danish-sounding name in the belief that it conjured up a feeling in the consumer of an exotic European brand. By 1984, when the confrontation with Ben & Jerry's took place, Häagen Dazs held a 70% share of the super-premium ice cream market.

When Hurley discovered that both Dari-Farms and Paul's were distributing Ben & Jerry's as well as Häagen Dazs, he rang both Dennis Silva and Chuck Green. Although Ben & Jerry's still only had a tiny share of the market compared to Häagen Dazs, Hurley was determined that the distributors he used were not going to help a competitor. "We didn't say to the distributor 'You can't carry Ben & Jerry's', but 'We're asking you to make a choice'," said Hurley. "We just told them [Silva and Green] that they couldn't sell Ben & Jerry's *and* Häagen Dazs." This 'it's us or them' ultimatum took the two distributors by surprise and it presented a distressing dilemma. "We were just stunned at this comment coming from Häagen Dazs, this huge company where we were selling trailer loads of ice cream versus this minuscule amount of Ben & Jerry's we were selling," said Chuck Green of Paul's Distribution. "They had drawn this line in the sand saying that we had to make a decision."

When Ben and Jerry heard of Hurley's threat, they arranged a meeting with the distributors to discuss the situation. In view of the potential of Ben & Jerry's, neither distributor wanted to stop taking their products but, at the same time, the thought of having Häagen Dazs withdraw their supply could prove very damaging indeed. The three parties agreed that they would need legal representation if they were to take on the might of Pillsbury and they chose Howie Fuguet, a business lawyer who had spent his professional life defending large organizations.

Like Ben and Jerry, Howie was an eccentric. He was said to have cared little for his appearance and had holes in his shoes. He agreed that Pillsbury had behaved in a curious way and sent off a letter to Pillsbury setting out the nature of Ben & Jerry's grievance. Protesting that Hurley had acted unfairly, Howie wrote to the Board of Pillsbury: "It would be wishful thinking on the part of your subsidiary's officers [Häagen Dazs] to imagine that it can bully Ben & Jerry's, stifle its growth and cause it to roll over," wrote Howie. "Ben & Jerry's is a classic entrepreneurial success and its owners are aggressive. Häagen Dazs will have to learn to compete on their merits in the market place. That is the American way and that is what competition is all about."

Notwithstanding the apparent 'rightness' of Ben & Jerry's case, the legal odds were clearly stacked against them. If they couldn't beat the 'bullying' Häagen Dazs through normal legal channels, then another weapon would be needed.

The 'dough boy' campaign

The key move was to make Pillsbury the target of the campaign and not Häagen Dazs – Pillsbury was bigger and had more to lose. Since the mid-1960s, the symbol of Pillsbury was the Pillsbury 'dough boy'. The dough boy was used by Pillsbury in its advertising and other corporate communications and was a valuable symbol of the company's identity. In order to avoid the appearance of an ice cream war between two competitors, Howie proposed that they attacked the Pillsbury company by specifically targeting the dough boy.

Accordingly, the 'What's the dough boy afraid of?' campaign was launched, intentionally designed to appear as a 'David versus Goliath' conflict in which a small company (Ben & Jerry's) had been unfairly treated by a large 'bully' in the shape of Pillsbury. "We didn't really know a thing about PR. We were just trying to survive," said Ben Cohen. "If we were going to go down, we wanted to let as many people as we could know what was going on. [We wanted to say that] the reason why you can't find Ben & Jerry's on the shelf is because this big corporation [Pillsbury] is trying to prevent you, the consumer, from having a choice about what kind of ice cream you want to buy."

The campaign included T-shirts, bumper stickers, bill posters and other media, which all bore the statement: 'What's the dough boy afraid of?' Jerry launched a one-man campaign outside the Pillsbury headquarters in Minneapolis, Minnesota, and it wasn't long before the local television news programmes started carrying the story on a regular basis. This proved not only to make the public sympathize with Ben & Jerry's, but also to provide a lot of free publicity for the company and its products.

From its seventeen-strong legal department, Pillsbury assigned Richard Wegener to "get rid of the Ben & Jerry problem". Wegener quickly realized the size of the task facing Pillsbury. "The publicity became bigger than the dispute itself," said Wegener. The reputation of Pillsbury was at stake and Wegener sought to bring a rapid end to the controversy. Realizing that the campaign had grabbed the public's attention and the sympathies were predominantly with Ben & Jerry's, Wegener advised Hurley to back down.

Kevin Hurley was persuaded to sign an out-of-court settlement agreeing not to coerce any distributors. The campaign was over and Ben & Jerry's had won. The controversy not only ensured the defeat of Pillsbury, it also acted unwittingly as an enormous amount of publicity for the Ben & Jerry's brand.

After the victory

The success of Ben & Jerry's after the Pillsbury confrontation was marked. The distribution channels were widened still further until Ben & Jerry's ice cream was supplied through supermarkets, grocery stores, convenience stores and food service operations, as well as through licensed scoop shops, franchised scoop shops and company-owned scoop shops. By 1992, the company's turnover exceeded $130 million and it was on the verge of international development into the UK.

In the super-premium ice cream sector, a number of new and distinctive product flavours were launched, including 'Milk chocolate ice cream and white fudge cows swirled with white chocolate ice cream and dark fudge cows', 'Chocolate comfort low fat ice cream', 'Mocha latte' and 'Triple caramel chunk ice cream'.

In addition, non-ice-cream frozen sweets were introduced, including a range of ice cream 'novelties', frozen yoghurts and sorbets, such as 'Chunky monkey frozen yoghurt – banana frozen yoghurt with fudge flakes and walnuts'. The Ben & Jerry's name and the company's reputation for quality meant that the new products became quickly adopted by the market.

The personalities of the founders helped to frame the company's culture and its mission. Two important statements were released which described the company's approach to its approach to business.

In 1988, the company stated that, "We are dedicated to the creation and demonstration of a new corporate concept of linked prosperity." This was articulated via its philanthropy statement and its mission statement.

Ben & Jerry's philanthropy statement

Ben & Jerry's gives away 7.5% of its pretax earnings in three ways: the Ben & Jerry's Foundation; employee community action teams at five

Vermont sites; and through corporate grants made by the Director of Social Mission Development. We support projects that are models for social change, projects which exhibit creative problem-solving and hopefulness. The Foundation is managed by a nine-member employee board and considers proposals relating to children and families, disadvantaged groups, and the environment.

Mission statement

Ben & Jerry's is dedicated to the creation and demonstration of a new corporate concept of linked prosperity.

Our mission consists of three inter-related parts:

- To make, distribute and sell the finest quality all natural ice cream and related products in a wide variety of innovative flavors made from Vermont dairy products.
- To operate the Company on a sound financial basis of profitable growth, increasing value for our shareholders, and creating career opportunities and financial rewards for our employees.
- To operate the Company in a way that actively recognizes the central role that business plays in the structure of society by initiating innovative ways to improve the quality of life of a broad community – local, national, and international.

Underlying the mission of Ben & Jerry's is the determination to seek new and creative ways of addressing all three parts, while holding a deep respect for the individuals, inside and outside the company, and for the communities of which they are a part.

Who owns Newcastle United?

Newcastle United's league season had not been a good one. The 1997–98 season had started with much promise, with a recently appointed new manager (Kenny Dalglish), new player signings and a place in the European Cup. In addition, the recent flotation of over a third of the company's stock on the stock exchange had provided the club with capital with which to improve the ground and invest in new players.

Despite beating Barcelona in the opening rounds, the team did not get through to the second phase of the European Cup and the league season went from bad to worse. By March 1998, a run of bad results saw the team slip to a league position that was perilously close to the relegation zone. The intensely loyal but increasingly frustrated Newcastle fans began to openly vent their disquiet.

The new transfers had made disappointing contributions to the club's efforts on the pitch, and the faith that had been placed in Kenny Dalglish was beginning to show signs of breaking. Doubts also crept in that the financial pressures being exerted on the club from its new masters in the City may have had a detrimental effect on the club's ability to bring in the new players that the fans thought might help the team's performance.

Frustrations came to a head in mid-March 1998. The *News of the World* published a story reporting some alleged behaviour by the club's most senior two directors, Freddie Shepherd (Chairman) and Douglas Hall (Deputy Chairman, whose family owned 58% of the company's shares). It was reported that the two men had, on a trip abroad, frequented brothels and had made some indiscreet comments regarding the club, some of the players and the fans. In discussions with a reporter posing as a Middle-Eastern businessman, the two directors reportedly ridiculed the Newcastle fans for paying £50 for a replica shirt that only cost £5 to buy in. Star player Alan Shearer was compared to Mary Poppins and the directors allegedly described the women of Tyneside as dogs. The two directors also allegedly boasted that they had sacked Kevin Keegan, the former manager.

The report went down very badly among the fans on Tyneside. A local television poll asked whether the two directors should resign and 97% of callers voted that they should. The former Newcastle striker Malcolm MacDonald weighed in to the controversy by insisting on local television news that Shepherd and Hall should go.

In the days following the disclosure, the company's share price started to slip as investors registered their discomfort with the internal controversies at the strategic level in the company.

Shepherd and Hall remained silent for a few days, but eventually decided to issue a public apology in an attempt to defuse the row that had taken hold among the fans and in the City. It was issued to local newsrooms on the morning of a crucial relegation match against Crystal Palace. The lunchtime news bulletins carried the statement and then cut to street interviews where fans were asked if they accepted the apology. All of them said that they would not accept it and the insistence that they should resign was repeated.

The home game against bottom-of-the-table Crystal Palace was a disaster – the team lost two-one. It was a dreadful end to a bad week. After the game, some of the vocal and frustrated fans congregated outside the offices section of the ground and chanted, 'Sack the board, Sack the board, Sack the board' – scenes that were recorded and broadcast on national television.

Malcolm MacDonald repeated his demand that Shepherd and Hall should resign and Kevin Keegan added his weight to the calls to resign by commenting that "The fans own the club."

As the weekend of 21 March approached, the directors still refused to resign. After all, Douglas Hall (via his holding company) was the majority shareholder and was thus technically in control of the club. The *News of the World* published another batch of damaging allegations against the two directors on Sunday 22 March. They were alleged to have said that they liked the fans to get drunk because they owned the bars in which the fans drank and hence were able to extract more profit from the same fans.

On Monday 23 March, the non-executive directors of Newcastle United plc met in an all-day meeting. It was later announced that Shepherd and Hall had resigned. Local television news carried more interviews with fans in the town centre, all of whom said that they were pleased to see the two directors go. The following day, Sir John Hall, Douglas's father and the former club chairman, was re-appointed Chairman until the end of the current season.

Sir John held a press conference on the Tuesday in which he expressed anger at the way that the two directors had been treated by the press and by the fans. It was pointed out that both Douglas and Freddie had made a massive contribution to the development of the club, including much of the behind-the-scene work involved in bringing both Alan Shearer and Kenny Dalglish to the club. Sir John conceded that the two directors had acted foolishly but he deeply resented their being hounded from office by 'mob power'.

As the league season progressed, the team's performance showed little sign of improvement. The one high point was the FA Cup semi-final defeat of Barnsley which guaranteed Newcastle a place in the 1998 FA Cup Final. At the conclusion of the game, team manager Kenny Dalglish defiantly dedicated the win to Douglas and Freddie.

During the summer of 1998, the fans' attention was drawn away from Newcastle United and towards the World Cup in France. Then there was a development in the week following the end of the World Cup. On 15 July, the Board of the plc met at a secret location and speculation grew among the fans that the secrecy may be because Hall and Shepherd were about to be reinstated as directors.

A press release was issued on 24 July that the two directors had indeed been reinstated. The two men issued a statement to the fans. Freddie Shepherd said that he and Douglas had been very stupid but qualified their statement by saying that, with them sharing 65% of the company's stock, it was always going to be difficult with them on the outside.

The news was reported on the national as well as local television, and cameras focused on their reserved parking spaces outside the office section of St James Park, the company's home ground. The point was made that, even although they had technically resigned in the spring, in reality the two had never really left.

When the fans were interviewed for the television news, opinion was somewhat more divided than it had been when they had previously called for the resignations. Some maintained their defiance while others seemed to accept that the club needed good management and that Hall and Shepherd had proved to be competent in the past.

Food retailing in the UK

As at the year 2001, Britain's big four supermarket groups (Tesco, Sainsbury's, Safeway and Asda) had achieved a position that was in part enviable but at the same time open to some criticism. Throughout the 1990s, they had, for the most part, maintained steady increases in sales and profits, and a gradual increase in their combined market share. The 'out-of-town' strategy, which all four had followed for the most part, had paid off as sales grew against 'town and suburb' competitors such as Somerfield and Iceland.

Furthermore, the market research evidence pointed to a situation in which consumers were generally happy with what was offered. With a typical store offering in excess of 35,000 product lines, the choice for shoppers was unprecedented. Completely new entrants were very little threat owing to the huge costs of store development, the labyrinthine complexity of supplier relationships, the arduous tasks associated with gaining planning permission for store developments and, to a limited extent, customer loyalty. Suitable sites for new stores became expensive and hard to find, especially in key locations within easy reach of large car-owning centres of population. High share prices over most of the decade acted as an effective deterrent for predatory takeovers, although Wal-Mart from the USA proved it could be done when it acquired Asda in 1999.

By the year 2001, however, there was evidence that the future may not be all rosy for the big supermarket groups. There were signs that they had reached the peak of their power and influence. Food sales were not growing rapidly and, as a proportion of total consumer spending, had dropped by more than 10% (to just over 10.5% of all spending) during the 1990s. It was predicted that food sales as a proportion of consumer spending would 'flatline' for many years to come. Profit margins had been slipping in recent years, partly because of the entry of discounters and partly because rivalry between the big chains was bringing them into direct competition with each other.

Regulatory and legal changes arising from the opening up of the single European market in 1993 made inward investment easier for foreign 'invaders'. The impact of a small number of such foreign-owned supermarket chains entering the UK market was felt by most industry players during the 1990s. Although companies such as Carrefour, Lidl, Netto, Metro and Aldi had been successfully building international businesses that included the UK market, the British-based supermarket companies, including the 'big four', had made little or no foreign investments of their own. Their expansion strategy was limited to building as many stores as possible within the British Isles and gaining as much geographical coverage as possible. As this geographical expansion continued, however, the distribution of goods to the stores became an increasingly complex process. With stores covering the UK mainland and, increasingly, Northern Ireland and the Republic of Ireland, it became vital that supermarket chains utilized the most sophisticated and reliable supply-chain management methods. One way in which the companies dealt with such problems was to centralize their administrative activities and consolidate their supply-chain management. Sainsbury's succeeded in reducing costs by £20 million in the last few years of the decade by improving its ordering and supply control systems. Rising fuel prices in the late 1990s posed a cost challenge to the road-based distribution systems, however, especially those with outlying stores and a diverse geographic base. Although the Exchequer welcomed the increased fuel tax revenues, designed in part to discourage vehicle usage for environmental reasons, the more vocal environmental lobby groups argued that fuel prices should have been even higher.

The introduction of home and Internet shopping put pressure on the supermarket chains to deliver local orders as quickly as possible. The ease by which most customers could switch supermarkets – especially as prices and product offerings were so similar – made home delivery one of the key factors in winning and keeping a share of this growing sector. Some companies attempted to manage home delivery in-house, whereas others employed existing logistics companies (Marks & Spencer, for example, awarded a contract for its same-day delivery service to Exel Logistics Ltd in 1999). Internet shopping also necessitated substantial investment in information technology services, which only the largest competitors could afford. In most locations, Tesco and Sainsbury's were pioneers in Internet shopping, although Asda and Safeway were close behind. Most other supermarket companies had no Internet shopping facilities at all as at the year 2000.

Not surprisingly, food manufacturers were the most important out-side suppliers to the industry. These ranged in size from small-scale local manufacturers of specialist products to major international producers such as Nestle and Philip Morris. What all suppliers clearly understood was that the large supermarket chains had immense buying power owing to their vast economies of scale. As a result of consumer demands and the huge diversity of the product lines carried in the stores, the large supermarket chains were able to source goods from around the globe. The idea of fresh produce seasonality became a thing of the past as the international reach of the supplier networks meant that shoppers could enjoy fresh strawberries at Christmas and brussels sprouts in August. In addition to the power that the large supermarkets had over the suppliers of well-known brands, the high volumes of 'own label' products meant that they were also able to gain favourable terms from the likes of Dalgety plc and Associated Foods plc, who derived a large proportion of their business from manufacturing own-brand goods for the big supermarket chains. Overseas companies, such as South African-based Spring Valley Foods, were asked to, and succeeded in providing, UK-based stores with retail packs of fruit within four days of the fruit being harvested.

All was not rosy for the big four supermarkets, however. They were criticized for the effects that their out-of-town investment strategy had had on high streets and town centres. Town planners came under pressure from some politicians and trade bodies to limit new planning permission applications for out-of-town developments so as to provide some support for suburban local shopping parades, independent retailers and non-car-owning shoppers. Then they were investigated for alleged monopolistic practices by the UK Competition Commission.

The 1999 investigation by the UK competition authorities was seen as a 'let off' for the 'big four', but it highlighted the extent to which each was exposed to potential criticism from one corner or another. Added to this were the challenges that industry financial performance was below the FTSE average, and year-to-year volume growth in the market was tiny. This maturity of the market meant that, in food at least, any gain by one company had to come from someone else's market share. Given the low margins and the high capital intensity of the industry (i.e. the high fixed costs that each company was carrying), nobody in the industry could afford a price war.

In terms of strategy, therefore, short-term advantage lay in fundamental retailing skills – making their space work for them, squeezing out costs while maintaining availability, improving quality while preserving profit margins at attractive prices, innovating in the total mix of products and services. Perhaps the greatest (and least familiar) challenge was to make information technology deliver a better understanding of consumers and use this to improve marketing.

As at 2001, two areas were noted as key to the development of strategy in the supermarket industry. First, there was the lack of a truly distinctive personality – the store groups were considered to be virtually all the same. Asda claimed to offer 'service with personality', but there was little evidence of 'personality' over and above that found in any other store. Even Marks & Spencer was finding it difficult to show the differences between itself and leading rivals. Fresh food and ready-made meals were thought to be a key competitive battleground, but any innovation by one competitor was quickly copied by the others. 'Craft skills' re-emerged, such as on-the-premises bakeries, butchers and fishmongers, but no company stood out from the others as a result.

Second, there was a belief that there was little that could be done with the basic retail formula that could create competitive advantage over others. Shopping for food had been much the same for 30 years – it was self-service. Although the supermarkets transformed the shopping experience in the late 1960s with this innovation, any changes since then were at the margin. Compared to ten or twenty years previously, the modern superstore had more car parking, was more emotionally warmer and physically more pleasant with a wider range of products, but was, in its basic formula, exactly the same. For most shoppers, shopping was seen as clinical and unexciting, and being in one shop was much the same as being in any other. Furthermore, the companies were well aware that the relationship between consumer and store was dangerously shallow and impersonal.

Tesco's rise to the top of the pile (in terms of market share) in the mid-1990s caused consternation at Sainsbury's but presented Tesco's management with the challenge to stay ahead. Its challenge was to remain – if not all things to all people, then attractive to all main demographic segments. Its international strategy was distinctly unproven, but there seemed to be a coherent philosophy behind its intentions; it had learned from past errors and its track record was improving. It was also noted that Tesco would be a hugely attractive ally for any big continental group that wished to enter Britain.

Sainsbury's had an entirely different challenge. Having been leader for so long then lost the plot a little, it had to summon up new drive. It fell behind in a whole range of innovations, notably loyalty cards, and its priorities were to rediscover the business authority and certain feel for food-standards leadership that once motivated it. Asda had the clearest positioning of the big groups but had to deliver on its promises from a tightly controlled cost and staff base. Safeway was perhaps the most vulnerable of the big four as it had a 'mixed store' base. This meant it competed with the other big three for out-of-town market share, but the fact that it had some smaller suburban stores meant it also had to take on Somerfield, Iceland and other companies in that part of the market. Safeway had always been willing to be innovative, however, and was the first to introduce self-scanning and crèches, for example.

Finding the key to success in the supermarket industry was elusive, however. The decade 2000–2010 promised as much, or maybe even more, change than the 1990s. Finding the right strategy and understanding the retail environment was unlikely to get any easier.

Appendix 1

Retail sales of food in supermarkets and superstores, 1993–1998 (source: *Business Monitor* SDM28, Key Note)

	1993	1994	1995	1996	1997	1998
Sales (£ million)	51,689	54,920	59,362	63,400	67,096	70,786

Figures include some sales through convenience stores and food halls.

Appendix 2

Leading supermarket and superstore chains in the UK food industry by value, 1998 (source: company information, Key Note)

Company	Market share (%)
Tesco	15.2
Sainsbury's	12.6
Safeway	7.8
Asda	7.2
Somerfield/Kwik Save	4.5
Marks & Spencer*	3.1
Morrison	2.3
Iceland	1.7
Waitrose	1.3
Others	44.3
Total	100.0

*Food sales only.

Appendix 3

Leading UK supermarket and superstore retailers by number of outlets, 1998 (source: company information, Key Note)

Somerfield/Kwik Save	1,400
Tesco	568
Safeway	500
Sainsbury's	391
Marks & Spencer*	285
Co-operative Wholesale Society	268
Asda	218
Gateway Foodmarkets	132
Aldi	130
Waitrose	113
Netto	113
Budgens	108
Iceland	108

*Food sales only.

Appendix 4

Form of transport used by adults to travel to regular grocery purchasing point, 1998 (source: Target Group Index)

Form of transport	000s	%
Car	31,985	74.2
Bus	3,443	8.0
Train	113	0.3
Bicycle, motorcycle, moped	473	1.1
Walk	5,732	13.3

© BMRB International, 1998.

Appendix 5

Consumer choice of supermarket by social grade, 1998 (source: BMRB Access)

'At which, if any, of the following supermarkets do you shop for groceries on a regular basis?'

	Social grade (% of adults)				
	AB	CI	C2	D	E
Tesco	52	44	40	37	36
Sainsbury's	52	39	38	29	32
Asda	22	30	29	38	20
Marks & Spencer	31	30	27	17	19
Safeway	24	28	24	23	17
Iceland	14	19	24	35	28
Co-op	19	14	20	25	20
Somerfield	10	20	16	16	17
Kwik Save	9	10	20	23	26
Wm Morrison	11	8	14	20	9
Aldi	4	7	12	15	11
Waitrose	18	9	5	2	5

Base: 1015 adults aged 16+.

Appendix 6

Analysis of the UK grocery trade by turnover, 1998 (source: *Business Monitor* PA1003 – size analysis of UK businesses)

Turnover (£000)	Number of enterprises	%
1–49	1,390	6.0
50–99	4,365	18.7
100–249	10,040	43.0
250–499	4,735	20.3
500–999	1,840	7.9
1000–4999	820	3.5
5000+	155	0.7
Total	23,345	100.0*

*Does not sum due to rounding.

Appendix 7

Forecast sales by supermarkets and superstores, 1999–2002 (source: Key Note estimates)

	1999	2000	2001	2002
Sales (£ million)	74,326	78,042	82,724	87,274

Appendix 8

Summary company financial information, 1992–2001 (source: FAME)

Tesco plc	2001	2000	1999	1998	1997	1996	1995	1994	1993	1992
Turnover (UK£ billion)	20.988	18.796	17.158	16.452	13.887	12.094	10.101	8.599	7.581	7.097
Profit (loss) before tax (UK£ billion)	1.054	0.933	0.842	0.728	0.750	0.675	0.551	0.435	0.580	0.545
Net tangible assets (liabilities) (UK£ billion)	7.189	6.246	5.512	4.726	4.521	4.214	4.127	3.735	3.471	3.148
Shareholder funds (UK£ billion)	5.356	4.769	4.382	3.876	3.890	3.588	3.104	2.748	2.752	2.447
Return on sales (%)	5.02	4.96	4.91	4.42	5.40	5.58	5.45	5.06	7.66	7.69
Return on shareholder funds (%)	19.68	19.56	19.21	18.78	19.28	18.81	17.75	15.84	21.10	22.29
Return on capital employed (%)	14.35	14.62	14.97	15.40	16.59	16.02	13.35	11.66	16.73	17.32
Liquidity ratio	0.20	0.17	0.16	0.13	0.11	0.09	0.16	0.19	0.27	0.38
Gearing (%)	63.48	51.58	47.28	38.03	24.09	26.78	43.49	37.01	27.56	29.40
Number of employees	152,210	134,896	172,712	185,580	153,198	135,037	182,926	93,339	86,066	87,033

J Sainsbury plc	2001	2000	1999	1998	1997	1996	1995	1994	1993	1992
Turnover (UK£ billion)	17.244	16.271	16.433	14.500	13.395	12.627	11.357	10.583	9.685	8.695
Profit (loss) before tax (UK£ billion)	0.434	0.509	0.888	0.719	0.609	0.712	0.809	0.369	0.733	0.628
Net tangible assets (liabilities) (UK£ billion)	5.768	5.516	5.501	5.123	4.482	4.235	3.996	3.708	3.759	3.236
Shareholder funds (UK£ billion)	4.911	4.742	4.644	4.112	3.671	3.534	3.289	3.040	3.029	2.640
Return on sales (%)	2.52	3.13	5.40	4.96	4.55	5.64	7.12	3.49	7.57	7.22
Return on shareholder funds (%)	8.84	10.73	17.65	17.49	18.10	20.15	24.60	12.14	24.20	23.78
Return on capital employed (%)	7.18	8.73	14.90	14.03	14.82	16.81	20.25	9.95	19.50	19.40
Liquidity ratio	0.68	0.55	0.61	0.52	0.18	0.17	0.20	0.21	0.23	0.33
Gearing (%)	30.73	41.02	32.77	35.19	47.70	42.73	28.46	31.84	27.01	31.99
Number of employees	111,600	116,946	178,958	107,226	165,992	154,661	131,298	124,841	120,119	112,784

Asda Stores Ltd	2001	2000	1999	1998	1997	1996	1995	1994	1993	1992
Turnover (UK£ billion)		9.680	8.178	7.601	6.883	6.010	5.257	4.794	4.396	4.308
Profit (loss) before tax (UK£ billion)		0.418	0.324	0.320	0.270	0.334	0.216	0.080	0.131	−0.079
Net tangible assets (liabilities) (UK£ billion)		2.112	1.856	1.641	1.498	1.406	1.189	1.330	1.332	1.281
Shareholder funds (UK£ billion)		1.969	1.817	1.565	1.417	1.288	1.071	0.990	0.993	0.943
Return on sales (%)		4.32	3.96	4.21	3.93	5.56	4.11	1.66	2.99	−1.84
Return on shareholder funds (%)		21.23	17.81	20.43	19.09	25.91	20.17	8.06	13.23	−8.35
Return on capital employed (%)		19.79	17.44	19.50	18.06	23.74	18.17	6.00	9.87	−6.15
Liquidity ratio		0.67	0.40	0.47	0.41	0.77	0.65	0.85	0.85	0.71
Gearing (%)		34.72	3.60	5.55	8.71	47.45	52.10	50.48	50.72	46.98
Number of employees		89,981	80,101	76,350	74,625	73,581	67,604	69,228	65,621	66,500
Safeway plc										
Turnover (UK£ billion)	8.151	7.659	7.511	6.978	6.589	6.069	5.815	5.608	5.196	4.729
Profit (loss) before tax (UK£ billion)	0.314	0.236	0.341	0.340	0.421	0.429	0.176	0.362	0.417	0.364
Net tangible assets (liabilities) (UK£ billion)	3.128	3.070	2.946	2.845	2.455	2.294	2.070	2.149	1.974	1.619
Shareholder funds (UK£ billion)	2.190	2.051	2.123	2.007	1.887	1.939	1.755	1.776	1.644	1.446
Return on sales (%)	3.86	3.08	4.53	4.87	6.38	7.07	3.03	6.46	8.03	7.71
Return on shareholder funds (%)	14.36	11.51	16.04	16.95	22.28	22.14	10.03	20.38	25.38	25.20
Return on capital employed (%)	10.05	7.69	11.56	11.96	17.13	18.72	8.50	16.85	21.14	22.51
Liquidity ratio	0.18	0.17	0.19	0.20	0.19	0.22	0.18	0.26	0.53	0.65
Gearing (%)	55.65	66.20	53.76	45.16	40.60	21.89	24.05	24.72	37.72	28.40
Number of employees	57,904	137,661	75,904	75,193	70,423	66,681	67,323	68,546	65,937	65,635

Derwent Valley Foods Ltd

The early years (1981–88)

Beginnings

The story of Derwent Valley Foods (DVF) began in the early 1980s when Roger McKechnie left Tudor Foods (potato crisp manufacturers) in County Durham seeking a new challenge within the crisps and snacks industry.

Roger had enjoyed a successful career in fast-moving consumer goods (FMCGs), first with Proctor and Gamble and then for fourteen years at Tudor, where he had become marketing director. He was responsible for establishing Tudor as the brand leader in the crisps sector in the north-east region. When he was presented with the opportunity to become the company's managing director, he decided to take his expertise out of Tudor to attempt to establish his own company.

One of Roger's longstanding friends, Ray McGhee, was a product group manager with the foods group Lyons. Ray was persuaded to join Roger in the new venture and they decided to explore the possibility of setting up the new business within the sector that Roger knew best – crisps and snacks.

In April 1981, Roger set out his ideas for the company:

> The company will manufacture and sell a wide range of high-quality pre-packaged savoury snack food products. It will be positioned as a small, caring, totally committed manufacturer of high-quality products able to give its customers remarkable service and value for money due to low overheads and the personal involvement of key management.

As Roger and Ray developed their ideas, two of Roger's former colleagues from Tudor expressed an interest in joining the embryonic company. Keith Gill, formerly Tudor's group product manager, was energetic and good at generating ideas; John Pike joined with a view to overseeing production.

In January 1982, as the four were still formulating their initial strategy, Roger McKechnie went to the USA to attend the Annual Snacks and Crisps Convention. Roger noted that, in contrast to packaging designs in the UK, premium crisps and snacks for the US market were often presented in high-quality metallized polythene packets. This not only assured greater freshness, but also allowed for the possibility of imprinting distinctive and attractive designs on the packaging. At the same convention, Roger identified a range of production machinery, unavailable in the UK, that could be used to manufacture a wide range of textures and shapes of corn- and bread-based snacks.

A major theme at the conference was the growth of the upmarket savoury snack market. Unlike in the UK, where premium non-potato savoury snacks accounted for only a fraction of 1% of total savoury snacks, the Americans had developed this segment, which accounted for about 8% of their total sales – and at higher gross margins than in the traditional 'crisps and nuts' markets.

Brand and product development

From the outset, Roger was aware of these changes in the market for savoury snacks and he and his fellow founder directors began looking for ideas on products and market positioning, particularly at the premium and specialist end of the market. The traditional market for potato crisps was in maturity and offered limited opportunity for high profits, so they set about developing products that were both distinctive and could sell at a premium price.

One product idea that was relatively new at the time was to base snack products on corn rather than potato. Corn was known to be the basis of a popular snack in South and Central America, and the tortilla chip was the first of a number of ideas that formed the basis of DVF's first tranche of products. A range of exotic flavours from different parts of the world was developed and, together with the unique foil packaging, the idea for the distinctive brand was born.

The name *Phileas Fogg* was suggested as the name of the brand after Jules Verne's character in the novel *Around the World in 80 Days*. A design was based on this concept that would not only accommodate the early product range but also others that might be added later. Before long, the Phileas Fogg brand comprised a number of products, including 'Tortilla Chips', 'California Corn Chips' (cheese flavour) and 'Punjab Puri' (spicy flavour). The products were packaged in 100-gram packs, compared to the more usual 25-gram packs of potato crisps.

Such a specialized product range necessitated a clear identification of DVF's target market. The original strategy had made it clear that it was in the relatively unexploited 'adult' sector that DVF saw its clearest opportunity for innovation. DVF set out to create a range of high-quality products that were distinctive in shape, texture and flavour, and especially appealing to people who had acquired a taste for foreign foods. A wholesome, appetizing and, at same time, slightly exotic taste experience was what they wanted to offer.

An insight into possible consumer reaction to product and packaging was obtained by arranging for small groups, drawn from the relevant market segments, to meet in a social setting where reactions could be observed and impressions and comments recorded. It was noted that the most likely target market segment for the range would be adults in AB households, aged under 35 years with experience of foreign travel. The favours were often an 'acquired' taste and the products were typically consumed with alcoholic beverages.

Production and distribution

With the new product idea now well developed, the new company set about finding suitable premises for production and as a base for operations. Given that the four all lived in the north-east of England, the most obvious option was to see what was available in that region.

A site in the former steel town of Consett, County Durham, was eventually selected. John Pike explained the reasons for choosing Consett.

There were a number of reasons [for choosing Consett]. Given that we were unprepared (nor in truth would any great advantage have been gained) to move house, we reviewed a number of locations within the North East which carried maximum grant support. Consett offered a suitable rent-free factory as well as space to expand. The support from DIDA [Derwentside Industrial Development Agency] – then run at British Steel Corporation's cost, was a significant factor. There was a

council and a town happy to welcome us who could provide the labour
we required.

The production facility on the Number One Industrial Estate in
Consett offered 12,000 square feet of production space – an adequate
area for the start up. Employees were drawn largely from the large
pool of unemployed people in the town, which had suffered since the
closure of the large steel works in 1979. The machines that Roger had
identified as being suitable in the USA were imported to form the
basis of the plant.

A relaxed and informal style was maintained against a background
of close personal involvement by the partners in every aspect of the
company's work. First-name relationships, shared canteen facilities
and the absence of status symbols helped to encourage an atmosphere
that was friendly and informal, and they took particular trouble to
ensure that everyone was fully briefed on the company's progress and
problems. The fast efficient service they wanted to offer to their customers demanded the greatest possible flexibility and everyone was
expected to carry out any task within their capacity that the situation
demanded.

The company policy was to pay wage rates higher than average for
comparable work in the area. The legacy of closure at British Steel,
and other companies in the area, ensured a good supply of key skills
in the operation and maintenance of electronically controlled
machinery.

Channels of distribution were identified as supermarket chains
with a high proportion of AB householders among their customers
and delicatessen stores, of which there were some 4000 at that time in
the UK. Sainsbury's, Safeway, Waitrose and Marks & Spencer represented the chief possibilities among the supermarket chains. After
some careful detective work, small specialist distributors were identified as supplying the delicatessen stores. The network was completed
by March 1983.

Changes

It wasn't long before demand for the Phileas Fogg brand exceeded
the capacity of the original factory and the company was able to
secure a second factory just across the road from the first. As well
as expanding production space from 12,000 to 40,000 square feet, this

offered a more modern facility for both production and office accommodation. The four directors set up a large shared office in one corner of the new building to enable them to discuss strategy with each other in an open and inclusive way.

In order to consolidate its position in its market niche, DVF made a number of acquisitions in the 1980s. Anglo-Oriental Foods was a London-based ethnic food specialist and was a typical DVF's acquisition as the company sought to buy in increased capacity, geographical coverage and expertise. Roger expressed his personal vision for the group as wanting, "to become the number one upmarket snack food manufacturer in the UK. We want to be the Rolls Royce of the snack food industry."

By 1988, DVF had experienced four years of consistent growth and, in addition to its acquisitions, had introduced new products, some of which were based on nuts and on bread. From a standing start, turnover had grown to £14 million and the company employed 200 people. It was noted, however, that one of the most urgent needs was to appoint good managers, "to give us [the directors] the time to do the things we are best at, such as strategic thinking and creativity in spotting new products and ideas".

At that time the £1 billion snack food market was growing at around 5% per year in real terms, with the adult sector growing faster still. DVF was a "piddling little force in a huge market" with a 1–2% market share in a market growing faster than DVF's turnover. The big players in the market "have not yet attacked us head on", said McKechnie.

Culture and management style

From the outset in 1982, the four directors sought to cultivate a unique corporate culture into DVF. It was described as 'informal' and was encapsulated in the maxim 'make it fun.' Unlike other employers in the industry, DVF's directors dressed informally and encouraged their managers to do the same. It was important, they believed, to keep employees 'on a high'. The idea behind the culture was eventually articulated in the mission statement:

We will become the best UK adult snack company through dedication to quality, the bold use of new ideas, and the determination to succeed. As we strive to achieve this goal, it is important that we maintain an environment of friendship, cooperation and respect.

The idea of friendship and cooperation was considered pivotal to the success of the company. The directors believed that, through this cultural approach, an environment of creativity and innovation could be cultivated – something that would be vital if DVF was to continue its growth and success.

At that time, possible future options were many. Outlining the partners' aspirations, McKechnie said they were not in the business of seeking a flotation or selling up. "It's too early to cash in on our investment. We are still enjoying it," he said. "We are in the business of developing the business. We want to become the number one upmarket snack food manufacturer in the UK. We want to be the Rolls Royce of the snack food industry." The partners also looked at maintaining the quality of the product and their ethics of doing business in an increasingly complicated company environment.

Kwik Save Group plc (A)

An introduction to the UK retail industry

The total sales through UK supermarkets in 1997 exceeded £62 billion. Of this total, the majority was food (approximately £45 billion); the remainder comprised sales of household goods and clothing. The total UK food sales (from supermarkets and other outlets) in 1997 amounted to £81 billion.

The grocery sector underwent a number of changes during the 1990s. Among the most important of these was the increasing concentration of market share among the largest companies. By 1996, the four largest competitors in the sector controlled in excess of 60% of the total market by value (Table 1). Five years previously, the same companies had controlled less than half of the total market.

Table I
Market shares of the leading UK
supermarket and superstore chains by
value, 1996 (source: Key Note)

Company	Market share (%)
Tesco	20.3
Sainsbury's	18.1
Asda	12.2
Safeway	9.9
Kwik Save	4.5
Somerfield	4.5
Marks & Spencer*	3.6
Wm Morrison	3.3
Waitrose	2.0
Iceland	1.8

*Food sales only.

Table 2

Leading UK supermarket and superstore retailers by number of outlets in the UK, 1997 (source: Key Note)

Company	Number of outlets
Kwik Save	979
Tesco	545
Safeway	500
Somerfield	400
Sainsbury's	378
Marks & Spencer*	285
Co-operative Wholesale Society	268
Asda	213
Gateway	132
Aldi Stores	130
Netto Foodstores	113
Waitrose	113
Budgens	108
Iceland Group	108
Wm Morrison	86
Food Giant	28
Savacentre	12
Lidl	10
Dales	7

*Food sales only.

The history and philosophy of Kwik Save

What later became the Kwik Save Group plc started life in 1959 in the North Wales town of Rhyl. In 1965, when the company had four stores, it changed its name from Value Foods Ltd to Kwik Save. The name change was thought appropriate to reflect the philosophy of the company: to provide foods at discounted prices. "We do not compromise on quality," the company said, "but simply achieve savings on operating costs by efficiencies and adherence to our no-nonsense trading philosophy."

The company's outlets grew steadily in number. Although prepackaged goods remained the core of Kwik Save's product offering, in-store franchises allowed the products offered for sale to be substantially widened. Branded wines, beers, spirits and tobacco were retailed through such an arrangement, as were in-store franchised departments for meats and greengrocery. In this context, 'franchise' referred to a nominated independent supplier selling specialized products within Kwik Save stores. It was argued that by franchising out the retailing of non-prepackaged goods, the core Kwik Save retailing formula could be focused upon. Some of the franchisees were eventually acquired by Kwik Save, although they remained operationally independent despite their change in ownership.

In 1970, with the company having expanded to a total of 24 stores, it was floated on the London Stock Exchange. This provided the capital required for further expansion and, over the next decade, the company increased its stores to a total of 260. Eleven years later, the company opened its 750th store and, by 1995, it owned a total of 990 outlets (see Table 3).

Table 3
Number of Kwik Save
outlets (source: Kwik
Save Group plc)

Year	Number of stores
1965	4
1970	24
1975	71
1980	260
1885	420
1990	661
1991	730
1992	780
1993	814
1994	860
1995	990

In the mid-1990s, the chief executive, Graeme Bowler, set out Kwik Save's underlying approach as one of "providing shoppers with unbeatable value from conveniently located stores". He continued: "Outstanding value will remain the cornerstone of Kwik Save's retailing philosophy".

The company had a succinct mission statement:

> To operate clean, bright, efficient, friendly and socially responsible 'no nonsense' foodstores which give to the discerning shopper the best value anywhere.

In addition, a 'charter' was published in its annual report:

- The more efficiently we operate, the more our customers benefit from the best prices.
- We sell top brands and top sellers – we never compromise on quality.
- We always use our buying power to obtain the keenest costs and pass on the savings through everyday low prices.
- We operate smaller, efficient stores that are conveniently located and easy to shop in.
- We don't insult our customers with frills or gimmicks for which, ultimately, they pay the price.

We believe all this adds up to the best value shopping in the United Kingdom.

Acquisitions and growth

Beginning in 1981, the company began a programme of non-organic expansion. On 1 May 1981, Kwik Save completed the purchase of the Coleman Meat Company Ltd, which subsequently became Kwik Save's first wholly owned in-store franchise operator. Coleman's was at the time an independent meat producer and butcher, and Kwik Save used its expertise to operate the meat sections in most of its larger stores, thus adding to its own offerings of prepackaged products. Eventually, Coleman's also operated the greengrocery concessions and some other 'specialist' counters in Kwik Save stores.

In 1986, Kwik Save purchased 29 Arctic freezer centres – a company that concentrated on the growing frozen food market, thus providing Kwik Save with a new range of frozen products. Tates Ltd was purchased in August 1986 – a company that operated the Tates Lateshopper 'convenience' outlets. Kwik Save's geographical coverage was expanded with the 1987 purchase of 43 stores in London, thus increasing the group's presence in the South East. Further expansion in the London area was limited, however, as the target demographic sectors (mainly socio-economic groups C2, D and E – see Appendix 4) were less concentrated in that region than in others.

In 1989, the Victor Value chain of 'limited-assortment' supermarkets was acquired. The majority of these 'conveniently located' stores were converted into Kwik Save format shops, and a number of others were closed because they were not deemed to be economically viable. This acquisition continued Kwik Save's strategy of buying existing retail premises rather than investing in more expensive new-build investments. Victor Value was typical of those acquisitions that were bought for the premises rather than for the value of the 'name', enabling the company to increase the proportion of target segments it could reach.

The acquisitions continued into the 1990s. In 1991, 42 former Gateway properties were added to the Group in the previously under-represented North East of England. Seven Grandways stores were purchased and 18 stores previously operated by RT Willis (Food Distributors) Ltd. In the same year, Kwik Save bought the off-licence chain Liquorsave, to operate the wines, beers and spirits franchises in the larger Kwik Save stores. In 1992, twelve stores were purchased from William Jackson to enable Kwik Save to develop its presence in the Yorkshire and Humberside region, and, in 1994, 100 stores were added by the acquisition of the Shoprite chain of discount retailers – a company with a broad geographic coverage within the UK.

Although a few of the acquisitions continued to operate under their own name, the majority were bought for their location and were refitted under the Kwik Save format. One of the results of this programme of expansion was a significant widening of the company's geographic base.

Shops and locations

Unlike some of its competitors, Kwik Save did not develop large out-of-town superstores. Its focus from the outset was on smaller local town centre or suburban developments which the majority of its customers could reach on foot or by a short bus ride. The average size of its stores in 1995 was less than 10,000 square feet – very small in comparison to the major food multiples such as Tesco, Asda and Sainsbury's.

By geographic area, the overwhelming majority of Kwik Save out-lets were opened or acquired in areas of the country that had suffered de-industrialization over recent decades. The stores were largely located in Wales, the North West, the North East and the Midlands. A number of stores were opened in selected parts of London and the South West. There was a small presence in Scotland.

Products

Kwik Save's product range comprised both branded products from the major food manufacturers and a range of the company's own-branded products. In order to develop the market among the more cost-conscious customers, the 'No Frills' own brand was launched in 1993. The 'No Frills' range was packaged in simple black and white and was designed to appeal to those customers to whom value for money was more important than premium features. Within a year of the launch of 'No Frills', sales of the 100 products in the brand accounted for 7% of total sales and was growing. Despite new product launches, Kwik Save's total product offering was small in comparison with the larger multiples. A typical Asda or Sainsbury's store typically carried 35,000 different product lines. In a Kwik save store, the figure was approximately 5,000 – mainly basic and staple goods that could be expected to have a short residence time on the shelf (thus favouring stock turnover over customer choice).

The company claimed that, by stocking different quality grades of products, the customer was given the maximum choice (three 'grades' of instant coffee, for example), although in other areas of the product offering Kwik Save offered only a fraction of the choice of its larger rivals. This disparity was particularly marked with fresh produce and in more exotic and premium products (of which these were very few).

The focus of the product range was firmly on 'the fastest selling brands, varieties and sizes'. This emphasis meant that Kwik Save made no secret of its aim to provide cost savings (and hence lower prices) by stocking a smaller range of products than its major 'superstore' com-petitors, but that the faster stock turnover would, it was hoped, result in lower stockholding costs.

Technology and systems

Kwik Save was one of the earliest adopters of scanning technology and EPOS in the retail industry. Investment in scanning began in 1988 and was designed to exploit the new (at the time) bar code information on product packaging. In addition to speeding up the checkout process, scanning technology facilitated rapid transfer of stock-flow information to decision-makers. The company described its technology as enabling the company to "manage a product range tailored to customers' needs and to operate an efficient and cost-effective supply chain". Specifically, EPOS (electronic point of sale) was designed to optimize stockholding, to increase the stocking of fast-moving items and to reduce or eliminate the holding of slow-moving or obsolete stock items. Electronic links from stores back to the central warehouse meant that stockholding and ordering was informed by data from the EPOS system.

In the mid-1990s, the group-wide computer systems were upgraded with a view to offering a number of additional advantages. In summary, the new systems were designed to "lock in a low-cost operating base".

The company detailed the advantages:

- upgrading our point of sale equipment to facilitate electronic payment and special promotions;
- developing new systems to fit the product range and promotions to local needs;
- developing new stock and re-ordering systems to let us refill shelves daily – essential to our fresh and chilled food plans;
- extending the computerization programme within our distribution centres.

In order to gain economies of scale in product purchasing and distribution, a new purpose-built warehousing centre was developed in central England in 1995. Located close to the M1 motorway in Wellingborough, Northamptonshire, phase 1 of the warehouse facility comprised 250,000 square feet of multi-temperature storage.

The company described the benefits of the new facility:

This centre enables us to supply chilled, frozen and dry products together, on a daily basis. We are starting to see the benefits in better availability of products on the shelves, lower stock levels, lower costs and less damage to goods through handling orders less frequently.

Competition in the mid- to late 1990s

Over the course of the 1990s, a number of changes occurred both in the retail sector's external environment and in the industry itself. All of these were to challenge Kwik Save's competitive position.

First, the major 'big four' multiples (Sainsbury's, Tesco, Safeway and Asda) focused their new developments on very large new-build stores in edge-of-town or out-of-town locations where land was cheaper and large plots were more available compared to town centres or in suburbs. These larger stores with ample parking were designed to fit the lifestyles of customers who tended to shop on a weekly or monthly basis rather than day to day and whose average spend per visit was much higher than those visiting smaller stores.

The second noticeable change in the sector was the apparent reduction in purely price-based competition. The evidence suggested that consumers became more concerned about other features of stores they shopped at rather than just price. The provision of free parking, crèches, on-site petrol stations and a wide range of in-kind benefits (e.g. points-based loyalty cards, etc.) all had an influence on shopping habits. Kwik Save found itself unable to offer most benefits of this type.

Third, there was a significant expansion in the number of non-food products that the major multiples offered. The idea of a superstore as a 'one-stop' shop grew over the decade as the key 'cash-rich-time-poor' customers sought to spend less time shopping. Accordingly, many of the larger retailers added clothing, music, electrical goods, banking services, pharmacies and holiday/travel agencies to their product portfolios. The development of large stores with space for such in-store shops was a significant factor in this trend.

Finally, the distinction between 'mainstream' and 'discounting' supermarkets was blurred as the 'big four' expanded ranges to include 'basic' own brands in addition to their main own brands and other branded goods. Tesco, Asda and Safeway all pursued this option with their ranges of such products (such as Safeway's 'Savers'). By offering these cheaper ranges, the retailers in question sought to broaden the demographic profile of their customer bases, including segments targeted by the 'discounter' retailers such as Kwik Save.

Appendix I

Consolidated profit and loss statements, 1987–96 (figures in £ millions)

	1996	1995	1994	1993	1992	1991	1990	1989	1988	1987
Sales including VAT	3,511.6	3,228.3	3,020.3	2,858.4	2,498.2	1,894.6	1,520.4	1,238.8	974.1	862.03
VAT	(257.5)	(236.2)	(220.3)	(207.2)	(179.2)	n/a	(74.8)	(47.4)	(42.46)	(35.92)
Sales excluding VAT	3,254.1	2,992.1	2,800.0	2,651.2	2,319.0	n/a	1,445.6	1,181.4	931.634	826.1
Cost of sales	(2,796.8)	(2,551.9)	(2,403.6)	(2,278.7)	(1,984.6)	n/a	(1,226.4)	(1,002.0)	(792.07)	(708.5)
Gross profit	457.3	440.2	396.4	372.5	334.4	n/a	219.2	179.3	139.564	117.59
Distribution costs	(349.5)	(297.4)	(249.2)	(232.9)	(206.9)	n/a	(131.8)	(106.4)	(81.45)	(69.98)
Administration expenses	(44.8)	(36.2)	(35.4)	(33.8)	(31.2)	n/a	(19.9)	(15.5)	(13.8)	(10.45)
Trading profit	63.0	106.6	111.8	105.8	96.3	n/a	67.5	57.4	44.3	37.16
Other income (concessions and other sources)	32.2	27.5	23.7	20.5	16.8	n/a	12.9	11.2	8.69	7.75
Operating profit	95.2	134.1	135.5	126.3	113.1	n/a	80.4	68.6	53.0	44.9
Provisions	–	(6.8)	–	–	–	n/a	–	–	–	–
Profit on divestments	–	–	0.2	–	–	n/a	–	–	–	–
Interest payable/receivable	(4.9)	(1.8)	(0.1)	(0.2)	(2.5)	n/a	4.86	4.6	2.186	1.701
Profit before tax	90.3	125.5	135.6	126.1	110.6	101.7	85.3	73.2	55.176	46.6
Tax	(31.6)	(45.5)	(47.1)	(40.5)	(36.4)	n/a	(29.9)	(25.0)	(19.755)	(16.408)
Profit after interest and tax	58.7	80.0	88.5	85.6	74.2	n/a	55.4	48.2	35.421	30.2

Appendix 2

Consolidated balance sheets, 1987–96 (figures in £ millions)

	1996	1995	1994	1993	1992	1991	1990	1989	1988	1987
Fixed assets										
Tangible assets	635.4	626.2	517.4	465.3	405.3	n/a	253.72	217.48	183.13	168.12
Investments	–	–	–	–	–	n/a	3.721	3.721	–	–
Current assets										
Stocks	179.0	180.2	148.4	154.9	116.5	n/a	70.751	61.277	43.9	37.86
Debtors	51.7	36.6	7.9	16.2	15.9	n/a	13.913	10.683	6.5	6.05
Short-term investments	9.5	9.7	41.6	–	3.6	n/a	11.833	22.217	37.5	18.3
Cash at bank and in hand	11.4	19.5	14.7	31.2	14.7	n/a	7.536	6.651	6.3	5.9
	251.6	246.0	212.6	202.3	150.7	n/a	104.033	100.828	94.24	68.16
Creditors: amounts falling due within one year	(460.6)	(431.4)	(285.4)	(318.5)	(260.3)	n/a	(153.46)	(148.8)	(104.5)	(91.2)
Net current liabilities	(209.0)	(431.4)	(72.8)	(116.2)	(109.6)	n/a	(49.428)	(47.97)	(10.24)	(23.06)
Total assets less current liabilities	426.4	440.8	444.6	349.1	295.7	n/a	208.013	173.227	172.9	145.06
Creditors: amount falling due after more than one year	–	–	(0.1)	(0.2)	(0.3)	n/a	(3.441)	(3.441)	(14.9)	(12.1)
Provisions for liabilities and charges	(44.2)	(5.3)	(34.3)	(1.1)	(1.0)	n/a	(0.7)	(0.5)	(0.5)	(0.5)
Net assets	**382.2**	**435.5**	**410.2**	**347.8**	**294.4**	**244.3**	**203.9**	**169.3**	**157.5**	**132.4**
Capital and reserves										
Called-up share capital	15.6	15.6	15.5	15.4	15.4	n/a	15.33	15.26	15.2	15.15
Share premium account	19.0	18.4	14.9	14.1	12.6	n/a	10.6	9.25	8.9	7.5
Profit and loss account	347.6	401.5	379.8	318.3	266.4	n/a	177.9	144.8	133.3	109.8
Shareholders' funds	**382.2**	**435.5**	**410.2**	**347.8**	**294.4**	**244.3**	**203.89**	**169.3**	**157.5**	**132.4**

Appendix 3

Selected operational statistics

	1996	1995	1994	1993	1992	1991	1990	1989
Number of Kwik Save stores at year end	979	979	861	814	768	745	661	643
Average store size (square feet)	7,442	7,282	6.950	6,620	6,440	6,240	6,050	5,910
Total sales area, including concessions (million square feet)	7.3	7.1	7.2	7.3	6.5	6.1	5.3	5.0
Total number of concessions	1,849	1,864	1,664	1,560	1,507	1,472	1,113	1,062

Appendix 4

Consumer choice of supermarket by social grade, 1998 (source: BMRB Access)

'At which, if any, of the following supermarkets do you shop for groceries on a regular basis?'

	Social grade (% of adults)				
	AB	C1	C2	D	E
Tesco	52	44	40	37	36
Sainsbury's	52	39	38	29	32
Asda	22	30	29	38	20
Marks & Spencer	31	30	27	17	19
Safeway	24	28	24	23	17
Iceland	14	19	24	35	28
Co-op	19	14	20	25	20
Somerfield	10	20	16	16	17
Kwik Save	9	10	20	23	26
Wm Morrison	11	8	14	20	9
Aldi	4	7	12	15	11
Waitrose	18	9	5	2	5

Base: 1015 adults aged 16+.

Kwik Save (B): Somerfield

The end of Kwik Save's independence

On 19 February 1998, it was announced that Kwik Save was to merge with Somerfield. City commentators said that is was "relentless competition" that had forced Kwik Save "into the arms of Somerfield". Although it was announced as a merger, most thought that the £1.26 billion 'all-paper' merger plan was in fact a thinly disguised takeover of Kwik Save by Somerfield.

Although the initial reactions to the announcement's were favourable – both companies' share prices rose on the news – the deal did not win universal praise. Analysts questioned whether putting together two mediocre chains would in fact create a superior 'new' trading entity. Somerfield's management claimed that savings, estimated at £50m a year would result from the deal, but there were concerns about how Somerfield's management would cope with Kwik Save, a company whose retail formula had been attacked by competitors from both the cost and middle parts of the industry. "Avoid the merged company," was the advice of Paul Smiddy, retail analyst at Credit Lyonnais Laing, the broker.

Somerfield

Somerfield was a much older company than Kwik Save. It began life in 1875 as JH Mills – a family grocery store in the English city of Bristol. JH Mills was incorporated as a limited company in 1900, by which time it had grown into a small chain of twelve shops in the Bristol area. By 1950, the chain had grown to fourteen shops when control passed from the Mills family to Tyndall's – a Bristol finance house.

Tyndall's changed the name to Gateway because, it was suggested, Bristol was the 'gateway to the West Country'.

During the 1960s, 1970s and 1980s, the company underwent a number of changes as it was acquired and restructured by three separate parent companies (Dee Corporation, Linfood Holdings and Isosceles). By 1990, the Isosceles group, itself the product of several previous mergers and acquisitions, owned a number of well-established high street supermarket chains, including Keymarket, Lennons, International Stores, Fine Fare and Carrefour. The first 'Somerfield' store was opened in 1990, with the first Somerfield own-label products being launched in August of that year; the first 'Food Giant' store was opened in 1991. Somerfield plc was demerged from the Isosceles group in 1996 and floated in its own right on the stock exchange.

Somerfield in the 1990s

The flotation in 1996 was not a great success. Investors needed some convincing that the Somerfield chain, with its chequered history, could be an investment success story. David Simons, the CEO appointed in 1993, claimed to have proved the pessimists wrong when, in the year after the stock market listing, Somerfield shares outperformed the market by nearly 30% (albeit helped by a low starting point). Simons 'rolled out' the Somerfield name, changing the names and fascias of all stores previously under other names (such as Gateway, Fine Fare, etc.). Despite the efforts at rebranding the company's 'front end', however, city analysts were growing wary about Somerfield's pretensions to be (or become) a retailer with sufficient muscle to take on the 'big four' (Tesco, Sainsbury's, Safeway and Asda).

It had already shown itself to be more vulnerable than its competitors in the recession of the early 1990s. It was all but bankrupted when the recession hit and it had to go through several refinancings and changes of management as executives tried to revive its fortunes. At the end of the process, Gateway stores (as they were then called) were still a big presence on the high street, but suffered from no investment and a poor image. It was only when Simons was appointed that some semblance of purpose seemed to return to the company's strategy.

One way in which Simons stayed true to the strategy of his predecessors, however, was in choosing to keep Somerfield as a chain of 'local' retailers which customers could reach by a short car journey or on foot. In the early to mid-1990s, the 'big four' were all making a dash for the best out-of-town (more like 'edge-of-town') sites, where very large stores were built with large car parks and much larger floor areas than would be possible in more suburban stores where shop space and parking were much more limited.

Simons complained that the City was unwilling to acknowledge the potential for the Somerfield chain because it was obsessed with the big out-of-town superstore chains. 'They have not yet got their minds around the fact that you can get a very good retail concept that is not out-of-town,' he said. Despite the City's misgivings about the 'local shop' and 'high street' strategy, Somerfield continued with this approach.

Kwik Save in the mid-1990s

By 1996, Kwik Save's performance had reached a new low due to a number of changes in the food retailing sector. The retailing philosophy that had underpinned Kwik Save's growth in the 1970s and 1980s was under severe pressure and was threatening the future of the company itself. The 1997 accounts reported a profit before tax figure of £73.7 million against a turnover of £3.25 billion – a return on sales of just over 2%, which was the worst in the company's history.

A number of challenges faced Kwik Save. First, a number of European discounters such as Aldi, Netto and Lidl, had arrived in the UK, providing tough competition for Kwik Save within their target markets (more cost-conscious, non-car-using, higher-frequency convenience shoppers). Second, the more upmarket 'big four' retailers introduced cheaper and 'better value' lines into their product offerings. Sold in plain packaging and at cheaper prices than branded and own-brand lines, the cheaper products attacked Kwik Save's retail formula head on, especially its 'no frills' unbranded products. Third, the increase in numbers of out-of-town hypermarkets meant that more shoppers could reach one or more of them within a convenient walk or bus ride, just as they previously did to reach a Kwik Save store.

In the mid-1990s, Graeme Bowler, CEO of Kwik Save, attempted to address these challenges by creating a number of 'new-generation' Kwik Save stores with a broader product range, possibly in an attempt to take on the 'big four' with more upmarket products. Product rationalization and the closure of more than a hundred under-performing stores were also announced and the City waited to see if results would improve. They didn't.

It was Kwik Save's seeming reluctance to accept the importance of these challenges that caused the departure of Bowler in 1997. No replacement was named, fuelling speculation of a change in the ownership structure of the group. Dairy Farm, the retailing arm of the Jardine Matheson empire in Hong Kong, had long held a 29.2% stake in Kwik Save and had had enough of its under-performing stock in Kwik Save by the beginning of 1998.

With the merger announcement in 1998, Kwik Save 'slipped in' a profits warning:

> Efforts to re-establish sales momentum and improve service and standards have led to an acceleration in advertising expenditure and to increased investment in store wages and cleaning cost. This, combined with the necessary increases in costs of developing new systems and implementing the 'new-generation' strategy, will depress profitability in the first half to a greater extent than anticipated at the start of the financial year.

Dairy Farm and PDFM, the fund manager that was Kwik Save's second-largest shareholder, were in no doubt the company needed a saviour, but it was difficult to know where one might come from. Most other large retailers had no interest in Kwik Save-style shops, preferring to continue the out-of-town investment strategy. Rather than big out-of-town stores, Kwik Save stores were small and concentrated on local high streets, often in poorer areas (those with a higher proportion of socio-demographic segments C2, D and E).

The merger/take-over

Somerfield emerged as a possible saviour owing to the similarity of, among other things, the location strategies of the two companies. Acting on behalf of the major shareholders, SBC Warburg's Dillon Read approached David Simons of Somerfield. Simons was on the look-out for a partner to provide a step change in size so as to increase scale economies. Simons, however, was reluctant to give up control of the business he had done so much to turn round. Furthermore, Kwik Save, with its poor recent performance record, was not the ideal partner, but it was available and it was certain that Somerfield would emerge as the clear leader in any talks.

Based on the values at the time of the integration, it worked out that Somerfield shareholders would own more than 60% of the joined company, hence the suggestion that it was an acquisition rather than a merger. Andrew Thomas became chairman of the merged group and David Simons became CEO – the same positions they had held previously in Somerfield. It was announced that the merged company would be called Somerfield and would retain both big brand names (Kwik Save and Somerfield) for the foreseeable future (although this later changed).

In the 1998 Somerfield annual report, Andrew Thomas gave a statement to shareholders on the move:

> The most exciting and far-reaching step [this year] was the merger with Kwik Save Group plc which was formally concluded on 20 March 1998. Under the terms of the merger, Somerfield shareholders retained their shares while Kwik Save shareholders received seven new Somerfield shares for every six of their Kwik Save shares.
>
> The Board firmly believes that this new grouping transforms the business, giving Somerfield the weight and scale to move forward as a major player in the highly competitive UK food retailing market. Following the merger, we are now the country's leading high street grocery retailer.
>
> The merger brings us three important and immediate benefits:
>
> - Significant cost savings, amounting to at least £50 million a year.
> - Strong national and regional positions arising from the excellent geographic 'fit' between Kwik Save's strength in the North and Somerfield's strength in the South [of Britain], South-West and Anglia; the amount of overlap is remarkably small.
> - Improved trading performance as we transfer products, skills and best practice.
>
> Even more importantly, over the medium term it brings the opportunity to build on our leadership in neighbourhood retailing. We aim to make our stores focal points in their local communities . . . .

The 1998 annual report also provided a 'two-minute guide' to the 'merger' on a question-and-answer basis:

> *How big is the merged business?*
> The combined market capitalization of the two companies before the merger was £1.26 billion. Immediately following the merger, the value of the company grew £500 million to £1.76 billion and has since grown to over £2 billion. We now have over 1400 stores and 68,000 employees.
> *What is the logic behind the merger?*
> In the short term it provides the increased buying and marketing power that comes from greater size, cost savings, and a good fit in market positioning and the geographic distribution of stores. In the

longer term it creates the opportunity to realize a new vision that will enable us to compete more vigorously with the 'Big Four' supermarket chains. [It eventually transpired that the local 'overlap' between Somerfield and Kwik Save shops was about 120 stores and total store closures amounted to about 300.]
What is this 'new vision' that the merger makes possible?
    We intend to focus on one distinctive brand: Somerfield. Over the next five years, we want to build our stores into the fabric of Britain's local communities. We'll become a focal point in the neighbourhood, so that people think of us as "my friends around the corner who have the things I need at just the right price".

David Simons added the following:

We have made substantial progress towards integration of the two businesses . . . We have already started to negotiate better buying terms with our suppliers. Integration programmes for the finance and systems departments have been developed and implementation has begun. The transfer of operations from Kwik Save's headquarters in Prestatyn to Bristol will be complete by April 1999, when the Prestatyn office will close [resulting in several hundred job losses].

What went wrong?

Despite the encouraging noises from the Board of Somerfield, industry watchers had their doubts. "The deal will deliver short-term cost savings," said Richard Perks at Verdict, the retail research company. "But in the longer term the business will be stuck in the middle, squeezed between the superstore and the discounters."

Simons conceded that Kwik Save will have to re-evaluate its place within the supermarket hierarchy, but he denied that the Somerfield brand was lost in no-man's land. "The secret of turning those Kwik Save stores into a success will be to get the right balance between price and fresh food," he said. He cited a recent trend by the supermarket giants to develop smaller inner-city and 'petrol station' stores as further evidence that the high street is not dying. Despite this, research in 1998 showed that the 'second-division' food retailers had seen their market share fall from nearly 16% in 1998 to nearer 13.5% at Christmas 1999. Perhaps not surprisingly, therefore, other smaller food retailers were also facing pressure. Iceland, the frozen food retailer in mainly high street locations, had already suffered problems and was seen as a weakened competitor and a possible take-over target. Budgens, another discount retailer, had talks with Somerfield in 1999 about a possible merger, but the two could not agree terms.

The first hints that all was not well with the merger came in Somerfield's 1999 corporate report. David Simons said that, "conversion of the Kwik Save stores and the rejuvenation of the Kwik Save business have not gone as smoothly as expected".

The 1999 annual report went on to describe part of the company's strategy:

> Our strategy since flotation in 1996 has been to position Somerfield as a national chain of dependable, good quality, friendly local stores; extend its appeal to more ABC1s, family groups and younger shoppers; leverage the Somerfield brand; improve customer service and dependability; and build customer loyalty. We aim to keep prices low by keeping costs down.

The annual report continued:

> The sales performance of the Kwik Save fascia stores was disappointing with like-for-like sales for the year declining by 5.7%. Like-for-like sales deteriorated from a decline of 3.1% in the first half, to a decline of 8.7% in the second half of the year as increasing price competition affected these stores. Too many Kwik Save stores suffer from a poor store environment and poor on-shelf availability ... Prices on own-label products have been frozen and we have stepped up promotional activity with our 'Price Fighters' campaign and money-off vouchers. Price competitiveness remains a key driver of success and we have invested significantly to reaffirm the discount price positioning of the Kwik Save brand.
>
> By the year end the former Kwik Save head office at Prestatyn was closed ... We have now embarked on the next stages of integration, which will yield further cost savings and increased efficiency. We believe that, a year on from merger, it is an appropriate time to assess the way in which we do things and to review the efficiency of the evolving processes. We have also begun a major programme to rationalize the depot network and unify the supply chains into a single, highly efficient whole. The Somerfield and Kwik Save own brand ranges are being harmonized and common specifications and sole supply for many lines are being progressed. Virtually all of Kwik Save's fresh food space – covering meat, fish, deli, bakery, and fruit and vegetables – is operated by [outsourced] concessionaires.

The trade paper *Retail Week* reported the following in November 2001:

Under intense pressure from the likes of Sainsbury's and Tesco, Somerfield had been losing sales for some time. To try and reverse this trend, the group bought the equally troubled Kwik Save business. The company's 'one brand' vision – to rebrand the shops as Somerfield – proved flawed and led to a further fall in sales. Not surprisingly, when management tried to sell many of its stores, it found few takers.

With a sprawling chain of more than 1300 supermarkets – made up of around 550 Somerfield outlets, 730 Kwik Save and 19 petrol forecourt stores – [new directors] John von Spreckelsen [Chairman] and Alan Smith [CEO] were faced with an enormous task when they joined the company in May and April last year, respectively. Smith had previously been chief executive of Punch Taverns and von Spreckelsen had joined from Budgens. [Thomas and Simons were forced to resign in 2000 because of the company's poor post-merger performance.]

But now, 18 months down the road, they are confident that they are well on the road to recovery, but admit there is still much to do. "The picture was not perfect when I first visited the stores. I was happy with 30% of them. Now it's 80%, but that's still not enough," says Smith.

ING Barings retail analyst Clive Black praises what has been done so far: "Every part of the business needed attention and they've kept their heads down and slowly got on with it. They are two talented guys."

Appendix 1

Profit and loss statements for Somerfield (figures in £000s) (source: FAME)

	1996	1997	1998	1999	2000	2001
Turnover	3,161,000	3,200,600	3,483,600	5,897,900	5,465,700	4,612,500
Cost of sales	−3,013,300	−3,024,200	−3,280,400	−5,548,000	−5,415,500	−4,523,500
Gross profit	147,700	176,400	203,200	349,900	50,200	89,000
Other expenses	−47,000	−61,300	−99,200	−114,200	−129,700	−95,300
Total expenses	−3,060,300	−3,085,500	−3,379,600	−5,662,200	−5,545,200	−4,618,800
Operating profit	100,700	115,100	104,000	235,700	−79,500	−6,300
Other income	2,300	800	3,000	9,200	2,200	6,800
Exceptional items	−3,800	200	−101,200	−9,300	84,900	2,000
Profit (loss) before interest	99,200	116,100	5,800	235,600	7,600	2,500
Interest paid	−7,200	−10,700	−16,900	−27,100	−22,100	−15,600
Profit (loss) before tax	92,000	105,400	−11,100	208,500	−14,500	−13,100
Taxation	−4,100	−17,200	−300	−50,000	−100	6,500
Profit (loss) after tax	87,900	88,200	−11,400	158,500	−14,600	−6,600
Dividends	−590,800	−37,500	−48,100	−63,900	−7,300	0
Retained profit (loss)	−502,900	50,700	−59,500	94,600	−21,900	−6,600

Appendix 2

Share price histories for Kwik Save and Somerfield (source: Datastream)

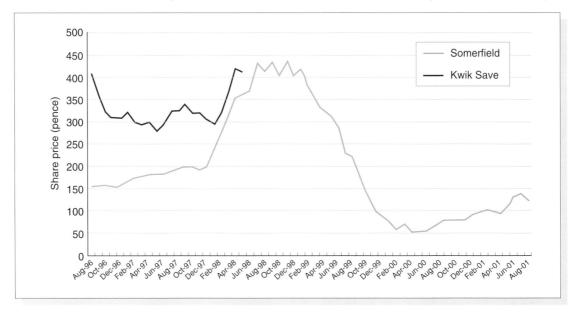

Appendix 3

Retail sales of food in supermarkets and superstores, 1993–98 (source: *Business Monitor* SDM28, Key Note)

	1993	1994	1995	1996	1997	1998
Sales (£ million)	51,689	54,920	59,362	63,400	67,096	70,786

Note: figures include some sales through convenience stores and food halls.

Appendix 4

Leading supermarket and superstore chains in the UK food industry by value, 1998 (source: company information, Key Note)

Company	Market share (%)
Tesco	15.2
Sainsbury's	12.6
Safeway	7.8
Asda	7.2
Somerfield/Kwik Save	4.5
Marks & Spencer*	3.1
Wm Morrison	2.3
Iceland	1.7
Waitrose	1.3
Others	44.3
Total	**100.0**

*Food sales only.

Appendix 5

Leading UK supermarket and superstore retailers by number of outlets, 1998 (source: company information, Key Note)

Somerfield/Kwik Save	1,400
Tesco	568
Safeway	500
Sainsbury's	391
Marks & Spencer*	285
Co-operative Wholesale Society	268
Asda	218
Gateway Foodmarkets	132
Aldi	130
Waitrose	113
Netto	113
Budgens	108
Iceland	108

*Food sales only.

Appendix 6

Form of transport used by adults to travel to regular grocery purchasing point, 1998 (source: Target Group Index)

Form of transport	000s	%
Car	31,985	74.2
Bus	3,443	8.0
Train	113	0.3
Bicycle, motorcycle, moped	473	1.1
Walk	5,732	13.3

© BMRB International, 1998.

Appendix 7

Consumer choice of supermarket by social grade, 1998 (source: BMRB Access)

'At which, if any, of the following supermarkets do you shop for groceries on a regular basis?'

	Social grade (% of adults)				
	AB	**C1**	**C2**	**D**	**E**
Tesco	52	44	40	37	36
Sainsbury's	52	39	38	29	32
Asda	22	30	29	38	20
Marks & Spencer	31	30	27	17	19
Safeway	24	28	24	23	17
Iceland	14	19	24	35	28
Co-op	19	14	20	25	20
Somerfield	10	20	16	16	17
Kwik Save	9	10	20	23	26
Wm Morrison	11	8	14	20	9
Aldi	4	7	12	15	11
Waitrose	18	9	5	2	5

Base: 1015 adults aged 16+.

Appendix 8

Number of product lines in store (source: Press Office, Somerfield plc)

Company	Number of product lines per store
Asda, Sainsbury's, Safeway and Tesco	Over 35,000
Somerfield	Approx. 12,000
Kwik Save	Approx. 5,000

The UK outbound tour operations industry

Nigel Evans

The 'package' concept

Tourists travelling abroad can purchase each separate component of a holiday – accommodation, transportation, activities, ground handling, etc. – as individual items. During the 1960s, however, the foreign inclusive tour or 'package' holiday became established in Western Europe and brought with it a substantial expansion in the numbers of tourists venturing abroad.

A 'package' was defined by the European Commission in 1990 as a pre-arranged combination, sold or offered for sale at an inclusive price, of not less than two of the following three elements: transport; accommodation; and other tourist services not ancillary to transport or accommodation and accounting for a significant part of the package.

The role of the tour operators was the key element in the expansion of the package concept, which has continued to grow since it began in the 1950s. This role goes beyond that of the wholesaler, in that tour operators not only purchase or reserve the separate components in bulk but, in combining these components into an 'inclusive tour', they also become producers, since a new product – the inclusive tour or package holiday – is created. The traditional appeal of the tour operators' product has been to offer a complete holiday package at the lowest price to a population often lacking the linguistic knowledge or the knowledge and confidence to organize independent travel. As a result, tour operation has become the dominant feature of the holiday market, not only in the UK but also in most tourist-generating countries.

Benefits of the package concept

Despite some industry commentators' comments over the years suggesting that the package holiday's days may be numbered (because many tourists have become more 'worldly wise' and are prepared to travel independently), growth in the industry has been fuelled by three key selling points:

- the convenience of purchasing all the elements of the product in one purpose-designed 'bundle';
- delivery of product quality assurance, reliability and protection;
- prices perceived to be good value.

But although the future of the 'package' seems assured, changes in consumer preferences and in the business environment are changing the characteristics of these packages, which will, in turn, will have an effect on the future structure of this industrial sector. The tour operating sector as a whole (and the independent sector in particular) is facing a number of pressures, which has led to marked differences in recent performance.

The growth of UK outbound tour operations

Vladimar Raitz, a Russian émigré, is widely credited with operating the first air inclusive tour (AIT) charter to Corsica in 1950, at an all-inclusive price of £32.10. Part of his original company, Horizon, continued until recent years as a trading name of Thomson. Others who pioneered AITs during the 1950s in the UK were: Captain Ted Langton, who set up Universal Skytours (which was also later to become part of Thomson); Joe and Syril Shuman, founders of Global Holidays; Christopher and Stephen Lord, whose Lord Brothers firm was later absorbed by Laker Airways; George Jackman and Wilf Jones, who built up Cosmos; and Harry Chandler, whose family continues to control The Travel Club of Upminster, founded in 1936.

Other companies missed out on the early market opportunities. Thomas Cook never achieved the market leadership in air holidays that it had in rail holidays, and British European Airways (BEA), a forerunner of British Airways, was slow to react to the threat posed by the charter airlines. In the 1950s, foreign travel remained a luxury commodity within the reach of only a privileged few who had plenty of free time and considerable purchasing power. The market changed during the 1960s, from that of a privileged 'niche' market to a 'mass' tourism market as a result of innovations in aircraft technology, changes in labour legislation (which provided for paid holidays in most European countries) and changes to the structure of the tour operating industry itself. Large companies had begun buying into tour operating as early as 1956 when Great Universal Stores acquired Global, but the industry remained highly fragmented during the 1950s and early 1960s.

The industry of the early 1960s was also beset by a number of company failures, including the failure in 1964 of Fiesta Tours – a major tour operator of the period. The Association of British Travel Agents (ABTA) had to step in to rescue customers stranded abroad and, in the aftermath, calls were made for statutory controls of the burgeoning tour operating sector. ABTA responded from November 1966 with the introduction of the so-called 'Stabiliser Resolution'. Stabiliser was an attempt by ABTA to regulate the UK travel industry whereby ABTA member agents could sell only the foreign inclusive tours of ABTA tour operators, while ABTA tour operators could only sell through ABTA agents (or direct). It thus became impossible to build up a major market presence without belonging to ABTA. The Stabiliser Resolution did indeed help to stabilize the industry as the rate of failures fell after its introduction. Stabiliser remained in force until 1993 when ABTA relinquished the requirement upon the introduction of the European Commission directive on package travel, one effect of which was to require tour operators to provide financial protection to customers under law.

New entrants and consolidation

The strategic entry into the marketplace of the International Thomson Organization (ITO) in 1965 proved to be a major turning point for the industry. It represented the initiation of a period of consolidation within the industry which continued until the late 1980s. The introduction of ITO meant the entry to the UK tour operations industry of a large, sophisticated and diversified international group of companies. During the summer of 1965, Thomson had around 100,000 holidays on offer. The AIT market [which is regulated in the UK by the Civil Aviation Authority (CAA) through the Air Travel Organisers' Licences (ATOLs) it issues each year] grew enormously during the period, but detailed figures are only available from 1976. Although many operators do not use their full ATOL allocation, the licences issued give an indication of the size of the total market and relative market shares.

The reasons for the rapid growth of the UK outbound AIT market and that of the operators are inextricably linked, but perhaps two major factors stand out. First, many UK residents travel abroad for their holidays in order to obtain reliable sunshine and warmth. The UK's island location has necessitated the development of well–organized, packaged transportation to service this need. Second, UK residents accord holidays and travel a high priority in terms of their discretionary expenditure, even in times of relative economic hardship.

Relatively low barriers to entry and continual striving among operators for increased market share led to price wars (particularly in the early 1970s and the mid-1980s), which resulted in a highly volatile record of profitability over the period. The price wars, low margins and the vulnerability of the travel industry to external economic and political factors inevitably took their toll on operators. For example, Clarksons, which had expanded rapidly in the late 1960s, was losing money by 1971 and was taken over by the Court Line Group. The Court Line Group invested heavily in jet aircraft, but the 1973 oil crisis and economic recession led to the collapse of the company at the height of the summer season in August 1974. Parallels can be drawn between the International Leisure Group (ILG), which, when it failed in March 1991, was Britain's second largest tour operator, and Clarksons. The downturn in business at the time of The Gulf War exposed ILG's strategy of using strong tour operating cash flows to diversify into scheduled air services through its airline Air Europe.

During the 1970s and the 1980s, the large tour operators came to increasingly dominate the AIT market, as mass market operators were determined to increase their market share and to reap the anticipated rewards of market dominance. Thomson, the market leader, had since its inception faced major challenges to its market leadership position, but had hitherto always successfully defended its position. Major competitors had disappeared from the scene: Clarksons collapsed in 1974; ILG collapsed in March 1991. Thomson's major challengers in the current marketplace are of more recent prominence. Owners Abroad (now re-named First Choice) was founded in 1972, and, as its name suggests, was a 'seat-only' specialist serving the needs of expatriate overseas property owners. Airtours started in 1978 as Pendle Airtours, a small operating division of David Crossland's travel agency Pendle Travel. The demise of ILG removed from the industry a privately held company that had targeted Thomson through aggressive pricing in a bid for an ever-greater share of the market. Both Airtours (since 1989) and First Choice are public limited companies. Their status as public limited companies necessitated the targeting of profitability rather than market share as the primary objective of the two companies and, as a result, competition since 1991 has focused on matching supply much more closely to demand and thereby avoiding damaging price wars.

By 1990, a marked polarization had occurred in the industry, dividing competitors into a relatively small number of 'mass' tour operators and a much larger number of 'independent' operators largely serving specialized niche markets. The term 'independent' tour operator has become widely used in the UK but it has no precise meaning. The term is often used loosely to describe any operator that is not one of the largest mass tour operators. One of the key features of independent tour operators is that they are not vertically integrated and they therefore rely on the supply in the market place for individual components of the package. With regard to the distribution of the products, the choice depends very much on the size of the organization in terms of the number of passengers carried. Many of the smaller tour operators choose to apply direct sell methods. As one of the components of an air inclusive package is transport by air, the independents also need to secure capacity with either charter or scheduled airlines in order to assemble their products. In the UK, the term 'independent' tour operator also has a more precise meaning, in that it can refer to those companies that are members of the Association of Independent Tour Operators (AITO). AITO was formed in 1976 in the wake of the Clarksons crash primarily to represent the views of smaller tour operators during the setting up of the CAA's bonding scheme. The association has grown to represent about 150 members that collectively carry some 1,500,000 customers per annum.

AITO members range from those carrying fewer than 500 customers per year to those carrying in excess of 100,000. The membership includes well-known companies that are part of the second tier of operators, such as Balkan Holidays and Simply Travel and less well-known names such as Sunvil Holidays. The membership also includes many tour operators that predominately use cars and ferries as means of transport. These companies, particularly a large number of French specialists, include well-known names such as Eurocamp (which is a subsidiary of Holiday Break which has the status of a public limited company and carries over 250,000 customers a year), but do not appear in the ATOL listings, which solely cover AITs.

Competition, therefore, took place in two competitive arenas: the larger AITs competed with each other for the major 'volume' business, whereas the independents, usually smaller companies, offered specialist products to niche markets. The temptation among the AITs to acquire within the independent sector was, however, limited by two factors: the constant threat of anti-monopoly legislation and a fear that the larger tour operators may be unable to 'think small' and flexible in a way that maintains quality for clients.

Clearly, given the scale and complexity of their operations, and the vertically and horizontally integrated structure of their businesses, the four largest operators in the UK can now be viewed as constituting a category of their own. Increasingly, however, given the size and international complexity of the companies concerned, it is apparent that a pan-European view of competition issues in the tour operating sector will need to be taken in future. Expansion through integration does not only apply to the UK, but the travel industry is also experiencing rapid internationalization of ownership. If a company wants to be regarded as a major player in this sector, it now needs to be part be part of a pan-European partnership, alliance or ownership structure of some sort. The aim of such international integration is to increase buying power abroad together with improvement of margins through airline fleet integration and combined ground handling.

The take-over of Thomson by its German rival Preussag during 2000, which required European Commission approval (that was granted during August 2000), is indicative of this trend. This purchase signalled a further round of merger and acquisition activity. C&N Touristic (Germany's second largest tour operator) gained control of Thomas Cook in December 2000 after Preussag had been forced to sell its controlling stake as a consequence of its purchase of Thomson.

Industry features

Economies of scale

One of the reasons often cited for ever-greater concentration by a few large suppliers of activities for an industry is that larger companies enjoy the advantages to be derived from economies of scale. These economies clearly exist in tour operating, in terms of marketing and purchasing economies for instance, but perhaps the influence of such economies is on the wane. The trend away from standard 'summer sun' packages towards a more diverse range of package options in the UK means that such economies of scale are harder to achieve. Tour operators are increasingly being forced to respond to a much more complex holiday market than has hitherto existed, through diversification, narrower market segmentation, catering for independently minded travellers and increasingly experienced customers. All of these trends reduce, to some extent, the advantages to be derived from economies of scale.

Furthermore, it is by no means clear that economies of scale are great beyond a certain size threshold in the industry. The increasing bureaucracy, expense of systems and the inflexibility of a larger scale of operations can lead to diseconomies of scale, resulting in higher not lower unit costs. The tour operating industry may well have many of the same characteristics as the airline industry. In the USA, the lowest cost 'producer' that other airlines seek to emulate is not one of the major carriers, but a medium-sized airline called Southwest.

The four largest tour operating companies operating in the UK have become vertically (as well as horizontally) integrated in recent year – that is to say, they own both inputs to the operating process and control a part of the distribution channels for their products. To this end, the largest four tour operating brands of Thomson, Airtours, First Choice and JMC are part of groups that own airlines: Britannia; Airtours; Air 2000 and JMC, respectively. The four companies also have extensive interests in travel agency. Thomson, Airtours and JMC are part of groups that control the country's first, second and third largest travel agency chains: Lunn Poly, MyTravel (a re-branding of the former Going Places chain) and Thomas Cook, respectively. First Choice, as well as owning the Travel Choice and Bakers Dolphin chains, has also developed a successful 'out-of-town' format with its Holiday Hypermarket concept which is spreading across the country.

The larger travel agency chains (which have themselves expanded their aggregate share of the total travel agency market) have increasingly favoured the larger operators that are able to offer bulk capacity and sufficient brochures to 'rack'. This trend has intensified as vertical integration and has led to travel agencies favouring the operating brands of their owners, and operators seek preferential terms with agents. The tour operators have also developed direct forms of distribution through the development of dedicated call centres where staff are able to earner higher salaries than most travel agents if sales targets are met.

Regulatory investigations

The increased concentration in the industry resulted in referral to the UK Mergers and Monopolies Commission (MMC, now known as the Competition Commission) on two occasions in 1989 and 1997. The MMC sought to investigate the issues arising out of possible anti-competitive behaviour by the largest tour operators in the UK. Later, in year 2000, the European Commission investigated the UK industry in relation to the proposed take-over of First Choice plc by Airtours plc.

In 1989, the Thomson Travel Group was investigated for its take-over of Horizon plc as the industry worried that the long-term effects of the merger would cause the withdrawal of a number of operators from the industry, thereby increasing concentration and leading to adverse effects on price, choice, availability and standards of service. The take-over (of the UK's third largest tour operator of the time by the first largest) was allowed to proceed. The sector was investigated again in 1997 owing to the increase in the level of vertical integration by the larger tour operators. Smaller tour operators and travel agents again argued that this increase would bring about anti-competitive practices that would eventually squeeze them out of the market, leading to higher prices and less choice for consumers. However, in both investigations, the Commission found that the industry was broadly competitive and saw no significant reason to intervene although, in relation to vertical integration, recommendations were made in the 1997 report to:

- prevent tying discounts to the purchase of travel insurance;
- make travel agency ownership links more explicit;
- outlaw the practice of specifying discount levels to travel agencies by major operators.

The smaller tour operators were worried not only about the distribution of their products but also the supply of charter seats. In this regard, the MMC concluded that, "while there may be a shortage of capacity at weekends, there appears to be no shortage during the week". One industry observer noted that the 1997 MMC investigation effectively gave a go-ahead for further consolidation in the industry.

Many of the smaller companies have successfully developed a niche in the market, usually by targeting particular customer types or by focusing on specific destinations. Furthermore, a number of niche operators have been acquired by the 'big four'. Innovative companies, which have created new products and discovered new destinations, have fallen to their more predatory competitors searching for greater economies of scale and scope. In doing so they have tried to combine the benefits of scale with the higher margins to be derived from the exploitation of successful niche markets. Nevertheless, many middle-ranking operators remain vulnerable since, on the one hand, they fail to derive the benefits of scale and, on the other, they have failed to develop a niche market they can effectively defend. This vulnerability is likely to be greatest in the short-haul markets due to the structural characteristics of the industry. Concentration specifically in key short-haul markets is even higher than the figures indicated for overall concentration, a point that was to be emphasized by the European Commission investigation.

In November 1999 the European Commission prohibited a merger of two of the largest tour operators within the UK AIT market (Airtours and First Choice), on the grounds that the three largest operators effectively would control a large share of the short-haul market. The report stated that: "the four large integrated suppliers already sell between them, over 90% of all packages to mainland Spain, the Balearic Islands, the Canary Islands and Tunisia and 80% to [most] other significant short-haul summer destinations". Concern was given in the report to the position of the remaining smaller tour operators since they would become further marginalized with regard to distribution, flight capacity and general competitiveness in the industry. The European Commission indicated that an excessively concentrated industry structure would emerge as a result of the proposed take-over. The potential removal of First Choice from the market would, the commission argued, remove the last remaining medium-sized tour operator (and the only one with the potential to grow rapidly to the size of the three major suppliers). Finally, the take-over would have reduced competition at all three levels of the supply chain.

New technologies

Tour operators in the UK have played an important part in the development of computerized bookings for tour packages. The investment in on-line interactive view-data systems (during the 1970s and 1980s) resulted in the majority of the larger tour operators relying on this technology for most of their bookings. Other smaller operators have chosen not to automate and to rely instead on using conventional telephone calls as the main vehicle for bookings. This has worked to the advantage of the larger tour operators as travel agents have endeavoured to reduce telephone call charges and improve efficiency.

Foremost among the newer technologies is the development of computerized reservation systems (CRSs). CRSs were first developed in the USA in the 1960s and 1970s as databases and booking systems for US airlines. They continued to develop and now include vast amounts of information on other transport providers, hotels, car hire provision, attractions and so on. Additionally, the reach of systems such as Amadeus and Galileo has expanded throughout the developed world as non-US airlines have forged partnerships with the US instigators of the systems.

In the USA, 96% of travel agents are linked to a CRS. CRSs give travel agencies the ability to flexibly package exactly what the consumers want, thereby undermining the role of the traditional mass market tour operator. They can combine hotels, flights, car hire and so on using the CRS database. However, the role of the CRS in a British 'leisure traveller' context should not be overstated. There is a marked polarization of business and leisure travel agencies with a low level of CRS penetration in the leisure travel agency sector. Many leisure travel agents are owned by tour operators that have invested heavily in their own view-data technology, and therefore have a vested interest in delaying the diffusion of CRSs to the leisure travel agent sector.

Other technological developments are also important. Distribution options include home shopping, point-of-sale multimedia booths, mail order and particularly booking through the Internet.

The emerging tools of the Internet enable consumers to search on-line for information, to access reliable, accurate and up-to-date information, and to compare comparative product offerings quickly. Furthermore, the availability of such information enables consumers to make reservations in a fraction of the time necessary for some other methods and with a minimum of inconvenience. The Internet is driven by both the increasing volume and diversity of tourism demand and by the power it gives consumers to buy personalized 'bundles' of tourism products. In some cases, this leads to the avoidance of the traditional tourism 'packages', leading instead to consumers assembling their own packages from individual component parts on offer.

Booking habits, however, are slow to change, and use of the Internet for international travel requirements (other than flights) is comparatively small compared to other forms of distribution – as at the year 2002 at least. Most Internet users, however, match the profile of the most desirable market segments in that they tend to be relatively well-educated professionals who travel frequently and have a higher disposable income. Furthermore, the Internet allows (at reasonable cost) suppliers an unprecedented opportunity to communicate globally with their target markets and to establish direct relationships with consumers.

Legal and regulatory developments

The EC Directive on Package Travel, Package Holidays and Package Tours was adopted on 13 June 1990 and EU member states were required to implement its measures prior to 31 December 1992. The main provisions of the directive are outlined below:

- Article 2 – definitions. The directive covers 'packages' that are defined as a pre-arranged combination of not less than two of three elements: transport; accommodation; and other tourist services.
- Article 3 – descriptions and advertising. The directive does not impose a legal obligation to provide a brochure, but where one is available it must contain in a legible, comprehensive and accurate manner both the price and adequate information concerning certain specified items such as the itinerary and the meal plan.
- Article 4 – the package travel contract. Certain information is specified, such as information relating to passport and visa requirements, that the tour operator and/or the travel agent must provide to the consumer prior to travelling.
- Article 5 – liability. The tour operator becomes responsible for ensuring that all services under the package are rendered effectively and efficiently (whether rendered directly or by a third party).

    ■   Article 7 – financial security. The tour operator must provide evidence of security for the refund of money paid over and for repatriation of the consumer in the event of insolvency.

The goal of the directive was to codify and harmonize existing EC legislation relating to package travel. In so doing much of the detailed implementation of the directive was left to the discretion of member states. In the UK, the Department of Trade and Industry took the view that it wanted to place a minimum of additional burdens on the sector and consequently opted for a self-regulating system.

As a result, 'bonding' in the UK is undertaken by a number of 'approved' schemes, including those operated by ABTA, AITO, the Federation of Tour Operators (FTO) and the CAA. Under these systems, a tour operator has to pay for a bond representing the value of an agreed proportion of their licensed capacity. The bond is forfeited in the event of failure to help reimburse customers. One effect of the implementation of the directive in the UK has been to include surface transport and domestic packages as 'packages' requiring financial protection for the first time. The directive, in requiring financial protection and greater scrutiny of activities, has raised the entry barriers to the tour-operating sector in Europe and forced some of the smaller, specialized tour operators to carry heavy additional financial burdens.

Changing consumers

Mass tourism can be seen as a phenomenon of large-scale packaging of standardized leisure services at fixed prices for sale to a mass clientele. Clearly, such tourism remains central to the outbound tourism product of the UK and several other north European countries, but underlying trends towards a new type of more independent and experienced traveller have been discerned.

These 'new tourists' have been described as consumers who are flexible, independent and experienced travellers, whose values and lifestyles are different from those of mass tourists. Six key attributes are characteristic of these 'new tourists':

    1   *New consumers are more experienced.* In the UK, the proportion of adults who had ever been on holiday abroad rose sharply from the 1960s through to the mid-1980s, reaching 67% in 1985. The figure has stayed close to this level ever since. In other words, first-time buyers with sufficient income to enter the market had been captured and future growth (or decline)

would reflect the motivations of experienced travellers. More experienced travellers are more knowledgeable and consequently more quality and value conscious, they demand greater choice and flexibility and are more certain of what they want and what they find unacceptable

2 *New consumers have changed values.* Values of conservation, health and nature are being reflected in the tour operators' products and there are growing signs that the fashion for the sun is beginning to fade.

3 *New consumers have changed lifestyles.* One industry-watcher argued that society has moved through three key phases between the industrial era and today. First, from the industrial era in which people live to work, to the post-industrial era in which they worked to live, to the third phase where a new unity exists between work and leisure, and travel and leisure become integral aspects of daily life. These changes in the role of travel and leisure in society have implications for the travel industry. People who live to work have simple holiday and travel motivations; people who work to live view leisure as the counterpoint to everyday life. Those seeking unity of everyday life want to reduce the polarity between work and leisure and are looking for fulfilment throughout all sectors of life, during working time, through 'humanized' working conditions, and at home through more habitable cities and a more colourful everyday life. The varying motivations of these three groups are summarized in Table 1.

4 *New consumers are the products of changing population demographics.* Population demographics in the tourism-generating countries are changing. In particular, the population is ageing. These demographic changes will have profound effects upon buyer behaviour in tourist-generating countries. It has been forecast that the early years of the twenty-first century will witness demographic shifts in Europe, including a slight growth in the proportion of elderly people over 65 years, a large growth in the middle-age categories and a relative decline in the 18–35 age category. A significant European demographic trend was the rise of the 'baby boomers' – i.e. those born between the end of the 1939–45 war and the mid-1960s, who are currently aged in their mid-thirties to mid-fifties. This category is inheriting wealth on a large scale, leading to the higher net worth of middle-age households. They take wealth for granted, have higher expectations of the

Table I
Motivations for travel

People who live to work	People who work to live	People seeking a unity between work and leisure
▪ To recover ▪ To recuperate ▪ To rest ▪ To be served ▪ To switch off	▪ To experience something different ▪ To explore ▪ To have fun ▪ To play ▪ To be active ▪ To relax without stress ▪ To enjoy proximity to nature ▪ To do as one pleases	▪ To broaden their horizons ▪ To learn something new ▪ To encourage introspection and communication with other people ▪ To discover the simple things in life and nature ▪ To foster creativity ▪ To experiment ▪ To take personal risks

products and services that they buy and are likely to buy such products and services for their intrinsic qualities rather than for their status.

5   *New consumers are more flexible.* Consumers are becoming 'hybrid' in nature in that they may consume in an unpredictable way, making the traditional stereotypical categories of rich, poor or middle-income people no longer sufficient to segment holiday markets. Some consumers may, for instance, take the cheapest charter flight available but stay in the most luxurious accommodation available at the destination. Other consumers may stay in relatively modest accommodation but partake in expensive sporting activities such as heli-skiing or hot-air ballooning. Another aspect of the flexible consumer is the spread of impulse buying to the travel industry. There are shorter lead times before booking and paying for holidays – a changing consumer preference that partially explains the growing number of shorter and more frequent breaks.

6   *New consumers are more independent.* Consumers are increasingly asserting their individuality and independence, and seeking more flexible and custom-made travel and leisure options. They tend to resist the standardized and sanitized product options. This trend towards independence, indivi-

duality and more experimentation in travel and leisure is clearly underpinned by the value, lifestyle and demographic changes. Such changes are likely to manifest themselves in the continuing demand by consumers for the core advantages provided by packaged travel products relating to pricing, convenience, reliability and easy access. However, consumers are likely to increasingly reject some of the traditional drawbacks of packaged travel products relating to the inflexibility of products and show resistance to travelling in organized groups.

Appendix 1
Total ATOL capacity (source: CAA, various)

Year	Total ATOL capacity (000s)
1976	8,345
1977	7,424
1978	8,578
1979	5,303
1980	6,164
1981	6,661
1982	7,067
1983	7,938
1984	8,623
1985	8,647
1986	9,843
1987	12,598
1988	14,567
1989	13,982
1990	13,065
1991	10,061
1992	14,920
1993	15,468
1994	18,539
1995	22,723
1996	22,951
1997	24,980
1998	27,926
1999	27,942
2000	30,652
2001	32,470

Year	Market share of five largest tour operators (000s)	Tour operators in order of market share
1976	1,553	Thomson, Cosmos, Silverwing, Laker Air, Horizon-Midlands
1977	1,502	Thomson, Cosmos, Silverwing, Horizon-Midlands, Laker Air
1978	1,521	Thomson, Cosmos, Silverwing, Horizon-Midlands, Laker Air
1979	1,875	Thomson, Silverwing, Cosmos, Horizon, Laker Air
1980	2,165	Thomson, Silverwing, Horizon, Cosmos, Owners Services
1981	2,263	Thomson, Silverwing, Horizon, Cosmos, Owners Services
1982	2,913	Thomson, Silverwing, Intasun, Horizon, Cosmos
1983	3,142	Thomson, British Airways, Intasun, Horizon, Rank
1984	3,076	Thomson, Horizon, Intasun, British Airways, Rank
1985	3,456	Thomson, Horizon, Intasun, Rank, British Airways
1986	5,041	Thomson, Horizon, Intasun, Rank, British Airways
1987	8,493	Thomson, ILG, Horizon, British Airways, First Choice
1988	8,985	Thomson, ILG, Horizon, Redwing, First Choice
1989	10,022	Thomson, ILG, First Choice, Redwing, Airtours
1990	8,899	Thomson, ILG, First Choice, Airtours, Yugotours
1991	6,088	Thomson, First Choice, Airtours, Yugotours, Sunworld
1992	8,353	Thomson, First Choice, Airtours, Cosmos, Sunworld
1993	8,600	Thomson, First Choice, Airtours, Cosmos, Sunworld
1994	10,719	Thomson, Airtours, First Choice, Cosmos, Sunworld
1995	11,799	Thomson, Airtours, First Choice, Cosmos, Sunworld
1996	10,253	Thomson, Airtours, First Choice, Cosmos, Unijet
1997	11,952	Thomson, Airtours, First Choice, Thomas Cook, Cosmos
1998	16,009	Thomson, Airtours, First Choice, Thomas Cook, Carlson
1999	15,921	Thomson, Airtours, Thomas Cook, First Choice, Cosmos
2000	18,218	Airtours, Thomson, Thomas Cook, First Choice, Cosmos
2001	18,518	Airtours, Thomson, Thomas Cook, First Choice, Cosmos

Note: Tour operator figures are for the group of companies if an operator has more than one operating brand.

Appendix 3

Capacity of the largest tour operators (source: CAA, various)

Tour operator	ATOL capacity (000s)											
	1990	1991*	1992	1993	1994	1995	1996	1997	1998	1999	2000	2001
Thomson	4,348	3,015	3,326	3,488	3,801	4,281	4,032	4,440	5,080	5,080	4,725	4,568
ILG	1,798	a										
First Choice	1,798	1,621	2,275	1,939	2,042	2,373	2,029	1,917	3,164	3,068	3,210	3,557
Airtours	635	828	1,488	1,692	2,438	2,946	2,671	3,083	3,841	3,930	5,330	5,540
Cosmos	b	b	822	1,081	1,805	1,453	831	1,049	b	1,132	1,294	1,269
Yugotours	320	340	b	e								
Sunworld[c]/Thomas Cook	b	284	442	400	633	746	b	1,463	2,711	2,711	3,659	3,584
Unijet	b	b	b	b	b	b	690	b	d	d		
Carlson	b	b	b	b	b	b	b	b	1,213	f		
Total (largest five)	8,899	6,088	8,353	8,600	10,719	11,799	10,253	11,952	16,009	15,921	18,218	18,518
Total (all tour operators)	13,065	10,061	13,575	14,545	17,136	18,813	21,995	19,819	22,231	23,264	24,039	25,362

*Gulf War.
[a] ILG was placed in receivership in March 1991.
[b] Not placed in the top five tour operators. Airtours' 1994 and 1995 figures include Aspro, which was acquired in June 1993.
[c] Became Thomas Cook after 1997.
[d] Part of First Choice after 1997.
[e] Ceased trading.
[f] Traded as part of Thomas Cook from 1999.

Appendix 4

Actual carryings (source: CAA, various)

Tour operator	Carryings (000s)										
	1991	1992	1993	1994	1995	1996	1997	1998	1999	2000	2001
Thomson	2,850	3,247	3,481	3,950	4,208	3,657	3,917	4,679	4,869	4,037	3,917
First Choice	1,658	2,094	1,878	1,915	1,928	1,992	1,875	2,919	2,973	2,844	2,949
Airtours	993	1,437	2,135	2,427	2,720	2,488	2,877	3,618	3,961	4,338	5,087
Cosmos	600	864	1,135	1,562	1,091	931	965	957	991	1,084	1,134
Sunworld/ Thomas Cook	239	461	429	661	705	a	1,050	2,352	2,901	3,232	3,292
Unijet	a	a	a	a	a	649	b				
First tier subtotal	6,340	8,103	9,058	10,515	10,652	9,717	10,684	14,525	15,695	15,535	16,379
Others	4,040	4,807	5,192	6,085	7,648	10,983	11,416	9,975	10,605	11,965	12,821
Total	10,380	12,910	14,250	16,600	18,300	20,700	22,100	24,500	26,300	27,500	29,200

Figures relate to all licences for twelve-month periods to the end of September.
Not placed in the top five tour operators.
[b]Part of Thomas Cook

Since 1990, the CAA has published data on the actual carryings of the total AIT market and since 1991 these data have been broken down to itemize the actual carryings of individual ATOL holders. The CAA data on actual carryings can be categorized in order to distinguish between two groupings of tour operators:

- first tier operators – consisting of the largest five tour operators;
- other operators – which include all remaining actual carryings by ATOL holders.

Following the introduction of new ATOL regulations in May 1995, three kinds of businesses are specified in licences. These are:

- fully bonded – scheduled or charter-based inclusive packages and seat-only travel on charter flights (1406 licences December 1996);
- lower bonded – scheduled seat-only tickets covered by a bond. These are bonded at a lower level than packages and charters, usually 5% (186 licences December 1996);

■ agency – scheduled seat-only tickets where an airline guarantees the business of a consolidator and provides a 'deed of undertaking' to the CAA (63 licences December 1996).

The introduction of lower bonded and agency ATOLs from 1995 accounts for a large part (although not precisely quantifiable) part of the increase in ATOL capacity between 1995 and 1996.

Appendix 5

Number of ATOL holders (source: CAA, various)

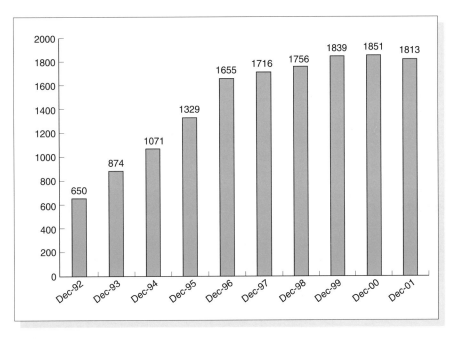

Appendix 6

Average prices, total revenue and retail price indices (source: CAA, various)

	1992	1993	1994	1995	1996	1997	1998	1999	2000	2001
Average holiday price	£318	£346	£356	£361	£388	£415	£415	£421	£438	£447
Total revenue (£ billions)	4.1	4.9	5.9	6.6	7.8	9.2	10.2	11.0	12.0	13.1
Retail price index (1987=100)	138.5	140.7	144.1	149.1	152.7	157.5	162.9	165.4	170.3	173.3

Note: table shows actual average prices charged by tour operators for 12 months to September.

References

Buhalis, D. (2001) The tourism phenomenon: the new tourist and consumer. In: Waha, S. and Cooper, C. (eds), *Tourism in The Age of Globalisation*. London: Routledge.

Civil Aviation Authority. *ATOL Business, 1992–2001*. London: Civil Aviation Authority.

European Commission. *Council Directive of June 13 1990 on Package Travel, Package Holidays and Package Tours* (90/314/EEC).

Krippendorf, J. (1986) Tourism in the system of industrial society. *Annals of Tourism Research*, 13(4).

Krippendorf, J. (1987) *The Holidaymakers: Understanding the Impact of Leisure and Travel*. London: Heinemann.

Middleton, V.T.C. (1991) Whither the package tour? *Tourism Management*, September.

Poon, A. (1993) *Tourism Technology and Competitive Strategies*. Wallingford: CAB International.

Ryan, C. (1991) UK package holiday industry. *Tourism Management*, March.

Smith, C. and Jenner, P. (1998) Travel agents in Europe. *Travel and Tourism Analyst*, 4, 5–15.

Travel Trade Gazette (1998) The year that shook the travel world. *Travel Trade Gazette*, 6 January.

MyTravel plc (formerly Airtours)

Competing in the travel industry big league
Nigel Evans

An entrepreneurial beginning

David Crossland's introduction to the business world was not very promising. On leaving Burnley Grammar School in 1963 he took a job as a glorified coffee boy in a local travel agent and it was difficult to imagine that he would in time become the chairman of what became one of the world's leading travel companies and rank 86th in *The Sunday Times* 'Rich List' of Britain's wealthiest 1000 people. From acorns oak trees grow, and so it was with this Lancastrian entrepreneur.

During the 1970s, Crossland developed his own travel agency business, Pendle Travel, together with his brother-in-law Tom Trickett. Entry costs were at the time relatively low and the powerful multiple chains were far less the threat to the independent travel agency business that they were later to become. Trickett backed Crossland in 1972 with an £8000 investment in the first travel agency, and he remained a large shareholder in the Airtours business until the mid-1990s. What later evolved into the MyTravel group emerged with the Airtours name in 1978 when Pendle Travel launched a tour operations division within the successful travel agency business. When the first tours took to the air the company operated from a tiny office above a travel agency in the small Lancashire village of Haslingden.

The initial specialization of the company was low-cost package holidays to Malta, which found a ready market in north-west England. The speed of development of the tour-operating business outstripped that of the travel agency chain and the competitive pressures on independent travel agents were becoming ever greater with 'the march of the multiples' as it was later termed.

From 1985, Crossland, recognizing that the development of the business required professional inputs from others, started to draw around him a strong management team to help him build the business. The sale of the 22-branch chain to Hogg Robinson (which operated a nation-wide branch network) was concluded in 1986 and in that year Airtours carried 300,000 holidaymakers. This period culminated the following year with a major step in the company's strategic development. The company was floated on the London Stock Exchange to become a public limited company (plc), making it one of a very small number of tour operators to have a full stock market listing at that time.

After flotation

As Airtours plc, the management could raise capital for investment and although this allowed opportunities for expansion, it also imposed financial disciplines on the management team. As a public limited company, every move was carefully scrutinized by the City and by the media. The company had to deliver satisfaction to customers, shareholders and bankers, and balancing these competing demands was not always easy. Still based in its north-west England heartland (the company today has its corporate headquarters in the Manchester suburbs), Airtours had established a reputation throughout the travel industry for its relatively low staffing costs and the loyalty it was able to engender in its staff. "They stay a long time because they are determined that one day they will get to the office before me," Crossland once joked. Although he became less 'hands-on' as he approached retirement in the late 1990s, he remained as chairman, and the days on which he regularly arrived at the office by 5.30 a.m. are still fondly remembered by staff.

Despite many developments in the company, tour operations remained at the core of the group's activities, with airline, distribution networks and accommodation developing largely to service the needs of the tour operations activity. The Aspro brand was positioned at the value for money or price-led end of the market, whereas Airtours was positioned as the main market brand with particular appeal to families.

A large number of different brochures were produced in the UK using the Airtours name and representing a variety of holiday types. The brochures included: Summer Sun, Far and Away, Turkey, Greece, Florida, Fly-Drive USA, Cruises, Florida and Caribbean Cruise and Stay Holidays (featuring Carnival Cruises), All-Inclusive Suncenters, City and Short Breaks and Lakes and Mountains. The Tradewinds brand offered more exclusive and exotic holidays, mainly utilizing scheduled flights to destinations all over the world.

In 1990, Airtours introduced EuroSites by establishing a subsidiary operating self-drive holidays with pre-arranged camping locations. By the late 1990s, EuroSites had become the second largest company (after Eurocamp) in this area of the market. EuroSites offered tent and mobile home holidays across Europe, selling since its launch in the UK and more recently in the Dutch and German markets. Further capacity was added progressively from one season to the next by increasing the capacity at sites and adding additional camp sites to its portfolio. Demand for the product proved to be strong, with good levels of profitability, high levels of customer satisfaction and high levels of repeat business. During 1990, 'The Cottage Directory' product, selling UK country cottages, was also developed. However, sales levels achieved were lower than forecast and the product proved operationally difficult, involving as it did close liaison with a large number of individual property owners and a comparatively low value of sales per brochure page. After the end of its first season an offer for the business was received and accepted, thereby incurring a relatively limited loss overall.

Throughout the 1990s, the UK outbound tour-operating sector was characterized by intense competition and was highly seasonal and cyclical in its booking patterns. A number of factors combined to create a substantial imbalance between supply and demand for the summer of 1995. Tour operators had anticipated the arrival of the much talked about 'feel good factor' in the UK economy and sales in the pre-Christmas selling period were encouraging. However, this did not continue into the peak booking months of January–March, although all operators maintained capacity in the expectation of an upturn in demand. Several companies also declared their aim of gaining market share in 1995. Onto this market position was added the effect of the excellent, record-breaking UK weather during the summer months. With supply greater than demand in the increasingly important 'late sales' market, many prices fell to unprofitable levels across the industry and discounting was substantially higher than in most years.

The alternatives indicated by the 1995 market were straightforward. The industry could either downsize by offering fewer holidays at realistic margins or continue on the same basis as pre-1995 with higher and higher late sales discounts giving customers little incentive to book early.

Launched ahead of schedule on 18 March 1991, Airtours International was set up. Unlike some other charter carriers, Airtours International's airline capacity was intended solely to serve the group's tour operations. Its capacity was fully utilized on Airtours business and was not dependent upon third-party customers. The growing needs of the Airtours' tour operations required assurance that sufficient seat capacity could be acquired at the right price and of a consistent quality. The airline's growth, however, was limited by Airtours' winter tour operations since it was during the winter that any excess charter capacity was likely to become apparent. With this factor in mind, the airline provided over 90% of the winter tour operations flying programme, dropping to between 60% and 70% for the summer programme.

Airtours' northern roots were emphasized by the position of Manchester airport. In 1986, 76% of Airtours' bookings were for Manchester departures and, although growth from the airport continued in terms of absolute numbers, its relative position declined since it represented only 46% of UK departures in 1991 and this proportion subsequently fell further. The company's in-house airline, Airtours International, was, from its inception in 1991, based at the airport.

In September 1992, Airtours re-entered the UK retail travel agency business with the purchase of 335 branches of the third largest retail chain, Pickfords. This was followed by the purchase in June 1993 of 210 branches acquired from Hogg Robinson, moving the group to second position behind Lunn Poly in UK retail distribution. The branches served as outlets for the distribution of Airtours products and importantly provided market intelligence on customer preferences and market trends. A major re-branding exercise took place during December 1993 in which the division was re-launched under the Going Places name. Within seven days every one of the company's 545 retail shops had been fitted out with new fascias, signage and stationery. Later in the year, the forty-strong Winston Rees chain was added to the Airtours network.

The merging of the large retail networks inevitably resulted in a degree of duplication, with some shops being closer to others than would be considered ideal. Little merit was seen in closing branches despite the close proximity of a second Going Places outlet, as long as each shop continued to make a satisfactory contribution to central overheads. Nevertheless, the profitability of each shop was continually reviewed and, although many new sites were subsequently developed by Going Places, several poorly performing shops were closed and sold off. In 1995, Going Places had over 650 branches operating in the UK compared with 795 operated by Lunn Poly, the market leader. Late Escapes, a telephone sales business specializing in the sales of holidays within eight weeks of departure, was purchased in 1994. Late Escapes, based in north-east England, made extensive use of the tele-text information services for the marketing of its services directly to customers in their homes.

In January 1993, Airtours launched a hostile take-over bid for Owners Abroad (later known as First Choice Holidays), another large tour operator, which served many of the same destinations. The acrimonious battle fought over several months and widely reported by the media led to a narrow defeat for Airtours and incurred costs of some £9 million.

International expansion

After 1994, the group expanded internationally, most significantly in Scandinavia and subsequently in North America. The acquisition from Scandinavian Airways in June 1994 of the Scandinavian Leisure Group (SLG) gave Airtours ownership of the largest leisure travel company in Scandinavia, albeit one that served many of the same destinations as Airtours in the UK market. SLG operates the Ving, Always and Saga brands, with particular strengths in Norway and Sweden. 70% of its sales were made directly to the public either by 'direct sell' methods or through dedicated retail outlets, with the remaining 30% of bookings being made through third-party travel agents.

During the winter of 1994–95, SLG undertook a major restructuring exercise of its operations, which together with an improvement in the Scandinavian economies resulted in a greatly enhanced performance by this division. SLG carried 915,000 customers in 1995, increasing to 1,028,000 in 1996. The acquisition of the Spies group, Scandinavia's third largest tour operator, during 1996 added a further 397,000 customers under the Spies and Tjaerborg brands. The Spies group was extensively reorganized and re-focused on acquisition, with most administrative functions being integrated into SLG's Stockholm headquarters and respective overseas resort offices being rationalized. Following its major expansion, SLG had approximately 50% of the Scandinavian market, with the leading position in each of the Scandinavian countries. The acquisition of Spies gave Airtours full control of Scandinavia's largest charter airline Premiair.

The Scandinavian acquisitions brought with them hotel and holiday complex portfolios of sixteen properties in the case of SLG and twenty-five properties in the case of Spies, located in many of the principal resorts served by the group's tour operations. Accommodation ownership allowed retention within the group of a higher proportion of resort expenditure and allowed the company to monitor customer tastes and preferences more accurately. By limiting hotel ownership to less than 20% of total accommodation requirements within any one area, the group was able to ensure high occupancy levels. Distinct accommodation brands were developed in order to satisfy the differing demands of the group's tour operations. The successful Sunwing brand was primarily designed for Scandinavian customers, whereas the Suncenter product was marketed through Airtours Holidays and catered largely for the needs of the UK market. Suncenters offered families an action-packed home-from-home with many activities, lots of entertainment and children's clubs.

The acquisition of Sunquest Vacations in August 1995 established Airtours' presence in the North American market through its tour-operating businesses in Ontario and western Canada. This was followed by the acquisition of Alba, another significant Canadian tour operator, in August of the following year. Airtours also made its first foray into the vast US market during 1996, deciding that the most cost-effective entry vehicle would be through a 'greenfield' start-up operation capitalizing on the Sunquest brand name. Accordingly, Sunquest Holidays was formed under the leadership of John Trickett, who had previously held management positions within the Airtours group in the UK prior to moving to California in 1989, where he had subsequently worked for other tour operators. The company operated its first programme of holidays in 1997, flying largely from California and focusing on Mexico, the Caribbean and Hawaii, all of which were also served by existing tour operations within the Airtours group. In 1996, Airtours' North American Leisure Group had built a business carrying almost 500,000 customers a year.

Cruising as a holiday choice grew in popularity during the 1990s in most Western economies. The UK market was still relatively small (representing about 500,000 customers in 1994) due to its image of high cost, exclusivity and older age group appeal, but this market doubled in size between 1994 and 2000. It also grew elsewhere in Europe but accounted for only 2% of European package holidays as at the year 2000. The North American cruise market developed in a different way, with rapid growth in the late 1990s, a much younger customer base, specialist targeted cruise programmes and a product that offered high standards at competitive prices.

In 1994, Airtours created a cruise product, Sun Cruises, at a price level that would appeal to its existing customer base and two ships containing a total of 1900 berths were purchased. Passengers flew from local airports in the UK, Scandinavia and North America to their point of embarkation (mainly in traditional Mediterranean resort areas and the Caribbean). The operational management of the ships was subcontracted to an experienced cruise operator. Utilizing many of the services of the group's tour-operating businesses and taking advantage of its distribution network substantially reduced costs and enables a high-quality product to be offered at prices significantly below those offered by traditional cruise operators. In only its second year of operation Sun Cruises achieved load factors approaching 100% and a UK market share of 18%.

The principal risks usually perceived by external observers of the travel industry for a group such as Airtours are those of underutilized aircraft and excess hotel accommodation for which payment has already been made. The reality was that Airtours, in common with other major tour operators, had considerable flexibility in its contracting of both of these services. Aviation contracts with third-party suppliers usually had a variety of cancellation options, which could be exercised once booking patterns had been established. This provided a margin of comfort when coupled with the way in which Airtours' in-house flying capacity was tailored to provide 60–70% of expected summer requirements. With regard to accommodation, only 10% of Airtours' requirements were booked on an irrevocable basis.

Perhaps more critical to the business, and common to other businesses dealing with international conditions, were changes in exchange and interest rates and aviation fuel. Airtours' developed a policy of 'hedging' against all major risks on the financial and commodity markets prior to each brochure launch. Specifically, the group developed the practice of negotiating a range of forward contracts and options. In this way, the costs of hedging these risks were built into the brochure selling prices.

The holiday business is well known for generating substantial cash flows as customers traditionally pay in advance and the holiday companies pay their suppliers in arrears. There is a degree of seasonality to this cash flow but, even at its lowest point, substantial cash balances are usually held by the tour-operating companies. Effective 'cash management' of these balances therefore became a very important part of managing the business and interest receivable as, with other tour operators, this represented a significant source of income. Surplus funds were placed on deposit with established international banks, but other investment opportunities were examined at times of falling interest rates.

Airtours competing in the big league

For many years Airtours was seen as the darling of the City – a travel company that was professionally run and which reported steadily increasing turnover and profits. Its shares peaked at 540 pence in mid-1999 but then languished at prices of between 200 and 300 pence as a series of problems beset the company over 2000 and 2001. Europe-wide consolidation of the sector led to the emergence of powerful new competitive groupings while its own deals largely failed to impress. The years 1998 and 1999 saw a flurry of take-over activity in the UK tour-operating sector, with Airtours and other large groups consolidating their leading positions following an investigation by the Monopolies and Merger Commission (now the UK Competition Commission). Thus, Airtours added to its portfolio of activities by acquiring medium-sized British operators (such as Cresta, Bridge, Panorama and Direct Holidays and the Bridge Travel Group), Thomson added Crystal Holidays and First Choice added Unijet.

Problems began for the group in 1999 when Airtours bought Travelworld, a 120-strong Yorkshire-based travel agency, for £12 million. Airtours had to beat off competition from rival companies to buy Travel world, and post acquisition it re-branded the shops and bolted them on to its existing Going Places chain. Travelworld's financial position was less robust than it had been hoped at the time of the purchase and this raised questions about Airtours management's astuteness in making the deal. Of greater strategic significance to the group, however, was the impact of the consolidation that swept through the sector.

"Scale matters in a business where the better performers only make a 4% profit margin," said John Donaldson, Thomas Cook's chief executive. "If you can get cost efficiencies of 1 to 2% through better buying, such as hotel rooms and aircraft fuel, that has a very material impact on profitability. That's what's driving consolidation." Tour operating has always been viewed as a risky business, where most profits are made during a short summer period. The tour operators responded to this in several ways. In the 1990s, the sector increasingly became vertically integrated and horizontal expansion followed first at the national level and then internationally when domestic opportunities became more limited. The new century, however, has been characterized not by the largest players purchasing smaller, weaker rivals, but by consolidation among the largest players themselves, which has seen the emergence of four key groups: Preussag and Thomas Cook based in Germany and Airtours and First Choice based in the UK.

The European industry was largely shaped at corporate headquarters in Toronto in Canada and Hanover in Germany by the changing strategies of two large industrial companies. Thomson, the Canadian Media group, withdrew from the sector by floating its Thomson Holiday group in the UK during 1998. Preussag AG, a German industrial and logistics group, decided to withdraw from these sectors in order to concentrate its activities on the travel industry. In 1999, Preussag purchased Germany's largest travel group (TUI) and followed up this purchase a year later with the acquisition of Thomson Travel. The TUI purchase left Preussag with a stake in Thomas Cook, a first-class brand-name in the travel industry. European Community rules meant that the Thomas Cook holding had to be sold by Preussag when Thomson was subsequently purchased. C&N Touristic, Germany' s second largest tour-operating group (which was owned jointly by Lufthansa and Karstadt, a department store group), subsequently purchased Thomas Cook and later changed its name to Thomas Cook AG.

Airtours purchased its means of entry into the German market in 1998 when it bought a minority stake in Frosch Touristik International (FTI), Germany's fourth-ranked tour-operating group. That sun-starved Germany and Britain emerged to dominate the industry in Europe is not surprising. They are the two largest European markets, with the Germans, who typically have six weeks annual holiday, spending £40 billion on international tourism – 20% more than the British. Airtours, however, in common with other British companies expanding in Germany, found the going difficult. Airtours discovered it had bought trouble in that the 2000 season produced losses of some £100 million for FTI, which resulted in

Airtours taking full control of the company in late 2000. The difficulties were attributed to the over-estimation of capacity requirements for the summer season and being left with unfilled allocations.

Although (as at 2002) further consolidation remained likely, there were legal constraints upon further consolidation. In 1999, Airtours' £950 million bid for First Choice plc was blocked by the European Commission on the grounds that it would have left three vertically integrated tour operators (Thomson, Airtours and Thomas Cook) controlling over 80% of some short-haul tour operating destinations. Although Airtours did not rule out a further bid in the future, and lodged an appeal against the decision, First Choice emerged re-invigorated having modified its strategic positioning. First Choice's emphasis began to shift away from high-volume, low-margin businesses towards a portfolio of individually branded more specialist products offering potentially higher returns. Nevertheless, cost efficiency was maintained through the utilization of centralized systems and corporate buying power.

The vertically integrated model, whereby a single group became the full owner (or had equity in) of airline operations, tour operations and travel retailing was, however, the subject of further development. Until the late 1990s, most groups avoided investment in accommodation, believing that the high capital costs and inherent interest rate and property risks involved were at variance with the types of businesses they had traditionally run. Competition from operators around Europe, the growth of new markets in Eastern and Central Europe, and a slow-down in the rate of new building led to a shortage of good-quality accommodation at key resorts (particularly in the Balearic and Canary Islands). The shortage increasingly led to a re-assessment of the position with regard to property and hotel ownership on the part of the big travel groups.

Airtours became hoteliers with the purchase of Scandinavian Leisure Group and then further embraced accommodation ownership with the purchase of several hotels and apartment complexes. In January 2000, for example, the company purchased for £63.4 million the Bellevue apartments, Europe's largest complex situated in Majorca. This not only gave the company access to high-quality accommodation in an important location, but it also denied others such access at a time when increasingly stringent planning procedures prevented large-scale new developments.

In 1997, Airtours and Carnival Cruise Line (the world's largest) agreed to jointly purchase the Costa cruise line based in Florida at a cost (to Airtours) of £59 million. Sales through Airtours' distribution network were significant but far from spectacular and the sale of the assets to the partner Carnival in summer 2000 for £350 million represented an opportunity to realize the value of a non-core asset at a time when a large amount of additional cruising capacity was about to enter the market. The transaction left Airtours better positioned to exploit its business model in Europe and North America and to seek investments that would further support and enhance the group's core activities.

Management, staff and systems

The transition from its single business core of tour operating into an integrated international travel business was rapid, and this placed considerable demands on management, staff and systems. Considerable resources were devoted to staff recruitment, management training and the procurement of the necessary computer hardware and software in order to enhance the group's competitive position. As at the year 2002, Airtours, now renamed the MyTravel group, was managed on a decentralized basis with a small head office team and a separate board of directors for each of the main divisions: UK tour operations, UK retail, Scandinavian Leisure Group, North American Leisure Group, aviation division, and cruise and hotels division.

Such rapid development did not always run smoothly. Airtours was a long-time favourite target for attacks by sections of the media, attracting poor ratings by reports from The Consumers' Association, and attracting more than its share of press criticism over quality standards. During the late 1990s, Airtours made strenuous efforts to ensure that customers knew what they are buying and that they got what they were promised. Each of the group's divisions operated its own quality-control initiatives, relying heavily on customer feed-back, and, although it remained an area for some concern relative to competitors, there was a marked reduction in the proportion of complaints relative to holidays sold.

Management clashes led to a series of high-profile departures from Airtours. A new director was brought from a cinema chain to shake up the UK retail division during 2000 and subsequently sacked five directors of Going Places. The sacked directors launched actions in the High Court to recover money they claimed they were owed, with two of them later being re-employed by First Choice plc. Meanwhile, at the group level, Harry Coe and Hugh Collinson, longstanding board members and Airtours' founder David Crossland's 'right-hand men', both retired. Perhaps the most damaging, however, was the defection of two senior executives during 2001 to arch-rival, Thomson.

The imponderable factor for all firms was the future of direct dealings with customers as opposed to dealings through intermediaries such as travel agents. Airtours invested heavily in call centres, and channels such as TV text services and TV channels dedicated to travel grew in importance, but capturing e-commerce business remained the elusive prize. Airtours chief executive, Tim Byrne, hoped to make huge savings by persuading people to book direct rather than on the high street. Just two years after a big UK retail expansion (of Going Places) he closed 120 of 867 shops in 2001, and more were expected to follow. Airtours struck a £20 million deal with TV text service, teletext, to distribute holidays on digital channels, but it was the £240 million purchase of US Travel Services International (which included mytravel.com) in 2000 that was viewed as the key deal in distribution.

The acquisition brought expenditure by Airtours on its net strategy to more than £340 million, with few discernible signs of success. The MyTravel brand was launched in Autumn 2001 and was rolled out across the shops and brochures to raise visibility. The Airtours name had served the group well and continued to be the largest tour-operating brand, Airtours Holidays, but it was thought that benefits could be gained from aligning the plc name with the new branded distribution. The new name was placed on each of the 115 million brochures produced each year, the 1000 retail outlets and on each piece of stationery.

Although it cost 15% of turnover to book through travel agents and just 5% online, everything hung on persuading people to book their holidays in this way. Consumer purchasing behaviour was deeply embedded and slow to change. Travel agents, like shoe shops, were often found clustered on a high street, allowing comparisons to be made and bargains to be struck by customers. Going to buy the holiday was associated with the excitement of the holiday itself and so the change to online booking was not expected to be fast growing. Internet bookings struggled to get off the ground in the UK as elsewhere, with, as at 2002, package holidays bought in this way only accounting for 1% of business.

Appendix 1

MyTravel plc group structure (2002)

Products	Markets			
	UK	**Scandinavia**	**Germany**	**North America**
Distribution	Going Places Late Escapes MyTravel	Spies Tjaerborg Ving Shops MyTravel	FTi Touristik	WorldChoice Travel MyTravel Cruises Only
Tour operations	Airtours Aspro Tradewinds EuroSites Direct Holidays Manos Panorama Cresta	Ving Always Saga Spies Tjaerborg	FTi Touristik	Sunquest Vacations Alba tours Vacation Express
Aviation	Airtours International	Premiair		Skyservice*
Cruise and hotels	Resort hotels: Sunwing, Tenerife Sol**, Hotetur** Cruise: Sun Cruises			

*Long-term contract.
**Joint ventures.
Note: The board of directors comprises the chairman (David Crossland), chief executive (Tim Byrne), the group finance director, chairmen of the operating divisions (UK Leisure Group, Scandinavian Leisure Group, German Leisure Group, MyTravel North America and the Aviation Division) and three non-executive directors. Each operating division has its own board of directors chaired by a main board member.

Appendix 2

Some comments by David Crossland – MyTravel chairman

Speaking in 1992, chairman David Crossland said: "I certainly can't claim that I sat down 20 years ago and created a master plan for a travel business, but I did always believe that if you really wanted to achieve something you could." From the earliest days, Crossland wanted to give holidaymakers a good value-for-money product and believed that if they received such a product they would come back for more. That desire is something that has not changed and it proved to be correct. He recently said that "[the only people] I really worry about are those who buy our products, the end users. I care passionately about them."

Initially, Airtours was very much a family business. It had very little capital and Crossland knew the only way the company would grow was through reinvestment and hard work. Today it is a big organization, but Crossland argues that the management and staff all share that original commitment towards passengers and they work extremely hard and show great loyalty. "My enthusiasm seems to be infectious and rub off on them," he said. "It is still a family business, but now it has become the Airtours family rather than the Crossland family."

Crossland has said that he only really has one talent and that is the ability to appoint managers who are far cleverer than he is – people who are extremely professional and absolute experts in their fields. The success of the company has a great deal to do with them. Another key to the success, he said was that 'we believe in our product. We believe we have a really good product, that our brochures are clear, clean and easily understood, and that our advertising is effective. We have grown and changed, but our roots are in travel retailing and we understand, from inside knowledge, just how retailers work.'

In 2002, David Crossland appointed Tim Byrne, Airtours' managing director, as chief executive to oversee the day-to-day running of the company. Crossland's plan was then to concentrate on exploring new opportunities. This came in the wake of news that Airtours' underlying profits had fallen 30% against the previous year. Pretax profits were up to £211.4 million from £125.9 million, but the problem with FTI, its German business (which lost £100 million during these two years), is still being addressed. MyTravel's mistake was entering the German market with a minority stake. It acquired control only during 2001, but not in time to reverse the damage caused by excess capacity in the local holiday market. Yet Crossland saw the problems as a blip. "You've got to get it into perspective," he said. "When we floated in 1987 we were making £2 million and when we started we employed two people."

A key mistake was made in 1999 when the company thought it was taking a low-risk route by only buying 30% of FTI, but it actually turned out to be worse because, in Crossland's words: "We did not have control and if we had had control this year, which has been a difficult year in the German market, the losses would not have been as bad." Airtours finally took full control of FTI in September 2001 and big changes were made in the German subsidiary. Overseas bed rates were renegotiated using the MyTravel bargaining strength, the cost of sales were brought down and the company was restructured. Crossland added that: "It grew very fast. It had an entrepreneur who would not take advice about putting a structure in and was trying to manage all the divisions himself."

Having been the driving force behind MyTravel's growth and then the architect of its move into Germany, Crossland's challenge became to restore investor confidence. It has been suggested that MyTravel is a one-man band, but Crossland responds by saying that "we have some strong managers and directors who run big businesses all over the world . . . but I'm the front person and take responsibility when we have a difficult year." The appointment of Tim Byrne was clearly important for the group, as Crossland explained: "We need one guy sitting on the top of each division and driving out the costs and sweeping the synergies across the matrix rather than just down it. It will leave me able to spot opportunities, which is what I'm good at."

Appendix 3

Preussag AG

According to Dr Michael Frenzel, the boss of German holiday giant Preussag, the package tour must become more European. Although there will still be room for diversity, and differences in national tastes will still be important, Preussag believes that further integration at a European level will take place. Preussag's GBP 1.8 billion take-over of Thomson Travel in August 2000 made it the largest package holiday firm in the world. Frenzel's opinion is one that cannot be ignored.

Frenzel, 53, manages Preussag from an austere headquarters in Hanover, where for the past six years he has plotted the company's transformation from an industrial conglomerate into a more focused package holiday giant. After joining the company in 1994, Frenzel has embarked on a high-risk strategy. While rapidly withdrawing from the group's poorly performing industrial interests, he has set about acquiring prized assets among European holiday companies. As an industrial group, there were about 50 separate businesses, but, importantly, Preussag was not number one at anything.

Leisure and tourism presented major opportunities for growth. Rivals cannot help but admire the single-mindedness demonstrated in his plans for the tour group. In 1998, the German travel giant Tui and airline Hapag-Lloyd were acquired, followed by British holiday and financial services group Thomas Cook. Then, after acquiring a couple of travel agency chains, Frenzel went for his holiday dream in the form of Thomson Travel. He snatched it at the eleventh hour from C&N Touristic, Germany's second-biggest travel company. He had promised to turn Thomas Cook into the British market leader ahead of Thomson and Airtours (MyTravel), but sold Thomas Cook to another German tour operator as soon as Thomson came on the market. Thomson represented the bigger opportunity.

Control of two of the UK's biggest tour companies make the two German operators the two most powerful holiday firms in Europe. This is all a far cry from just a few years ago, when British firms such as MyTravel were homing in on German companies. After a period of aggressive selling and buying, Preussag is concentrating on digesting and integrating the companies. Twelve teams of executives have been established to ease the integration of the various new companies in what has been dubbed Operation Titan.

"It's not a question of cost savings", Frenzel maintains. "It's about being more flexible in our destinations, in buying fuel for our airlines and negotiating on hotel beds. Shifting over-capacity of tourists from one subsidiary's resort to another to take advantage of synergies also offers opportunities."

Appendix 4

MyTravel financial statements

MyTravel financial summary, 1986–2001

	2001	2000	1999	1998	1997	1996	1995	1994	1993	1992	1991	1990	1989	1988	1987	1986
Turnover (£ million)	5061.4	3949.0	3309.3	2753.4	2235.6	1717.9	1317.8	971.7	615.6	405.6	289.5	183.0	155.6	102.5	68.3	55.0
Profit before tax (£ million)	81.3	211.4	125.9	125.7	117.2	86.8	59.1	75.8	45.6	36.5	27.5	6.3	5.2	4.1	2.0	2.0
Earnings per ordinary share (pence)	6.28	35.98	19.74	21.14	20.62	45.63	32.76	41.79	29.22	24.47	24.68	6.69	5.12	17.43	8.55	8.53
Dividends per ordinary share (pence)	9.50	9.00	8.25	7.50	6.67	16.00	14.00	12.00	9.00	7.25	5.75	2.03	1.72	6.25	n/a	n/a
Number of employees	27,868	24,316	20,226	17,354	14,565	12,198	9,896	6,337	3,819	1,349	946	571	389	310	212	283

MyTravel business segment analysis

		Turnover (£ million)		Profits before tax (£ million)		Net assets (£ million)	
		2001	2000	2001	2000	2001	2000
UK	Continuing	2672.2	2323.8	110.6	279.9	106.9	282.6
Other Europe	Continuing					286.5	273.3
	Scandinavia and The Netherlands	1018.3	926.8	31.2	20.7		
	FTi	684.4	92.8	−52.6	−13.3		
	Acquisitions	14.0	−	0.8	−		
	Discontinued	22.3	143.3	−2.0	−36.1		
North America	Continuing	641.8	462.8	−10.8	−19.3	128.5	−12.3
	Acquisitions	8.4	−	−	−		
Joint ventures	Continuing						
	FTi	−	293.9	−	−49.6		
	Other	28.1	8.5	4.1	2.2		
	Discontinued						
	Costa Cruises	−	183.4	−	26.9		
	Total	5089.5	4435.3	81.3	211.4	521.9	543.6

MyTravel balance sheet

		2001	2000	1999	1998	1997
Fixed assets	Tangible	431.1	513.5	417.8	310.7	261.4
	Intangible	540.2	534.8	36.9	–	–
	Investments	83.7	55.3	116.9	82.7	63.0
	Total	1055.0	1103.6	571.6	393.4	324.4
Current assets	Stock	13.3	17.2	11.4	17.0	6.4
	Debtors	838.5	712.2	550.5	403.5	331.7
	Investments	0	0	0	0	0
	Bank and deposits	378.6	793.3	554.2	364.2	406.6
	Total	1230.4	1522.7	1116.1	784.7	744.7
Current liabilities	Creditors	−359.0	−462.6			
	Loans/overdraft	−16.9	−33.8			
	Other	−827.4[a]	−777.5[a]			
	Total	−1203.3	−1273.9	−948.8	−802.0	−747.2
Non-current liabilities		−560.2	−695.4	−490.8	−210.1	−562.6
Total assets less liabilities		521.9	543.6	248.1	166.0	240.7
Shareholders funds	Share capital	49.3	49.1	47.8	47.5	47.2
	Reserves	263.0	285.7	200.3	118.5	193.5
Non-equity preference shares		209.6	208.8	–	–	–
Total		521.9	543.6	248.1	166.0	240.7

[a]Of which revenue received in advance: 310.8 (2001), 333.4 (2002); accruals and deferred income: 330.2 (2001), 250.5 (2000).

Appendix 5

Major competitors' financial statements

Major competitors' turnover and profits

		2000	1999
Turnover	Preussag (Euro million) of which tourism (Euro million)	21854.0 10562.1	16,501 7164.8
	First Choice (£ million)	1880.7	1465.8
	Thomas Cook (DM million)	9740.8	9073.9
Profit before tax	Preussag (Euro million) of which tourism (Euro million)	402.5 423.3	345.4 307.5
	First Choice (£ million)	68.9	38.0
	Thomas Cook (DM million)	220.4	209.5

Note: Euro/£=1.70, DM/$=3.30.

Balance sheet of First Choice Holidays plc (£ million)

		2000	1999	1998	1997	1996
Fixed assets	Tangible					
	Intangible					
	Investments					
	Total	462.1	134.3	58.3	51.3	58.9
Current assets	Stock					
	Debtors					
	Investments					
	Bank and deposits					
	Prepayments					
	Total	704.9	417.6	380.9	264.4	238.5
Current liabilities	Creditors					
	Loans/overdraft					
	Other					
	Total	−660.1	−375.2	−325.4	−227.2	−206.2
Non-current liabilities		−89.6	−57.5	−45.7	−28.1	−30.8
Total assets less liabilities		417.3	119.2	68.1	60.4	60.4
Shareholders funds	Share capital	213.2	13.1	13.1	13.1	7.1
	Reserves	204.1	106.1	55.0	47.3	53.3
	Total	417.3	119.2	68.1	60.4	60.4

Note: Royal Caribbean Cruise Lines invested £200 million in a strategic alliance with First Choice during 2000. The alliance provides the cruise line with a 20% stake and enhanced distribution while providing First Choice with access to high-quality cruising products.

Honda–Rover: how successful was it?

British Leyland

The history of the Rover Group goes back to the turn of the nine-teenth century. In the first half of the twentieth century, the West Midlands of the UK was home to a number of independent motor companies and became one of the most important centres of motor manufacturing outside the USA. As the independents started to 'feel the heat' from foreign competitors in the 1950s and 1960s, some of the locally based producers saw the logic of merging in order to take advantage of economies of scale in purchasing and production.

Austin and Morris MG joined together in 1952 to become the British Motor Company (BMC) and were joined in 1965 by Pressed Steel Ltd – a producer of sheet steel, one of the key inputs into the car production process. The company structure changed to a divisiona-lized holding company in 1966 when BMC purchased Jaguar Daimler. Two years later, in 1968, BMC Holdings merged with its rival Leyland Motor Corporation (LMC) to form the British Leyland Motor Company. LMC was itself the result of several mergers in the 1960s and owned the marques Rover, Land Rover, Triumph and Leyland.

By 1975, when the Group simplified its name to British Leyland (BL), it had three major production sites: two in the West Midlands, at Longbridge (the UK's largest car plant) and at Solihull, and one in Oxfordshire (the Cowley plant).

Rover in the 1970s

The 1970s was a bad decade for BL. Between 1968 and 1978, its share of the UK car market fell from 40% to 23% and it was overtaken for the first time by Ford motors (USA). The trades unions at the Rover plants, particularly at its main Longbridge plant near Birmingham, had a reputation for militancy, and productivity had plumbed to new depths through a series of wildcat strikes and work-to-rule measures.

The company's major products were as unsuccessful as its industrial relations. Although the top-of-the-range offerings held up well (the Land Rover and Range Rover), the mid-range Austin Allegro and Morris Marina faired badly against the equivalent Ford Escort, Vauxhall's Viva and Chevette, and the VW Golf. The high-volume Rover products were not known for their design, their build or their longevity. Some of Rover's products from the 1970s have entered motoring folklore as objects of ridicule, such as the Austin Ambassador, the Princess and the Rover 3500. In order to set out the company's position to its staff, the then chairman of BL, Donald Stokes, said: "Workmanship and finish of British Leyland cars must be improved. If we don't do this I think our jobs are at risk."

The one high-volume segment that showed some promise was the growing supermini market. The Ford Fiesta, launched in the mid-1970s, had demonstrated a market for this design format and, by the end of the decade, BL's Mini Metro was showing some promise in this sector. The traditional Mini had faired reasonably within its small niche market.

In 1977, Donald Stokes' warning finally came true. The British Labour government acquired a controlling stake in the company to prevent it from becoming bankrupt with the inevitable loss of over 60,000 direct jobs, with many more being threatened in the service and supply industries in the West Midlands area. It was the last nationalization of the 1974–1979 Labour administration.

When the Conservatives came to power in 1979, one of Prime Minister Thatcher's first acts of industrial policy was to privatize BL. The UK defence company, British Aerospace plc (BAe), was persuaded to purchase the company as a wholly owned subsidiary. Despite the fact that motor manufacturing didn't fit naturally into BAe's product portfolio, plans were already in hand to bring about a radical improvement in its fortunes.

The company described its situation at the end of the 1970s:

> In the late 1970s, the world automotive industry was starting to stagnate after decades of consistent growth. All manufacturers were moving swiftly to find ways of adjusting to the new climate. They were looking to use research and development money more effectively, and looking to spread the risk associated with the manufacture of major components in a high-volume plant.
>
> They were also looking at new ways of gaining access to markets which were difficult, or seemingly impossible, to [enter]. Increasingly, manufacturers worldwide were reaching the conclusion that a joint venture was the best way of meeting these objectives and, at the same time, remaining independent. Honda also reached that conclusion.

Worldwide joint ventures and Honda

It was import restrictions in the form of import duties and quotas that had limited transnational growth in many markets, and the automotive sector was no exception. Some producers, seeking to circumvent these restrictions, opted for the higher-risk international strategy of direct investment. Most, however, decided to investigate the possibility of linking up with a local producer with a view to collaboration on research and production. By assembling cars in local factories, the cars could be sold as locally produced. Other benefits included synergies in product design, purchasing and distribution.

By 1980, most of the world's major motor manufacturers had entered into, or were considering, international joint ventures or similar collaborative arrangements. The US-based General Motors (the world's largest motor company) established collaborative relationships with Saab, Daewoo, Isuzu, Lotus and Suzuki and it was not untypical in its approach. Ford entered into similar arrangements with Jaguar, Kia, Mazda and Nissan. In some cases, international joint ventures eventually led to acquisition, such as that of Jaguar by Ford.

Honda, the Japanese motor company, had been well known in the UK for its motorcycles but less so for its cars. Like other Far Eastern manufacturers in its position, Honda had enjoyed only limited success in developing the large European market through exporting into the region, but import restrictions had placed a limit on the extent to which it could develop the European market. Honda's cars had a good reputation for quality, and many observers considered its design capability to be its key strength.

Of the three main automotive market areas (the Far East, the USA and Europe), Honda's presence was conspicuously small in Europe. It had a strong presence in its home area and had already successfully developed the North American market. Given the potential of the European market, Honda considered it a strategic priority to make some inroads into it.

The beginning of the alliance

Following meetings between Honda and BL in late 1978, a formal agreement was signed on 27 December 1979. Both parties entered into the 'partnership' warily, reluctant to expose too much to each other until a culture of mutual trust could be established. Accordingly, the initial agreement was for the joint production of a single model – the Triumph Acclaim (Triumph being a marque owned by BL). The Acclaim included parts and technology from both companies and proved to be a successful model, selling 130,000 units across Europe.

In 1981, 'Project XX' was launched to enable the two companies to develop, in tandem, an executive model under each marque. The Rover 800 series and the Honda Legend were essentially similar 'under the skin'. They shared the same body platform and both companies contributed to the design and styling.

The success of the Acclaim and Project XX persuaded both parties that they were, together, capable of producing a quality product that would enjoy success in the European market. In June 1984, two medium family cars were launched that were also essentially the same 'under the skin'. The Rover 200 and the Honda Ballade were designed mainly by Honda, and Rover's knowledge of the European markets proved to be valuable in terms of styling and specification. Both cars were produced by Rover at its Longbridge plant.

In 1984, BL took the decision to demerge its premium marques Jaguar and Daimler. It was thought that the sale of shares in the demerged company would be useful in developing the company's core high-volume products. Two years later, in order to identify the company with what it saw as its strongest marque, BL changed its name to Rover Group.

The reversal in Rover's fortunes was evidenced by the award of Car of the Year in 1989 for the Rover 200 series. Rover went on to manufacture the Honda Concerto for the European market and to launch a new mid-range car, the Rover 400 series. Despite these apparent successes (particularly its improvements in product design), Rover products continued to lose market share against its larger international competitors. In 1988, Rover's share of the UK market fell below 12% and it was overtaken by Vauxhall motors – the UK subsidiary of the US-based General Motors.

The alliance in the 1990s

In the late 1980s, Honda invested in its own assembly plant in the UK. The £200 million plant at Swindon in Wiltshire was smaller than those built at around the same time in the UK by Toyota and Nissan, but Rover's Longbridge and Cowley plants were able to pick up any extra volumes that Honda might require.

Following the success of the alliance in the 1980s, the two companies signed a new ten-year extension in 1989. The first fruits of the new alliance were the Rover 600 series and the Honda Accord. Like the models launched in the 1980s, these two models shared the same 'under-the-skin' components and were aimed at the upper- to mid-range market. Panels for both cars were produced by Rover and the cars were assembled at the two companies' respective factories.

Honda assisted Rover in its international market development by distributing Rover products through its dealership network in the Far East. The Land Rover Discovery, for example, was badged as a Honda for sale in Japan.

In early 1990, the two companies made a gesture to each other as a sign of their mutual trust and 'friendship'. A 20% stake in share capital was exchanged between Rover Group motors and Honda UK. Rover Group commented that, "This advanced the relationship to a more formal and permanent basis and helped both companies, while preserving their separate identities, to develop long-term strategies to meet the demands of an increasingly global market."

The two companies also formalized a joint strategy on purchasing and component supply for the expanded alliance. This was designed to take advantage of economies of scale and to ensure that quality assurance standards could be guaranteed in respect to purchased parts and other inputs.

Events in 1994

In the early 1990s, British Aerospace, Rover Group's parent company, began to review Rover's place in its portfolio of businesses. BAe is an international aircraft and armaments business and had, among other things, a strategic interest in the Eurofighter project. The fact that BAe had accepted ownership of Rover only reluctantly in the 1970s (when it was privatized by Prime Minister Thatcher) was also a key consideration at this time. Honda was not made aware of these discussions.

On 31 January 1994, a press statement was issued by BAe to the effect that it had sold the Rover Group in its entirety (apart from Honda's 20% share) to the German car manufacturer BMW for £800 million. For BAe, this disposal was seen as an opportunity to refocus on its core areas. Honda found out about the sale at the same time as the press and made its anger at the move clear.

Rover's new owner, BMW, made clear that it intended to keep the manufacturing plants in the UK but that it was unlikely that it would wish to maintain the alliance with Honda in the long term. On 21 February 1994, Honda announced that it had sold its 20% share-holding in the Rover Group.

Amazon.com

Colin Combe

Introduction

In 1995, Jeff Bezos was a young Wall Street executive who had become interested in the business opportunities presented by the development of digital technology. By the summer of that year he had returned to his native Seattle to set up an online book-selling business in the garage of his home. Using contacts gathered from his time in the financial hub of America, Bezos was able to attract sufficient investment capital from investors excited about the prospects of Internet selling to initiate the business concept behind Amazon.com. Initially, Bezos handled customer service himself and hired specialists to distribute books. By becoming the first mover in the e-retailing market, Amazon became the business model most used as a benchmark for analysing the development of e-commerce. By the end of 2000, Amazon's quarterly turnover had soared to $960 million yet the company was still trading at a loss, with Bezos facing criticism from many sources of the company's strategies.

The Amazon concept

The basis of the Amazon strategy was to create a virtual bookshop on its website. Bezos believed this would offer several sources of competitive advantage. These included a greater range of titles to choose from: convenience; twenty-four-hour access; quick and efficient search capability; and a competitive price through lower transaction costs. Another important aspect of Bezos's vision was the personalization of the service. The more customers interacted with the Amazon website, the greater Amazon's knowledge of their requirements would become. Accordingly, Amazon would become able to make customer-specific recommendations, reviews of particular genres of books and interaction with other customers and publishers. The customer database was also used as a marketing tool in targeting existing customers and pursuing potential new ones. Customer loyalty was a key asset for the company. The customer base of Amazon included both book buyers and publishers. Book buyers constituted the business to consumer (B2C) market, publishers and other sectors of the book trade were business to business (B2B).

e-tailing

In the early days of e-commerce, many analysts believed that the role of the middleman in the supply chain had come to an end. It was thought that manufacturers would by-pass retailers and deal directly with customers online (a process called *disintermediation*). As it transpired, however, manufacturers were reluctant to break up the traditional supply chain through e-commerce. The gap was filled by a new generation of 'dot.com' retailers (or 'e-tailers') and online divisions of traditional companies (a process referred to as *reintermediation*). This trend created opportunities for online retailing pioneers such as Amazon.com to establish brand recognition and develop a strong position in the supply chain.

A typical supply chain comprises raw material suppliers, manufacturers, distributors, retailers and customers – each element of which constitutes a value-adding as well as a cost-adding stage. The e-tailing concept aimed to eliminate traditional retailers from the supply chain (together with their associated costs). Thus, with the help of venture capital, e-tailers saved on the cost of building or leasing elaborate premises and used the capital instead for marketing and web development purposes. In the book industry, most e-commerce activity has been at the retailer level. Amazon.com, as first mover in the new economy book-selling market, was able to build a significant market share through Internet trading. However, as at 2001, the number of books sold online remained small compared with traditional methods (most books were still sold through 'impulse buying' in bookstores), leading most established bookstores such as Waterstones to approach e-commerce with caution.

Flotation and development

Amazon.com was floated on the Nasdaq in 1997 and used the capital to become one of the leading online bookstores in the world. Whereas physical bookstores are limited in the number of books they can stock, the virtual world inhabited by Amazon.com meant it could offer buyers an unprecedented range of titles. By 1998, the company had a catalogue of some three million books. Alongside the sale of books, the company had a book search service, ordering and payment system, delivery services and book information service. This latter aspect of the company's strategy was self-perpetuating as it fed on book buyer's opinions, book reviews, author feedback, publishers' statistics and information from the trade press. The huge array of data was customized by Amazon.com for easy access to potential clients whether they were book buyers, literary agents, publishers or authors. Each request for a book or 'click of interest' helped to build the database of customer profiles and to build a 'virtual community'. Thus, one of Amazon's key strengths became its ability to organize and disseminate book information for both consumers and businesses in the book trade.

As the first mover in the new online book-selling arena, Amazon enjoyed a near monopoly from 1995 to 1997. Even after the arrival of the closest rivals (Barnes & Noble in 1997), Amazon enjoyed strong sales growth. Despite this, however, profits on its trading remained elusive.

In 1997, the net sales of the company were $148 million; the following year this figure had risen to $540 million. By 2001, it had ten million customers worldwide and had expanded into other media sales such as CDs and videos. The company also expanded into garden implements, kitchenware and health products. Some critics questioned this proliferation of product offering as being one of the reasons for its lack of profitability.

Redesigning the book publishing supply chain

The traditional book publishing supply chain was redesigned by the advent of trading on the Internet. Previously books underwent a linear process incorporating authors, publishers, distributors, bookshops and then on to customers. While all these parties still have a role to play in the publishing of books, the selling aspect has changed significantly. Authors still write books and publishers bring them to the attention of consumers. However, the Internet has broken down the linear relationships in the supply chain and replaced it with a value network. The characteristics of the network ensure that value is added to Amazon. Value-adding activities include: community building; direct customer ordering and registration of customers; information value added by building up and providing access to catalogues and payment and processing across the supply chain; and providing delivery services.

Information to authors and customers forms the basis for building up the community within the publishing and book-selling process. The sales interface relies on building up a bank of knowledge from each and every sale whether from readers (through Amazon.com) or resellers (through Amazon Associates). Core information management builds and provides access to the Amazon catalogue of books and is linked to Amazon Advantage. The customer database also provides added-value information. Core handling and processing maintains payment services between the company and its customers whether they be readers, publishers, resellers or authors. This function also covers shipping and delivery administration. From this configuration, the process of publishing and book selling became much more dynamic than the linear model that was the traditional industry model. The Internet has allowed each party in the process to interact with each other with more intensity.

Products, markets and customers

The initial strategy of Amazon.com was to create two distinct customer bases: the business to customer sector (B2C) and the business to business (B2B) sector. The former would concentrate on selling books to consumers (book buyers). The latter included publishers and resellers. To add value to the latter customer group Amazon.com set up specialist groups within the organization to cater for these markets. Amazon Advantage focused on publishers, whereas Amazon Associates concentrated on book resellers.

The 'Amazon Advantage' service was designed to offer a centralized catalogue for publishers. The development of the book catalogue lies at the heart of the company's strategy. Publishers add information to the catalogue which is absorbed and customized by Amazon for registered members. Publishers benefit from the service by having their books catalogued on the website with added graphics and feedback material designed by Amazon. They also benefit from the reductions in cost associated with having their book list included on the Amazon website. This gives the publishers an outlet towards Amazon's customer base. It also adds value by offering inventory control through updated information on re-ordering or books out of stock. The profits from the service are split 45% to the publisher and 55% to Amazon.

'Amazon Associates' is a service for online bookstores. The online bookstore *refers* customers to the Amazon catalogue while Amazon undertakes the process of distribution, ordering, payment and shipping. The registration process for associates is quick and easy, thereby allowing bookstores ease of access to online operations or to add online book sales to an existing website. This referral system ensures that much more web traffic is routed through the Amazon site, thereby increasing exposure of the Amazon brand-name. The referral site can be localized and maintained in the user's local language. This ensures that Amazon can have not only a global reach but one that is, up to a point, culture-specific. The advantage to bookstores of this is the savings in transaction costs by selling books via the Internet. Associates also save on administrative costs since this element is processed by Amazon; 15% of the profit is secured by the online bookstores and the rest goes to Amazon.

The number of associates grew rapidly after 1997, as shown in Table 1.

Table I
Number of Amazon associates

September 1997	March 1998	July 1998	September 1998
15,000	30,000	60,000	150,000

Competition

By 2001, the B2B aspect of Amazon faced competition from a number of sources. Other leading booksellers were building online systems for customers within the book trade. In October 2000, Amazon saw the demise of an alliance with Internet service provider (ISP) Yahoo!, as Yahoo! decided to form a new alliance with booksellers Barnes & Noble instead. This setback was compounded by news that Borders Bookshops had overtaken Amazon as the leading internet bookseller. The influential Forrester Research consultancy analysed Internet booksellers' performance based on categories such as transaction efficiency, cost and delivery/returns. The findings showed a close rivalry, as shown in Table 2.

Table 2
Forrester Research rankings

Bookseller	Power ranking
Borders Bookshops	66.83
Amazon.com	66.76
Barnes & Noble	65.46
Buy.com	55.52

The Forrester findings showed that the competitive advantage built up by Amazon during the late 1990s had been eroded by competitors. In the early years of Internet book selling (1995–98) Amazon benefited from being 'first movers'. Other booksellers then entered the market and adopted similar strategies to gain market share. One important feature of competitors' strategies was the convergence of the retailing and online businesses. Barnes & Noble and Borders set up strategic links between the traditional method of book selling and the new one in the form of the Internet. Barnes & Noble set up hundreds of Internet counters in their retail shops, broadening the choice for customers in terms of purchase arrangements, delivery and collection. Borders fared well principally because of its focus on the sort of detail customers want. Order totals were posted to customers before any credit card details were requested and they had a comprehensive and up-to-date list of book stocks.

Other competitive pressures came from publishers and booksellers who maintained and built upon their own in-house catalogues. In terms of distribution, Amazon had to operate in a highly competitive world market for shipping and transportation of goods – an area of business that does not constitute one of the company's core strengths.

Human resources

Despite the fact that the company was at the leading edge of 'new economy' business, the majority of the jobs performed by workers were distinctly 'old economy' in nature. Most work involved handling customer service calls and packing in warehouses. Many Amazon workers were part-time or temporary staff working long shifts.

There was no recognized trade union in Amazon. Jeff Bezos argued: "everybody is an owner so we don't need unions". The basis of this argument was that Amazon workers were given the option to buy stocks in the company after completing a set period of working tenure. However, since dot.com shares dipped in value in 2000–2001, this option became less attractive. As a result, the appetite grew amongst workers for trade union recognition.

The central human resource problem facing Amazon was the different views taken by management and workers. Workers wanted job security but this is sometimes seen to be at odds with the ethos of risk and flexibility that is the cornerstone of Internet entrepreneurs. Maintaining worker satisfaction in a transformed workplace is an ideal that is proving to be elusive in the new economy and Amazon is just one of many Internet businesses struggling to placate potential disquiet in the workplace.

The Amazon strategy

The Amazon Advantage and Amazon Associates programmes were geared towards low cost and easy financial benefits as a result of the high volume of online traffic from its publishing and book-selling customers. It is the Amazon brand-name itself, however, that attracted the high volume of online traffic to the Amazon website. Thus, in the initial development of the Amazon strategy towards its business customers (B2B), the company set out to become the lowest cost provider of books in the industry. This differed from the strategy adopted for its consumer market (B2C), where book buyers sought additional services, wider choice, efficient delivery and a host of book information services as well as a low price.

Corporate partnerships became an important part of the Amazon strategy. In particular, the company formed alliances with portals (Internet search engines) and ISPs. These offered access to heavily trafficked websites which could play an important role in directing customers to the Amazon website thereby increasing the company's brand awareness and market share. Mutual benefits arose from this arrangement. The high profile of Amazon offered 'corporate' sponsors such as the Star Wars franchise the opportunity to gain exposure from the website. Amazon's corporate partners included Internet Movie Database, AOL Netfind, Adobe, Star Wars, C-SPAN, Ivillage, Motley Fool and Magellan Internet Guide. Other followed. Barnes & Noble set up an alliance with erstwhile Amazon partners Yahoo!.

Barnes & Noble also had partnerships with, among others, AOL, Microsoft Network (MSN.com), *The New York Times*, Lycos and Disney.

Amazon also sought income from other sources such as 'co-op money'. Publishers have traditionally given 'co-op money' to retail bookshops for prominent display sites in the shop or for advertising titles. In print advertising such as newspapers, this is deemed a 'co-operative' venture since the bookshop and the publishers share the cost of the advertisement. Both are being advertised simultaneously. Amazon, as a virtual bookshop, received 'co-op money' from publishers for high visibility on the website. Publishers also had their titles placed in prominent book reviews. Critics of Amazon argued that this practice is unethical because it blurs the line between editorial and advertising. These 'paid for placement' titles could command up to $10,000 and became an important source of revenue for Amazon.

Despite the undoubted promise of the Amazon strategy, three years on from its stock market flotation the company hit crisis. On 23 June 2000, Lehman Brothers reported that Amazon would run out of money within a year. Debts had built up significantly since 1997 and the company was yet to show signs of profit despite encouraging revenue streams.

Along with many other dot.com businesses, Amazon found investors offloading its stock in early 2000, thereby reducing the share price by some 20%. New Internet businesses soaked up investment capital like a sponge based on little more than potential future profits from clever Internet applications rather than using physical resources. The success of Amazon was built on its knowledge and expertise in book selling. Essentially, this was the core business – both B2C and B2B. The initial business strategy did not include ventures into other areas of retailing. After a series of acquisitions and partnerships, Amazon entered other markets as diverse as kitchenware and healthcare. Fuelled by deficit spending, Amazon drifted from the core activity of book selling, where it had built up much of its goodwill. By diversifying into other areas of retailing (albeit using the same medium), the company diluted the effect customer that loyalty played in attaining investment credibility. The expectation that the company would be self-sustaining by the time the market corrected itself proved to be optimistic.

Problems with the model

The outworking of the e-commerce model proved somewhat different in practice than its designers had suggested, and this engendered an element of reluctance to fully commit to it both by buyers and investors. It was suggested, for example, that goods delivery after an Internet order remained sluggish. Also, maintaining inventory and warehousing meant Amazon was incurring a relatively high level of cost in order to guarantee availability of goods. This problem was exacerbated by the expansion of its product portfolio. The business model formulated by Amazon was heavily dependent on the e-commerce aspect of operations and the benefits that lower transaction costs would bring. The network of publishers, authors, bookshops and customers relied on the Internet for the dissemination of information within their cyber-community. To the extent that publishing and book selling was information-driven, this business model fitted the objectives of the company. That Amazon became an internationally known brand-name in such a short period of time was testimony to the success of the community-building exercise.

The Amazon business model was not a static one. Changes became necessary as the company extended its core business activities beyond book selling. The way the company positioned itself prior to expansion suggested a clear vision, which attracted investment funds. Maintaining expansion required new investment funds, which in turn necessitated changes in the business model. In effect, the company had drifted from a business model designed to achieve growth and profits to one that would facilitate expansion through attracting investment.

The future for Amazon

In 2000, Jeff Bezos was quite clear as to the future for Amazon. He stated that he intended to continue the expansion of the Amazon concept not only in terms of products but also across geographical areas. Growth through acquisition of Internet and distribution specialists was a key theme in the expansion, as was the search for suitable partnerships that offered economies of scale in management, technology and distribution. The ethos of risk-taking remained central to the Amazon strategy, alongside innovation and being responsive to changes in the business environment. As the Amazon empire grew, a more decentralized management structure evolved, with key personnel organizing and running the business ventures in each country.

As Bezos saw it, the key to future success for Amazon was to continue to find ways of adding value for customers. As the number of competitors increased, a priority was to maintain its position as market leader through increasing the product range, entering new markets and offering quality in customer service. Underpinning these was a commitment and a pro-active approach to new technology applications in e-commerce. In particular, the efficiency of distribution was a key area of concern for customers and goods delivery.

Amazon's future strategy had to be carried out within the financial constraints brought about by the decline in confidence in Internet stocks. Although future share issues are likely (to lessen the burden of debt, which is undermining expansion plans), take-up is likely to be lower than in previous issues. As the biggest brand-name in e-commerce, Amazon.com is the business most new economy analysts are watching closely. Should it fail, alongside some other previously celebrated dot.com businesses, it could prove to be a decisive blow to the whole e-commerce model in its present form.

Appendix I

Amazon.com consolidated profit and loss statements (figures in US$ 000s)

	9 months ended September 30	12 Months ended December 31				
	2000	1999	1998	1997	1996	1995
Sales	1,789,623	1,639,839	609,819	147,787	15,746	511
Cost of sales	1,358,146	1,349,194	476,155	118,969	12,287	409
Gross profit	431,477	290,645	133,664	28,818	3,459	102
Operating expenses						
Sales and marketing	408,266	413,150	132,654	40,077	6,090	200
Technology and content	199,535	159,722	46,424	13,384	2,313	171
General and administrative	80,730	70,144	15,618	6,741	1,035	35
Stock-based compensation	25,909	30,618	1,889	1,211	0	0
Goodwill amortization	242,562	214,694	42,599	0	0	0
Acquisition and related	16,259	8,072	3,535	0	0	0
	973,261	896,400	242,719	61,413	9,438	406
Operating profit/(loss)	(541,784)	(605,755)	(109,055)	(32,595)	(5,979)	(304)
Other income						
Interest received	29,842	45,451	14,053	1,901	202	1
Investment income (expense)	12,366	0	0	0	0	0
Other	(4,693)	1,671	0	0	0	0
	37,515	47,122	14,053	1,901	202	1
Profit before interest	(504,269)	(558,633)	(95,002)	(30,694)	(5,777)	(303)
Interest paid	94,827	84,566	26,639	326	0	0
Profit/(loss) before ELEMI	(599,096)	(643,199)	(121,641)	(31,020)	(5,777)	(303)
ELEMI*	(267,037)	(76,769)	(2,905)	0	0	0
Net profit (loss)	**(866,133)**	**(719,968)**	**(124,546)**	**(31,020)**	**(5,777)**	**(303)**
Earnings (loss) per share	(2.48)	(2.20)	(0.42)	(0.12)	(0.31)	(0.02)

*Equity in losses of equity-method investees. Amazon.com made the following statement in its Annual Report for 1999:

Appendix 2
Amazon.com consolidated balance sheets (figures in US$ 000s)

	Sep-30	Dec-31	Dec-31	Dec-31	Dec-31
	2000	**1999**	**1998**	**1997**	**1996**
Fixed assets					
Tangible assets	352,290	317,613	29,791	9,726	985
Goodwill	383,996	534,699	174,052	0	0
Other intangibles	136,474	195,445	4,586	0	0
Investments	91,131	226,727	7,740	0	0
Equity method investees	73,345	144,735	0	0	0
Other assets	54,306	40,154	8,037	2,409	146
	1,091,542	1,459,373	224,206	12,135	1,131
Current assets					
Cash and equivalents	647,048	116,962	25,561	1,876	6,248
Securities	252,976	589,226	347,884	123,499	0
Inventories	163,880	220,646	29,501	8,971	571
Other current assets	99,181	85,344	21,308	3,363	321
	1,163,085	1,012,178	424,254	137,709	7,140
Creditors: amounts falling due within one year					
Accounts payable	304,709	463,026	113,273	33,027	2,852
Accrued expenses	160,073	126,017	34,413	6,570	1,420
Accrued advertising	0	55,892	13,071	3,454	598
Deferred revenue	142,046	54,790	0	0	0
Interest payable	35,056	24,888	10	0	0
Current debt	17,213	14,322	808	1,500	0
	659,097	738,935	161,575	44,551	4,870
Net current assets	503,988	273,243	262,679	93,158	2,270
Total assets less current liabilities	1,595,530	1,732,616	486,885	105,293	3,401
Creditors: amounts falling due after one year					
Long-term debt	2,082,697	1,466,338	348,140	76,702	0
Net assets	**(487,167)**	**266,278**	**138,745**	**28,591**	**3,401**

Shareholders' equity					
Share capital	3,561	3,452	3,186	1,449	165
Share premium account	1,342,574	1,195,540	298,537	66,586	9,873
Note receivable for common stock	0	(1,171)	(1,099)	0	0
Stock-based compensation	(19,504)	(47,806)	(1,625)	(1,930)	(612)
Unrealized investment losses	(65,637)	(1,709)	1,806	0	0
Reserves	(1,748,161)	(882,028)	(162,060)	(37,514)	(6,025)
Total shareholders' funds	**(487,167)**	**266,278**	**138,745**	**28,591**	**3,401**

Strategic alliances in the airline industry

Nigel Evans

Introduction

The airline sector has a long history of working in partnerships. In 1999, 513 international alliances existed between airline companies, an increase of about 80% from the 1994 level. Under the auspices of the International Air Transport Association (IATA), a tradition of cooperation between airlines was built up, and on individual routes cooperation has commonly included revenue-pooling agreements between the carriers operating a route.

During the 1990s, airlines rushed to form alliances in the fear of being left behind, and the stage has now been reached where the international airline sector is coalescing into a small number of large alliance groupings such as the Star Alliance, which includes Lufthansa, United Airlines and Scandinavian Airlines System (SAS), the Oneworld Alliance which includes British Airways, American Airlines and Qantas, and the long-standing alliance between KLM and Northwest Airlines. It is not only the number of airline alliance agreements being made that is significant, but the deepening relations between partners in these alliances. "No longer are alliances mere loose arrangements between a couple of carriers to share flight codes and cross-sell tickets." The alliances are now so wide ranging that "they are aiming at virtual mergers, despite national rules forbidding foreign ownership" (*The Economist*, 1998).

Motivations for alliance formation in the airline sector

British Airways attempted to introduce a degree of empiricism to the analysis of the external forces driving alliance formation. It used scenario-planning techniques to develop strategies for the future given the uncertainties in the macroenvironment. Scenarios representing possible futures were developed which sought to identify the key driving forces shaping the world economy and in turn the airline industry. Enormous changes have occurred in technology, education, world trade and finance over the last fifty years with a quickening pace of change. The combination of these forces has helped to bring about the information 'revolution', global economic restructuring and global competition.

External drivers

The information 'revolution'

In the 1960s and 1970s, information technologies mainly played a facilitating role in international tourism. The US Airline Deregulation Act of 1978 introduced airlines operating in the USA to a new world of competitive threats and opportunities. The key change, whereby price-regulating power was removed from the Civil Aeronautics Board (CAB), enabled airlines to increase the variety of fares offered, and the increased frequency by which fares were changed necessitated the extensive development of advanced computer reservations systems (CRSs). The CRSs allowed airlines to monitor, manage and control their capacity through yield management and their clients through 'frequent flyer' programmes. The growth in CRSs, first in the USA and then in Europe and elsewhere, created a marketing tool of considerable power, given travel agents' preferences for booking flights on their screens as the customer is waiting. In the past, the airlines that owned the CRSs undoubtedly favoured their own flights (or those of their code-sharing partners), but to a significant extent such bias has now been eliminated, at least in Europe and North America, through codes of conduct. The power given to airlines by the CRSs has now been replicated by the power given directly to consumers by the Internet. A vast amount of information is available to allow consumers to compare prices, and the Internet's growth has allowed airlines to communicate directly with consumers, thus cutting out the need for intermediaries to be involved. Some airlines such as Easyjet are making extensive use of the technology, reporting that over 80% of bookings are being made through the Internet.

Economic restructuring

Economic restructuring through the philosophy of 'economic disengagement' by governments in many parts of the world has, since the 1970s, had a major impact on airline industry structure. This philosophy, influenced by the widespread adoption of the theory of 'contestable markets' (which advocated the removal of restrictive industry entry barriers) from the early 1980s, manifested itself in the forms of deregulation and privatization. The Chicago Convention of 1944 established the bilateral system of air service agreements (between pairs of national governments), which have since governed international air transport. The international industry that developed was characterized by national airlines from each country serving routes, with airlines charging the same fares, and often sharing markets and revenues. Some bilateral agreements also involved agreement on such matters as ground handling. The terms of the bilateral agreements reflected the negotiating power and current aviation policies of the countries involved and the resulting productivity was often low and costs were high.

Deregulation of domestic services occurred in the USA in 1978, followed by Canada, the UK, Australia and New Zealand in the 1980s, and the completion of deregulation within the European Union in April 1997. However, parallel liberalization in international air services has taken place much more slowly. Notwithstanding the change that has occurred in some markets, even the liberalized structures are restrictive on industry entry. Requirements for designated airlines to be owned by nationals of the states involved are common and airport congestion and slot allocation practices often further impede effective industry entry. There was some evidence, however, that the removal of bilateral agreements and similar intervention barriers can reduce fares.

Another, and linked, aspect of economic disengagement is the worldwide movement towards the privatization of state-owned airlines. Despite this gradual process, however, many international airlines remain publicly owned or have major government shareholdings. Controls on foreign ownership remain in most national industries, but some foreign ownership now exists and, with planned privatizations, this will increase.

The EU's third air transport package (implemented from April 1997), for instance, sets no limit on the stake an EU national or EU airline can hold in an airline registered in another EU state. With limited exceptions, however, non-EU investors cannot hold a majority stake in any EU airline. In the USA, foreign shareholdings of up to 49% of equity under certain circumstances and 25% of voting stock is possible, although the US government also imposes an ad hoc control test to determine whether the foreign shareholder would substantially influence decision-making irrespective of equity held.

Liberalization, privatization, foreign ownership and transnational mergers will have a major impact upon the future structure of the airline industry, but many regulatory and ownership barriers remain in force worldwide. As a result, alternative methods of strategic development – namely, internally generated growth and mergers and acquisitions – are often precluded as viable growth strategies for international airlines, and consequently the formation of strategic alliances is, in many cases, the only available form of new market entry.

Global competition

Organizational 'type' has been dramatically influenced by the rise of globalization, and it has been argued that success or failure of larger businesses in the future will depend upon their ability to compete globally. Certainly many industries in the post-war era have seen a rapid concentration of activity, with the emergence of a few dominant companies. Global competition is clearly well advanced in industries such as motor vehicles, pharmaceuticals, soft drinks and, more recently, financial services, but globalization is a more recent phenomenon in the airline business, having been restricted for so long by regulation, government ownership and consumer preferences.

Airlines are seeking to maximize their 'global reach', in the belief that those that offer a global service (with a competitively credible presence in each of the major air travel markets) will be in the strongest competitive position. The importance of the 'triad' markets of Japan, North America and Europe is shown in Appendix 6. In a global airline context, the triad is modified so as to broaden the Japanese leg of the triad to include the wider Asia-Pacific region and for the crucial markets to include not only the constituent markets of the triad but also the flows between them. Thus, globalization, and particularly developments in the key markets, is an important external driver for alliance formation.

Internal drivers

Risk sharing

Strategic alliances are seen as an attractive mechanism for hedging risk because neither partner bears the full risk and cost of the alliance activity. The need to spread the costs and risks of innovation has increased as capital requirements for development projects have risen. Developing new or existing routes, for instance, becomes far less risky if the partners operating the routes have firmly entrenched marketing strengths in the two markets at either end of the routes.

Economies of scale, scope and learning

A prime driver for alliance formation is for airlines to achieve cost economies, which can be categorized as economies of scale, scope and experience. Economies of scale exist where the average cost per unit of output declines as the level of output increases. Empirical evidence reveals little evidence of economies of scale, however, except for the smallest operators and in specific areas such as marketing. Indeed, one study of US domestic aviation suggests possible diseconomies at the largest airlines. Furthermore, the evidence also suggests that airlines' unit costs do not fall greatly as they expand their networks. Cost savings stem from attracting more traffic to a given network rather than expanding it to cover more destinations.

The airline industry may lack substantial scale economies, but other economies related to the size and nature of operations exist, which helps to explain the growing industry concentration and the move towards alliances. Economies of scope occur when the cost of producing two (or more) products jointly is less than the cost of producing each one alone. Such economies can be achieved if alliance partners link up their existing networks so that they can provide connecting services for new markets, and where marketing costs can be shared between alliance partners.

For example, the alliance between KLM and Northwest formed in 1989 has had a substantial impact on passenger numbers, market share and both airlines' financial performance. Through the alliance, KLM has gained access to Northwest's extensive North American route network based on its Minneapolis, Detroit and Boston hubs, and Northwest can advertise that it serves KLM's sizeable international network.

A number of observers have suggested that an important motivator in forming alliances is the benefit to be derived from economies of learning (or experience). Incumbent suppliers have more information on the market being served and can tailor their services to specific customer needs. New entrants would have to sink resources to acquire such information in order to win market share, but alliances allow the information to be gained from existing suppliers.

Access to assets, resources and competences

Specific resource, skill or competence inadequacy can be addressed by collaborating with partners that have a different set of such attributes and can therefore compensate for internal deficiencies. The regulatory framework of 'bilaterals' and landing rights means that slots at congested airports are important and marketable assets that are attractive to alliance partners. Alliances can thus offer relatively easy access to a route through allowing access to a partner's assets that may have been established over prolonged periods and which may have been previously protected by government intervention.

Shape competition

Strategic alliances can influence the companies that a firm competes with and the basis of competition. They can also reduce the likelihood of retaliatory behaviour by binding two firms together as allies. Furthermore, current strategic positions may be successfully defended against forces that are too strong for one firm to withstand alone. Strategic alliances may, therefore, be used as a defensive ploy to reduce competition, since an obvious benefit of strategic alliances is converting a competitor into a partner. Smaller and weaker airlines may view alliances as the only viable way in which to compete with larger, more sophisticated rivals. The announcement in March 1998 by Air Lanka that it was to sell a 40% stake to Emirates Airlines, for instance, was viewed as part of a defensive alliance strategy aimed at retaining international competitiveness through allying with a commercially stronger rival.

Alternatively, alliance formation may form part of an offensive strategy. By linking with a rival pressure can be put on the profits and market share of a common competitor. The proposed alliance between British Airways and American Airlines announced in June 1996 was seen as such a case since it represented the combining of (arguably) the two strongest airlines on the transatlantic routes. It therefore attracted widespread criticism from competing airlines and later failed to win regulatory approval from either the US or EU authorities.

Alliance structure and scope

Considerable time and effort may be expended in developing the structure and scope of an alliance. The unique nature and operating environment of the airline sector means that alliances must be structured around diverse requirements. Determining the structure and scope of an alliance requires detailed consideration of issues across a broad spectrum. Issues that must be taken into account include marketing, products, computer system technologies, equipment and equipment servicing and logistics.

Evaluation of alliance performance

Evaluating the performance of alliances is complex given the multifaceted objectives of many alliances and the difficulties involved in ascribing financial measures. The situation is often further complicated by the asymmetric performance: one firm achieves its objectives whereas others fail to do so. For instance, several alliances have resulted in a situation where one partner raced to learn the other's skills whereas the other partner had no such intentions.

Despite these evident measurement obstacles, several observers have attempted empirical studies of alliance performance primarily through examining the factors leading to the termination of alliance arrangements. These contributory factors include partner asymmetry, competitive overlap between partners, the presence of other concurrent ties and the characteristics of the alliance itself, such as autonomy of operations and flexibility. It should be borne in mind, however, that not all alliance terminations can be viewed as failures since in some cases they may have been intended as time-limited arrangements. Furthermore, it should not be assumed that all continuing alliances are successful since inertia or high exit costs may provide an explanation for their continuation.

Examples of airline alliance success and failure

The 'Alcazar' alliance involving Scandinavian Airline System (SAS), Swissair, Austrian Airlines and KLM failed in the early 1990s partly because the individual airlines were technologically incompatible (they used different CRSs). In another example, British Airways held discussions at various times with KLM, Sabena and United Airlines regarding strategic alliances before forming such an alliance with US Airways in July 1992 as part of its strategy of building up several key global collaborative agreements.

The agreement between British Airways and US Airways (which involved the acquisition of approximately 44% of US Airways' equity share capital by British Airways) has now been broken with British Airways writing off 50% of its initial investment. The British Airways/ US Airways alliance provides an example of poor long-term positioning in that the alliance stood in the way of more recent strategies by both partners. In June 1996, British Airways announced its intention to form a wider alliance with American Airlines (which still awaits regulatory approval as at year 2002), and US Airways responded with a lawsuit seeking damages. US Airways is said to have been anxious to extricate itself from its alliance with British Airways because it failed to deliver the projected earnings enhancement. British Airways, on the other hand, viewed American Airlines as a larger strategically more important alliance partner. The long list of failed airline alliances, supposedly bolstered by equity stakes, includes Air Canada/Continental Airlines, Scandinavian Airlines System/ Continental Airlines and Sabena/Air France.

Political sensitivities lay behind the failure of another proposed airline alliance between the Dutch airline KLM and Belgian airline Sabena in the early 1990s. Both airlines had held talks with British Airways before talking to each other about a possible alliance or merger. Both were loss-making and feared absorption by larger competitors, but the failure to cement an alliance highlighted the uniquely political nature of the airline sector. Political considerations are transparent when both companies involved are 'national flag carriers' carrying the prestige of the home country around the world. For Sabena to ally with KLM would have created a predominantly Dutch-speaking company which would have proved politically unacceptable in bilingual Belgium. Sabena had to bow to political pressure from Belgium's French-speaking community and pull out of negotiations.

The airline alliance between KLM and the American airline Northwest dating from 1989 can claim to be a success, at least in part, since it has shown uncharacteristic sustainability and appears to have been revenue-enhancing for the two partners. The alliance, which encompasses collaboration on a broad front, including code-sharing, flight scheduling, joint marketing, and integration of frequent flyer programmes, had generated additional revenues of between $125 million and $175 million for Northwest and $100 million for KLM by 1994. Through the alliance KLM gained access to Northwest's extensive North American route network based on its Minneapolis, Detroit and Boston hubs, whilst Northwest can advertise that it serves KLM's sizeable international network through its Amsterdam hub.

The alliance was borne out of necessity when KLM (in return for a 20% equity stake) contributed $400 million to the $700 million that was required when senior Northwest executives put together a leveraged buyout of the airline. Notwithstanding the financial success of this strategic alliance, cultural differences and personal incompatibilities between the two parties have repeatedly threatened to force them apart and have at times soured the relationship. One writer noted that: "the alliance has been a saga of personal spats, fights over 'creeping control' and threats of separation that until recently were hidden behind a marriage that works well on a daily basis." KLM, it is said, is inclined to be quiet, stay out of the limelight and focus on strong operational expertise, whereas the US partner (Northwest) is more inclined to Hollywood lifestyles and a financial engineering approach to management.

Conclusion

Clearly, the growth of airline strategic alliances is one of the most fundamental developments in the airline industry over recent years. Airlines have rushed to form alliances in the fear of being left behind, and many have later changed their partners as they have become more sophisticated at identifying the potential 'strategic fit' between partners. To some degree alliance formation can be viewed as an inevitable result of the regulatory framework within which the international airline industry operates. Regulatory and legal restrictions often prevent the full ownership of airlines by foreign companies and consequently alliances have been perceived as the only viable market entry mechanism, at least in the short to medium term. However, some observers view strategic alliances as inherently unstable and transitory forms of organization, a 'second-best' solution that is disturbingly likely to break up under commercial pressure.

The airline industry is littered with examples of alliances that have been broken up (the alliance between British Airways and US Airways, for instance) and planned alliances that failed to materialize.

However, the role and characteristics of the strategic alliances have continued to evolve. In the late 1980s, strategic alliances were seen as a rather crude way in which to grow quickly through the avoidance of bilateral restrictions and some airlines rushed to form alliances in the fear of being left behind. The cyclical slump and heavy losses of the early 1990s turned attention to the efficiency improvements made possible by alliances, and consequently airlines focused more clearly on the strategic logic of the particular partners that had been chosen. The importance of 'strategic fit' thus came to be stressed – that the proposed partner should have a culture, management style and geographical coverage that are compatible.

Consumers receive several benefits from those alliances that are successful in producing integrated products. Consumers are provided with an enhanced choice of destinations through the marketing of alliance partners' route networks. Schedule coordination between partners often produces shorter transfer times between connections, and coordination of flight timings can avoid bunching of flight schedules. Additionally, consumers benefit from one-stop check-in for passengers, the pooling of frequent-flyer programmes, shared airport lounge facilities, ground handling arrangements and the improvement in technical standards brought about through the sharing of expertise.

A number of trends relating to strategic airline alliances are discernible:

- The number of airlines involved in alliances has continued to grow. Four key alliances have emerged each headed by one of the major American airlines. The focus in the coming years will be on these alliances adding further airlines so as to fill gaps in their global coverage. Equally, second-level feeder airlines will be added to the existing alliances.

- Substantial new alliances may be difficult to form since the major international players from the 'triad' countries are all now involved in alliances and new alliances would therefore lack the substantial marketing presence that appears to be necessary to ensure success.

- Airlines from outside the 'triad' countries will increasingly become involved with the established alliances. To date, airlines from Africa, South America and parts of Asia have largely been excluded from the major alliances. Although many such airlines are currently operating in highly protected domestic markets, the degree of protection will progressively decrease and these airlines will increasingly want to secure their commercial future through involvement with the major alliance groupings.

- Increasing consumer pressure is likely to be evident. Although the case for alliances has robustly been made by the airlines, less attention has been focused on consumers. This has started to change with the intense investigation into the effects of British Airways/American Airlines alliance and possible retrospective investigation of the Star alliance by competition authorities. Increasingly, international regulators will be attempting to ensure that the supposed cost savings (which the airlines argue result from alliance activity) are passed on to consumers and that the dominant positions at hub airports are scaled down so as to allow more 'contestability' of markets.

- Competition between the alliance groupings as entities (as opposed to the individual airlines comprising them) is likely to increase. The alliances will start to look more like 'umbrella' brands with the individual airlines being sub-brands, offering similar service standards and an increasing level of integration between the constituent airlines will be evident.

Appendix I

Airline alliances in the global airline industry, 1994–99 (source: *Airline Business*, 1999)

	1994	1995	1996	1997	1998	1999	Change 1999/1994
Number of alliances	280	324	389	363	502	513	+183.0%
with equity stakes	58	58	62	54	56	53	−8.6%
non-equity alliances	222	266	327	309	446	460	+207.2%
New alliances	–	50	71	72	121	26	
Number of airlines	136	153	159	177	196	204	+150.0%

Appendix 2

Major international airline alliances as at July 1999 (source: adapted from *Airline Business*, 1999)

Alliance members	Date joined	Passenger traffic 1998 (RPK, billions)	Passenger traffic 1998 (% world share)	Passenger numbers (millions)	Revenue (US$ billions)
Atlantic Excellence/Qualiflyer					
Atlantic Excellence					
Austrian Airlines	Jun 96	7.3	0.3	3.4	1.3
Delta Air Lines	Jun 96	166.3	6.3	105.4	14.4
Sabena	Jun 96	15.3	0.6	8.7	2.4
Swissair	Jun 96	28.0	1.1	11.9	7.8
Subtotal		*216.9*	*8.2*	*129.5*	*25.9*
Qualifier					
Air Europe	May 99	5.8	0.2	0.8	0.2
AOM	Mar 98	8.5	0.3	2.9	0.6
Austrian Airlines	Mar 98	7.3	0.3	3.4	1.3
Crossair	Mar 98	2.7	0.1	4.4	N/a
Lauda Air	Mar 98	2.9	0.1	0.8	N/a
Sabena	Mar 98	15.3	0.6	8.7	2.4
Swissair	Mar 98	28.0	1.1	11.9	7.8
TAP Air Portugal	Mar 98	9.4	0.4	4.5	0.9
THY Turkish Airlines	Mar 98	13.0	0.5	9.9	1.4
Subtotal		*93.0*	*3.5*	*47.4*	*14.6*
Total		**259.3**	**9.9**	**152.8**	**29.0**
Oneworld					
American Airlines	Sep 98	175.2	6.7	81.4	19.2
British Airways	Sep 98	116.0	4.4	36.6	14.6
Canadian	Sep 98	26.9	1.0	8.3	2.1
Cathay Pacific	Sep 98	40.7	1.5	10.3	3.4
Qantas	Sep 98	56.9	2.2	16.4	5.2
Subtotal		*415.7*	*15.8*	*153.0*	*30.0*

Future members					
Finnair		10.2	0.4	6.8	1.5
Iberia		32.5	1.2	21.8	3.6
Lan Chile		8.7	0.3	4.0	1.1
Total		**467.1**	**17.8**	**185.5**	**36.2**
Star Alliance					
Air Canada	May 97	37.3	1.4	15.0	4.0
Lufthansa	May 97	75.4	2.9	38.5	12.8
SAS	May 97	20.8	0.8	21.5	5.2
Thai International	May 97	34.4	1.3	15.6	2.5
United Airlines	May 97	200.4	7.6	88.6	17.6
Varig	Oct 97	27.1	1.0	11.0	3.0
Ansett Australia	Mar 99	13.1	0.5	11.7	2.0
Air New Zealand	Mar 99	19.4	0.7	6.2	1.7
Subtotal		*428.0*	*16.3*	*206.3*	*48.8*
Future members					
All Nippon Airways		54.4	2.1	42.3	7.1
Singapore Airlines		58.2	2.2	12.4	2.7
Total		**540.6**	**20.6**	**261.0**	**58.6**
Northwest/KLM					
Alitalia	May 99	35.6	1.4	24.2	5.0
Continental	Jan 99	86.7	3.3	43.6	8.0
KLM	1989	57.3	2.2	15.0	22.0
Northwest Airlines	1989	107.4	4.1	50.5	9.0
Total		**287.0**	**10.9**	**133.3**	**44.0**

RPK – revenue passenger kilometres.

Appendix 3

External driving forces underpinning strategic alliance formation in the airline industry (source: Moyer, 1996)

Appendix 4

Market share of computerized reservation systems in European countries (source: Humphreys, 1994)

Country	Percentage of locations			
	Amadeus	Galileo	Sabre	Worldspan
Austria	34.8	60.4	3.1	1.6
Belgium	21.1	30.1	16.0	32.8
Denmark	54.2	14.1	6.9	24.8
Finland	98.1	–	1.7	0.2
France	81.7	4.1	10.1	4.1
Germany	91.6	1.4	4.7	2.3
Greece	–	39.9	34.9	25.2
Hungary	–	97.6	2.4	–
Ireland	–	84.6	6.0	9.4
Italy	–	76.9	17.8	5.3
Luxembourg	57.1	–	42.9	–
Netherlands	–	61.6	10.3	26.8
Norway	74.5	11.2	7.7	6.6
Portugal	6.0	65.5	0.2	28.3
Spain	88.7	5.2	2.6	3.5
Sweden	77.0	–	13.0	10.0
Switzerland	–	87.7	9.9	2.4
UK	0.2	65.6	20.0	14.2

Amadeus: developed by Air France, Lufthansa, Iberia, Sabena.
Galileo: developed by British Airways, KLM, Swissair, Austrian, Aer
    Lingus, Air Portugal, Olympic.
Sabre: developed by American Airlines.
Worldspan: developed by Delta, Northwest, TWA.

Appendix 5

Foreign ownership of selected airlines (source: *Airline Business*, 1999)

Country	Airline	Stake held by	Stake (%)	Date first acquired
Europe				
Austria	Austrian	Air France Group All Nippon Airways Swissair	1.5 9.0 10.0	1988 1989 1988
	Lauda Air	Austrian Lufthansa	35.9 20.0	1996 1993
Belgium	Sabena	Swissair	49.5	1995
France	Air Liberté	British Airways	70	1992
Germany	Deutsche BA	British Airways	100	1992
Luxembourg	Luxair	Lufthansa	13.0	1992
Spain	Spanair	SAS	49.0	1986
Switzerland	Swissair	Delta Air Lines Singapore Airlines	4.5 2.7	1989 1991
Ukraine	Ukraine International Airlines	Austrian Airlines Swissair	14.3 4.1	1996 1996
UK	British Midland	SAS	40.0	1988
North America				
USA	Delta Airlines	Singapore Airlines Swissair	3 3	1991 1989
Canada	Canadian Airlines	American Airlines	33.0	1994
Asia/Pacific				
Australia	Ansett Australia Qantas	Air New Zealand British Airways	50.0 25.0	1996 1993
China	Dragonair	Cathay Pacific	25.5	1990
Malaysia	Malaysia Airlines	Royal Brunei	10.0	Not reported
Singapore	Singapore Airlines	Delta Air Lines Swissair	2.7 0.6	1991 1991
Other				
Argentina	Aerolinas Argentinas	Iberia Airlines American Airlines	10.0 10	1990 1997
Mauritius	Air Mauritius	Air France Air India British Airways	12.8 8.8 12.8	1975 1975 1975
Kenya	Kenya Airways	KLM	26.0	1995

Appendix 6

Share of world revenue passenger kilometres (RPKs) and world RPK growth (source: Boeing 1999)

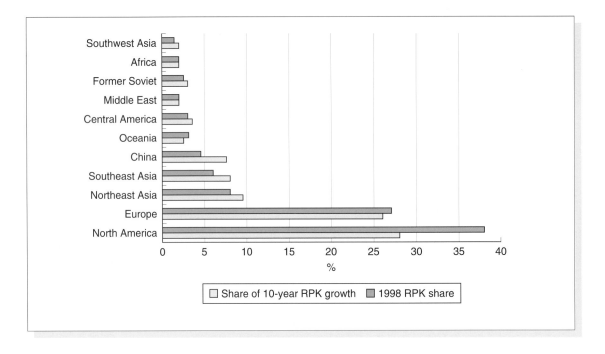

The Gulf War (1990–91)

The invasion

The BBC World at One news on 1 August 1990 was among the first bulletins to break the news that Iraq had invaded Kuwait, its southern neighbour in the Middle East. It was reported that, after a military build-up by the Iraqi army on the Kuwaiti border, President Saddam Hussein, the allegedly despotic Iraqi leader, had finally ordered his troops into the Emirate of Kuwait – an oil-rich but relatively defenceless state situated between Iraq and Saudi Arabia. The evening television news carried pictures of Iraqi tanks and armoured personnel carriers establishing themselves in the capital, Kuwait City.

Political leaders across the world were quick to condemn the invasion. Prime Minister Thatcher in the UK and President Bush in the USA were among the first to record their disapproval of the Iraqi 'aggression'. An emergency session was called at the United Nations headquarters in New York, where resolutions were quickly passed not only condemning the invasion but also demanding an immediate and unconditional Iraqi withdrawal. It was agreed by the UN that a peaceful or diplomatic resolution to the conflict would be preferable to a military confrontation.

Formulating a response

When the full picture of the invasion was emerging, US President George Bush assembled a 'war cabinet' in the White House to consider the USA's possible responses to the Iraqi actions. The key players in the early days of President Bush's deliberations included Vice President Dan Quayle, Secretary of State James Baker, Defence Secretary Dick Cheney, National Security Advisor Brent Scowcroft and the Chairman of the Joint Chiefs of Staff General Colin Powell. At the early meetings, the possibility of military action was considered in the event that diplomatic efforts failed.

The political complexity of the Middle East, with its numerous tensions and potential flash points, meant that the objectives of any military campaign would have to be very carefully formulated. President Bush proposed that any military exercise in the Gulf should be mounted by a coalition of nations, each of which had strategic interests in the relative stability of the status quo in the Gulf (as a key supplier of oil to the West). This would offer the advantage of avoiding an image of the USA and the West 'policing' the region with its military superiority. The disadvantage (to the USA) of a coalition would be that any military action would necessarily have more limited objectives than otherwise it might. It was well understood by media observers, for example, that President Bush and other Western leaders would probably have wanted to bring Saddam Hussein to trial, but this outcome would be unlikely if a coalition including Iraq's Arab neighbours was to remain intact.

The allied coalition took shape through intense top-level diplomatic negotiations until a total of thirty nations either agreed to take part in a military campaign or offered their full support. It was then agreed, by the coalition participants, that any military campaign should have very specific and immediately measurable aims – to eject Iraqi militia from Kuwait and no more.

Once the overall 'grand plan' objectives had finally been established, the US 'war cabinet' appointed its key military personnel to oversee the military part of the campaign should it became necessary. The allied powers agreed that the USA should lead the campaign and the US government appointed General Norman Schwarzkopf as the commander of forces in the theatre of war.

Over the next few days, Schwarzkopf entered into intense discussions with Dick Cheney and Colin Powell to put plans in place that would work towards the achievement of the coalition's limited overall objectives. The plans had to include the inputs from the other countries that had offered military assistance to the campaign: Britain, France, Syria, Egypt, Saudi Arabia and others. Countries who offered financial support but no military personnel were also offered the chance to put in their ideas.

In November 1990, political upheaval in the governing British Conservative party led to the replacement of Margaret Thatcher by John Major as Prime Minister and he immediately made clear that there would be no change at all in Britain's policy in respect to the

Iraqi 'crisis'. Mr Major, in consultation with the Americans, appointed General Peter de la Billière as the commander of the British forces in the proposed Gulf campaign. General de la Billière joined Schwarzkopf in the Gulf to contribute to the planning of the military campaign.

As the year turned it became clear that the diplomatic efforts were unlikely to bring about the Iraqi withdrawal. Saddam Hussein had invested much in the Kuwaiti invasion and he had succeeded in uniting most of the Iraqi people in support of his actions. Diplomatic activity by Javier Perez de Cuellier, the UN General Secretary had come to nothing and, as a last resort, President Bush dispatched his Secretary of State, James Baker to engage in face-to-face meetings with the Iraqi Deputy Prime Minister, Tariq Aziz. Secretary of State Baker carried a letter to the Iraqi leadership from President Bush in which the President stated bluntly that: "There can be no reward for aggression. Nor will there be any negotiation . . . You and your country will pay a terrible price."

This 'last gasp' meeting predictably failed to change the Iraqi leadership's mind and Mr Baker returned to Washington empty-handed. With this news, President Bush consulted the allies and the decision to finalize preparations for a military solution was made.

Operation Desert Storm

From the earliest meetings in the White House, the possibility that the situation would need to be resolved through a military campaign was openly acknowledged. Accordingly, throughout the intervening months, military planning had been taking place in parallel with the diplomatic efforts.

In consultation with the allies, President Bush negotiated access to bases in countries neighbouring Iraq. Iran and Jordan decided to remain neutral in the campaign, but Iraq's neighbours – Syria, Saudi Arabia and Turkey – all agreed to allow their military bases to be used for Operation Desert Storm. Israel was encouraged to remain neutral in the campaign because of the sensitivity of its relationships with its Islamic neighbours, particularly with the Palestinians and the Egyptians.

Generals Powell, Schwarzkopf and de la Billière formulated a military strategy that would meet the allies' strategic objectives for the war. The overall aims of bringing about a 'rapid and decisive' victory were tempered with the need to keep Israel out of the conflict and the political need to reduce collateral damage to Iraqi civilians and civilian property.

Accordingly, it was decided to place an emphasis upon gaining an immediate superiority in the air. The USA moved 48 bombers and 1000 strike aircraft into the theatre; 200 other aircraft were provided by the UK, Saudi Arabia, France and Kuwait. In support of the air capability, six aircraft carriers and over 100 warships were positioned in the waters in and around the Mediterranean, the Red Sea and in the Gulf itself. These were armed with a range of high-technology sea-launched weapons, including the satellite-navigated Tomahawk cruise missile.

Ground-based troops were mobilized into the area just behind the Iraqi borders of the collaborating countries of Turkey, Syria and Saudi Arabia. The US army assigned 350,000 troops to the campaign, the UK assigned 20,000, Saudi Arabia 20,000, Egypt 30,000, Syria 20,000, and other countries a total of 20,000 between them.

The balance of power in the area was overwhelmingly biased towards the allies. Although the Iraqi army boasted 350,000 troops, Western intelligence experts estimated that their state of readiness would not be as high as that of the allies. Iraq had an estimated 500 military jets and a small number of ground-based Scud missiles.

On 16 January 1991 President Bush ordered the allied forces to prosecute the operation. Saddam Hussein defiantly declared that: "The devil Bush and his treacherous gang have begun the great show-down – the mother of all battles between triumphant good and doomed evil." The Soviet leader, President Gorbachev, was one of the few world leaders to openly express regret over the beginning of the conflict. "I want once again to underline," he said, "that we did everything feasible to solve the conflict by peaceful means." France's President Mitterand spoke for the majority of leaders when he admitted that diplomacy had failed and said that: "It is now time for the guns to speak."

Within the first few hours of the military campaign, allied forces had launched hundreds of bombing air raids to take out the Iraqi communications systems. The priorities also included the destruction of Iraq's air capability and raids were made over known Iraqi air force sites.

Saddam Hussein's main weapons became his adroit news management and his secreted land-based Scud missiles. In an attempt to appeal to the sympathy of the West, he released film footage of a basement in which many Iraqis had been killed and which he claimed had been struck by an American Cruise missile. Meanwhile, on 18

January, he attempted to destabilize the allied coalition by launching a series of Scud missile attacks on Israel in the hope that Israel would be tempted to retaliate. Although Israeli tolerance was tested, its government was persuaded to maintain its neutrality in the interests of the cohesion of the allied forces. More Scud attacks on Tel Aviv followed on 25 and 31 January, killing several.

The ending

As it became clear that the allied forces were successfully winning the campaign, it was reported that the Iraqi air force was flying its remaining military jets into neighbouring Iran for safe keeping. Meanwhile, the Iraqi command ordered the spillage of large quantities of crude oil into the waters of the Gulf – a move that caused concern in the West that it could cause a sizeable environmental disaster.

On 22 February, with Iraq's air defences knocked out by allied missiles and air attacks, President Bush set an immediate deadline for Iraq's withdrawal from Kuwait. Failure to comply would, according to Mr Bush, bring about "an instant and sharp response". Prime Minister Major added: "We are not prepared to be strung along any longer." The Iraqi army in Kuwait and southern Iraq had had their supply lines cut off by the allied air strikes and morale in their ranks was reported to be very low. Saddam Hussein, determined to the end, dismissed Bush's "high noon" deadline and condemned the US President as "God's enemy and the Devil's friend".

As the allied troops entered Kuwait to finally evict the Iraqi army, Saddam ordered the withdrawing troops to set fire to Kuwait's oil wells. The first explosion on the night of 22 February was seen from HMS Brave, 40 miles away. The officer of the watch, Lt Paul Hanson, said: "A massive sheet of flame suddenly leapt into the sky. It was a huge orange fireball which lit up the sea for miles." In the Saudi capital, Riyadh, the US military spokesman, Brig.-Gen. Richard Neal, said: "This is orchestrated, systematic destruction . . . he [Saddam] intends to destroy Kuwait."

Within 100 hours of the ground war starting, the Iraqis had completely surrendered Kuwait and agreed to the allied terms of surrender. Advancing allied troops found the Iraqi army demoralized and unable to put up a defence. Many of them had abandoned their hardware in their haste to get home and the allied forces entered as far as Southern Iraq without experiencing any resistance.

On 27 February, with the key objective of liberating Kuwait accomplished, President Bush ordered the end of the campaign. Saddam Hussein, in negotiation with the allied high command, agreed to a programme of weapons inspections by the UN to ensure that Iraq's stock of weapons of mass destruction could be monitored and destroyed. Meanwhile, the allied forces faced the task of extinguishing the burning oil wells and clearing up the oil spill in the Gulf. The British forces lost a total of sixteen people in the conflict, and the Americans lost 35. The Iraqi casualties were estimated at over 150,000, of whom a third were killed.

In financial terms, the cost of the war was considerable. Within the first two weeks of Operation Desert Storm, the cost had reached £1.25 billion and was increasing at the rate of £30 million a day. In addition to the allied powers' expenditure, Saudi Arabia made £8 billion available and Japan £5 billion. The total cost of the war to the allies was estimated at over £40 billion.

Glossary of key terms

Acquisition

The purchase of a controlling interest of one business's shares by another. The acquired business becomes a subsidiary of the acquirer but may be subsequently absorbed fully into the parent's structure.

Added value

The difference between the full cost of a product and its financial value to the market. High added value is one of the objectives of strategy. It tends to be measured in terms of profit.

Annual report and accounts

Audited annual communication between a limited company and its shareholders. In the UK, it has five compulsory statements by law (the chairman's statement, the auditors' statement, the profit and loss statement, the balance sheet and the cash-flow statement).

Augmented benefits

Benefits added to core (or basic) benefits that are intended to differentiate a product.

Backward vertical development

The acquisition of one or more parts of the backward direction in the supply chain. This is typically done by acquisition of or merger with a supplier.

BCG matrix (Boston Consulting Group matrix)

Framework used to rationalize and understand a business's product portfolio. It divides products according to their market share and the rate of market growth. Four categories are identified: stars (high market share in high-growth market), cash cows (high market share in low-growth market), question marks (low market share in high-growth market) and dogs (low market share in low-growth market).

Benchmarking

A collection of techniques used to compare certain aspects of business practice and the transfer of good practice procedures from benchmark companies to 'followers'.

Business ethics

An area of research in which the nature of the relationship between business organizations and their role as moral agents is explored. It also describes research into the interface between business organizations and their social constituencies.

Capital

The finance used to invest in a business with a view to making a return from it in future years. It is used to purchase the other resource inputs that enable an organization to carry out business activity.

Change agent

One of the models of change management wherein the change process is overseen and managed by a single individual (the change agent). Offers the advantages of specialist management of a change process and the personification of the need for change.

Collaboration

Businesses are said to collaborate when, instead of (or perhaps as well as) competing, they choose to work together in pursuit of both parties' strategic objectives.

Competences

The abilities that an organization possesses that enable it to compete and survive in an industry. It includes an element that is tangible (its physical resource base) and another that is intangible (know-how, networks, etc.).

Competitive advantage

The ability of an organization to outperform its competitors. It can be measured in terms of superior profitability, increase in market share or other similar performance measures.

Competitive positioning (school of thought)

The approach to business strategy that argues that an organization's success in strategy rests upon how it positions itself in respect to its environment. This is in contrast to the resource-based approach.

Consortia/consortium

Collaborative arrangements in which more than two organizations join together for the duration of, usually, a project.

Core competences

Competences are core when they become the cause of the business's competitive advantage. Also called distinctive capabilities.

Corporate reports – same as annual report and accounts (see above)

Cost–benefit analysis

One of the non-financial tools sometimes used in evaluating strategic options. It involves weighing up the benefits that will arise from a course of action against its costs.

Cost leadership (in generic strategy framework)

The approach to business that seeks to achieve higher than industry-average performance by keeping unit costs lower than those of competitors. It is characterized by an emphasis upon the high-volume production of standard products.

Critical success factors (CSFs)

Those features owned by an organization that are the cause of its superior performance. Management approach to CSFs is to lock them in as far as possible.

Culture

The character or personality of an organization. A culture can be understood by examining its manifestations under the categories of the cultural web.

Deliberate strategy

Strategy that is planned in advance and which follows a rational process through each stage from analysis through to implementation.

Demerger

The disposal of a business (usually a subsidiary) by making it into a stand-alone business and selling it off, usually via a flotation.

Differentiation (in generic strategy framework)

The approach to business that seeks to achieve higher than industry-average performance by being distinctive rather than cheap (more distinctive than competitors). It presupposes that markets will pay more for extra product features.

Distinctive cability – see core competence

Diversification

Business growth that involves developing new products for new markets.

Earnings

Profit after interest and tax. Attributable to the company's shareholders who may elect to not withdraw the total earnings as dividends in order to leave some retained profit for future investment.

Economies of scale

The benefits gained in unit costs (cost per item) of increases in size and, hence, the dilution of fixed costs.

Emergent strategy

Strategy that is not planned in advance and which arises from a consistent pattern of behaviour.

Entry barriers

The obstacles that a new entrant to an industry needs to negotiate in order to gain market entry. Examples include the cost of capital, the legal and regulatory obstacles, access to supply and distribution channels, the costs of competing (especially lack of scale economies), etc.

Environmental analysis

Essentially, the same as strategic analysis – an analysis of an organization's internal environment and its external macroenvironment and microenvironment.

External analysis

The analysis of the external environments in which an organization exists (micro and macro) with a view to identifying opportunities and threats.

External growth

Growth of a business by merger or acquisition (in contrast to organic or internal growth).

Factors of production

Inputs into an organizational process that make normal operation possible (otherwise called resources).

Fiscal policy

Regulation of a national economy by the use of government revenues and expenditure.

Five-forces analysis

A conceptual framework for understanding an industry's or organization's position with respect to the forces in its microenvironment. Can be used to explain the structure of the industry and the performance of competitors within it.

Focus strategy (in generic strategy framework)

Competitive advantage gained through serving one (or few) market segments.

Forward vertical development

The acquisition of one or more parts of the forward direction in the supply chain. This is typically done by acquisition of, or merger with, a buyer.

Franchising

An arragement for business growth where the idea or format is rented out (from a franchiser to a franchisee) rather than directly developed by the originator of the idea.

Generic strategy

A distinctive posture that an organization adopts with regard to its strategy. It is suggested that superior performance arises from adopting a cost leadership or differentiation strategy with either a narrow or broad product and market scope.

Globalization

The most extensive stage of business development in which an organization's interests are spread throughout the world and are configured so as to compete and respond to differing customer requirements in many different national and local cultures.

Horizontal development

Merger with or acquisition of a competitor or a business at the same stage of the supply chain. Increase in market share.

Hostile take-over

An acquisition attempt that is not supported by the board of the target company.

Human resource

One of four resource inputs that can be deployed to help create competitive advantage. Comprises the employees and any other people whose skills are used by the organization (such as consultancy skills that it has access to).

Hybrid strategy

An approach to generic strategy that adopts elements of both cost leadership and differentiation.

Implementation

The part of the strategic process that involves carrying out the selected strategy. It involves making the requisite internal changes and reconfiguring the organization's resource base to make it possible.

Incremental change

Organizational change that is carried out in many small steps rather than fewer large steps.

Industry

A group of producers of close substitute products. The players in an industry compete against each other for resource inputs and in product markets.

Industry analysis

Part of strategic analysis. The analysis of an industry, usually using the five-forces framework, with a view to gaining a greater understanding of the microenvironment.

Intangible resources

Sometimes called intellectual resources – resource inputs that are not physical but which can be among the most important at causing competitive advantage. Examples includes patents, legal permissions, licences, registered logos, designs, brand-names, etc.

Intellectual resources – see intangible resources

Internal analysis

Part of strategic analysis (along with external analysis) wherein the internal parts are examined for strengths and weaknesses. The value chain framework is often used to assist the process.

Internal growth

Growth in the size of a business without the use of mergers and acquisition. It involves the reinvestment of previous years' retained profits in the same business venture.

Internationalization

Business growth involving development across national borders. Can be achieved by using market entry strategies such as exporting, direct investment, international joint ventures, alliances or franchising.

Joint ventures

A collaborative arrangement between two or more companies. Joint ventures tend to be for limited time periods, usually for a project or similar. Can also take the form of multi-partner consortia.

Just in time

An operational philosophy which aims to carry out (usually) production without any waste. Sometimes called stockless production.

Key issues

The issues that 'fall out of' the SWOT analysis which is, in turn, the summary of the strategic analysis. In practice, key issues are those issues that are the most pressing, the most important and the most critical.

Licensing

The renting-out of a piece of intellectual property so that the licensee enjoys the benefits of the licensor's innovation upon the agreement of a royalty payment. Most commonly applied to recipes, formulations, brands (such as lager brands), etc. Not to be confused with franchising.

Macroenvironment

The outer 'layer' of environmental influence – that which can influence the microenvironment. It comprises five categories of influence: socio-demographic, political, economic, natural and technological influences.

Market

The group of customers that a business or industry can sell its outputs to. Can also mean the specific part of a total market that an individual business sells to. In economics, market is taken to mean the 'place' or arena in which buyers and sellers come together.

Market segmentation

The practice of subdividing a total market into smaller units, each of which shares a commonality of preference with regard to a buying motivation. Markets are segmented by applying segmentation bases – ways of dividing customers in a market from each other.

Market share

The proportion (usually expressed as a percentage) of the market for a product type held by a supplier to the market. Can be defined in terms of value or volume.

Mergers

A form of external growth involving the 'marriage' of two partners of (usually) approximately equal size. The identities of both former companies are submerged into the new company.

Microenvironment

The near or immediate business environment that contains factors that affect the business often, and over which individual businesses may have some influence. Usually comprises competitors, suppliers and customers.

Mission statement

A formalized statement of the overall strategic purpose of an organization.

Near environment – see microenvironment

Objectives
The state of being to which an organization aims or purposes. It is the end to which strategy aims.

Operational objectives
To be distinguished from strategic objectives. The level of objective that tends to be short to medium term in timescale and which has the sole purpose of helping to achieve the higher-level strategic objective.

Organic growth – see internal growth

Paradigm
The worldview or way of looking at the world held by an individual or organization. It is a very powerful determinant of the culture and behaviour (and hence performance) of a business.

Planned strategies – see deliberate strategy

Portfolio
Can refer to the spread of interest with respect to products and markets. The principle behind any portfolio is to spread opportunity and risk with a view to making the organization less vulnerable to trauma in any one product or market segment and to enable it to be in the position to exploit any opportunities quickly.

Prescriptive strategy – see deliberate strategy

Price elasticity of demand
The relationship between the price of a product and the quantity of the product sold. Price-elastic products are those whose quantity sold is relatively price responsive. Price-inelastic products are those for which a change in price would be expected to bring about a proportionately lower change in quantity sold.

Product
The output of an organization intended for consumption by its product markets. The result of the adding-value process.

Profit
The surplus of sale against total costs. Tends to be measured before tax.

Profit and loss account

One of the three compulsory financial statements in a company annual report. The profit and loss statement reports on the total sales, the costs incurred in creating those sales and hence (by subtraction) the profit made over a reporting period.

Quality

Usually defined as 'fitness for the purpose'. It is not to be defined in terms of luxury or premium.

Related diversification

External growth by developing new products for new markets. Related diversification suggests that the new products or markets have something in common with existing products or markets such that the risk of the diversification is lessened. Related diversification is in contrast to unrelated diversification.

Resource-based approach

A way of understanding the source of competitive advantage as arising from the way in which an organization obtains and deploys its resources to build and develop core competences.

Resource markets

The markets in which a business competes with other businesses for resource inputs. Examples include labour markets, real estate and property markets, finance markets (for capital), etc.

Resources

The key inputs into an organization that enable normal functioning to take place. There are four categories of resource: physical (e.g. stock, land, buildings, etc.), financial, human and intangible (or intellectual).

Retained profit

A balance sheet measure of the profit that is attributable to the shareholders once all other allocations are accounted for – i.e. profit after interest, tax and extraordinary items.

Selection of strategy

The second stage in the overall strategic process which takes the information gained in the strategic analysis and uses it to evaluate options and to decide upon the most appropriate option.

SPENT analysis

The key stage in macroenvironmental analysis. It involves auditing the macroenvironment for socio-demographic, political, environmental, natural and technological influences.

Stakeholder theory

The belief that the objectives of an organization are determined by the relative strengths of the various stakeholders.

Stakeholders

'Any group or individual who can affect or [be] affected by the achievement of an organization's objectives' (Freeman, 1984, p. 46).

STEP analysis – see SPENT analysis

Stockholder position

The belief that business objectives should be determined predominantly for the financial benefit of the owners (shareholders). In practice, this position is taken to mean that the objectives of a business should be to maximize its profits.

Strategic alliances

A collaborative arrangement between (usually) two businesses where part or all of the two companies' value chains are shared for a mutually beneficial strategic purpose.

Strategic analysis

The first part of the strategic purpose. Its purpose is to gather information about a business's internal and external environments so that sufficient information is avilable to make possible the informed evaluation of options.

Strategic groups

The subgroups within an industry that compete head on with each other for the same types of customers or for similar resource inputs. The members of a strategic group will normally consider an ongoing monitoring of each others' activities to be an essential part of their strategic analysis.

Strategic implementation – see implementation

Strategic objectives
In contrast to operational objectives, strategic objectives are those pursued at the highest level of an organization. They concern the whole organization, are concerned with the overall product and market scope, and tend to concern longer timescales than operational objectives.

Strategic options
Generated as part of the second stage of the strategic process (evaluation and selection). The options that are considered as possible courses of action for the future.

Strategic process
One way of looking at strategy is to conceptualize it as an iterative process. According to this view, the process has three distinct stages: strategic analysis, strategic evaluation and selection and then, finally, strategic implementation. In practice, all stages are carried out continually.

Strategic selection – see selection

Strategy
There are a number of definitions of strategy, perhaps best understood in terms of Mintzberg's five Ps: plan, ploy, pattern, perspective and position. A strategy is usually taken to mean the process that is performed in order to close the gap between where an organization is now and where it aims to be in the future.

Strengths
Those internal features of an organization that can be considered to add to its ability to compete in its strategic group (or industry) and to increase its competitive advantage. Strengths are positive attributes that an organization owns.

Structure
The terms used to describe the shape of an organization. In strategy, a consideration of structure usually refers to its height, width, complexity and the extent to which it is decentralized.

Stuck in the middle

A phrase used to describe the position of an organization that, in respect to the generic strategy framework, is neither purely cost leadership nor differentiation. It has been argued that to be stuck in the middle is to expose an organization to the probability of returning below-average profits because the organization experiences competition from those pursuing all other competitive strategies (narrow and broad, cost and differentiation). This view has been challenged.

Substitute products

Products that provide identical or comparable benefits to those of the organization's products.

Supply chain

Not to be confused with the value chain. Usually refers to the entire path that a product and its component parts takes from the primary industry stage to when it is sold to the final consumer on the chain.

Synergy

The effect that is observed after two or more parties (e.g. businesses in a merger) come together and the whole becomes greater than the sum of the parts. Sometimes expressed as '2+2=5'.

Unrelated diversification

External growth by developing new products for new markets. Unrelated diversification suggests that the new products or markets have little or nothing in common with existing products or markets such that the risk of the diversification is increased, but that portfolio benefits are maximized. Unrelated diversification is in contrast to related diversification.

Value adding – see added value

Value chain analysis

A conceptualization of the internal activities of an organization. The framework divides the internal activities of an organization into two categories: those that directly add value (primary activities) and those that support the primary activities (support or secondary activities). The analysis of an organization's value chain is intended to show up the strategic importance of any key linkages or any blockages – points where value is added less efficiently than it might be.

Vertical development

The acquisition of forward or backward competences such as through merger with, or acquisition of, a supplier (backward vertical development) or a customer (forward vertical development).

Waste

Anything that does not add value in an organizational process (such as machine inefficiencies, tooling up and tooling down, bad quality, stock, etc.).

Weaknesses

Those internal features of an organization that can be considered to detract from its ability to compete in its strategic group (or industry) and to reduce its competitive advantage. Weaknesses are negative attributes that an organization owns.

Index

Page numbers in italics refer to definitions in the Glossary. Abbreviations: Fig = Figure; Tab = Table.